PUFFIN BOOKS
INDIA AT 70

Roshen Dalal was born in Mussoorie, and lived in various places in India, including Hyderabad, Mumbai and Delhi, before settling in Dehradun, where she now resides along with several rescued cats and a dog. She has an MA and a PhD in ancient Indian history from Jawaharlal Nehru University, New Delhi. She has taught both at school and university level, and has been involved in research in the fields of history, religion, philosophy and education.

She is the author of the bestselling two-volume *Puffin History of India*; *The Puffin History of the World*, also in two volumes; *The Religions of India: A Concise Guide to Nine Major Faiths*; *Hinduism: An Alphabetical Guide*; *The Vedas: An Introduction to Hinduism's Sacred Texts* and *The Compact Timeline History of the World*. Apart from books, she has written numerous articles and book reviews. Having been an editor for many years, she is now a full-time writer and is currently working on a book on the Upanishads.

ALSO IN PUFFIN BY ROSHEN DALAL

The Puffin History of India:
Volume 1 (3000 BC to AD 1947)

The Puffin History of India:
Volume 2 (1947 to the Present)

The Puffin History of the World: Volume 1

The Puffin History of the World: Volume 2

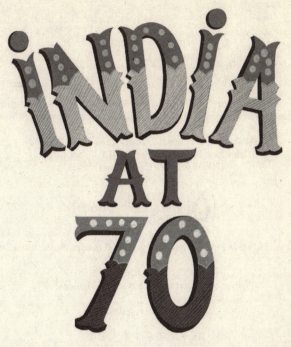

INDIA AT 70

SNAPSHOTS SINCE INDEPENDENCE

ROSHEN DALAL

Illustrations by Sayan Mukherjee

PUFFIN BOOKS
An imprint of Penguin Random House

PUFFIN BOOKS

USA | Canada | UK | Ireland | Australia
New Zealand | India | South Africa | China

Puffin Books is part of the Penguin Random House group of companies whose addresses can be found at global.penguinrandomhouse.com

Published by Penguin Random House India Pvt. Ltd
7th Floor, Infinity Tower C, DLF Cyber City,
Gurgaon 122 002, Haryana, India

First published in Puffin Books by Penguin Random House India 2017

Text copyright © Roshen Dalal 2017
Illustrations copyright © Sayan Mukherjee 2017

All rights reserved

10 9 8 7 6 5 4 3 2 1

The views and opinions expressed in this book are the author's own and the facts are as reported by her which have been verified to the extent possible, and the publishers are not in any way liable for the same.

The international boundaries on the maps of India are neither purported to be correct nor authentic by Survey of India directives.

ISBN 9780143428718

Typeset in Adobe Caslon Pro by Manipal Digital Systems, Manipal
Printed at Replika Press Pvt. Ltd, India

This book is sold subject to the condition that it shall not, by way of trade or otherwise, be lent, resold, hired out, or otherwise circulated without the publisher's prior consent in any form of binding or cover other than that in which it is published and without a similar condition including this condition being imposed on the subsequent purchaser.

www.penguin.co.in

For Shahnaz

CONTENTS

Introduction   xi

1. 1947: A Rainbow in the Sky   1
2. 1948: Beginning with a Tragedy   7
3. 1949: Integration of the States   13
4. 1950: India Becomes a Republic   19
5. 1951: Counting the People   25
6. 1952: The First Elections   30
7. 1953: The Paradise of Kashmir   36
8. 1954: India and China Are Friends   42
9. 1955: India Becomes a World Leader   49
10. 1956: Reorganizing the States   56
11. 1957: Elections Again   63
12. 1958: Panchayati Raj   69
13. 1959: The Dalai Lama Enters India   74
14. 1960: Bombay Is Divided   79
15. 1961: The Liberation of Goa   84
16. 1962: The Indo-China War   90
17. 1963: The Language Problem   95
18. 1964: The Death of Nehru   100
19. 1965: War with Pakistan   105

Contents

20.	1966: The Rise of Indira Gandhi	110
21.	1967: The Fourth General Elections	116
22.	1968: The Green Revolution Begins	121
23.	1969: The Congress Splits	125
24.	1970: The Lok Sabha Is Dissolved	130
25.	1971: Bangladesh Is Born	135
26.	1972: Assembly Elections	141
27.	1973: Economic Problems	146
28.	1974: Total Revolution—the JP Movement	150
29.	1975: The Emergency	156
30.	1976: The Twenty Point Programme	161
31.	1977: A New Government—the Janata Party	165
32.	1978: The Forty-Fourth Amendment	170
33.	1979: Charan Singh	175
34.	1980: The Seventh General Elections	180
35.	1981: Internal Developments	185
36.	1982: The Asian Games	190
37.	1983: The Demand for Khalistan	196
38.	1984: Indira Is Assassinated	200
39.	1985: Rajiv Gandhi—a Young Prime Minister	205
40.	1986: Peace in Mizoram	210
41.	1987: Sri Lanka and the IPKF	217
42.	1988: Attempts towards Peace	224
43.	1989: V.P. Singh—a New Prime Minister	229
44.	1990: Another Government—Chandra Shekhar	236
45.	1991: Rajiv Gandhi Is Assassinated	242
46.	1992: Narasimha Rao—Economic Reforms	249
47.	1993: Narasimha Rao Continues as Prime Minister	254

Contents

48. 1994: Economic Growth — 259
49. 1995: The Eighth SAARC Summit, New Delhi — 264
50. 1996: The Eleventh General Elections — 270
51. 1997: I.K. Gujral—a New Prime Minister — 275
52. 1998: A BJP-Led Government — 281
53. 1999: The BJP Again — 287
54. 2000: Three New States — 294
55. 2001: Three Tragedies — 299
56. 2002: A New President—A.P.J. Abdul Kalam — 306
57. 2003: Improving Relations with Pakistan — 313
58. 2004: A New Government—the UPA — 320
59. 2005: The Right to Information Act Is Passed — 325
60. 2006: The Twenty Point Programme Is Restructured — 330
61. 2007: Pratibha Patil—the First Female President — 337
62. 2008: A Terrorist Attack in Mumbai — 344
63. 2009: The UPA Government Again — 351
64. 2010: Maoist Attacks in West Bengal and Chhattisgarh — 356
65. 2011: Anna Hazare against Corruption — 362
66. 2012: Sixty Years of the Indian Parliament — 367
67. 2013: The Mars Orbiter Mission Is Launched — 374
68. 2014: Narendra Modi Becomes Prime Minister — 380
69. 2015: The Aam Aadmi Party Wins in Delhi — 386
70. 2016: Demonetization — 392
71. 2017: India at Seventy — 399

Conclusion: A Cultural Revolution Begins — 405
Acknowledgements — 407
Index — 409

INTRODUCTION

In 2017, India's spacecraft Mangalyaan is orbiting Mars, satellites are regularly sent into space, the economy is growing rapidly and India's diverse art and culture is appreciated globally. And, most importantly, India is the largest democracy in the world.

The story of India as an independent nation began seventy years ago, in 1947, when the country gained independence after almost 200 years of British rule. For the first time, India became a united political entity, a nation with clearly defined boundaries. What type of country would the new India be? Would it remain united and strong?

At this time, the territory known as India consisted of eleven British provinces and some additional areas directly under British rule as well as 565 Indian states (also called princely states) where the British had overall control. The Muslim League, led by Muhammad Ali Jinnah, wanted a separate state of Pakistan, and finally it was decided that this demand would be granted. On 14 and 15 August 1947, two new nations were created, but the boundary lines between them were known only on 17 August. Pakistan was in two parts; West Pakistan was formed in the western half of Punjab while East Pakistan was created from the province of Bengal. As the lines for dividing the area were drawn on a map, districts, canals and even villages were divided.

INTRODUCTION

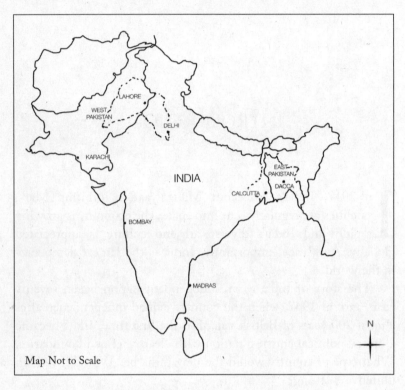

India and Pakistan after Partition, 1947

This partition of one country into two created many problems. In the west, 10 million migrated across the new borders, and as anger arose between Muslims on one side and Hindus and Sikhs on the other, about 1 million were killed. There were other issues too, as the entire administration and all its possessions—including tables, chairs, books, musical instruments, cars, pencils and pens as well as the army, police, railways, postal services, money and other items—had to be divided.

The process of integrating the different states to form one India began before Independence. While some of the states were

Introduction

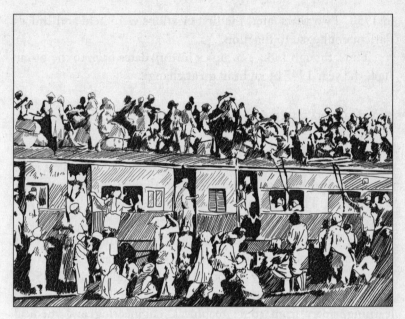

Refugees boarding a train, 1947

in the region of Pakistan, 554 states were in Indian territory. These states had different kinds of rulers. Some controlled huge areas and had vast quantities of wealth, land, buildings, money, gold, jewels, cars and elephants; others had small territories of just a few square kilometres. There were actually 425 small states. By 31 July, two types of agreements had been worked out for the Indian states to sign, by which they agreed to join India and give up some of their powers.

At the time of Independence, the Constitution of India was being prepared. A constitution consists of the rules and ideas according to which a nation is governed. The Constituent Assembly, a group of people who would discuss and write India's constitution, first met on 9 December 1946. The Constitution was ready by the end of 1949, after which India became a republic

❋ INTRODUCTION ❋

in 1950. Two years later, the first elections were held and India's Parliament began to function.

Thus, though India's complex history dates back to the Stone Age, the year 1947 brought in great change.

❋ WHAT WAS INDIA LIKE IN 1947?

The basic structure of the government and administration already existed in the British provinces. From 1937 onwards, Indians were elected to legislatures in the provinces, though the right to vote was limited. There was also a judicial system with a hierarchy of courts, and an army, a navy and an air force.

The literacy rate at the time was just 12.1 per cent. That means only twelve people in every 100 could read. There were about 1,70,000 primary schools, 12,000 middle schools, 5000 high schools, and twenty-five universities and institutes of higher learning, apart from some technical, engineering and medical colleges. Newspapers, books, printing presses and publishing houses existed in English and most Indian languages. Scientific institutions included the Survey of India (founded in 1767), the Geological Survey of India (1851), the Archaeological Survey of India (1861), the India Meteorological Department (1875), the Forest Research Institute (1878), the Zoological Survey of India (1916), the Indian Statistical Institute (1931), the Council of Scientific and Industrial Research (1942) and the Tata Institute of Fundamental Research (1945)—the last two being set up by Indians. There were other scientific and technological organizations too, as well as libraries, museums and some hospitals.

Agriculture was widespread, caste differentiation was prevalent, and the zamindari system and bonded labour still existed. Peasants were poor and there were many landless labourers. Terrible famines had taken place, one of the most recent being the Bengal famine of 1943–44.

Introduction

Electricity and piped water were available in large towns and cities, and some villages had electricity for public buildings and spaces, though most had neither. Industry was being developed, but heavy industry—which could produce machines or large items—was limited. Transport and communication were well developed. Air travel had started—though flights took much longer than today, and not many used them. In fact, in 1945, all the different airlines together had just over 24,000 passengers. For travel by sea, there were ships, ports, lighthouses and a merchant navy. Motor vehicles were few (1,42,172 in 1945), but trains were widely used, and railway tracks were quite extensive. Television, of course, did not exist, but there were nine radio stations by 1947. India had a postal service with 26,130 post offices, a telegram service and 1,23,000 telephone connections. (There were only landline connections in those days.)

Social changes that had started in the late nineteenth and early twentieth centuries continued after Independence. India had some traditional sports and games, such as wrestling and kabaddi, but many new ones, such as hockey, football, cricket, badminton, tennis and golf, began to be played. As for indoor games, an international style was established in chess. On the whole, food habits remained traditional, but new food items such as biscuits, tea, coffee, cakes and bread were introduced in the twentieth century. Men in cities started wearing Western clothing.

From ancient times, India had a rich tradition of literature, dance, music, art, sculpture and crafts of all kinds. By 1947, there were new trends in culture, with further innovations after the migration of artists and writers from across the border.

It was against this background that India had to build a new nation. After a shaky beginning, India gradually gained strength and became a functioning democracy and a stable state.

❋ INTRODUCTION ❋

India has a total land area of 32,87,263 sq. km, which is just 2.42 per cent of the world's land. However, according to the 2011 Census of India, the country's population was 1,21,01,93,422, amounting to 16.7 per cent of the world's population, the second highest in the world. By the same year, there were 497 cities with a population of over 1,00,000 and forty-seven with over 10,00,000. Since 2011, India's population has risen further, amounting to approximately 17.8 per cent of the world's population. As this book will show, India has achieved a lot in its first seventy years of being a nation. However, more remains to be done to ensure health, education, sanitation and welfare to every citizen.

❋ ABOUT THIS BOOK

This book contains snapshots of each of these seventy years. Against India's political backdrop, it provides glimpses of the country's vast and rich culture, its diversity and many languages, its eminent personalities and its achievements in all spheres. Each chapter begins with a brief account of the main political events of the year. It then looks at select personalities and cultural events that are key to that year. At the end of each chapter is a short timeline of some additional events of the year.

Many individuals had a role in creating the new India, and the government contributed too, setting up and financing new institutions of education, science, sports, literature and art, establishing awards of all kinds, organizing Festivals of India across the world and making India a part of the global scene.

It has, of course, not been possible to include every accomplishment, event and great personality in this book, as a choice had to be made from the thousands of significant people and incidents of each year. The main criterion for the selection was to provide a balance among the different categories included. The eminent personalities, in particular, have been chosen from the many award winners of every year or because of their extraordinary contribution. Cinema, literature, music, dance and art reflect the happenings in India, sometimes directly, and some of the best or most relevant portrayals of the last seventy years have been described.

In literature, the book provides accounts of authors, poets and works in many of the twenty-two languages recognized in the Constitution. It is hoped that this glimpse will lead you to find out more about the writers and read some of the books. In cinema, select actors, films and directors have been chosen out of thousands, again across various languages. Then there are details of television and tele-serials, artists, musicians, dancers, and types of art, music and dance. Musical instruments are included. Sports, sportspersons and medal winners find a place too, along with a lot more—including science and space research, humanitarian activities and some of India's unique wildlife and ecosystems. The book also indicates how tradition is gradually giving way to new forms of culture, and showcases some of the latest trends.

To sum up, this volume presents an idea of the vibrant and ever-changing nation of India, and of the people who provide its vitality.

❋ A NOTE ON SOURCES

Sources consulted for this book are numerous and varied, but some of the main ones are listed here:

Bipan Chandra, et al, *India after Independence*; Patrick French, *Liberty or Death: India's Journey to Independence and Division*; Ramachandra Guha, *India after Gandhi: The History of the World's Largest Democracy*; Shashi Tharoor, *Nehru: The Invention of India*; S. Gopal, *Jawaharlal Nehru: A Biography* (Volumes 1–3); Myron Weiner, *State Politics in India*; V.P. Menon, *Integration of the Indian States*; B.N. Mullik, *My Years with Nehru:*

INTRODUCTION

The Chinese Betrayal; Stanley Wolpert, *Nehru: A Tryst with Destiny*; Andrea L. Stanton, *Cultural Sociology of the Middle East, Asia & Africa*; Vijaya Ramaswamy, *Historical Dictionary of the Tamils*; Paul R. Brass, *The Politics of India since Independence*; A. Ghosh, *Planning, Programming and Input–Output Models: Selected Papers on Indian Planning*; B.R. Tomlinson, *The Economy of Modern India*; M.L. Sondhi (ed.), *Towards a New Era: Economic, Social and Political Reforms*; several publications of the Sahitya Akademi, particularly Amaresh Dutta (ed.), *The Encyclopaedia of Indian Literature* (Volumes 1–6) and K.M. George (ed.), *Modern Indian Literature: An Anthology* (Volumes 1–3); Anil Sehgal (ed.), *Ali Sardar Jafri: The Youthful Boatman of Joy*; Ravi Shankar, *My Music, My Life*; Pradeep Thakur, *Indian Music Masters of Our Times*; Amjad Ali Khan, *Master on Masters*; Avanthi Meduri (ed.), *Rukmini Devi Arundale (1904–1986): A Visionary Architect of Indian Culture and the Performing Arts*; Neville Tuli, *Indian Contemporary Painting*; Gayatri Sinha, *Indian Art: An Overview*; Renu Saran, *History of Indian Cinema*; Ashish Rajadhyaksha, *Indian Cinema: A Very Short Introduction*.

In addition to the above, official websites of Government of India organizations and other reputed sites have been accessed, as well as various print publications.

All dates have been checked and verified to the extent possible, and where the dates differ across sources, the more authentic one has been chosen.

India at 70 is a companion volume to *The Puffin History of India: Volume 2*, which focuses on the history, politics and economy of India after Independence.

1947: A RAINBOW IN THE SKY

It was midnight on 14 August 1947. At one minute past, as the 15th dawned, India became free. In front of numerous guests in the assembly hall of the Council House, Jawaharlal Nehru, the prime minister of free India, gave a speech celebrating India's independence. '[As] the world sleeps, India will awake to life and freedom,' he began. Conches were blown, shouts of 'Mahatma Gandhi ki jai!' were heard and everyone rejoiced. While it rained outside, thousands danced in the lit and decorated streets of Delhi. The next day too, there were people all over the roads, cheering and dancing. There was another ceremony in the Council House, to inaugurate the new government, and in the evening, all moved towards India Gate. There were huge crowds, at least half a million people. Our national flag, the tricolour, was raised. It was the rainy season, and a rainbow appeared in the sky like a blessing.

Independence Day celebrations at India Gate

And the day after that, the 16th, there was a ceremony at the Red Fort. Even more people had gathered there, probably a million. Jawaharlal Nehru spoke, beginning with the words 'Jai Hind!', and all roared in response, repeating those words with joy. Bismillah Khan, the great musician, played on his *shehnai*.

And a new era began.

But there was still a lot to be done. The integration of the states had to be completed and the Constitution had to be finalized. There were many problems in the new India, but Independence also brought hope, excitement, a sense of strength and pride, and a desire for innovation and change.

● INTEGRATION BEGINS

By 15 August, all except five states—three large and two small—had signed agreements that made them part of India. The first step towards integration had been achieved. Even by the end of August 1947, three important states had not yet joined India: Kashmir, Junagadh and Hyderabad.

Maharaja Hari Singh, ruler of Kashmir, did not sign the agreement and retained his independence while both India and Pakistan were keen to get Kashmir to join them. On 22 October, Pathan tribes, unofficially backed by Pakistan, invaded Kashmir. To get help from India, the maharaja joined India on 26 October. A war broke out in Kashmir between Indian troops and the invaders, continuing into the next year, even though Kashmir was now part of India.

● THE CONSTITUTION AND THE GOVERNMENT

After Independence and until the Constitution was ready, there was a central government with a governor general, a prime minister and other ministers. The Constituent Assembly functioned as the legislative assembly from 15 August 1947 onwards, with Jawaharlal Nehru as the first prime minister and Lord Mountbatten, previously the viceroy, as the governor general. The Viceroy's House was renamed the Government House, and later Rashtrapati Bhavan. What was known as the Council House later became the Parliament.

THE NATIONAL FLAG

The national flag was flown for the first time on the night of 14 August 1947. A different form of the flag had been used since 1930 but the final design was approved by the Constituent Assembly on 22 July 1947. This flag has three horizontal stripes, of deep saffron, white and dark green, with a navy blue wheel with twenty-four spokes in the centre. This wheel, or chakra, is a Buddhist symbol, which appears on the capital of one of Mauryan emperor Ashoka's (ruled 269–232 BCE) pillars. It is called the dharmachakra, or the wheel of law, and indicates that change should take place through right actions and peaceful means. The colours too have meanings: saffron represents renunciation and holiness; white indicates light, truth and simplicity; the green at the base reflects the relationship with the earth.

BISMILLAH KHAN

Bismillah Khan, who played on the occasion of Independence, came from a family of shehnai players. His father was a musician in the court of Maharaja Keshav Prasad Singh of Dumraon, now in Bihar. His maternal uncle, Ali Baksh Khan, played the shehnai at the Kashi Vishwanath Temple and others in Varanasi.

Bismillah performed many more times on special occasions, including Republic Day. He lived in Varanasi, where his music could be heard at several temples, particularly the Kashi Vishwanath. He used to practise at the Balaji Temple in Varanasi. In an interview, he said, 'For us here, there has always been one God . . . call Him Allah or Ishwar or Ram.'[1] When he died on 21 August 2006, a day of national mourning was declared. His beloved shehnai was buried with him, and a twenty-one-gun salute sounded in his honour. During his lifetime, he received many awards, including the Bharat Ratna in 2001. He held concerts not only in India, but in countries across the world.

WIND INSTRUMENTS AND THE SHEHNAI

The shehnai is a wind instrument, made largely of wood, with a range of two octaves. It normally has eight holes, though the number can vary from six to nine. The instrument is tube-like and tapered, and 45–60 cm long. Notes are produced by blowing through it while closing one or more holes with the fingers. Variations in notes are produced by control of the breath. Making the shehnai is an art, requiring special raw materials. The pala reed, found in marshlands near River Ganga, is the basic material required. A mouthpiece, tube or pipe of smooth black wood and a metal bell-shaped end are added. The sound of the shehnai is considered auspicious, and from medieval days it has been played in temples and at marriages. The name 'shehnai' is said to mean 'royal flute'. There are different views on its origin. It may have developed from existing flutes or from the pungi, the snake charmer's instrument, or, according to other sources, it may have come from Iran in the sixteenth century. The nagaswaram in south India is a similar instrument.

---

[1] Sharat Pradhan, 'Even the Heavens Have Wept: Bismillah Khan', *Rediff.com*, 12 March 2006, http://www.rediff.com/news/report/up/20060312.htm.

> Bismillah Khan had several shehnais, some having been gifted to him. He played on a unique silver and wooden shehnai on special occasions.

INDIAN CLASSICAL MUSIC

Indian classical music has two main streams: Hindustani, from north India, and Karnatic (Carnatic) from the south. Both are based on ragas. A raga consists of a melody created from a series of notes that are believed to be pre-existent in nature. A raga, therefore, is revealed or discovered, not invented.

Sanskrit was originally the language used for music, but in medieval times it was largely replaced in the north by Braj Bhasha, a Hindi dialect. In the south, apart from Sanskrit, local languages such as Tamil and Telugu were used.

Some ragas of the north have different names in the south, and some with the same names are actually different ragas! An example of the former category is Malkauns of the north, known in the south as Hindolam; and of the second type, Todi, which, though it has the same name, is an entirely different raga in the south than that in the north. Karnatic music has more fixed compositions and less improvisation.

❈ NICHOLAS (NIKOLAI) ROERICH

The great Russian mystic and painter Nicholas Roerich died on 13 December 1947 in Naggar, in present-day Himachal Pradesh. Born in 1874 in St Petersburg, Russia, he and his wife, Helena, settled in Naggar in 1928, after extensive travels in the Himalayas and other parts of the world. Roerich believed in the ultimate spirituality of creation, and this is depicted in his paintings with themes of majestic mountains, prophets and female deities. His paintings can be viewed in museums and galleries in India and across the world.

ALSO IN 1947

18 January: Death of actor and singer K.L. Saigal (b. 11 April 1904)

August–December: Migration; 5 million Hindu and Sikh refugees reach India from West Pakistan, and about 1 to 5 million from East Pakistan.

December: The second stage of integration begins, merging the states into larger units.

1948: BEGINNING WITH A TRAGEDY

Mahatma Gandhi had led India to freedom through the path of non-violence and truth, but as Independence approached, he felt that most people had forgotten his ideas and were no longer listening to him. At the time of Independence, he was in Bengal, and because of his presence, there was peace in the region. He came to Delhi in September 1947, and on 13 January 1948, began a fast. His main aim was to end all violence in Delhi, but he also wanted the Government of India to act fairly towards Pakistan. After Independence, the money reserves had to be divided between the two new nations. Pakistan's share was Rs 75 crore, of which Rs 20 crore had been paid. Since Pakistan had started the war in Kashmir and occupied some territory, India did not want to pay the remaining amount. But Gandhi said this was not right and that the money must be paid.

When he began his fast, there was not much response, but gradually, as he became weaker, leaders of all political parties came to him and promised to put a stop to the violence. The Indian government too promised to follow his wishes and pay the money to Pakistan. Gandhi then ended his fast. But some remained angry with him, thinking he was favouring Muslims and Pakistan.

Nehru and Gandhi sharing a happy moment

He was shot dead by Nathuram Godse on 30 January as he was walking to his evening prayer meeting. As the news spread, there was shock and grief everywhere. Jawaharlal Nehru wept, but then as he spoke on the radio, he said that Gandhi's light would not die—it would be seen by India and the world 'for that light represented the living truth'.

Despite this terrible disaster, life in India had to go on. Refugees from Pakistan still had to be provided food and shelter. And so vast refugee camps were set up.

🟎 INTEGRATION CONTINUES

The task of integrating the states had to continue, and progress was made with the two states in Indian territory that had not joined India, as well as in Kashmir.

The nawab of Junagadh, in Gujarat, joined Pakistan, but the people did not want to and in February 1948, voted to join India. The small state of Manavadar also joined India.

Under Nizam Mir Osman Ali Khan, Hyderabad, in central India, retained its independence for some time. All attempts at negotiation failed, and by 18 September 1948, Indian troops took over the state. To maintain friendly relations, the Nizam was made rajpramukh, or the constitutional head of the state.

The war in Kashmir ended on 31 December 1948, but a large part of the territory of Kashmir remained with Pakistan.

❈ CHANGES IN THE GOVERNMENT

Meanwhile, there were some changes in the government. Lord Mountbatten left India on 21 June, and Chakravarti Rajagopalachari (popularly known as Rajaji) became the first Indian governor general. Rajaji remained the governor general till the introduction of India's new Constitution on 26 January 1950. By then, he had had a long career in politics, beginning with his participation in the freedom movement. After his stint as governor general, he became minister of home affairs in 1951 and was chief minister of Madras from 1952–54. Later, he gradually moved away from the Indian National Congress and was a founder member of the Swatantra Party in 1959. Rajaji was not only a politician, but also a writer in English and Tamil. He died in 1972.

Among other political changes, a new socialist party was formed. It had been established in 1924–25 as the Congress Socialist Party. In 1948, it broke away from the Indian National Congress, forming a separate party.

This year also saw the first batch of the Indian Foreign Service being recruited through the Civil Services Examination, while the Atomic Energy Commission was set up to develop nuclear energy for peaceful use.

❈ THE 1948 SUMMER OLYMPICS

Indians had been participating in the Olympics from 1900, when the only Indian participant, Norman Pritchard, won a silver medal in the 200-metre sprint, and another in the 200-metre hurdles. There were other participants in succeeding Olympics, but in the 1948 games held in London, India entered as an independent nation for the first time. With seventy-nine male participants, India took part in athletics, boxing, cycling, field hockey, football, weightlifting, wrestling, swimming and water polo. The country won a single medal, a gold, in field hockey. In athletics, most did not advance to the finals, though Gurnam Singh ranked 18th in the men's high jump.

India's first Olympic gold medal is celebrated in a film called *Gold*, starring Akshay Kumar, to be released on Independence Day 2018. Hockey also figures in other films, including *Chak De! India* (2007). Though hockey is not a traditional game, hockey tournaments in India date back to the nineteenth century, while the All India Hockey Federation was formed in 1925. The first nationals were held in 1928 in Calcutta (Kolkata). Dhyan Chand was one of the best hockey players in the early days.

❉ THE TOP FILMS

The first Indian talkie, in Hindi, was *Alam Ara*, produced in 1931, and the same year saw talking films in some other Indian languages. After this, films in Indian languages flourished.

Among the notable films made in 1948 was Raj Kapoor's *Aag*, in which he played the lead role, Kewal, who was pushed into studying law by his family but left it to follow his dream and open a theatre company. Raj's brother, Shashi Kapoor, acted as the young Kewal, and Nargis, as Nimmi, a woman who had lost her home to Partition. Though the film was not a box office hit, it had several firsts: it was the first film produced and directed by Raj Kapoor and the first film in which he and Nargis acted together. The film was also very close to Kapoor's heart, and he wrote, 'I'll never forget *Aag* because it was the story of youth consumed by a desire for a brighter and more intense life.'[2]

---

[2] 'Aag (1948): Raj Kapoor's Burning Idealism', *Let's Talk about Bollywood* (blog), accessed 11 June 2017, http://www.letstalkaboutbollywood.com/article-21928919.html.

The top box office hits of 1948 included *Shaheed*, *Chandralekha*, *Pyar ki Jeet*, *Mela* and *Ziddi*.

The Films Division of India was founded in 1948 to promote film production in India. It is the main film organization of the Government of India. At that time, India had 3003 cinema theatres, out of which 908 were touring theatres.

RAJ KAPOOR

Born on 14 December 1924, Raj Kapoor, the son of Prithviraj Kapoor, went on to make many more films. He began working as a child actor in 1935. At first, he worked for films produced by other companies. Later, he started his own company, R.K. Studio. Other notable films of his include *Barsaat* (1949), *Awara* (1951), *Boot Polish* (1954), *Shree 420* (1955), *Jagte Raho* (1956), *Jis Desh Mein Ganga Behti Hai* (1960), *Mera Naam Joker* (1970) and *Kal Aaj aur Kal* (1971). Known as the Indian Charlie Chaplin, he gained popularity not only in India, but in other countries too, including the Soviet Union and China as well as West Asia. He received many awards, including three National Film Awards, several Filmfare Awards, the Padma Bhushan in 1971 and the Dadasaheb Phalke Award in 1987. He died on 2 June 1988.

ALSO IN 1948

4 January: The Union of Burma, now Myanmar, gains independence from British rule.

4 February: Ceylon, now Sri Lanka, gains independence from British rule.

15 February: The state of Manavadar accedes to India.

20 February: A plebiscite is held in Junagadh and all but ninety-one people vote to join India.

1 May: The Armed Forces Medical College is set up in Pune.

15 July: The National Cadet Corps is formed.

11 September: Death of M.A. Jinnah (b. 25 December 1876), the founder of Pakistan, and earlier, a leader of the freedom movement in India

1949: INTEGRATION OF THE STATES

The second stage of integrating the states began soon after Independence, and was completed by the end of 1949. Sardar Patel, the then home minister, was in charge of supervising the integration along with V.P. Menon. The states were classified into parts A, B, C and D. Part A had nine states: Assam, Bihar, Bombay, Madhya Pradesh (previously the Central Provinces and Berar), Madras, Orissa, Punjab, the United Provinces (later Uttar Pradesh) and West Bengal. These states were formed from the former British provinces, with some Indian states added to them. Part B had eight states: Hyderabad, Jammu and Kashmir, Madhya Bharat, Mysore, Patiala and East Punjab States Union (PEPSU), Rajasthan, Union of Saurashtra and Travancore–Cochin. Part C included ten states: Ajmer, Bhopal, Bilaspur, Coorg, Delhi, Himachal Pradesh, Kutch, Manipur, Tripura and Vindhya Pradesh. And Part D had one: the Andaman and Nicobar Islands. Part A states were headed by a Governor. Part B states consisted of three large Indian states and five new unions, each headed by a rajpramukh who was one of the former rulers. In Jammu and Kashmir, the head of the state was known as the sadar-i-riyasat. Part C and Part D states were under chief commissioners.

Some territories still remained under the Portuguese and French. The Portuguese territories were on the western coast and included Dadra and Nagar Haveli, Diu and Goa. The French had four small territories in the south of India—Pondichéry, Mahé, Karikal and Yanaon.

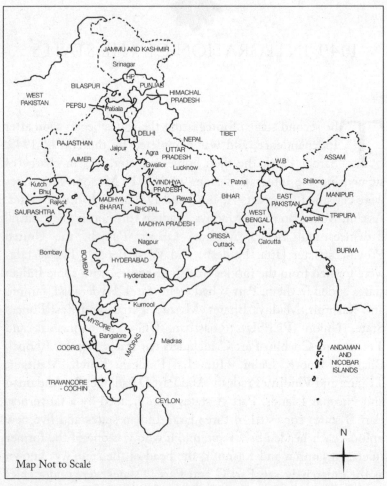

The states after the second stage of integration, 1949

INDIANS RISE IN THE ARMED FORCES

Another aspect of the new India was that gradually, Indian officials replaced the British in the top posts. The first Indian commander-in-chief of the army, General K.M. Cariappa (28 January 1899–15 May 1993), took over on 15 January 1949, succeeding General Sir Roy Bucher. He retired in January 1953, but continued to hold important posts.

The first Indian commander-in-chief of the Air Force, Air Marshal Subroto Mukerjee, was appointed on 1 April 1954, while the first Indian chief of the Naval Staff was Vice Admiral Ram Dass Katari (1911–83), appointed on 22 April 1958.

THE BOMBAY PROGRESSIVE ARTISTS' GROUP

There were new trends in art. Six artists, K.H. Ara, S.K. Bakre (the only sculptor), H.A. Gade, M.F. Husain, S.H. Raza and F.N. Souza, founded the Bombay Progressive Artists' Group in December 1947. Krishen Khanna and V.S. Gaitonde later joined as well. Their aim was to create art that was both Indian and yet modern. All these artists became famous, and their styles were very influential. They held their first exhibition in Bombay (Mumbai) in 1949. Among the works displayed was Ara's painting titled *Independence Day Parade*. Another artists' group founded in 1947 was the Shilpi Chakra, set up by refugees from Lahore.

PALAEOBOTANY AND BIRBAL SAHNI

Palaeobotanists help us understand the past by analysing ancient plant remains.

Birbal Sahni (b. 14 November 1891) was a pioneering palaeobotanist in India, who studied the plant fossils of India and, on 10 September 1946, set up the Birbal Sahni Institute of Palaeobotany (formerly the Institute of Palaeobotany) in Lucknow. Initially this was part of the botany department of Lucknow University. The foundation of the new building was laid on 3 April 1949 but, just a week later, Birbal died of a heart attack on the 10th.

Birbal was educated in India and England, and his research included both fossils and living plants. In addition, he had diverse interests, including archaeology, numismatics and geology. The Birbal Sahni Gold Medal for botany students was instituted in his memory. He published research papers and a textbook on botany (jointly with J.C. Willis), and received a number of awards.

INDIAN LITERATURE

India has a large number of languages and dialects. Out of these, originally fourteen and now twenty-two (along with English) are recognized by the Constitution. These are Assamese, Bengali, Bodo, Dogri, Gujarati, Hindi, Kannada, Kashmiri, Konkani, Maithili, Malayalam, Manipuri, Marathi, Nepali, Odia, Punjabi, Sanskrit, Santali, Sindhi, Tamil, Telugu and Urdu. Literature of all kinds has been written in these languages and dialects. Apart from the recognized languages, there are many more. Some of the tribal languages—Khasi, Mundari, Gondi, Bhili/Bhilodi, Kurukh/Oraon, Tulu and Ho—are spoken by over a million people each. Films also exist in many dialects, such as Bhojpuri, Rajasthani and Garhwali.

❋ THE NIGHTINGALE OF INDIA

Sarojini Naidu (19 February 1879–2 March 1949), a nationalist who participated in the freedom movement, became the second female president of the Indian National Congress in 1925 (the first was Annie Besant). After Independence, she was the first female Governor of an Indian state (the United Provinces), from 1947–49. But she is remembered for her poetry rather than her political life, and is known as the Nightingale of India.

Her poems are studied in schools and colleges today, and have been translated into several Indian and European languages. She was born in Hyderabad, and among her poems are some about the city. 'Nightfall in the City of Hyderabad' begins with the lines:[3]

> See how the speckled sky burns like a pigeon's throat,
> Jewelled with embers of opal and peridote.
> See the white river that flashes and scintillates,
> Curved like a tusk from the mouth of the city-gates.
> Hark, from the minaret, how the muezzin's call
> Floats like a battle-flag over the city wall.

❖ TENNIS: THE BEGINNINGS

After Independence, Dilip Bose won the first Asian International Championship in 1949. Naresh Kumar is another international player of the time.

Tennis began to be played in India from the late nineteenth century, mainly in army cantonments and clubs. All-India tennis championships started in 1910. Others among the noted early players were Ghaus Mohammad Khan, Sumant Mishra, Iftikhar Ahmad and Jimmy Mehta. Ghaus Mohammad Khan reached the quarter-finals at Wimbledon in 1939. He was the first Indian to do so. Jimmy Mehta and Sumant Mishra reached the doubles

---

[3] Quoted in *Mapping the Nation: An Anthology of Indian Poetry in English, 1870–1920*, ed. Sheshalatha Reddy (London: Anthem Press, 2012).

quarter-finals at Wimbledon in 1947 and 1948. Sumant won the first National Lawn Tennis Championship held in 1946 in Calcutta.

ALSO IN 1949

1 January: The Reserve Bank of India is nationalized. It takes over some of the functions of the Imperial Bank of India.

20 January: Death of Tej Bahadur Sapru (b. 8 December 1875), lawyer, nationalist, scholar and president of the Indian Council of World Affairs from 1943 until his death

28 April: The London Declaration is issued, enabling India to remain in the British Commonwealth, then renamed the Commonwealth of Nations.

15 August: The National Museum, New Delhi, is inaugurated in the Rashtrapati Bhavan. Its new building is inaugurated on 18 December 1960.

9 September: Queen Kanchanprabha Devi signs the Tripura Merger Agreement, an agreement to cede the state to India.

17 September: The political party of Dravida Munnetra Kazhagam (DMK) is founded in Madras (now Chennai) under the leadership of C.N. Annadurai by a breakaway group of the Dravida Kazhagam.

9 October: The Territorial Army is officially inaugurated. These forces assist the main army and civil administration when required.

15 October: Tripura becomes a part of India.

15 November: Nathuram Godse and Narayan Apte are executed for the murder of Mahatma Gandhi.

1950: INDIA BECOMES A REPUBLIC

India was already independent from 15 August 1947. But in theory, it still had to acknowledge the king of England, George VI, as the head. On 26 January 1950, India became a sovereign, democratic republic—that is, it was fully independent, with its own laws and systems. From this date onwards, India would be governed by its own Constitution, which was finally ready.

❋ CELEBRATIONS

India's first Republic Day was celebrated all over the country, and the celebrations were even more grand than those held on Independence Day. From the night before, the city of Delhi was decorated with arches, flowers and flags, and was glittering with multicoloured lights.

There was an elaborate ceremony in the durbar hall in the morning. The governor general, Rajagopalachari, read a statement announcing that India was now a republic. He would now be replaced by the first President of India, Rajendra Prasad. S. Radhakrishnan was chosen as vice president. The Constituent Assembly became the provisional Parliament until elections could take place. About a hundred more members were added, who were representatives of the Indian states that were now part of India. The provinces were now known as states, and the premiers or prime ministers as chief ministers.

On this occasion too, Bismillah Khan, who had played at the Red Fort upon Independence, performed with his shehnai.

❋ SARDAR PATEL

Vallabhbhai Jhaverbhai Patel (31 October 1875–15 December 1950) was born in Nadiad, Gujarat, and trained as a lawyer in England. After meeting Gandhi in 1916, he joined the Indian National Congress and the freedom movement, and was imprisoned several times. Mahatma Gandhi gave him the title 'sardar' in appreciation of his work in leading a satyagraha (civil disobedience) in Bardoli against the government in 1928. He and Jawaharlal Nehru worked closely together. After Independence, he held important posts, including that of home minister, and, together with V.P. Menon, was involved in the process of integrating the Indian states. Unfortunately, he died of a heart attack, after an illness that was probably cancer, just three years after Independence.

❋ NATIONAL SYMBOLS

A country is represented in the world by certain symbols: its national flag, national anthem and national emblem. The national flag was already chosen in 1947. In 1950, the national anthem and national emblem too were decided.

'Jana Gana Mana', written by Rabindranath Tagore, became the national anthem. Even before its official selection, this song had been used to represent India abroad and by the defence services.

The national emblem uses elements of Mauryan emperor Ashoka's Sarnath lion capital. At its base are three lions with a horse to the left, a bull to the right and a chakra in the centre. Below are the words 'Satyameva Jayate', meaning 'truth alone triumphs'. In later years, other national symbols were chosen. These were:

- National animal: Royal Bengal Tiger;
- National flower: Lotus*;
- National fruit: Mango;
- National river: Ganga;
- National tree: Banyan;
- National aquatic animal: River dolphin;
- National bird: Peacock;
- National heritage animal: Elephant;
- National reptile: King cobra;
- National game: Hockey.

The national emblem

*The lotus is also the national flower of Vietnam.

RAMANA MAHARSHI AND SRI AUROBINDO

This year saw the death of Ramana Maharshi and Sri Aurobindo, two great Indian philosophers.

Sri Ramana (30 December 1879–14 April 1950) was a philosopher and a guru, whose ashram was in Tiruvannamalai, Madras State (now Tamil Nadu), at the foot of the hill Arunachala. Ramana's philosophy was similar to that of the Advaita school. He maintained that only the atman (soul) is real and always remains pure. He advocated the realization of the atman by a constant inquiry into the nature of an individual through the question, 'Who am I?' He often communicated through silence, and saw all people, high and low, as the same. His love and sense of equality extended to animals and plants too. He would eat his simple food only after his favourite cow and dog had been fed. He was against people cutting trees or even plucking flowers, as he believed it caused the plants pain.

Sri Aurobindo (15 August 1872–5 December 1950) was initially involved in the freedom movement. When he was imprisoned in Calcutta, he had a divine experience. He then left British territory and founded an ashram in Pondicherry (Puducherry), which was under the French. There he started a new system known as integral yoga. He believed that human life was evolving towards a higher degree of spirituality, that each person should try to enter into communication with the divine and then act in the world according to that. Sri Aurobindo wrote a number of books which embody his philosophy, as well as an epic poem in 24,000 lines, *Savitri: A Legend and a Symbol*. In this work, he takes the traditional story of Savitri and Satyavan, but interprets it differently. To him, Satyavan represents the soul that has descended into death and ignorance, and Savitri the divine word, the supreme truth.

❋ THE GOLDEN VOICES: MUSIC IN FILMS

Once talkies began in India, music and dance became an integral part of films, just as they had been in early storytelling traditions.

Three of the most popular singers of the time were Talat Mahmood (24 February 1924–9 May 1998), Mohammed Rafi (24 December 1924–31 July 1980) and Mukesh (22 July 1923–27 August 1976), while K.L. Saigal and G.M. Durrani came slightly earlier.

In 1950, Talat Mahmood sang a song in the film *Arzoo*, and became famous. He was already known for his ghazals, and had started singing in 1939 at the age of sixteen on All India Radio,

Lucknow. He moved to Calcutta and sang in Bengali, and then to Bombay, where he sang for numerous films, sometimes duets with Lata Mangeshkar. Talat also acted in several films, from 1945–60.

Mohammed Rafi sang qawwalis, bhajans, romantic songs and ghazals in Hindi films, and also sang in other languages, including Indian languages, English, Dutch, Iranian and Arabic. One of his great songs was 'Bapuji ki Amar Kahani', composed after the Mahatma's death in 1948. His early songs were with the music director Naushad Ali, and later with composers S.D. Burman, Madan Mohan, O.P. Nayyar, Laxmikant–Pyarelal and others.

Mukesh sang for many films from 1941 onwards, for composers and music directors Anil Biswas, Naushad Ali and Shankar–Jaikishan, among others.

ALSO IN 1950

25 January: The Election Commission is set up. Sukumar Sen is the first chief election commissioner.

26 January: Earlier known as the Federal Court, the Supreme Court of India is established, with its inaugural proceedings held on 28 January. It is the highest constitutional court in the country and is located in Tilak Marg, New Delhi.

1 April: India is the first non-socialist-bloc country to recognize the People's Republic of China.

8 April: The Liaquat–Nehru Pact, an agreement, is signed between Pakistan and India to protect minorities and regulate the migration of refugees.

9 April: The Indian Council for Cultural Relations is founded to foster and strengthen cultural relations and mutual understanding between India and other countries.

31 July: The Indo-Nepal Treaty of Peace and Friendship is signed.

5 August: Death of Gopinath Bordoloi (b. 1890), prime minister of Assam in 1946, chief minister after Independence and recipient of the Bharat Ratna (1999, posthumous) for his contribution to the freedom movement and the development of Assam

15 August: The Assam–Tibet earthquake, on the border of Tibet (with its epicentre in Rima, Tibet, and a moment magnitude of 8.6), causes destruction and deaths in both countries.

5 November: Death of Hindustani classical vocalist Faiyaz Khan (b. 1886)

1951: COUNTING THE PEOPLE

The British had begun the process of counting the people in their Indian provinces back in 1881. This is known as a census. Along with the count, some details of the people were collected too. It helped in getting to know more about the population, including their literacy level, religion and languages spoken. A census is useful when planning development.

In the 1951 census, the first after Independence, the calculated population was 36,09,50,365. Even then, the entire population of the new India could not be counted; territories controlled by the French and the Portuguese, the state of Jammu and Kashmir—which was too disturbed—and some remote areas like the North-East Frontier Agency (now Arunachal Pradesh) were left out. In addition to the population count, the census figures showed:

- There were 4 million Indians living abroad.
- The male–female ratio was 1000 to 946.
- There were five cities with a population of over a million: Bombay, Calcutta, Madras, Hyderabad and Delhi.
- There were seventy-five cities with a population of over a lakh.

The two notable events of the year were the conclusion of the Telangana Movement, a peasant rebellion against landlords that had started in the state of Hyderabad in 1946, and the initiation of *bhudan*.

❋ THE BHUDAN MOVEMENT

Vinoba Bhave, a saintly person, wanted to build a new India where people would be more equal than before. He felt that wealthy people should share what they had with the poor and so he requested prosperous landowners to donate one-sixth of their land. This would be given to those who were landless. This was called 'bhudan', 'the gift of land'. The first gift of land was received on 18 April 1951 in the village of Pochampally, in Nalgonda district of Telangana. When Vinoba visited it, there were 700 families living there, mostly landless. Vedre Ramachandra Reddy, a local landlord, offered to donate 250 acres to those who had no land, thus starting the Bhudan movement.

Pochampally soon developed into a town and came to be known as Bhudan Pochampally. The town is famous for its textiles, particularly silk, woven with ikat patterns. Silk weaving in Pochampally dates back to the eighteenth century. Today, Pochampally's fabrics have both

Vinoba Bhave

SOME OTHER TYPES OF TEXTILES

Bandhani: It literally means 'tying' and is a term for coloured textiles created by tying knots in the cloth before dyeing it. The knotted areas remain free of dye. Red, blue and other bright colours are used. Simple patterns consist of spots and squares, but there are more complex designs too. The technique dates back to the eighteenth century. Textiles of this type are made mainly in Gujarat and Rajasthan.

Kalamkari: These are painted textiles. Such textiles began to be made in the seventeenth century, when designs were painted on cloth using a pen. There are different types of kalamkari. Some have block prints along with paintings, while others only have painted designs. Scenes from the Mahabharata and the Ramayana as well as images of deities are common. Kalamkari textiles are made at different centres, including Srikalahasti and Machilipatnam in Andhra Pradesh, Thanjavur, in Tamil Nadu, as well as in Gujarat.

Ikat: This is a technique where the warp and weft threads are tie-dyed before weaving.

Bleeding Madras: This type of fabric is handwoven checked cotton, dyed with non-permanent vegetable colours that have faded and spread upon being washed. It was extremely popular in the 1960s, and was exported to the USA, being especially in demand in California.

traditional and modern patterns, woven in silk, cotton and a mixture of the two. To create the patterns, the warp, and sometimes the weft too, are tie-dyed before they are woven.

❋ THE MUSICAL CLOCK

The Salar Jung Museum in Hyderabad was opened to the public by Jawaharlal Nehru on 16 December 1951. More than 40,000 objects are displayed in this grand museum, originally collected by Nawab Mir

Yousuf Ali Khan, Salar Jung III, the prime minister of the state of Hyderabad from 1912 to 1914. Salar Jung III acquired unique artefacts from all over the world as well as from India. There are swords and daggers belonging to the Mughal emperors, carpets from Bukhara and Shiraz, original paintings by European artists such as Edwin Landseer and a marble statue called the *Veiled Rebecca* by Giovanni Benzoni, as well as many more objects. The museum also has a vast library. Among the various items, it has a number of clocks, including a mechanical one called a British bracket clock. A figure comes out of a space in this and strikes a gong every hour. To this day, crowds gather to see it.

ABANINDRANATH TAGORE

Abanindranath Tagore (7 August 1871–5 December 1951), a noted artist, the great-grandson of Dwarkanath Tagore and the nephew of Rabindranath Tagore, developed the style of painting known as the Bengal school of art, based on Indian traditions and spirituality. Many later artists studied with Abanindranath, including Nandalal Bose, Asit Kumar Haldar, Kshitin Majumdar and Suren Ganguly.

Abanindranath was also a writer, and wrote books for adults and children. *Khirer Putul*, first written in 1896, with later translations, is the story of a queen, a monkey and a sugar doll.

The Bengal school of art was associated with nationalism while the Calcutta group of artists, an offshoot of the Bengal school, formed in 1943, was inspired by impressionist, post-impressionist and expressionist schools of art. Pradosh Das Gupta, Paritosh Sen and Nirode Mazumdar were among this group.

THE ASIAN GAMES

The Asian Athletics Federation was founded on 13 February 1949, and was also known as the Asian Games Federation. It was formed to bring unity among newly independent Asian nations. The First

Asian Games were held in Delhi from 4–11 March 1951. India did well, winning sixteen gold medals (athletics: eleven; aquatics: four; football: one), as well as sixteen silver and twenty bronze medals. In these games, India was second only to Japan.

● FILMS ROUND-UP

The total number of feature films produced in 1951 is: Hindi: 100 (including Urdu and Rajasthani); Bengali: 38; Telugu: 30; Tamil: 26; Marathi: 16; Malayalam: 7; Gujarati: 6; Punjabi: 4; Kannada: 2.

In addition to these, there were documentaries and short films.

ALSO IN 1951

20 January: Death of Amritlal Vithaldas Thakkar (b. 29 November 1869), also known as Thakkar Bapa, who was a tireless worker for Dalits and tribals

May: Visva-Bharati, located in Santiniketan, West Bengal, is recognized as a university.

18 June: The first amendment is made to the Constitution. This has several provisions, including modifications to the right to freedom of speech as well as protection for the laws for the advancement of backward castes.

August: The first Indian Institute of Technology (IIT), in Kharagpur, starts its first academic session.

21 October: Bharatiya Jana Sangh, a political party, is founded by Shyama Prasad Mukherjee.

27 October: The Delhi Public Library is established jointly by UNESCO and the Government of India.

5 November: The Central Railway and Western Railway are formed by merging smaller railways.

1952: THE FIRST ELECTIONS

The first election of free India was held between 25 October 1951 and 21 February 1952. An election commissioner had been appointed and now an electoral roll (a list of all the people who could vote) had to be prepared. It had been decided that everyone over the age of twenty-one was eligible to vote. The electoral roll listed 176 million people. Many women were not part of that list as they were too traditional to provide their names.

The country was divided into territorial constituencies (areas from where candidates would be elected). Steel ballot boxes were constructed in different colours, with the party symbol pasted on top. Voters put a ballot paper into the box of the party or candidate they chose. The new Lok Sabha, the lower house of Parliament that governs the country and passes laws, would elect 489 people. There were:

* 2.5 million ballot boxes;
* 620 million ballot papers;
* 2,24,000 polling booths.

All the states too would elect their governments, and a total of 3283 people would be elected to the state assemblies.

In this first election there were 17,500 candidates and a number of political parties. Some, like the Indian National Congress, were founded before Independence, while others, such as the Bharatiya Jana Sangh, were founded after.

After the election, the Congress won the most seats and formed the central and state governments. It had 364 seats in the Lok Sabha and a majority in most states, but in four states, it needed the support of other parties.

After the election, the first Lok Sabha and the first state governments of independent India were formed.

Indian National Congress

Socialist Party

Kisan Mazdoor Praja Party

Communist Party of India

Bharatiya Jana Sangh

All India Scheduled Caste Federation

Ram Rajya Parishad

The election symbols

✦ RASHID JAHAN AND GHULAM AHMAD MAHJOOR

This year saw the death of two noted writers.

Rashid Jahan has been called Urdu literature's first 'angry young woman'. She was a doctor, a writer, a member of the communist party, of the Indian People's Theatre Association as well as a founder member of the Progressive Writers' Association. She was born on 25 August 1905 and her parents, Sheikh Abdullah and Waheeda Begum, sent her to a girls' school that they had started themselves. She wrote short stories and plays, many of these on the problems faced by women. She died in 1952 in Moscow and is buried there. She was only forty-seven years old, and had gone there for the treatment of cancer. On her grave is the epitaph 'Communist Writer and Doctor'.

Some of her stories are included in a collection called *Angaarey*, recently translated into English from the original Urdu. First published in 1932, it also contains stories in Urdu by Sajjad Zaheer, Ahmed Ali and Mahmud-uz-Zafar. Though the book was banned, it inspired more Urdu writers and led to the founding of the Progressive Writers' Association, which was joined by writers such as Chughtai, Manto, Premchand and Faiz.

Ghulam Ahmad Mahjoor (1885–9 April 1952) was a Kashmiri-language poet. His popularity was so great that when he died, he was given a state funeral. His poem 'Gris' Kur (A Peasant Girl) indicates his love for a simple rural life, 'Azadi' (Freedom) comments on the problems accompanying Independence while 'Sangarmalan' hopes for a new era of peace and friendship. He wrote many more poems.

THE OLYMPICS AND OTHER SPORTS

In 1952, India participated in the Summer Olympics in Helsinki. India took part in hockey and other sports, including aquatics, cycling, shooting, weightlifting, wrestling, football, athletics and boxing. Indian women participated for the first time in these Olympics. This time too, India won the hockey gold. K.D. Jadhav (d. 1984) won the first individual Olympic medal for independent India. This was a bronze in wrestling, in the 52-kilogram freestyle. He later died in a road accident at the age of fifty-eight.

The first National Volleyball Championship was held in Madras in 1952 and was won by Mysore (now Mysuru).

CHILDREN'S DAY

Every country observes Children's Day to celebrate the innocence and courage of childhood, and to remind one to work for the welfare of children. India's Children's Day is observed every year on 14 November, the birthday of India's first prime minister, Jawaharlal Nehru. He was known for his love for children. This day was chosen in 1952. Earlier it was known as Flower Day and was first celebrated on 5 November 1948.

❋ AAN

The 1952 Hindi film *Aan* was a box office hit. It was one of the first Hindi films made in Technicolor. An earlier film, *Kisan Kanya* (1937) was shot in Cinecolor, but did not become popular. *Aan* was directed and produced by Mehboob Khan, and the main actors were Dilip Kumar, Nimmi, Nadira and Premnath. It was perhaps the first Hindi film to have an international release, and was dubbed in English and French, as well as in Tamil. The music was by Naushad and the lyrics by Shakeel Badayuni, while the songs were sung by Mohammed Rafi, Lata Mangeshkar and Shamshad Begum.

Baiju Bawra was another great film of the year, directed by Vijay Bhatt and narrating the story of Tansen and Baiju Bawra.

The year also saw the passing of the Cinematograph Act on film censorship, which replaced an earlier law of 1920.

WOMEN IN HINDI CINEMA

Nimmi (b. 1933) and Nadira (1932–2006), two female actors, had both acted in *Aan*. In fact, it was Florence Ezekiel Nadira's debut, while Nimmi began her career with Raj Kapoor's *Barsaat* in 1949. Among other women actors at this time, Madhubala made her debut as a child actress in the film *Basant* in 1942. She came to be known as a great beauty, and her role as Anarkali in *Mughal-e-Azam* (1960) is considered to be her greatest. Nargis and Suraiya were among other stars.

In many circles in India, acting was still not considered a respectable profession for women. These stars, however, did not face problems, nor did some who debuted earlier, such as Durga Khote and Devika Rani. But at least two early artists, Gulab Bai and Anusuya Bai (renamed Kamala Devi and Sushila Devi respectively), who were part of Prabhat Film Company, actually had to live in the studio after they were ostracized by their families.

● WILDLIFE

As wildlife was declining, an advisory body, the Indian Board for Wildlife, was set up in 1952. The chairperson was the prime minister. Over the years, more organizations for wildlife protection were added and brought under the Wildlife Division of the Ministry of Environment and Forests.

ALSO IN 1952

7 March: Death of Paramahansa Yogananda (b. 1893), who set up the Yogoda Satsang Society of India in Ranchi and founded Kriya Yoga

September: The Praja Socialist Party (PSP) is formed by the old Socialist Party and the Kisan Mazdoor Praja Party coming together.

2 October: Community development projects start.

December: The First Five-Year Plan is presented in Parliament and officially signed, though some of its programmes have been initiated from April 1951.

The first International Film Festival of India is held in Bombay, with Raj Kapoor's *Awara* as the Indian entry. This film later goes on to become popular in the Soviet Union.

1953: THE PARADISE OF KASHMIR

Kashmir is one of the most beautiful states of India. But ever since Independence, there were problems in the state. Pakistan had taken over some of the territory, which remained with the country. Kashmir was promised autonomy in its internal affairs, and that it would be allowed to make its own constitution. Karan Singh, son of Maharaja Hari Singh, who had ruled Kashmir before Independence, was made the sadar-i-riyasat in 1952. In 1953, Sheikh Abdullah, a popular leader who had earlier been the prime minister, was imprisoned and replaced by Bakshi Ghulam Mohammad. Abdullah was jailed because he wanted Kashmir to be independent. Except for a brief period in 1958, Abdullah remained in prison till 1964.

Meanwhile, Shyama Prasad Mukherjee, of the Bharatiya Jana Sangh, was among those who had a plan to reunite Pakistan and India. But when he went to Kashmir, he was imprisoned and died there on 23 June 1953.

❊ A NEW STATE

At this time, Madras was a large state covering much of south India, where people spoke different languages, including Tamil and Telugu. The Telugu speakers wanted a state of their own, and one of the leaders, Potti Sriramulu, who had been a freedom fighter, began a fast to pressurize the government into creating a new state. He fasted for fifty-eight days and died in December 1952. After this, agitation for a new state increased and was accompanied by violence. Finally, on 1 October 1953, the new state of Andhra was formed from the northern portion of Madras. The States Reorganization Commission was set up in 1953 to decide the boundary lines of other states.

● CLIMBING MOUNT EVEREST: TENZING NORGAY

Many had tried and failed to climb the highest mountain in the world. Tenzing Norgay (15 May 1914–9 May 1986), a Sherpa from Nepal who settled in Darjeeling, India, and the New Zealander Edmund Hillary were the first to reach the top of Mount Everest on 29 May 1953.

About that moment, Tenzing said, 'It was 11.30 in the morning, the sun was shining and the sky was the deepest blue I have ever seen.'[4]

Tenzing had no formal education, but loved the mountains and trained himself to climb. As a young boy, he took care of the family yaks, but later moved to Darjeeling and began his mountaineering career as a porter. After he reached the Everest summit, he became famous and received many awards, including the George Medal presented by Queen Elizabeth II, the Order of the Star of Nepal, the Cullum Geographical Medal of the American Geographical Society and the Founder's Medal of the Royal Geographical Society. Mountaineering institutes were

---

[4] Tenzing Norgay and James Ramsey Ullman, *Tiger of the Snows: The Autobiography of Tenzing of Everest* (New York: G.P. Putnam's Sons, 1955).

being established in India at the time, and Tenzing became the director of training at the Himalayan Mountaineering Institute in Darjeeling in 1954–55. After his retirement in 1977, he remained an adviser. He climbed mountains in other parts of the world, including some in the Swiss Alps and in Japan.

Books on him include two autobiographies: one with James Ramsey Ullman called *Tiger of the Snows* (1955) and the other, *After Everest* (1977) with Malcolm Barnes.

THE SANGEET NATAK AKADEMI

The Sangeet Natak Akademi, the national academy for music, dance and drama was set up in New Delhi in 1953. The academy presents awards to noted artists every year. Its highest honour is the Sangeet Natak Akademi Fellowship, known as the Ratna Sadasya.

DANCE IN INDIA

Dance is widespread in India, including classical and folk forms, as well as innovative modern dance. Dances are accompanied by rhythm and music, and there is both pure dance—in which movements create a work that has no story but evokes a mood—and dance that tells a story. Classical dance forms include Bharatanatyam, Kathak, Kathakali, Krishnanattam, Kuchipudi, Manipuri, Mohiniattam, Odissi, Ottanthullal, Yakshagana, Koodiyattam, Chakiarkoothu, Bhagavata Mela Nataka, Sattriya and Chhau. Folk and tribal dances also exist all over India, and some of the classical dances have absorbed elements of these.

Dance has been related to temple rituals, festivals and seasonal cycles such as harvests. Dance is linked with drama and storytelling too, particularly the retelling of myths from the epics. Dance was also performed for entertainment, both in courts and elsewhere.

In the late medieval days, dance and dancers began to be looked down upon, but after Independence, they regained their stature. After Independence, national and private dance schools were set up across the country.

KATHAK

Among the subsidiary institutes of the Sangeet Natak Akademi is the Kathak Kendra, also in New Delhi. Kathak, a classical dance form, has existed in India from ancient times; dance, song and drama were used to narrate stories from the Puranas and the epics, and Kathak (from the word *katha*, meaning 'story') was a dance form used for this. It was modified in Mughal times, and incorporated Persian and Turkish elements. Today, it is a prominent classical dance form of north India, with the three main gharanas or schools of Jaipur, Lucknow and Varanasi. One of the main and most influential dancers and teachers of Kathak in independent India is Birju Maharaj (b. 1938) of the Lucknow gharana. He learnt from his father, Acchan Maharaj (d. 1960), and his uncles, Shambhu (1910–70) and Lacchu Maharaj (1907–78). Birju Maharaj was closely associated with the Kathak Kendra, and thus has taught and influenced many dancers. He is also the choreographer of many dance dramas. He has received several awards, including the Sangeet Natak Akademi Award (1964), the Kalidas Samman (1986–87) and the Padma Vibhushan (1986).

Among the many other noted Kathak dancers are Shovana Narayan (b. 1949), who trained with Birju Maharaj and Guru Kundanlal Gangani (1926–84) at the Kathak Kendra, New Delhi; Rohini Bhate (1924–2008), who learnt with Lachhu Maharaj and Mohanrao Kallianpurkar (1913–85), and founded the Nrityabharati Kathak Dance Academy in Pune in 1947; Uma Sharma (b. 1942), who trained with Guru Hiralalji and Girvar Dayal of the Jaipur gharana and later with Sunder Prasad, Shambhu Maharaj and Birju Maharaj. Uma has created new dance forms by incorporating different elements, such as those of the Rasa Lila of Vrindavan. She also started a school of music and dance, and received several awards.

Kathak dancers

❋ A LIBRARY WITH A SECRET ROOM

India has over 60,000 libraries, and one of the most important is the National Library in Kolkata, which acquires a copy of every book published in the country. Its origins date back to before Independence, when the Imperial Library in Calcutta was inaugurated in 1903 by merging two existing libraries. After Independence, it came to be known as the National Library. It was moved to its present building on Belvedere Estate, Alipore, and opened to the public on 1 February 1953. It is the largest library in the country.

In 2010, when repairing the structure, it was found that the library building, dating back to British times, has a large hidden room. The room has neither an entry nor an exit; it is completely sealed. What had it been used for? No one really knows.

ALSO IN 1953

15 June: The Air Corporations Act (effective 1 August) nationalizes Air India and separates it into Indian Airlines and Air India International Limited.

September 1953: The Rajkumari Amrit Kaur Coaching Scheme for sports is founded.

The National Research Development Corporation is set up under the Ministry of Science and Technology to develop and coordinate inventions, patents and processes.

1954: INDIA AND CHINA ARE FRIENDS

India and China are two ancient Asian nations. While India gained independence in 1947, China formed a new government under Mao Zedong in 1949. India was one of the first countries to recognize the People's Republic of China.

Tibet lay between India and China. And in 1950, China claimed Tibet as part of its country. Though India had inherited some rights in Tibet from the British, it tried to remain friendly with China. In 1954, India and China signed an agreement, which was mainly a trade pact and recognized the Chinese occupation of Tibet. This also had five principles known as *panchsheel*, which included agreements to maintain peace and to respect each other's territory.

❋ OTHER KEY EVENTS

The small Portuguese-held territories of Dadra and Nagar Haveli succeeded in freeing themselves, and set up their own local government.

In 1949, a law had been passed on women abducted during Partition. This said that such women had to return to their own country, whether or not they wanted to. This law was withdrawn in 1954 as it had caused a lot of hardship to those who had settled down in new families and had even had children.

❋ THE NATIONAL GALLERY OF MODERN ART

Independent India needed new museums and art galleries. And so the National Gallery of Modern Art was established in New Delhi on 29 March 1954, located in what was once the residence of the maharaja of Jaipur. The first curator was the German art historian Hermann Goetz, who had also set up an art museum in Baroda. At the inauguration of the gallery, there was an exhibition of sculptures by all the major Indian sculptors of the time: Ramkinkar Baij (1910–80), Sankho Chaudhuri (1916–2006), Dhanraj Bhagat (1917–88) and Devi Prasad Roy Chowdhury (1899–1975), along with several others.

Today, the gallery includes the work of Indian artists from 1857 onwards, as well as those of European travellers. Among the well-known Indian artists whose works are preserved here are Raja Ravi Varma (1848–1906), Abanindranath Tagore (1871–1951), Nandalal Bose (1883–1966), Benode Behari Mukherjee (1904–80), Rabindranath Tagore (1861–1941), Gaganendranath Tagore (1867–1938), Jamini Roy (1887–1972), Amrita Sher-Gil (1913–41), Nicholas Roerich (1874–1947), M.F. Husain (1915–2011), Tyeb Mehta (1925–2009), Bhabesh Sanyal (1901–2003), Sailoz Mukherjee (1906–60), Ram Kumar (b. 1924), Krishen Khanna (b. 1925), J. Swaminathan (1928–94), Manjit Bawa (1941–2008), Anjolie Ela Menon (b. 1940) and many more. It has over 17,000 works, as well as prints, photographs and a large library.

Two branches of the gallery were later set up in Mumbai and Bengaluru (Bangalore).

THE LALIT KALA AKADEMI

Another important art institute, the Lalit Kala Akademi was established in the same year on 5 August. Its aim is to promote and propagate Indian art, both within and outside the country. The academy gradually set up numerous regional centres known as Rashtriya Lalit Kala Kendras. They hold exhibitions, bring out publications and have several awards and honours for Indian artists.

SHYAMCHI AAI AND THE NATIONAL FILM AWARDS

Shyamchi Aai, a Marathi film, received the first National Award for the best feature film.

All-India awards for films started being granted in 1954. These were known as the President's Awards and later as the National Film Awards. The President's Gold Medal was given for the best feature film and the best documentary, and the Prime Minister's Gold Medal for the best children's film. The films that placed second and third in each of these categories were awarded an all-India certificate of merit. In 1958, it was decided that cash prizes would be given to producers and directors of award-winning films. Separate awards were instituted for educational films in 1959. Apart from the all-India awards, the government also instituted regional awards from 1955 onwards.

In 1954, certificates of merit were awarded to Bimal Roy's *Do Bigha Zamin*, and to the Bengali film *Bhagavan Sri Krishna Chaitanya*. The best documentary was *Mahabalipuram*, with certificates of merit given to *Holy Himalayas* and *Tree of Wealth*. The Prime Minister's Gold Medal was not awarded, but the certificate of merit for the best children's film went to the Bengali film *Khela Ghar*.

Shyamchi Aai (Shyam's Mother) is based on a Marathi book by Sane Guruji (Pandurang Sadashiv Sane, 1899–1950) and is autobiographical. It consists of twelve short stories about a boy, Shyam,

A reproduction of the cover of *Shyamchi Aai*

and his mother, Yashoda. The stories depict cultural and family values, and provide an endearing portrait of Yashoda. For example, in one of the stories, Shyam's mother is ill with malaria. She wants to perform the Savitri *vrata*, for which she has to circle a banyan tree 108 times. Her fever has made her too weak to do it herself, and she asks Shyam to do it for her. He refuses at first. Vratas were for women, and his friends and everyone who saw him would laugh. But his mother convinces him that it is God's work and nothing to be ashamed of.

In another story, Shyam's mother offers stones to God as she has no money for sweets. She convinces Shyam that God will love her stones as He appreciates the love behind them. Yashoda is also kind and caring towards all living creatures. She looks after Mori the cow and Mathi the cat, who always eats near Yashoda's plate.

The film put together these stories, and it was screened again on Mother's Day 2010 in Mumbai.

❋ THE MOVEMENT OF LIGHT

What happens to light when it moves through something transparent? This is one of the problems C.V. Raman (7 November 1888–21 November 1970) worked on, and for which he won the Nobel Prize in Physics in 1930. He was the first Asian to receive the Nobel Prize in any field of science. He received many more awards and honours, including the Bharat Ratna in 1954. Born in Thiruvanaikoil, Tiruchirappalli (then in the Madras Presidency), he set up the Raman Research Institute in Bangalore. His work included the study of light, the vibration of musical instruments and the X-ray diffraction of liquids and crystals. The Nobel Prize was awarded 'for his work on the scattering of light and for the discovery of the [Raman effect]'.[5] He discovered that when light

---

[5] 'The Nobel Prize in Physics 1930', *Nobelprize.org*, Nobel Media AB 2014, accessed 11 June 2017, http://www.nobelprize.org/nobel_prizes/physics/laureates/1930/.

passes through transparent material, there are some changes in the wavelength of the deflected light.

❈ THE SAHITYA AKADEMI

The Sahitya Akademi, a literature academy, was set up by the Government of India on 12 March 1954 in New Delhi.

It promotes Indian literature in English and all Indian languages, has a vast library and an extensive programme of publications. These include surveys and very valuable translations, making literature in regional languages available to a wider audience. The academy also presents literary awards and fellowships. Krishna Kripalani (1907–92), a lawyer and educationist, was the first secretary of the Sahitya Akademi, from 1954–71. In recognition of his contribution to its development, he was awarded the Padma Bhushan in 1969.

❈ THE BHARAT RATNA

The Bharat Ratna, India's highest civilian award, was first awarded in 1954. The award is for exceptional work in art, literature or science, and in recognition of public service of the highest order. Apart from C.V. Raman, mentioned above, the other awardees of the year were S. Radhakrishnan and Chakravarti Rajagopalachari.

ALSO IN 1954

1 April: The first Indian air chief, Air Marshal Subroto Mukerjee, takes command. With the expansion of the Indian Air Force, the rank is elevated to air chief marshal in 1966. The first to hold this rank is Arjan Singh.

1–9 May: The Second Asian Games are held in Manila. India wins five gold (athletics), four silver and eight bronze medals.

3 August: The Department of Atomic Energy is formed. It conducts research and development, offers financial support to institutions engaged in nuclear research, looks after nuclear power production and industries and minerals.

22 October: Death of Jibanananda Das (b. 1899), Bengali-language poet, writer and essayist

1955: INDIA BECOMES A WORLD LEADER

A large part of the world, particularly Europe, was divided into two groups. They were not fighting, but neither were they friendly. This was known as the Cold War and lasted from 1945 to 1991. Jawaharlal Nehru did not want India to belong to either of these groups. He wanted the newly free nations of Asia and Africa to come together and act independently. In 1955, leaders of many of these countries met in Bandung, Indonesia. This was the beginning of the Non-Aligned Movement, which was formally set up in 1961.

❖ OTHER KEY EVENTS

In 1955, the new Socialist Party was founded by Ram Manohar Lohia after a split from the Praja Socialist Party.

A new Hindu Marriage Act was passed. The act stipulated the minimum marriageable age of fifteen for women and eighteen for men, and prohibited polygamy. It also included other clauses and laid out conditions for the registration of the marriage as well as for divorce.

Roshen Dalal

'RAGHUPATI RAGHAVA RAJA RAM'

Dattatreya Vishnu Paluskar (28 May 1921–26 October 1955), a great singer, died of encephalitis at the young age of thirty-four. His story begins with that of his father, Vishnu Digambar Paluskar (1872–1931), who was not only a well-known classical singer of Hindustani music, but the composer of the famous bhajan 'Raghupati Raghava Raja Ram' and the founder of many music schools, the Gandharva Vidyalayas. Dattatreya was born in Nashik and began his musical training early, though his father died when he was only ten years old. He continued training with other singers, including Narayanrao Vyas and Vinayakrao Patwardhan. He developed into a great singer and became an All India Radio artist at the age of seventeen. He belonged to the Gwalior gharana. The bhajans he sang include those of Meera, Kabir, Tulsidas and Surdas. In the film *Baiju Bawra* (1952), he sang a duet in raga Desi with Amir Khan that remains popular even today. The film is based on the legend of Tansen, the famed musician in the court of the emperor Akbar, who was challenged to a singing contest by Baiju Bawra. Amir Khan was to sing as Tansen, and he insisted that, even though it was just a story, he would accept loss in the contest only to D.V. Paluskar. This song brought Paluskar the most fame. In 1955, he went to China with a cultural delegation and sang in several cities, but died just two months later of an infection he picked up there.

Among other students of Vishnu Digambar Paluskar who went on to become great singers was Omkarnath Thakur (1897–1967), who became the first dean of the faculty of music at Banaras Hindu University, and had a melodious and powerful voice. He composed music under the name Pranav Rang, and wrote two books on music, *Sangeetanjali* and *Pranav Bharati*. Vinayakrao Patwardhan (22 July 1898–23 August 1975) was taught by Paluskar at the Gandharva Vidyalaya in Lahore, and later he himself taught at some branches of the Gandharva Vidyalayas. He received several awards, including the Padma Bhushan in 1972, and wrote books on music. Another one of Paluskar's notable students was Vishnudas Shirali (1907–84), vocalist, sitar player, composer and writer.

> **WHAT IS A GHARANA?**
>
> A gharana is a style of music. For example, the Senia gharana consists of those who follow Tansen's style of music. The word 'gharana' comes from 'ghar', meaning 'home'.

❋ CAT AND LOBSTER

Jamini Roy (1887–1972) was a renowned artist, initially a student of Abanindranath Tagore at the Government College of Art, Kolkata. He developed his own style influenced by folk art, particularly the Kalighat paintings of West Bengal and the early palm-leaf miniatures of western India. His paintings have different themes, including scenes from mythology, such as the Ramayana and the Krishna Leela, and from daily life. He received several awards, including the Padma Bhushan in 1955. Among his paintings in the National Gallery of Modern Art are *Gopini*, *Mother and Child*, *Santhal Girl*, *Santhal Dance* and *Cat and Lobster*.

❋ MANTO PASSES AWAY

Partition inspired many books, stories and films. Among the great authors was Saadat Hasan Manto (1912–55), who moved to Lahore from Bombay in 1947 and wrote several books and short stories. His most famous story, 'Toba Tek Singh', reflects the

A reproduction of *Cat and Lobster*

confusion and bewilderment of one man at the time of Partition. In the story, Bishan Singh, a Sikh in an asylum in Lahore, is to be transferred to India, though his village, Toba Tek Singh, is in Pakistan. He refuses to go, and when the truck with him and other Hindu and Sikh inmates reaches the Wagah border, he collapses between the barbed wire fences marking the boundaries of the two countries.

Manto married Safia in 1936, and after his death, was survived by his wife and three young girls. He deeply felt the tragedy of Partition and this sorrow led to alcoholism, which brought about his death at a young age.

❋ PATHER PANCHALI

Bengali cinema had an early start with two talkies being made in 1931, *Jamai Shashthi* and *Dena Paona*, but Satyajit Ray's *Pather Panchali* (1955) began a new era in Bengali films. Satyajit Ray (1921–92) initially studied art, and became a commercial artist. When he came across the novel *Pather Panchali* (Song of the Road), he obtained the film rights and began shooting the film with his personal funds. Later, the West Bengal government financed the production, enabling its completion. Its world premiere was at the Museum of Modern Art in New York.

Based on the book by Bibhutibhushan Bandyopadhyay, it tells the story of Apu, his elder sister, Durga, their parents, Harihar Roy and Sarbajaya, and an old cousin, Indir Thakrun, in a village in rural Bengal. The film realistically depicts the joys and problems of the children, but ends with the tragic death of Durga and a move away from the village. The film won the National Film Award in 1955, the Best Human Document Award in the 1956 Cannes Film Festival and several others. Chunibala Devi, who acted as Indir Thakrun, died in 1955 before the release of the film. Two sequels followed, *Aparajito* (1956) and *Apur Sansar* (1959).

Satyajit Ray went on to make more films, and was established as one of India's best directors. His other films include *Jalsaghar* (1958), *Nayak* (1966), *Pratidwandi* (1970), *Ashani Sanket* (1973), *Shatranj ke Khilari* (1977), *Charulata* (1964), *Kanchenjungha* (1962), *Teen Kanya* (1961), *Devi* (1960), *Goopy Gyne Bagha Byne* (1968), *Seemabaddha* (1971), *Jana Aranya* (1975) and *Agantuk* (1992), his last film. Before his death in 1992, he received an Oscar and the Bharat Ratna.

Other remarkable directors of early Bengali films include Ritwik Ghatak, who made several films from the 1950s onwards, and Mrinal Sen. Ritwik Ghatak's films deal with traumatic situations, including the plight of refugees. Among his films are *Meghe Dhaka Tara* (1960), *Komal Gandhar* (1961) and *Subarnarekha* (1965). Some of Mrinal Sen's films are *Bhuvan Shome* (1969), *Chorus* (1974), *Mrigayaa* (1976), *Ek Din Pratidin* (1979), *Akaler Sandhane* (1980) and *Genesis* (1986).

Other film-makers of Bengal include Tapan Sinha, Tarun Majumdar and Buddhadeb Dasgupta.

As for the Hindi films of 1955, *Shree 420*, starring Raj Kapoor and Nargis, was the highest-grossing film at the box office.

ALSO IN 1955

1 January: Death of Shanti Swarup Bhatnagar (b. 1894), scientist and director of the Council of Scientific and Industrial Research, who increased national laboratories

January: The National Defence Academy is established at Khadakvasla near Pune, Maharashtra.

30 April: The Imperial Bank of India, established in 1921, becomes the State Bank of India.

The Oil and Natural Gas Commission (ONGC) is founded.

The first Indian cultural delegation visits China, headed by the minister of external affairs A.K. Chanda.

The Bharat Ratna awardees of the year are Bhagwan Das, M. Visvesvaraya and Jawaharlal Nehru.

Baba Allauddin Khan is awarded the Sangeet Natak Akademi Fellowship for lifetime contribution to Indian music.

1956: REORGANIZING THE STATES

The States Reorganization Act was passed in November 1956. Now there were fourteen states and six territories administered by the Centre. The states were: Andhra Pradesh, Assam, Bihar, Bombay, Jammu and Kashmir, Kerala, Madhya Pradesh, Madras, Mysore, Orissa, Punjab, Rajasthan, Uttar Pradesh and West Bengal. The union territories were: Delhi, Himachal Pradesh, Manipur, Tripura, the Andaman and Nicobar Islands, and the Laccadive, Minicoy and Amindivi Islands. Another major change was that now all rajpramukhs were abolished and replaced by Governors.

French territories had been handed over to India, though legal documents for this were yet to be signed. In 1947, the loges or small French posts were returned. Chandernagore (now Chandannagar) was transferred to India in 1951, and Pondicherry and other areas in 1956, though they'd been effectively under Indian control from 1954.

❋ BABASAHEB AMBEDKAR

The end of the year saw the death of Bhimrao Ramji Ambedkar (14 April 1891–6 December 1956), one of the framers of the Constitution and a great Dalit leader. He was born in Mhow,

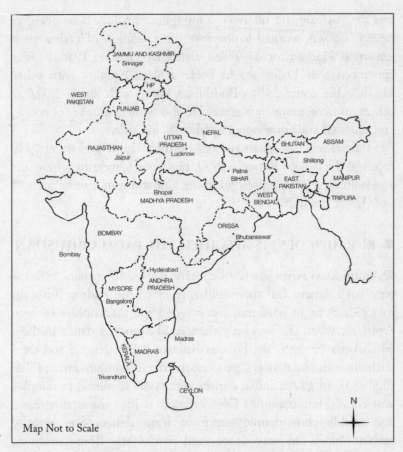

The states after reorganization, 1956

Madhya Pradesh, and was of the Mahar caste. He was lucky enough to complete school and receive a scholarship from the Gaekwad of Baroda to study further in the USA. After this, he went to England to study law and qualified as a lawyer. When he returned to India, he held several government and other posts, and in 1946, became a member of the Constituent Assembly and chairman of the committee for drafting the Constitution. After Independence, he was the law minister till 1951. Throughout his life, Babasaheb, as he was known, worked to improve the condition of Dalits, then known as Harijans or scheduled castes. By October 1956, he was convinced that Dalits would never achieve equality with other Hindus. He converted to Buddhism, along with about 2,00,000 others, in a ceremony in Nagpur. He also wrote a number of books, and founded and contributed to Marathi journals.

Babasaheb is a leader revered both by Dalits and others. He received the Bharat Ratna in 1990. His statues, wearing a blue suit and holding a book representing the Constitution, can be seen all over Uttar Pradesh.

❋ RUKMINI DEVI IS AWARDED THE PADMA BHUSHAN

Rukmini Devi Arundale (29 February 1904–24 February 1986), a renowned dancer and theosophist, received the Padma Bhushan in 1956. Born in Madurai, she married the theosophist George Arundale when she was only sixteen. She studied dance initially with Anna Pavlova, the famous Russian ballet dancer, and then with other Indian dancers, particularly Meenakshi Sundaram Pillai (d. 1954). In 1920s India, dance was mainly confined to temples and courts, but Rukmini Devi brought it into the mainstream, and middle-class people began to learn dance. She actually revolutionized the way dance, and particularly Bharatanatyam, was performed. E. Krishna Iyer (1897–1968) also contributed to this, encouraging girls from higher classes to learn dance. He and Rukmini Devi together chose the name Bharatanatyam for the temple dances earlier known as Sadirnatyam. In 1936, Rukmini set up Kalakshetra in Madras, a centre for the study of performing and creative arts. She also worked for animal welfare, and wrote and lectured on theosophy, art, dance and education. Apart from the Padma Bhushan, she received several other awards, including the Sangeet Natak Akademi Award (1957), the Queen Victoria

Silver Medal of the Royal Society for the Prevention of Cruelty to Animals, the Prani Mitra Award (1968) and the Sangeet Natak Akademi Fellowship in 1968. In 1977, Morarji Desai requested her to become President of India, but Rukmini refused.

● POTATOES AND CHOCOLATES

What is your favourite potato recipe?

Do you prefer an aloo paratha or a potato-stuffed masala dosa? Can you imagine life without potatoes? Originally, potatoes were only grown in the mountains of South America. Europeans brought them to India—either the Portuguese or the British—in the seventeenth century. Before Independence, they grew well only in hilly areas, but the Central Potato Research Institute developed varieties that could grow in the plains and warmer regions. The CPRI was first set up in 1949 in Patna, and transferred to Shimla in 1956. Today, potatoes are grown in all parts of India. And there are so many ways to eat them!

Other food items originally from South America include chocolates, cashew nuts, chillies and pineapples. None of these were in India before the sixteenth century.

CHOCOLATE PRODUCTION IN INDIA

1947: Cadbury starts producing chocolates in India.
1956: Cadbury milk chocolate is launched.
1957: Cadbury 5-Star is launched.
1970: Cadbury Eclairs is launched.
1974: Amul Chocolate is launched.
1986: Cadbury milk chocolate becomes Cadbury Dairy Milk.
1991: Nestlé Chocolate is launched.

🌸 SPORTS ROUND-UP

The 1956 Summer Olympics were held in Melbourne, Australia. India sent a seventy-six-member team, and participated in various events, including athletics, wrestling, weightlifting, swimming, hockey and football. India won the hockey gold but did not do well in other events.

Nandu Natekar (b. 1933) was the first Indian to win an international title in badminton. This was the Selangor International Tournament held in Kuala Lumpur in 1956. In 1953, he won the open nationals in Gwalior. He won six singles and six doubles national titles, receiving the first Arjuna Award (1961) and later, many other awards. In 1965, he gave up competitive badminton. Some other good badminton players of the time are T.N. Seth, Suresh Goel, P.M. Chawla and Manoj Guha.

CRICKET: HOW AND WHEN DID CRICKET START IN INDIA?

The first record of a cricket game is of one played by English merchants in Cambay as far back as 1721. The Calcutta Cricket Club was founded by the British in 1792. Parsis of Bombay formed the Orient Cricket Club in 1848, and later began playing against Europeans. By 1923–24, cricket was being played across the country. In Bombay, cricket was played between communities who formed teams, until Mahatma Gandhi protested against this in 1945.

C.K. Nayudu (31 October 1895–14 November 1967) was one of the best players; he was the first captain of the Indian cricket team, a good batsman, bowler and fielder. He retired in 1952–53, but resumed playing in 1956–57 as captain of the

Uttar Pradesh team, continuing to play matches till 1958. He was the *Wisden* Cricketer of the Year, 1933 and was called the Tiger on the Field. In 2003, the Board of Control for Cricket in India founded a cricketing award in his honour. He was the first cricketer to win the Padma Bhushan (1956).

India's first test win against England was in 1952 in Madras. Some of the captains of the Indian cricket team in the 1950s were Amarnath, H.R. Adhikari, Ghulam Ahmed, V.S. Hazare, V. Mankad, Pankaj Roy, G.S. Ramchand and P.R. Umrigar. Other early cricketers, active before Independence, were: K.S. Ranjitsinhji, or Ranji, after whom the Ranji Trophy is named; J.G. Navle; Wazir Ali; Colonel Mistri; Vijay Merchant; Shute Banerjee; M.J. Gopalan; K.R. Meherhomji; C. Ramaswami; Mushtaq Ali and Iftikhar Ali Khan, the nawab of Pataudi (Senior). Many princes of the Indian states supported the game.

● THE TOP FILMS

The top three Hindi films based on box office collections were *C.I.D.*, starring Dev Anand and Shakila; *Ek Hi Raasta*, with Ashok Kumar, Sunil Dutt and Meena Kumari; *Chori Chori*, with Raj Kapoor and Nargis.

ALSO IN 1956

20 March: Death of the modernist Marathi poet and writer B.S. Mardhekar (b. 1909)

21 July: An earthquake takes place near Anjar, in Kutch, Gujarat, with a surface wave magnitude of 6.1, causing widespread damage.

4 August: The first nuclear reactor in India, Apsara, starts functioning in Trombay, Bombay.

15 October: The Kerala Sahitya Akademi is inaugurated.

The All India Institute of Medical Sciences (AIIMS) is established by an Act of Parliament in New Delhi.

The National Crafts Museum is set up near Pragati Maidan, New Delhi.

The metric system in weights and measures is introduced.

1957: ELECTIONS AGAIN

In 1957, elections were held for the Lok Sabha and state assemblies between 24 February and 9 June. The electorate, or the number of people who could vote, now amounted to 193 million. Once again, the Congress won a majority of the seats. In the Lok Sabha, out of the 494 seats, it won 371. The party with the next highest number of seats was the Communist Party of India, with twenty-seven seats. In most of the state assemblies, the Congress could form the government, but in Kerala the communist party got a majority and formed the government with E.M.S. Namboodiripad as chief minister.

❋ WRITERS AND POETS: PUNJABI, HINDI AND ODIA

SUNDAR AND RANI RAJ KAUR

Rani Raj Kaur is the main character in the epic poem *Rana Surat Singh*, composed by the popular Punjabi-language poet and writer Bhai Vir Singh (5 December 1872–10 June 1957). Bhai Vir Singh was born in Amritsar, and wrote a number of works with a strong woman as the protagonist. His focus was also on Sikh heroic figures, the Sikh gurus and their holy writings. Vir Singh's first novel, *Sundari*, was published in 1898. *Sundari* is the story of Sundar Kaur. She became a Sikh and then lived with Sikh warriors in the forest—a life full of adventures. In *Rana Surat Singh*, set in the nineteenth to twentieth centuries, Rani Raj Kaur seeks the ultimate truth after the death of her husband in battle. Filled with grief for many years, she finally finds peace through the *bani* (compositions) of Sikh gurus. Bhai Vir's aim was to promote true Sikhism and so he wrote a commentary on the Guru Granth Sahib, the holy book of the Sikhs, as well as many novels, poems and biographies of Sikh saints and gurus.

He was awarded the degree of doctor of oriental learning by Panjab University, the Sahitya Akademi Award in 1955 for his book *Mere Saiyan Jio* and the Padma Bhushan in 1956.

HAZARI PRASAD DWIVEDI

Hazari Prasad Dwivedi (19 August 1907–19 May 1979) wrote several novels, essays and books on medieval saints and on the history of Hindi literature. He was born in Dube-ka-Chapra village in Ballia district of Uttar Pradesh and was educated in Ballia and Varanasi. He knew several languages, including Sanskrit. He taught at Visva-Bharati University, Banaras Hindu University and Panjab University, and was the rector of Banaras Hindu University (1968–70). He received several awards, among which were the Padma Bhushan (1957) and the Sahitya Akademi Award (1973). *Punarnava* and *Anamdas ka Potha* are two of his later novels.

BIDYUTPRABHA DEVI

Bidyutprabha Devi (1926–77) is recognized as one of the best female poets in Odia literature. In 1957, her poems were collected together as *Bidyutprabha Sanchayana*. They deal with different themes, such as the joy of writing and the problems faced by women. She also wrote plays as well as works for children, and gave speeches on the need for women's emancipation on All India Radio. She continued to write after 1957, but suffered from poor health from 1966 onwards. Bidyutprabha was married and had a supportive husband, but after her health problems started, she began to focus on spirituality and moved to the Sri Aurobindo Ashram in Pondicherry. In January 1977, her declining health led her to commit suicide by jumping in front of a train. *Bidyutprabha Sanchayana* won the Orissa Sahitya Akademi Award in 1962.

❋ THE TOP FILMS

Mother India, directed by Mehboob Khan, and starring Nargis, Raaj Kumar, Sunil Dutt and Rajendra Kumar, with music by Naushad, was the top Hindi film of the year. *Mother India* is the story of Radha, a poor village woman with strong ideals and good values. Radha is respected in the village, and is asked to inaugurate a new irrigation canal. As she thinks about her past, the story is told in flashbacks: She and her family have suffered, particularly because of Sukhilala, a moneylender. She loses her husband but her two sons, Birju and Ramu, survive. Birju wants to take revenge on Sukhilala, and kidnaps his daughter, Rupa, on her wedding day after shooting her father dead. To prevent him from taking the girl away, Radha shoots him, and he dies in her arms. The film's theme and the character of Radha have been variously analysed, both having been praised and criticized, and it is considered one of India's greatest hits.

Naya Daur tells the story of horse-cart drivers who are against the introduction of buses in their town. The film was directed by Baldev Raj Chopra.

Pyaasa is a romantic drama directed by Guru Dutt, who also acted in it. Vijay, the main character in the film, is an unpublished poet, whose poems gain fame even though Vijay remains unrecognized.

A reproduction of the poster of *Mother India*

❈ HARISH AND THE NATIONAL BRAVERY AWARD

Every year, courageous children and youngsters are presented bravery awards on Republic Day. These awards started because of a fourteen-year-old boy—Harish Chandra Mehra.

It was 2 October 1957. Jawaharlal Nehru and many others were watching a performance at Ramlila Ground when the shamiana in which they were sitting caught fire. Young Harish was the Boy Scout assigned to the area in which Nehru was seated. He immediately pulled Nehru by the hand and away from the fire. Then he climbed an electric pole and, using his scout's knife, cut off the burning portion, scorching his hands in the process. Because of his heroic action, Jawaharlal Nehru decided to start giving bravery awards to children. The first award, to Harish, was presented on 4 February 1958. As an extended honour, Harish took part in the 1959 Republic Day parade.

Harish was a celebrity for some time but he has not received further help from the government. He could not complete his studies because of financial problems, worked as a lower division clerk and retired in 2004.

❈ GURU DUTT

Guru Dutt (9 July 1925–10 October 1964), director and actor, was born in Bangalore. His original name was Vasanth Kumar Shivashankar Padukone but after a childhood accident, it was changed. Though he had a short life, he was a great director, producer and actor of the 1950s and early 1960s. His early films include *Baazi* (1951), *Jaal* (1952) and *Baaz* (1953). Among others, *Mr and Mrs 55* (1955), *Pyaasa* (1957) and *Kaagaz ke Phool* (1959) are still popular. He also wrote short stories. At the young age of thirty-nine, Dutt died suddenly in his sleep. His wife, Geeta Dutt, a playback singer, died in 1972 at the age of forty-one.

♦ MONEY

In the British days, the rupee was divided into sixteen annas. One anna had four pice, and one pice had three pies. After Independence, a new Indian coinage, based on the metric system, was introduced in 1957. This system of money, in which 100 naya paise made one rupee, replaced the old system of annas and pice. The change was based on the Indian Coinage (Amendment) Act of 1955. In 1964, the word 'naya' was dropped from usage.

ALSO IN 1957

20 January: The Atomic Energy Establishment, Trombay, is inaugurated. Renamed Bhabha Atomic Research Centre on 22 January 1967

1 August: The National Book Trust is set up by the Government of India, under the Department of Education, Ministry of Human Resource Development. It promotes literature by publishing low-priced books on a variety of subjects related to India.

30 August: Death of N.S. Krishnan, actor and playback singer

Balbir Singh (Senior) becomes the first hockey player to be awarded the Padma Shri.

The Bharat Ratna is awarded to G.B. Pant (1887–1961), a freedom fighter, premier of the United Provinces before Independence, chief minister of Uttar Pradesh and later the union minister.

1958: PANCHAYATI RAJ

A new panchayat system was approved in January 1958, based on the Balwant Rai Mehta Committee of 1957, and began to be implemented from 1959 onwards. The Constitution's Seventy-Third Amendment Act of 1992 also incorporated the details of the scheme. This system had three levels: the village panchayat elected by all the members of the village; the panchayat samiti consisting of the heads of the village panchayat, block development officers and others; the zila parishad at the district level for overall supervision. (In some of the north-eastern states, district councils were formed instead of panchayats.) Community development programmes were now linked to the panchayat system.

The year also saw advances in science and social welfare. The Scientific Policy Resolution of 1958 stated that technology was essential for prosperity, and that new technology could only emerge through the study of science and its applications. This policy led to the setting up of new agricultural, engineering and scientific institutes. New laws were passed to improve the condition of scheduled castes, scheduled tribes and women.

SPORTS AND GAMES

MILKHA SINGH: THE FLYING SIKH

Milkha Singh became famous when he won India's first-ever gold medal in the Commonwealth Games held in Cardiff in 1958. Milkha lost some of his family members at the time of Partition. Later, he joined the Indian Army, where his talent as a runner was recognized. He won two gold medals at the Asian Games in Tokyo that year (he won a total of four golds at two Asian Games—1958 and 1962), but was still relatively unknown. When he won the Commonwealth race, beating South Africa's renowned runner Malcolm Spence, there was joy across India. Vijaya Lakshmi Pandit was watching the race. After his win, she asked him to tell her what he wanted as a reward. He asked for a holiday to be declared, and Jawaharlal Nehru announced one throughout India in his honour! As the athletics team returned to India, bands greeted them at the airport and Jawaharlal Nehru hosted a reception for them. Milkha went on to win many more medals, though he narrowly missed the bronze at the 1960 Olympics.

How did he get the nickname of the Flying Sikh? Amazingly, it was Ayub Khan of Pakistan who gave him this name. In 1960, he was invited to participate in a 200-metre race at an international competition in Lahore, Pakistan. Milkha had painful memories of 1947 and did not want to go, but was persuaded by Jawaharlal Nehru. There, he received a great welcome, and after he won the race, General Ayub Khan, President of Pakistan, said that he actually 'flew' in the race!

Milkha Singh

Therefore, 'Pakistan [bestowed] upon [him] the title of the Flying Sikh'.[6]

Bhaag Milkha Bhaag was a film based on his life, released in 2013.

THE COMMONWEALTH AND ASIAN GAMES

Apart from Milkha Singh, there were other winners that year in the Commonwealth Games. In boxing, Hari Singh won a bronze in the middleweight category. In wrestling, the first gold was won in the 100-kilogram class by Lila Ram.

In the Third Asian Games, held in Tokyo, India won five gold, four silver and four bronze medals. All golds, as well as two silvers and two bronzes, were in athletics. Hockey was introduced in the 1958 Asian Games, and India won the silver medal.

❖ ARUNA ASAF ALI BECOMES THE FIRST MAYOR OF DELHI

Aruna Asaf Ali (1909–96), born Aruna Ganguly, was a freedom fighter, known as the Grand Old Lady of India's freedom movement. In 1928, she fell in love and married Asaf Ali (1888–1953) despite all opposition. Many years older than her, he was also a freedom fighter, who held important government posts after Independence.

After Independence, Aruna became the first mayor of Delhi (1958). She received a number of awards, including the Lenin Peace Prize (1964), the Indira Gandhi Award for National Integration (1987), the Jawaharlal Nehru Award for International

---

[6] Rob Brown and Rehan Fazal, 'The "Flying Sikh" Who Won India's First Commonwealth Gold', *BBC News Magazine*, 1 August 2014, http://www.bbc.com/news/magazine-28545882.

Understanding (1991), the Padma Vibhushan (1992) and the Bharat Ratna (1997). In 1998, a stamp commemorating her was issued.

❋ VALLATHOL

Narayana Menon Vallathol (16 October 1878–13 March 1958), a poet who wrote in Malayalam, was born in Chenara village, in present-day Kerala.

He wrote poems on different themes—ones against caste, on nationalistic and patriotic themes, as well as those based on the epics and the Puranas. He translated some Puranas and Valmiki's Ramayana from Sanskrit into Malayalam. A great admirer of Mahatma Gandhi, his famous poem about him is titled 'Ente Gurunathan' (My Master). He even wrote about Mary Magdalene ('Magdalana Mariam') and about Prophet Muhammad ('Allah', 'Pamsusnanam' and other poems), as well as of the problems he faced after losing his hearing. A number of his shorter poems are collected in the eleven-volume work *Sahitya Manjari*. He received the Padma Bhushan in 1954.

Vallathol is grouped together with Kumaran Asan (1873–1924) and Ulloor Parameswara Iyer (1877–1949) as the three *mahakavis*, or great poets, of Kerala.

ALSO IN 1958

8 January: Sheikh Abdullah is released from prison; reimprisoned on 29 April.

22 February: Death of Maulana Abul Kalam Azad (b. 1888), nationalist and freedom fighter, minister for education in India after Independence, author of *India Wins Freedom*

19 May: Death of the noted historian Jadunath Sarkar (b. 1870), known for his work on the Mughals and the Marathas

17 August: Death of Sir John Marshall, British archaeologist and the director of the Archaeological Survey of India (1902–28), who discovered the Harappan civilization

18 September: Death of Bhagwan Das, who helped found Hindu College (now Banaras Hindu University) and was a theosophist who wrote thirty books in Sanskrit

The National Children's Museum is founded as part of National Bal Bhavan.

The National Award for teachers is instituted.

The Bharat Ratna is awarded to Dhondo Keshav Karve (1858–1962), known as Maharishi Karve, a social worker, reformer and promoter of women's education.

1959: THE DALAI LAMA ENTERS INDIA

A new set of refugees came to India in 1959, after crossing the snow-covered borders in the north. These were the Dalai Lama (the political and spiritual leader of Tibet) and many other Tibetans. In 1950, after China declared that Tibet was part of its territory, the Chinese started moving into Tibet and interfering in the lives and religious practices of the Tibetans. In 1959, the Tibetans started a revolt against the Chinese. The Chinese soldiers attacked them, and so thousands of Tibetans entered India to escape. India allowed them to stay.

Gradually, Tibetans moved to different parts of India. The Dalai Lama made his home in Dharamshala, Himachal Pradesh as the head of a government in exile. And Buddhism returned to its homeland in the new form of Tibetan Buddhism.

As for other political events, an important new political party, the Swatantra Party, was formed in 1959 by C. Rajagopalachari and others. Its aims included a reduction of government control in industry. It was one of the major

The 14th Dalai Lama

political parties between 1959 and 1969, but in 1974, merged with other parties.

> ### THE DALAI LAMA AND TIBETAN BUDDHISM
>
> The Dalai Lama belongs to the Gelug sect of Tibetan Buddhism, founded in the fourteenth century by Tsong Khapa. The third head of the sect was given the title Dalai Lama by the ruler of Mongolia in 1578. After that, the title was applied retrospectively to the first two as well. The term means 'one whose wisdom is as great as the ocean'. It was the 14th Dalai Lama, known as Tenzing Gyatso, who entered India in 1959.
>
> Buddhism had spread to Tibet from India and Mongolia, but developed its own form in Tibet, along with elements of the religion practised in Tibet, Bon. Tibetan Buddhism includes rituals and the worship of deities, along with other Buddhist practices.

❋ RAJAB ALI KHAN

The year saw the death of Rajab Ali Khan (3 September 1874–8 January 1959), a khayal singer of Hindustani music, who specialized in singing complex *taan*s (sequences of notes). Born in Narsinghgarh, in present-day Madhya Pradesh, he was the son of sarangi player Mugalu Khan. He also played various instruments, including the *rudra* veena. He was a court musician in Dewas and Kolhapur, and performed in concerts too. He received the Sangeet Natak Akademi Award in 1954.

THE VEENA

The veena, or vina, is a stringed instrument with ancient origins. It has twenty-four frets, four main strings and three subsidiary strings. Its hollow body resonates with sound, and it often has two gourds. It is generally made of wood, but other materials are also used today, including glass fibre. The veena is associated with the goddess Sarasvati, and is depicted in sculptures, paintings and on coins. Samudragupta of the Gupta dynasty is shown on some of his coins playing the veena. The veenas used in north Indian classical music and those in Karnatic music are somewhat different. The various types of veenas include the Sarasvati veena, the rudra veena, the *vichitra* veena and the Mohan veena.

❋ THE TOP FILMS

The 1959 top box office hit in Hindi films was *Anari*, directed by Hrishikesh Mukherjee, and starring Raj Kapoor, Nutan, Lalita Pawar and Motilal. The music was by Shankar–Jaikishan, and the lyrics were mainly by Shailendra but also by Hasrat Jaipuri. The playback singers were Mukesh, Lata Mangeshkar and Manna Dey.

Paigham, starring Dilip Kumar, Vyjayanthimala and Raaj Kumar was second at the box office.

The President's Gold Medal for the best feature film of the year went to Satyajit Ray's *Apur Sansar*.

❋ LYRICIST SHAILENDRA WINS THE FILMFARE AWARD

Shankardas Kesarilal (30 August 1921–14 December 1966), who wrote under the name Shailendra, was one of the best composers of lyrics for early Hindi films. Shailendra wrote songs for Raj Kapoor's films, one of the most popular being 'Awara Hoon' for *Awara*. He also wrote for other films and worked with various composers, including Shankar–Jaikishan, Salil Chowdhury, Sachin Dev Burman and Ravi Shankar.

He won the Filmfare Award for the best lyricist in 1958, 1959 and 1968. The 1959 award was for the song 'Sab Kuch Seekha Hamne', from the film *Anari*. Shailendra later became involved in producing the film *Teesri Kasam* (1966). Even though this won the National Award for the best feature film in 1966, Shailendra lost money as it failed at the box office. Financial anxieties contributed to his death at a young age. Strangely, the day he died (14 December) was Raj Kapoor's birthday.

❋ THE NATIONAL ORCHIDARIUM AND BOTANIC GARDEN

Orchids are among the most beautiful flowers, and there are about 1600 species of the orchid family in India, mainly in the north-eastern states. The National Orchidarium, showcasing a variety of orchids, was founded in Shillong in 1959.

ALSO IN 1959

April: The National School of Drama is established by the Sangeet Natak Akademi in New Delhi. In 1975, it becomes an autonomous institution financed by the central government.

6 October: The Integrated Photo Unit, later renamed the Photo Division, is set up for the visual documentation of

Government of India activities. It is under the Ministry of Information and Broadcasting.

1 November: The Delhi Zoo, a 250-acre zoo, is opened in New Delhi; it is renamed the National Zoological Park in 1982.

1 November: Death of M.K. Thyagaraja Bhagavathar (b. 1910), actor and Karnatic music singer

1960: BOMBAY IS DIVIDED

How were the boundaries of the states decided? Jawaharlal Nehru was keen on forming states based on natural regions, but others believed they should be based on linguistic regions—areas where a particular language was spoken. This had already been done for some states, but Bombay remained a large one, where Marathi and Gujarati were the main languages. Gujarati speakers began agitating for a separate state. Finally in 1960, Bombay was divided into the two states of Maharashtra and Gujarat. The capital Bombay was given to Maharashtra, while Gujarat got the new capital of Ahmadabad.

❋ SPORTS AND GAMES

In the 1960 Rome Olympics, Milkha Singh came fourth in the 400-metre race, missing the bronze by a fraction of a second. India lost the hockey title to Pakistan. The only medal won was a silver in hockey.

❋ FLUTE PLAYERS

Flutes are known to have been around in India from the early days. One of the first wind instruments, the *bhorindo* is said to be the most ancient one of south India. It consists of a clay ball with three holes. Notes were played by blowing through one hole while covering the other two with the fingers. In India, the flute has a special place, being associated with a divine player, the god Krishna, who could soothe or lure both people and animals with it. The flute is known as bansuri in Hindi, and by other names in south India.

20 April 1960 saw the death of the flute player and composer Pannalal Ghosh (b. 1911), one of India's best.

Other great flute players of Hindustani music include Hariprasad Chaurasia and Ronu Majumdar. Among those from Karnatic music are Palladam Sanjeeva Rao (1882–1962), T.R. Mahalingam (1926–86) and N. Ramani (1934–2015).

Hariprasad Chaurasia

HARIPRASAD CHAURASIA: FROM WRESTLER TO MUSICIAN

Hariprasad Chaurasia (b. 1938), born in Allahabad, is a unique artist as he came from a family, not of musicians but, of wrestlers! He trained with his father as a wrestler but his heart was in music, and so he practised it secretly. At first he learnt with a neighbour, Rajaram, but his flute studies actually started in Varanasi with Bholanath Prasanna. Later, Annapurna Devi, daughter of Allauddin Khan, guided him. Chaurasia developed a unique style of playing, and composed new ragas, fusion and cross-cultural music, as well as music for films. His son, Rajeev Chaurasia, is also a musician, and has directed a documentary on his father, *Bansuri Guru* (2013).

Hariprasad received numerous awards, including the Sangeet Natak Akademi Award (1984), the Padma Bhushan (1992) and the Padma Vibhushan (2000). His music includes compositions titled *Call of the Valley* and *Music of the Rivers*. *Call of the Valley* (1967) is a Hindustani classical album, in which Chaurasia plays with Brij Bhushan Kabra (guitar) and Shivkumar Sharma (santoor). It tells the story of a day in the life of a Kashmiri shepherd, using a series of melodies in various ragas appropriate for the different times of the day.

❋ THE TOP FILMS

The three highest-grossing Hindi films at the box office in 1960 were *Mughal-e-Azam*, *Barsaat ki Raat* and *Kohinoor*.

Mughal-e-Azam was directed by K. Asif and produced by the Shapoorji Pallonji Group, starring Dilip Kumar, Madhubala, Prithviraj Kapoor and Durga Khote. It is based on the legendary story of Prince Salim (later the emperor Jahangir) and his love for the dancer Anarkali. The music in the film is considered to be among the best, including songs by Lata Mangeshkar and Bade Ghulam Ali Khan. The film had the highest collection at the box office up to that time. It was a black-and-white film but in November 2004, it was released again after being digitally coloured.

The Film Institute of India, located in Pune, was set up in 1960. In 1974, it was renamed the Film and Television Institute of India. The same year, it became an autonomous body.

The 1960 President's Gold Medal was awarded to the Hindi film *Anuradha*, produced and directed by Hrishikesh Mukherjee. Leela Naidu and Balraj Sahni were the main actors, and the music was composed by Ravi Shankar while Shailendra was the lyricist.

ASSAMESE LITERATURE

Two notable books were published in Assamese in 1960. These were *Surajmukhir Sapna* (The Dream of the Sunflower) by Syed Abdul Malik (1919–2000) and *Aai* (Mother) by Birendra Kumar Bhattacharya (1924–97). Birendra Kumar's first work was *Rajpathe Ringiyai* (The Call of the Highway) in 1957, where he looks at the poverty that continued to exist in India even after Independence. He also wrote a book on the Nagas and their struggle for an independent Nagaland (*Iyaruingam*). In 1979, he won the Jnanpith Award for his book *Mrityunjay*.

There have been many other Assamese novelists, as well as playwrights and poets, including Dinanath Sharma (1914–88), Hitesh Deka (1924–2000), Lakshminandan Bora (b. 1931), Homen Borgohain (b. 1931), Debendra Nath Acharya (1937–81), Jogesh Das (1927–99) and Prafulla Datta Goswami (1919–94).

RAJSHEKHAR BASU

The year saw the death of Rajshekhar Basu (b. 1880), Bengali-language writer, on 27 April. He wrote humorous and satirical stories, essays and poems, under the pseudonym Parashuram. Basu also compiled a Bengali dictionary and was the first to print a book in Bengali. He continued writing despite a full-time job as a chemist as well as his personal tragedies. He lost his son-in-law and only daughter on the same day, and his wife in 1942. Satyajit Ray directed two films based on his stories, and Basu received the Padma Bhushan in 1956.

RAMANATHAN KRISHNAN IS WORLD NO. 3

Tennis player Ramanathan Krishnan (b. 11 April 1937) was ranked third in the world in 1960. He won the Junior Wimbledon championship in 1954 at the age of sixteen, after winning the national junior title in 1950 at the age of thirteen. This was the start of a long tennis career. Ramanathan Krishnan reached the semi-finals of Wimbledon in 1960 and 1961, and received the Arjuna Award in 1961, the Padma Shri in 1962, and the Padma Bhushan in 1967. He also received the US Helms Trophy in 1966, awarded to the best amateur sportsman of Asia. He is a seven-time national champion and three-time Asian champion.

Nirupama Mankad (b. 1947) was India's best female tennis player in the sixties and seventies, and won the national championship seven times. She received the Arjuna Award in 1980.

ALSO IN 1960

2 February: Death of Acharya Chatursen Shastri (b. 1891), noted writer of Hindi literature

27 April: The National Defence College is established in New Delhi for the advanced training of senior defence officers.

1961: THE LIBERATION OF GOA

The Portuguese still refused to give up their territories in India. The people of Dadra and Nagar Haveli had already freed themselves, and in August 1961, the territory was officially taken over by India. Then on 18 December, Indian troops entered Goa, and it was liberated from the Portuguese on 19 December 1961. This day is still observed every year as Liberation Day in Goa.

❋ OTHER KEY EVENTS

India had to continue formulating plans for development. The Third Five-Year Plan (1961–66) aimed at making India self-sufficient in both agriculture and basic industry within the next ten years.

The second census of independent India was conducted, and this time the population of remote areas was also counted. The total population recorded was 43,90,72,582.

In Nagaland, Angami Zapu Phizo (1913–90), leader of the Nagas, had started an armed struggle for an independent state. After talks failed, Phizo left the country, and other Naga leaders agreed to a separate state within India. Thus, the state of Nagaland was created in 1961, though it officially came into being in 1963.

🟤 GOAN FREEDOM FIGHTERS

Many people worked to liberate Goa from the Portuguese. Among them was the writer and poet Telo de Mascarenhas (23 March 1899–October 1979). He was born in Majorda, Salcete (Mormugao), and went to Portugal in 1920, where he obtained a law degree from the University of Coimbra. He then worked as a magistrate in Portugal (1930–48) and at the same time wrote articles for local newspapers, praising India. Along with others who had come from Goa, he founded the Hindu National Centre and the periodical *India Nova* (New India). He also translated books from India into Portuguese. He returned to India in 1948, his involvement in the Goa freedom movement leading to him being under police watch. He moved to Bombay and lived there from 1950–58, where he published a political journal *Resurge Goa* and spoke on All India Radio, in Portuguese and Konkani, on the need to liberate Goa. When he entered Goa again in 1959, he was arrested and sent to Portugal, where he remained in prison till 1970. Finally, he was released and was allowed to return to Goa, where he spent the last days of his life in Panaji. His works include poetry, the collected sonnets *Goa, Terra Minha Amada* (Goa, My Beloved Land), the novella *Sinfonia Goesa* (Goan Symphony) and his memoirs, *Quando as Mangueiras Floriram* (When the Mango Tree Blossomed).

Tristao de Braganza Cunha (1891–1958) was another Goan freedom fighter and a writer, who studied in Pondicherry and Paris. Other activists of the movement included Peter Alvares, Evagrio George (1925–78), George Vaz (1919–99), the teacher Laxmikant Bhembre (1906–85), Pandurang Purushottam

Shirodkar (1916–2000), Purushottam Kakodkar (1913–98), noted surgeon Pundalik Gaitonde (1913–92) and another doctor, Rama Hegde (b. 1912). Non-Goans also joined the movement.

Reconciliation between India and Portugal came about with the invitation to Mario Soares, the then President of Portugal, to be the chief guest at the Republic Day parade in 1992.

> ### THE GOAN STRUGGLE IN FILM
>
> The story of *Saat Hindustani*, a film written and directed by Khwaja Ahmad Abbas, is based in Goa. Maria, waiting for surgery, looks back on how she and her six friends tried to free Goa from the Portuguese. Released in 1969, Amitabh Bachchan made his debut in this film.
>
> *Pukar* (1983), directed by Ramesh Behl, is another film on Goa's liberation struggle.
>
> *Trikal* (1985), directed by Shyam Benegal, looks back at the turbulent times in Goa.

❈ MOUNTAINEERING AND MOUNTAINEERING INSTITUTES

With the Himalayas to the north, mountaineering began to gain popularity in India, particularly after the first ascent of Mount Everest in 1953. Mountaineering institutes were established to provide basic and advanced mountaineering courses and organize expeditions, adventure courses, trekking and other mountaineering-related activities.

The Indian Mountaineering Foundation was founded in 1957 as the sponsoring committee of the Cho Oyu expedition. This 1958 expedition was a success, and on 15 January 1961, a permanent organization was set up, being registered in November.

The Himalayas

The other mountaineering institutions under the IMF are:

- The Himalayan Mountaineering Institute, Darjeeling, West Bengal, set up on 4 November 1954, to encourage mountaineering after Tenzing Norgay reached the summit of Mount Everest
- The Nehru Institute of Mountaineering, Uttarkashi, Uttarakhand, established on 14 November 1965, to honour Jawaharlal Nehru, who loved the mountains
- The Atal Bihari Vajpayee Institute of Mountaineering and Allied Sports, Manali, Himachal Pradesh, set up in 1961 as the Western Himalayan Mountaineering Institute. It has sub-centres in other parts of the state.
- The Jawahar Institute of Mountaineering and Winter Sports, in Aru, near Pahalgam, Jammu and Kashmir, established on 25 October 1983
- The Indian Institute of Skiing and Mountaineering, Gulmarg, Jammu and Kashmir, established in 1969
- The Pandit Nain Singh Surveyor Mountaineering Training Institute, Munsiyari, Pithoragarh district, Uttarakhand. Nain Singh Rawat (1830–95) had a major role in the Great Trigonometrical Survey, a project to scientifically measure the whole territory of India.

- The Sonam Gyatso Mountaineering Institute, Baluwakhani, Gangtok, Sikkim, set up in 1963
- The National Institute of Mountaineering and Allied Sports, Dirang, Arunachal Pradesh, set up in 2013

> **SEARCH AND RESCUE**
>
> Among these, the Nehru Institute of Mountaineering is the only institute which has a course in search and rescue. Its students did a great job of rescuing people after the 2013 floods in Uttarakhand.

BIDHAN CHANDRA ROY: DOCTORS' DAY

Bidhan Chandra Roy (1 July 1882–1 July 1962) became chief minister of West Bengal on 23 January 1948. A well-qualified doctor, Fellow of the Royal College of Surgeons, Member of the Royal College of Physicians, he joined politics and remained chief minister until his death. He received the Bharat Ratna in 1961. National Doctors' Day is observed in his memory on 1 July, which is both his birthday and his death day.

THE HUNGRY GENERATION

The Hungry Generation was a literary movement in Bengal, which challenged existing norms. Today it is known as the Hungryalist movement. It was officially launched in November 1961 and prevailed till 1965, though its effects were long-lasting and widespread. The four founders were Shakti Chattopadhyay, Malay Roy Choudhury, Samir Roychoudhury and Debi Roy. Many artists were associated with this movement, which influenced writers across India and even in other countries. The movement attacked traditional culture, and has been called outrageous, nihilistic and destructive. Malay Roy Choudhury (b. 29 October 1939) was even imprisoned for his poem 'Prachanda Baidyutik Chhutar', which has been translated as 'Stark Electric Jesus'. The poem was made into a short film in 2014, and won several awards. It begins with the following lines:[7]

> Oh I'll die I'll die I'll die
> My skin is in blazing furore
> I do not know what I'll do where I'll go oh I am sick . . .

ALSO IN 1961

7 March: Death of Govind Ballabh Pant (b. 1887), participant in the freedom movement, chief minister of Uttar Pradesh and a cabinet minister after Independence

September: The first conference of the Non-Aligned Movement is held in Belgrade, Yugoslavia, and attended by the heads of twenty-five countries.

The Arjuna Award is instituted by the Government of India to recognize outstanding performances by sportspersons.

From 1960 to 1961, Sainik Schools are established to train boys for entrance into the national defence academies. The first school is set up in 1960 in Lucknow, though the first schools under the Sainik School Society are founded in 1961 and are the idea of V.K. Krishna Menon, the defence minister. They are fully residential schools.

The National Council of Educational Research and Training (NCERT) is set up. Located in New Delhi, it is an advisory body to the Ministry of Education on school curriculum.

---

[7] Quoted in 'Malay Roy Choudhury Poems', *PoemHunter.com*, accessed 11 June 2017, https://www.poemhunter.com/poem/stark-electric-jesus/.

1962: THE INDO-CHINA WAR

There were three main events in 1962: the third general elections, the legal transfer of French territories to India and, the most important, the devastating Chinese invasion.

The third general elections took place between 16 February and 16 June. Once again, the Congress did well and won 361 out of a total of 494 seats. The party with the next highest number of seats, only twenty-nine, was the Communist Party of India.

French territories had been handed over to India in 1954, but the legal documents had not been signed. This was done in August 1962, thus completing the transfer of French possessions. The seventh union territory of Pondicherry, including Mahé, Yanam and Karaikal, was created.

While the elections were taking place, Jawaharlal Nehru fell ill with a kidney infection towards the end of March. Did this affect how he tackled the Chinese invasion? China had been encroaching on Indian territory and by 1959, had occupied over 30,000 sq. km of land in Ladakh in the west as well as Longju in the east. The then premier and foreign minister of China, Zhou Enlai (1898–1976), came to Delhi for talks in 1960 and wanted India to agree to giving up the region of Aksai Chin. But India refused. And by April 1962, Chinese troops were gathering at India's border.

On 8 September 1962, they crossed the border in the east, and on 20 October, they began a full-scale invasion both from the east and the west. Twenty thousand Chinese troops crossed the North-East Frontier Agency (NEFA) border, while in the western sector, they occupied thirteen border posts. Indian troops began retreating, but in the meantime, the US sent their Seventh Fleet to the Bay of Bengal in order to support India. Suddenly on the night of 20 November, the Chinese announced a ceasefire starting the next night and a withdrawal by 1 December. Though the war was over, China retained about 41,500 kilometres of the Aksai Chin region of Ladakh.

> ## HAQEEQAT
>
> The Indo-China War was depicted on-screen in *Haqeeqat*, a Hindi film directed by Chetan Anand and released in 1964. The main actors were Balraj Sahni, Dharmendra, Priya Rajvansh, Sudhir, Sanjay Khan, Sheikh Mukhtar and Vijay Anand. It received the National Award in 1965 for the second-best feature film. The story centres on Indian soldiers who are stranded in Ladakh and surrounded by the Chinese. Ladakhi Captain Bahadur Singh and his girlfriend, Angmo, lose their lives in an attempt to rescue them. There are several realistic scenes in the movie, one showing the endless hordes of Chinese soldiers crossing into India, far outnumbering the Indians, amidst the loudspeakers proclaiming, 'Hindi–Chini bhai–bhai!'

❈ THE STRENGTH OF THE ARMED FORCES

The strength of the army had increased from 2,80,000 at the time of Partition to 5,50,000 by 1962. The air force and navy had also been expanded.

A reproduction of the poster of *Haqeeqat*

❦ THE PARAM VIR CHAKRA IS AWARDED AFTER THE WAR

Three army men were awarded the Param Vir Chakra after the Indo-China War: Dhan Singh Thapa of the 1/8 Gorkha Rifles regiment, Joginder Singh Sahnan of the 1 Sikh regiment and Shaitan Singh of the 13 Kumaon regiment. The last two were awarded posthumously. Dhan Singh Thapa was also believed to be dead, but had in fact been taken prisoner and was returned. He was a major at the time of the war, and retired as a lieutenant colonel. He died in 2005 at the age of seventy-seven. A Hindi television serial was based on his life.

❦ TEACHERS' DAY

This is a day celebrated every year on 5 September, the birthday of the late President Radhakrishnan—who was a teacher himself, as well as a philosopher and writer. In 1962, friends and members of the public went to wish Radhakrishnan on his birthday, who had been elected as India's second President that year. He suggested that instead of being celebrated as his birthday, the day be celebrated as Teachers' Day.

The National Foundation for Teachers' Welfare was also founded in 1962 to provide financial assistance to teachers.

❦ THE NATIONAL PLEDGE

The national pledge was composed in 1962 in Telugu by P.V. Subba Rao, an author and government official. It was later translated into many languages. The pledge begins with:[8]

> India is my country.
> All Indians are my brothers and sisters.
> I love my country, and I am proud of its rich and varied heritage.

---

[8] Quoted in *The Everyday State and Society in Modern India*, ed. Christopher John Fuller and Véronique Bénéï (London: Hurst & Company, 2001).

The pledge is recited in schools and other institutes, particularly on days of national importance.

❃ BADE GHULAM ALI KHAN RECEIVES THE PADMA BHUSHAN

Bade Ghulam Ali Khan (1902–68), a renowned vocalist of Hindustani music, was born in Kasur, near Lahore. His three brothers, Barkat Ali Khan, Mubarak Ali Khan and Aman Ali Khan, were all good singers, and so was their father, Ali Baksh. He studied with his father and his uncle, Kale Khan Sahib, and later with Sindhi Khan in Bombay. He learnt vocal music as well as the sarangi, and gave a number of performances. He sang especially for Mahatma Gandhi in 1945, and also performed on All India Radio.

After Partition, Bade Ghulam Ali, though he was a Pakistani citizen, came to India and became an Indian citizen in 1957. He received the Sangeet Natak Akademi Award and the Padma Bhushan in 1962. He eventually settled in Hyderabad, where he died after a period of illness. His deep melodious voice, in which he sang khayals and thumris, accounts for his fame. He sang for only one film, *Mughal-e-Azam*.

ALSO IN 1962

8 June: Air India International is renamed Air India.

The Indian National Committee for Space Research is inaugurated, and a rocket launching facility is established in Thumba.

The Asian Games take place in Djakarta (later Jakarta), Indonesia, and India wins ten gold, fourteen silver and ten bronze medals.

The Socialist Party is united with part of the Praja Socialist Party to form the Samyukta Socialist Party (SSP).

The Bharat Ratna is awarded to Rajendra Prasad.

1963: THE LANGUAGE PROBLEM

Should the government use Hindi, English or some other language for their official communications? The Constitution had stated that for the first fifteen years i.e., up to 1965, both languages should be used, but after that, Hindi should be the official language. There were many states where Hindi was not spoken, and so they were against this change. As they protested, in 1963, the Official Languages Act was passed. This said that the use of English may be continued even after 1965.

❋ RAHUL SANKRITYAYAN

Rahul Sankrityayan (9 April 1893–14 April 1963) was one of the greatest scholars of India.

Born in Pandaha, in Azamgarh district of present-day Uttar Pradesh, his original name was Kedarnath Pandey. Inclined towards spirituality, he became a wandering sannyasi and changed his name to Baba Ram Udar Das. Later, out of a keen interest in Buddhism, he adopted the name Rahul Sankrityayan. He retained this name even though he became a communist in the next stage of his life.

In 1944, he became a teacher at Leningrad University (now St Petersburg State University), Russia, and later a professor at

Vidyalankara Pirivena University (now the University of Kelaniya), Sri Lanka. In 1958, he received the Sahitya Akademi Award for his book *Madhya Asia ka Itihas*, a two-volume work on the history of Central Asia.

Rahul was a great writer and traveller, who knew many languages. Over 125 of his works, in Hindi, Bhojpuri, Sanskrit, Pali and Tibetan, were published, apart from an autobiography. He is called the Father of the Hindi Travelogue as he wrote about his travels. One of his notable books in Hindi is *Volga se Ganga*, a collection of twenty short stories, which can be categorized as historical fiction. The first story is about the presumed migration of an Indo-European group from River Volga to India. Rahul died in Darjeeling, and his tomb is located there.

● ALLAUDDIN KHAN

Allauddin Khan (1881–6 September 1972) was one of the greatest musicians of Hindustani music. He belonged to the Senia gharana and was born in Shibpur, in present-day Bangladesh. Other than the sarod, he had learnt to play at least 200 instruments, including string, wind and percussion instruments. He was also a vocalist and composer, even creating and discovering new ragas. Though he trained under several musicians, one of the most important was Wazir Khan of Rampur (1851–1926), whose lineage can be traced to Tansen. Wazir Khan was one of the most renowned music teachers, known both for his strictness and expertise. Allauddin Khan recreated the Maihar gharana in Maihar, Madhya Pradesh, where he settled in 1918. He is often thought to be the originator of this gharana, as, though it was in existence from the nineteenth century, it was profoundly changed by him.

The Maihar gharana centres on him and his famous disciples, who played a number of different instruments. The sarod players included his son, Ali Akbar Khan, while the sitar players included Ravi Shankar and Nikhil Banerjee. Among other noted students who became great musicians are his daughter Annapurna Devi (originally named Roshanara), who played the *surbahar* and married Ravi Shankar; the flute player Pannalal Ghosh; Sharan Rani and several more. Allauddin Khan formed the Maihar Band in 1924, and in 1935–36 toured with Uday Shankar's dance troupe. He also founded the Maihar College of Music in 1955.

He received a number of awards, including the Sangeet Natak Akademi Award for Hindustani instrumental music (1952), the Sangeet Natak Akademi fellowship (1954), the Padma Bhushan (1958), the Desikottama award of Visva-Bharati (1961) and the Padma Vibhushan (1971). *Maihar Raag* (1993), a film directed by Sunil Shanbag based on the life and music of Allauddin Khan, won the National Film Award for the best non-feature film in 1994. In 1963, the documentary *Ustad Alauddin Khan* was made on his life by director Ritwik Ghatak.

The sarod

THE SAROD

The sarod is a stringed musical instrument, popular in Hindustani music, with a deeper sound than the sitar. There are some variations in the way the instrument is made, but it has a wooden body and steel or bronze strings. The instrument has no frets, and usually has four main and four subsidiary strings, two drone strings and nine to eleven sympathetic strings.

✻ THE TOP FILMS

The best-performing Hindi films at the box office were: *Mere Mehboob*, starring Rajendra Kumar, Sadhana and Ameeta; *Taj Mahal*, based on the story of the Mughal emperor Shah Jahan and directed by M. Sadiq; *Phir Wohi Dil Laya Hoon*, directed and produced by Nasir Hussain.

Bandini, directed and produced by Bimal Roy, ranked tenth at the box office but received the most awards. *Bandini* is about a woman in prison who is accused of murder. The prison doctor, Devendra, falls in love with her, though she is still pining for Bikash, a freedom fighter she knew in the past. The main actors were Nutan, Dharmendra and Ashok Kumar. The music was composed by Sachin Dev Burman, and the lyrics by Shailendra and Gulzar. Lata Mangeshkar, Asha Bhosle, Manna Dey, S.D. Burman and Mukesh were the singers. The film won the National Award for the best feature film of the year, and five Filmfare Awards. It was based on the Bengali novel *Tamasi* by Jarasandha, who fictionalized many of his experiences as a prison superintendent.

ALSO IN 1963

28 February: Death of Rajendra Prasad, the first President of India (1950–62)

October: Jawaharlal Nehru inaugurates the Bhakra Dam across River Sutlej in Bilaspur, Himachal Pradesh. On the occasion, he says, 'This dam has been built with the unrelenting toil of man for the benefit of mankind and therefore is worthy of worship.'[9]

The peacock is chosen as the national bird of India.

The Bharat Ratna is awarded to Zakir Husain, who later becomes the third President of India, and to the Indologist P.V. Kane.

---

[9] Vandana Asthana and A.C. Shukla, *Water Security in India: Hope, Despair, and the Challenges of Human Development* (n.p.: Bloomsbury, 2014).

1964: THE DEATH OF NEHRU

The year was a sad one for India, as Jawaharlal Nehru (b. 14 November 1889), India's first prime minister, died on 27 May in Delhi, having returned from Dehradun. He had not been keeping well since January. As the news of his death spread, thousands wept outside his home. They all loved Nehru, who had led India for so many years. At his funeral the following day, people lined up in the streets to get a last glimpse of their beloved leader. From across India and all over the world, messages came, praising him. After his cremation, some of his ashes were immersed in River Ganga, while the rest, according to his wishes, was scattered from a great height, so that it could mingle with the earth of the land he loved and served.

Nehru had a vision, a dream for the new India, and he had done his best to lead the country in the direction of his dreams. By the time he died, India was a

Nehru in his last days

functioning democracy, with a Constitution that upheld equality and human rights. His vision had laid the foundations for the future and for the development and growth of science, technology, industry, art and culture.

Jawaharlal Nehru had been involved in the freedom movement from 1912 onwards, and had been a close associate of Mahatma Gandhi. During the freedom movement, Nehru had been imprisoned for a total of nine years. While in prison, he lost his father, Motilal Nehru, in 1931, and his mother in 1938. His wife, Kamala, died of tuberculosis in 1936 in Lausanne, Switzerland, and he was released from prison to be with his wife in her last days. They had a daughter, Indira Priyadarshini Nehru (later known as Indira Gandhi).

Nehru was also a good writer and a learned man. He wrote *An Autobiography* (1936) while in prison, as well as *The Discovery of India* (1946) and *Glimpses of World History* (1934). The last was in the form of a series of letters to his daughter, Indira. His vast knowledge enabled him to write the latter while he was in prison with no access to books.

❋ A NEW PRIME MINISTER

On 2 June 1964, Lal Bahadur Shastri became the new prime minister.

He was a man of a short stature and was initially quite hesitant to assert himself, but gradually he began to take strong decisions.

❋ OTHER KEY EVENTS

A new plan for defence was being implemented. It included acquiring more weapons and equipment, ensuring better training and mountain divisions for high-altitude border areas.

In October 1964, the Agreement on Persons of Indian Origin was signed between India and Ceylon, Sri Lanka, allowing 5,25,000 stateless people of Indian origin to return to India. Ceylon would accept 3,00,000 residents as its citizens. This was later called the Sirima–Shastri Pact.

❋ URMILA

How many of you remember the character Urmila? Urmila was Lakshmana's wife in the Ramayana. Valmiki, whose Ramayana is the earliest available version, hardly mentioned her, merely saying that she stayed behind to look after her mothers-in-law when Sita accompanied Rama and Lakshmana to the forest. But Urmila has been portrayed by later writers differently, who have used their imagination to do so. Among these were two writers who died in 1964.

Maithili Sharan Gupt (3 August 1886–12 December 1964), considered to be one of the most important Hindi poets, was born in the small village of Chirgaon, in Jhansi district of present-day Uttar Pradesh. He used the Khari Boli dialect instead of Braj Bhasha, which was used by most other poets in those days. He wrote plays and poems, including those based on the epics and on Buddhism. Among his many works is *Saket*, which tells the story of Rama, but with special focus on Urmila. His poem 'Yashodhara' is about Gautama Buddha's wife, while his other compositions include *Bharat-Bharati*, a collection of patriotic poems against British rule. He also translated works from Sanskrit into Hindi. In 1947, he was nominated to the Rajya Sabha and he received the Padma Bhushan in 1954.

Bhargavaram Vitthal Varerkar (1883–1964) also wrote about Urmila. Born in Chiplun, in Ratnagiri district of Maharashtra, he was the author of several works in Marathi, including plays, short stories, novels and essays. He also translated books from English and Bengali into Marathi. *Bhumikanya Sita*, written in 1950 and published in 1955, is a play written for Natya Niketan, a theatre company. It depicts Urmila as a strong woman, protesting against Rama's actions in asking Sita to take an oath for a second time. He too received the Padma Bhushan, in 1959, and was also nominated to the Rajya Sabha.

❋ BHARATHIDASAN

Bharathidasan (29 April 1891–21 April 1964) was a great poet and writer. Born in Pondicherry, his real name was Kanaka Subburathinam. He took the name Bharathidasan as he was an admirer of the poet Subramania Bharati. He wrote lyrics, dramas, novels and epic poems in Tamil. He received the Sahitya Akademi Award posthumously in 1969 for his play *Pichirandaiyar*, the story of a Sangam poet and his friendship with the king Kopperuncholan.

❋ SPORTS AND GAMES

In the Tokyo Olympics held in October 1964, India reclaimed the hockey gold and participated in forty-two events. Fifty-three Indians competed, fifty-two of them men and just one woman. There were no other medals won apart from the one, but Gurbachan Singh Randhawa put up a good performance and finished fifth in the 110-metre hurdles.

❋ THE TOP FILMS

The top three Hindi box office hits were: *Sangam*, with Vyjayanthimala, Raj Kapoor and Rajendra Kumar; *Ayee Milan ki Bela*, directed by Mohan Kumar and about two friends who love the same woman; *Dosti*, directed by Satyen Bose and about the friendship between two differently abled boys.

The National Award for the best feature film went to *Charulata*, a Bengali film directed by Satyajit Ray.

ALSO IN 1964

6 February: Death of Rajkumari Amrit Kaur (b. 2 February 1889), a nationalist, social reformer and educationist, the first health minister in the union government (1947–57) and after that, a member of the Rajya Sabha

22 February: Death of Verrier Elwin (b. 29 August 1902), an eminent anthropologist and an authority on India's tribal people, particularly those of the north-eastern states

February: The National Film Archive of India is set up in Pune to acquire and preserve all films made in India, as well as film scripts, books, photographs and other records related to Indian cinema. It also conducts courses on film appreciation, and is a centre for research.

29 August: The Vishva Hindu Parishad is established. Its aims are to unify Hindu society and promote Hindu values.

September: Indian Oil Corporation Ltd is set up by amalgamating Indian Refineries Ltd with Indian Oil Company Ltd.

7 November: The Communist Party of India (Marxist) is formed after a split from the Communist Party of India.

November: The Essential Commodities (Amendment) Ordinance is passed in order to deal with food hoarding and shortages.

1965: WAR WITH PAKISTAN

In April 1965, Pakistan occupied some part of a disputed territory in the Rann of Kutch. India responded, but both nations agreed to maintain peace as Britain intervened to prevent a war. Then in August, Pakistan tried to start a revolt in Kashmir. This time, Prime Minister Lal Bahadur Shastri took decisive action and sent the army across the ceasefire line of 1948.[10] The passes of Tithwal and Haji Pir, through which Pakistan was sending its men, were soon occupied by India.

On 1 September, Pakistan attacked with tanks and infantry in the south-west region of Jammu and Kashmir. Indian troops launched a defence and started a counter-attack. The Indian Army almost reached the cities of Lahore and Sialkot in Pakistan, with the Air Force providing support. India's army had many successes. In one battle, that of Asal Uttar, almost a hundred Pakistani Patton and other tanks were captured or destroyed. This battle changed the course of the war, and eventually led to India's victory.

The United Nations asked both countries to stop the war, and a ceasefire was agreed to on 23 September. Shastri's strong leadership during the war inspired the people to look to him as a hero.

---

[10] This had been established after the India–Pakistan war of 1947–48.

Among other important events of the year were further changes in the socialist party. The Praja Socialist Party left the Samyukta Socialist Party, which had been formed in 1962.

> **INCREASE IN TECHNICAL EDUCATION: 1950–65**
>
> - The number of scientific and technical personnel rose from 1,88,000 to 7,31,500.
> - The number of students in engineering and technology institutions rose from 13,000 to 78,000.
> - The number of students of agriculture rose from 2600 to 14,900.

❋ *CHEMMEEN* AND *ODAKKUZHAL*

In 1965, the Malayalam film *Chemmeen*, directed by Ramu Kariat, won the President's Gold Medal. It was based on the novel of the same name by Thakazhi Sivasankara Pillai. The film, set in a fishing community, tells the story of Karuthamma, daughter of Chembankunju, a Hindu fisherman. She falls in love with a Muslim fish trader, Pareekutty, to whom her father sells his catch. When her mother discovers this, she persuades her to forget Pareekutty and marry a man called Palani instead, as going against the community's traditions would anger Kadalamma, the sea mother/goddess. Karuthamma remains loyal to Palani, but as her past becomes known in Palani's village, he is ostracized. One day, Karuthamma and Pareekutty meet again, reviving their love. Palani, alone at sea, dies in a whirlpool, and the two lovers are found dead too.

Chemmeen was the first film from south India to win the President's Gold Medal. It was dubbed in Hindi and English, and won a certificate of merit at the Chicago International Film Festival and a gold medal for best cinematography at the Cannes Film Festival. It is considered to be one of India's best films, with the novel becoming famous through the movie. The music was composed by Salil Chowdhury and the lyrics were by Vayalar Ramavarma. The singers were K.J. Yesudas, P. Leela and Manna Dey.

Another Malayalam writer, G. Sankara Kurup (3 June 1901–2 February 1978), won the first Jnanpith Award for his collection of poems *Odakkuzhal* (The Flute, 1950). Kurup was a great poet. Born in Nayathode, near Kaladi in Kerala, he began writing poems at the age of nine, but started his career as a teacher. He taught Malayalam in schools and later became a lecturer and professor, and then producer and adviser at All India Radio. Even before winning the Jnanpith, he was awarded the Kerala Sahitya Akademi Award (1961) and the Sahitya Akademi Award (1963). After 1965, even more recognition and awards came his way. He was nominated to the Rajya Sabha in 1968. He received the Soviet Land Nehru Award in 1967 and the Padma Bhushan in 1968.

His poetry combined mystical and social themes, and many of his poems have symbolic meanings. His poem 'Perumthachan' (The Master Carpenter) is a tragic tale of a carpenter jealous of his son, who is more talented. His chisel slips, leading to the death of his son, and he wonders ever after, *wasn't it an accident? Did he mean to do it?* Without his son, he is filled with sorrow and pain in his old age.

After winning the Jnanpith, Kurup founded his own award for writers in Malayalam literature, the Odakkuzhal Award.

THE JNANPITH AWARD

The Jnanpith Award is presented for the best and most creative piece of literary writing by an Indian citizen in any of the languages included in the Eighth Schedule of the Indian Constitution. The award was conceived and founded by the late Rama Jain. It is a prestigious literary award.

❋ THE JAL TARANG

The *jal tarang* is a musical instrument consisting of cups with water, filled to various levels and struck by sticks to create a melody. The cups can be made of metal or porcelain. The instrument was more popular in the past, but still has some players today. Seetha Doraiswamy (27 January 1926–14 March 2013), a Karnatic music exponent of the jal tarang, kept the dying instrument alive, receiving the Kalaimamani award in 2001. She started performing only at the age of forty-one. She also contributed to Karnatic music theory. Among other players of the instrument are Shashikala Dani, Anayampatti S. Ganesan, Nemani Somayajulu and Milind Tulankar. George Harrison used the instrument in his 1982 album *Gone Troppo*.

❋ MAHARISHI MAHESH YOGI

Maharishi Mahesh Yogi (12 January 1918–5 February 2008) began teaching a meditation technique in 1955 that he named Transcendental Meditation. This became one of the most widely practised method of meditation across the world, and from 1965 onwards, was introduced in some educational institutions. In this, trained teachers provide advanced techniques, which take the practitioner to deeper levels and are said to provide various siddhis (powers). The Beatles and other celebrities are among those who followed the yogi's programmes. Transcendental Meditation continued to be taught and practised after his death. The maharishi also founded schools, colleges, universities and charitable institutions in several countries.

ALSO IN 1965

January: The Food Corporation of India is established.

6 February: Partap Singh Kairon (b. 1901), three-time chief minister of Punjab after Independence, is shot dead. He was a member of the Indian National Congress, and had participated in the freedom movement.

September: The draft of the Fourth Five-Year Plan, for 1966–71, is prepared, with a focus on agriculture.

1 December: The Border Security Force, a paramilitary force to guard India's borders in peacetime, is set up.

The Jawaharlal Nehru Award for International Understanding is instituted by the union government as a tribute to Jawaharlal Nehru's dedication to world peace and international understanding. The first award winner, in 1965, is U Thant, a Burmese diplomat and secretary general of the United Nations.

The National Dairy Development Board is set up to start milk cooperatives all over India in the pattern of the Anand milk cooperative.

The Param Vir Chakra is awarded to Abdul Hamid of the 4 Grenadiers regiment and to Ardeshir Burzorji Tarapore of the 7 Poona Horse regiment, both posthumously.

20

1966: THE RISE OF INDIRA GANDHI

The war with Pakistan was over, but a peace treaty had not been signed. Prime Minister Alexei Kosygin of the Soviet Union invited President Ayub Khan of Pakistan and Prime Minister Lal Bahadur Shastri of India to Tashkent in the USSR (now in Uzbekistan) for talks. This took place from 3 to 10 January, and finally both Khan and Shastri agreed to withdraw to positions held on 5 August 1965. They also agreed to resume diplomatic relations and not interfere in each other's internal affairs.

For India, this meant a withdrawal from the passes of Tithwal and Haji Pir. Shastri believed this was necessary to maintain peace, in case China attacked India in support of Pakistan. The Tashkent Agreement was signed on 10 January, and Shastri, though tired, seemed well and calm. But he felt stressed when he heard of the unfavourable reactions to this agreement back in India. At 1.20 a.m. on 11 January, he called his doctor and the other officials who were sleeping in the next room. And as they rushed to his help, Shastri started coughing and he seemed to be in pain. At 1.32 a.m., he died of a heart attack.

Lal Bahadur Shastri

There was shock and grief both in India and Tashkent, and his body was flown home the same day. He had been prime minister for only nineteen months. Some wondered if there was something strange about his death, though doctors confirmed that it was a natural one. As a result of the peace treaty, India returned 2000 sq. km of territory captured from Pakistan.

❋ A NEW PRIME MINISTER

Shastri's death meant that a new prime minister had to be chosen. The choice in the Congress was between Indira Gandhi, daughter of Jawaharlal Nehru, and Morarji Desai, one of the most senior leaders of the party. An election was held and Indira won. She was sworn in as prime minister on 24 January 1966.

❋ OTHER KEY EVENTS

On 1 November 1966, the state of Punjab was divided into the two states of Haryana and Punjab. Chandigarh remained the capital of both states and was made a union territory.

The draft for the Fourth Five-Year Plan had been completed under Shastri, but changes had to be made to this because of the 1965 war. So, instead of a five-year plan, there were three annual plans from 1966 to 1969.

The Shiv Sena, a new political party based in Maharashtra, was founded by Balasaheb Thackeray. The Shiv Sena is still active in Maharashtra, where it tries to promote Hindu and Marathi culture.

❋ GUARDIANS OF THE RESERVE BANK: A *YAKSHA* AND A *YAKSHINI*

It was Jawaharlal Nehru's idea to decorate new public buildings with works of art created by Indian artists. And so it was decided that at the entrance of the Reserve Bank of India's new office in New Delhi, there would be two sculptures, one on either side, representing 'prosperity through industry' and 'prosperity through agriculture' respectively. A yaksha and yakshini, it was thought, would depict this best.

Ramkinkar Baij received the contract for the project and began working on the sculptures, but he took over ten years to make them and they were not ready till 1966–67. The images were based on the ancient sculptures of Parkham and Bisnagar, but by the time they were installed, the atmosphere in the country had changed. Politicians not familiar with art saw the yakshini as 'a naked woman' and wanted to know why it was in front of the Reserve Bank! Finally, they were convinced that the yaksha represented Kuber, the god of wealth, and the Yakshini, agriculture. The huge sculptures still stand outside the bank.

RAMKINKAR BAIJ

Ramkinkar received the Padma Bhushan in 1970. He was a noted artist and sculptor, who studied in Santiniketan with Nandalal Bose and became a professor of sculpture at Visva-Bharati University. He held several exhibitions of both sculptures and paintings. Among his other works are a bronze bust of Rabindranath Tagore, placed at a monument in Balatonfured, Hungary—a place where Tagore had received treatment for his cardiac problems—and an image of the Buddha and of a Santhal family, both preserved in Santiniketan. In fact, the Santhals find an important place in Ramkinkar's paintings and sculptures, as he had observed their simple lifestyles as well as their hardships in the neighbouring villages.

Ramkinkar's works are on display in the Lalit Kala Akademi and the National Gallery of Modern Art.

❋ NANDALAL BOSE

The year saw the death of Nandalal Bose, who had been Ramkinkar's teacher. Nandalal, a student of Abanindranath Tagore, belonged to the Bengal school of art. Nandalal used different styles in his paintings and became famous for his linocut of Mahatma Gandhi on the Dandi March. He was awarded the Padma Vibhushan in 1954 and was selected as a fellow of the Lalit Kala Akademi in 1956, among other honours. His paintings can be found in the National Gallery of Modern Art and have been exhibited all over the world.

❋ SADHU VASWANI MISSION AND THE MIRA MOVEMENT

Sadhu T.L. Vaswani (25 November 1879–16 January 1966) was a great educationist and social reformer. Born in Hyderabad, Sind (present-day Sindh), he wrote over a hundred books, and believed that all religions were different paths to the same truth. In 1933, he started the Mira Movement in Education in Sind, which was shifted to Pune after Partition. Today the Mira Movement has six educational institutions in Pune and some in other cities, as well as hospitals and dispensaries. Free education is provided to those who cannot afford it, as is free food. The mission works towards upliftment in villages. There is also an emphasis on spirituality, service to others, and kindness and compassion to animals and birds. 'For me not to love birds and animals would be not to love the Lord', Vaswani said,[11] and even after his death, his students feed birds and animals every day. His birthday is celebrated every year in India as Meatless Day and Animal Rights Day.

---

[11] 'Jiv Daya', *Activities of Sadhu Vaswani Mission*, accessed 11 June 2017, http://www.sadhuvaswani.org/svm/svmact.html.

After his death, the mission was continued by Sadhu Vaswani's nephew, Dada J.P. Vaswani (b. 1918), also an advocate for peace.

❋ REITA FARIA'S LOVE STORY

Reita Faria (b. 1943) of India was the first Asian to win the Miss World title, in 1966.

Born to Goan parents, Reita Faria was a medical student in Bombay when she entered the Miss India contest, and after a series of rounds, was crowned Miss India. The finals of the Miss World pageant took place in London on 17 November 1966, and to the astonishment of everyone, Reita won. She was only the second Indian to participate in the contest, and India's participation had not been organized well. A passport and visa had been arranged for her at the last minute, she had borrowed some of the clothes she would wear and she could take only £3 to London (that was the amount of foreign exchange allowed by the Indian government at the time).

Reita used her prize money to join King's College Hospital in London and completed her medical degree. And her win led to a great love story! David Powell, a junior doctor who was first attracted to her when he saw her on TV, met her and the two were married in 1971. By now their happy marriage has lasted more than forty-five years.

Strangely, another medical student, Yasmin Daji (b. 1947), studying at Lady Hardinge College, New Delhi, won the Femina Miss India contest in 1966 and participated in the Miss Universe contest that year. Though she did not win, she was the third runner-up. She became a model but also completed her medical studies, and now she lives in the USA, where she was born.

ALSO IN 1966

24 January: Death of Homi Bhabha (b. 30 October 1909) in a plane crash. He was the founder of the Bhabha Atomic Research Centre and known as the Father of Indian Nuclear Science.

In the Bangkok Asian Games, India wins seven gold, three silver and eleven bronze medals.

The Indian Forest Service, an all-India service, comes into existence for the management and protection of the forests of India. It is under the Ministry of Environment, Forest and Climate Change.

The Bharat Ratna is posthumously awarded to Lal Bahadur Shastri.

Tarashankar Bandyopadhyay wins the Jnanpith Award for his Bengali novel *Ganadebata*.

21

1967: THE FOURTH GENERAL ELECTIONS

The fourth general elections, as well as elections to most of the state assemblies, were held in February 1967. In these elections, the Congress got a majority, though it won only 283 seats, less than their count in earlier elections. In the states too, they suffered losses. The Congress did not get a majority in Bihar, Punjab, Rajasthan, Orissa, Uttar Pradesh, West Bengal, Kerala and Madras.

In Madras, the Dravida Munnetra Kazhagam formed the government, while in other states, there were coalition governments.

The Congress tried to get more support by suggesting reforms to improve the economy and reduce inequalities. These included more control over banking, the nationalization of general insurance, a public distribution system for foodgrains and the removal of privileges of former rulers. But some older congressmen were against these changes.

Among other important events of the year was the appointment of a new Planning Commission, and Zakir Husain being chosen as the new President.

🟖 THE MAOISTS AND THE NAXALITES

Today there are Maoists in various states, such as Chhattisgarh, who want to remove the government. Their aim is to have a different type of society, which is more equal. For this they use violent methods. So when did this movement start in India?

India saw peasant movements even before Independence. But in 1967, when the CPI (M) decided to participate in the general elections and to work for the people in a legal and peaceful way, some of their members left and founded the Communist Party of India (Marxist–Leninist), led by Charu Mazumdar. Members of the CPI (ML) started a peasant movement on 3 March 1967 in Naxalbari, a region in Darjeeling district of West Bengal, which is why they are known as Naxalites. They wanted to remove what they called the 'class enemies' of the peasants i.e., landlords and government officials.

An armed movement, it spread to other states, and many students and intellectuals joined in, most of whom later returned to mainstream life. The Naxalites were eventually suppressed by the police, though Naxalites, under different names, are still present in many states.

🟖 MIR OSMAN ALI KHAN: THE LAST NIZAM

Mir Osman Ali Khan (6 April 1886–24 February 1967) was the Nizam, or ruler, of the state of Hyderabad from 1911 to 1948. After the Indian government took over the state in 1948, he was the rajpramukh until 1956. However, he did not have much to do during the later years, as at first, there was a military government that had the

The last Nizam, Mir Osman Ali Khan

real power and after 1950, an elected government. In 1956, when Andhra Pradesh was formed, his role in the state was over.

He continued to live in his palace, now known as King Kothi, in Hyderabad, and received a sum of money (known as the privy purse) every year from the government to take care of his family and others who depended on him. After his death, a huge funeral procession passed through the city, the largest seen in independent India. He was one of the richest men in the world, and though many years have passed since the end of his rule, he is still remembered for setting up several institutions in Hyderabad, including Osmania University, the Hyderabad State Bank (now the State Bank of Hyderabad), a library, Osmania General Hospital and more.

❋ UMASHANKAR JOSHI AND KUVEMPU: JNANPITH WINNERS

Among writers in Gujarati literature, Umashankar Joshi (1911–88) stands out. He wrote short stories, poems, essays, plays and one novel. Here are a few lines from his poem 'Chinnabhinna Chum' (Fragmented), translated by himself:[12]

> I am fragmented—falling apart—
> Like rhythm striving to throb in a poem without metre,
> Like a pattern trying to emerge upon man's life canvas.
> Like breadcrumbs in several homes, not yet placed in a beggar's bowl.

He received the Jnanpith Award (1967) for his work *Nishitha*, the Sahitya Akademi Award (1973) and the Soviet Land Nehru Award (1979). He was nominated to the Rajya Sabha (1970–76) and was vice chancellor of Gujarat University, chancellor of Visva-Bharati University and president of the Sahitya Akademi.

---

[12] Quoted in *Modern Indian Literature: An Anthology; Surveys and Poems*, ed. K. M. George (Delhi: Sahitya Akademi, 1992).

Kuppali Venkatappa Puttappa, nicknamed Kuvempu (29 December 1904–11 November 1994), was a Kannada writer who also won the Jnanpith Award that year, for his work *Sri Ramayana Darshanam*, a new version of the Ramayana. Kuvempu was against the caste system and unnecessary rituals, and promoted women's equality. In his Ramayana, therefore, Rama too undergoes the agni *pariksha*, entering the fire along with Sita. Kuvempu also received the Padma Vibhushan (1988) as well as other awards.

❁ ANGELO DE FONSECA: A GOAN ARTIST

Angelo de Fonseca (1902–67) was a Goan artist, who studied with Rabindranath Tagore and Nandalal Bose. He painted Christian themes in an Indian style, and was expelled from Goa for painting the Madonna as a Goan woman in a sari. He moved to Pune and carried on painting, working with different media, including stained glass and wood, water colours, oils and pencil. He also painted murals.

❁ BADAL SIRCAR AND BENGALI THEATRE

Badal Sircar (15 July 1925–13 May 2011) wrote a number of plays in Bengali, among which *Ebong Indrajit*, *Baaki Itihash* and *Pagla Ghora* stand out, all written in the 1960s. *Ebong Indrajit* (And Indrajit, 1963) tells the story of the alienated loner Indrajit and three others, Amal, Bipal and Kamal. Sombhu Mitra, who formed the Bohurupee theatre group in Calcutta in 1948, produced these and other early plays of Sircar. In the 1970s, Badal Sircar was sympathetic to the Naxalite movement, and produced anti-establishment plays. In 1967, he formed the Shatabdi theatre group, and began producing plays himself. This became the Third Theatre movement, a form of performance in protest against commercial theatre. Third Theatre plays were performed in any open space, with audience participation. Sircar won a number of awards, including the Sangeet Natak Akademi's Ratna Sadasya in 1997. He declined the Padma Bhushan in 2010, but had accepted the Padma Shri in 1972. A five-day festival called Badal Utsav was held in July 2009 to celebrate his eighty-fifth birthday.

THE BOHURUPEE THEATRE GROUP

Sombhu Mitra (22 August 1915–19 May 1997), an actor, director and playwright, received the Sangeet Natak Akademi Fellowship in 1966, the Padma Bhushan in 1970 and the Ramon Magsaysay Award in 1976. His Bohurupee group produced a number of plays apart from those of Badal Sircar, including adaptations such as *Putul Khela* (based on Henrik Ibsen's *A Doll's House*) and *Raja Oidipous* (based on Sophocles's *Oedipus Rex*).

Ajitesh Bandopadhyay (1933–83) also produced a number of plays, many of them adaptations.

ALSO IN 1967

12 October: Death of Ram Manohar Lohia (b. 1910), founder of the Socialist Party

The Indian Air Force Museum, located at the Palam Air Force Station, New Delhi, is established.

22

1968: THE GREEN REVOLUTION BEGINS

In 1967–68, there was an increase in agricultural production, which came to be known as India's green revolution. The green revolution originally began in Mexico, when Norman Borlaug (1914–2009), an American who worked there, developed Mexican semi-dwarf wheat, a type of wheat that has high yields and is resistant to disease. Around that time, India was not producing enough food. M.S. Swaminathan (b. 7 August 1925), who was working with the Indian Agricultural Research Institute, was one of the main people responsible for bringing this wheat variety to India.

Swaminathan had begun research on potato, wheat, rice and jute seeds in 1949, and in 1963, he arranged for Borlaug's visit to India. After initial testing, Borlaug provided tons of seeds to India and Pakistan, even during the 1965 war. Fertilizers and more extensive irrigation helped expand the production of other crops. In addition to this, there were land reforms that helped the farmers.

Tractors increased in number during the green revolution

With the increase in yields, India became self-sufficient in all cereal grain production by 1974.

Swaminathan was director of the Indian Council of Agricultural Research from 1972 to 1979, minister for agriculture from 1979 to 1980 and director general of the International Rice Research Institute from 1982 to 1988.

✣ AUROVILLE: AN INTERNATIONAL CITY

Auroville, an international city, is a unique place where people of all nationalities live in harmony. It is near the Sri Aurobindo Ashram in present-day Puducherry, but extends into Tamil Nadu. The foundation stone for Auroville was laid on 28 February 1968, and representatives of 124 countries attended the inauguration ceremony. The Matrimandir, a golden circular meditation space, is in the centre of the city, with four zones around it, each for a different purpose (residential, industrial, cultural and international).

Auroville was conceived by 'The Mother', Mirra Alfassa Richard, who was associated with Sri Aurobindo in Pondicherry and ran the ashram after his death. Auroville gradually grew, and creative people from various countries settled there. The occupants grow crops, make handicrafts and express their creativity in other ways. They also have an agricultural department, a medical section and several other projects.

✣ VILAYAT KHAN REFUSES THE PADMA BHUSHAN

The sitar, a stringed instrument, has been popular since the eighteenth century. Where did the sitar come from? Did it develop from the veena? According to some sources, it was invented by Amir Khusrau in the thirteenth century. The sitar has seven main strings made of metal and eleven to seventeen strings below, all of which resonate when the instrument is played.

Among the great sitar players of the twentieth century were Ilyas Khan (1924–89) of the Lucknow gharana and Vilayat Khan (1928–2004) of the Etawah gharana. Vilayat Khan, son of Inayat Khan (1894–1934), also a brilliant sitar player, specialized in Gayaki Ang, a method of playing that was close to vocal music.

Vilayat played for some films too, among them *The Guru* (1969), directed by James Ivory. He was awarded but refused the Padma Shri (1964), the Padma Bhushan (1968) and even the Padma Vibhushan (2000).

A NOBEL PRIZE

Har Gobind Khorana (1922–2011), a biochemist originally from India, shared the Nobel Prize in Physiology or Medicine in 1968 with Marshall W. Nirenberg and Robert W. Holley, for his research on nucleic acids. The Nobel Prize–winning research helped discover the genetic components of the nucleus. Har Gobind was born in Raipur, West Punjab (now in Pakistan), and he studied at Panjab University, Lahore, and later at the University of Liverpool, England, from where he received a PhD. He continued his research at the University of Cambridge, and later in the USA. After 1947, he was an Indian citizen, but became an American citizen in 1966.

Khorana synthesized small nucleic acid molecules with a known structure. These combined with other materials, causing proteins to be synthesized. He continued his path-breaking research even after winning the Nobel Prize.

SUMITRANANDAN PANT WINS THE JNANPITH AWARD

Sumitranandan Pant (1900–78) was a Hindi writer and poet, who, along with Jaishankar Prasad and Suryakant Tripathi (known as Nirala), began the Chhayavaadi (romantic) school of Hindi poetry.

His first poetry collection, *Pallav*, published in 1926, dwells on the beauties of nature; 'Jyotsna' (1934) focuses on the plight of human beings in the world today; 'Svarna Kiran' (1947) portrays a vision for the future; *Lokayat* (1964), an epic in over 20,000 lines, sees man as he might be in the distant future. He also wrote a considerable amount of prose. This included a novel, written in his youth, a collection of short stories and of essays, a short autobiography and critical reviews of himself and some of his contemporaries. He received numerous literary awards and honours, including the Jnanpith Award in 1968. Ramdhari Singh 'Dinkar' and Mahadevi Verma were other Chhayavaadi writers. Though the Chhayavaadi period is considered to have lasted from 1918 to 1937, these writers continued to bring out related works after this.

Mahadevi Verma (1907–87) won the Jnanpith Award in 1982 for her poetry collection *Yama* (1936). Her other poetry collections include *Nihar*, *Rashmi*, *Niraj* and *Dipshikha*. She had an MA in Sanskrit, and became the principal of Mahila Vidyapith, Allahabad. Her memoirs are titled *Smriti ki Rekhayen*.

Ramdhari Singh 'Dinkar' (1908–74) won the Jnanpith Award for *Urvashi* (1972), apart from several others.

ALSO IN 1968

1 February: Death of A.R. Krishnashastry (b. 1890), writer and translator of Kannada literature

25 December: Forty-four Dalit women and children are attacked and burnt to death in the Keezhvenmani village of Tamil Nadu after landless peasants start an agitation.

The highest-grossing Hindi film of the year is *Ankhen*, directed and produced by Ramanand Sagar. A spy thriller, the story is based on terrorist attacks in Assam after Independence.

23

1969: THE CONGRESS SPLITS

Indira Gandhi wanted to bring in new policies, but she was opposed by the old Congress members, who came to be known as the Syndicate. The first conflict, in 1969, was over the choice of a new President after the death of Zakir Husain on 3 May. The Syndicate wanted Sanjiva Reddy as President while Indira was against this. Eventually, she managed the defeat of Sanjiva Reddy. Instead, V.V. Giri, the then vice president, who had contested as an independent, was elected on 20 August. The next step was to bring in the reforms Indira wanted implemented.

On 16 July 1969, Indira Gandhi took over the finance ministry from Morarji Desai, leading to his resignation. Following that, she passed an ordinance nationalizing banks. The Syndicate remained against her and, on 13 November, expelled Indira from the Congress. But Indira too had a number of supporters. After a meeting of the All India Congress Committee on 22 November, at least 440 out of 705 members supported her. There were now two groups and both sides claimed to be the real Congress party. Indira's Congress came to be called the Indian National Congress (R), the 'R' standing

Indira Gandhi

for 'requisitionist', and the other, Congress (O), the 'O' standing for 'organizational'.

❈ ANNADURAI: TAMIL ACTORS AND POLITICIANS

The year saw the death of C.N. Annadurai (b. 1909), who had broken away from the Dravida Kazhagam political party and founded the Dravida Munnetra Kazhagam. He became chief minister of Madras State in 1967, but died before completing a full term.

Annadurai was not just a politician, but an actor and a writer. The film *Velaikkaari* (1949), based on a play written by Annadurai, started a new era in Tamil cinema, as it centred on class conflicts and oppression by landlords. M. Karunanidhi, his assistant, who later became chief minister, also wrote screenplays. He wrote the screenplay for *Parasakthi* (1952), a notable film and a commercial success, through which the actor Sivaji Ganesan came to prominence. The original play was written by Pavalar Balasundaram, and the film is about a Tamil family at the time of World War II. M.G. Ramachandran, another chief minister, was also a popular actor. And he was succeeded by his protégée, J. Jayalalithaa, another prominent actor, as chief minister.

There were numerous other Tamil actors in the 1960s, but Gemini Ganesan stands out among them. Among directors, K. Balachander made new types of films, including *Ethir Neechal* (1968), which he also wrote, and *Arangetram* (1973). The latter is about a young woman who is forced to become a prostitute to support her poor, conservative Brahman family.

❈ KESARBAI KERKAR WINS THE PADMA BHUSHAN

Kesarbai Kerkar (13 July 1892–16 September 1977), one of the best vocalists of Hindustani music, was awarded the Padma Bhushan in 1969. She was born in Keri, a village in Goa, and studied with several teachers, particularly Alladiya Khan (1855–1946) of the

Jaipur–Atrauli gharana. Alladiya was a great singer, known as Sangeet Samrat or the emperor of music. He agreed to teach her only under certain conditions, which included a ten-year training period. Kesarbai followed everything he insisted upon, and even helped with his household tasks. She had a rich voice, and specialized in certain ragas, such as Bahar and Miyan Malhar. She received a number of other awards, including the Sangeet Natak Akademi Award (1953). She took on only one student, Dhondutai Kulkarni, and stopped singing a few years before her death.

Other noted female singers of Hindustani music at the time include Mogubai Kurdikar, Gangubai Hangal and Hirabai Barodekar. Mogubai Kurdikar (1904–2001), also born in Goa, won the Sangeet Natak Akademi Award (1968) and the Padma Bhushan (1974). Gangubai Hangal (1913–2009), of the Kirana gharana, mainly sang khayals. Born in Dharwad, she learnt Hindustani music with Sawai Gandharva. Upon her death, she was given a state funeral in Karnataka, and a music university in Mysuru is named after her. She was awarded the Padma Bhushan (1971), the Padma Vibhushan (2002), the Sangeet Natak Akademi Award (1973) and the Sangeet Natak Akademi Fellowship (1996). Hirabai Barodekar (1905–89) sang khayals, thumris and bhajans, and acted in films. She also received the Sangeet Natak Akademi Award (1965) and the Padma Bhushan (1970). Sureshbabu Mane and Saraswati Mane, her brother and sister, were also renowned singers.

❈ THE MAGIC KEY

Zakir Husain (b. 1897) was President of India from 1967 to 1969. An academic, he founded educational institutions and wrote on education, philosophy and other topics. He also wrote stories for children.

The Magic Key is a series of folk tales retold by him. Explaining the title, he wrote, 'For all children the first books they

A reproduction of the cover of *A Flower's Song*

read are the key to the magic of the world.'[13] The stories have been translated from Urdu into English by his great-granddaughter, Samina Mishra. *Blowing Hot, Blowing Cold* is about an ordinary woodcutter's magical breath. *A Flower's Song, Sunshine for Amma, The Bravest Goat in the World, The Poori that Ran Away* and *Little Chicken in a Hurry* are other entertaining stories in the series.

● THE BEST CRICKETERS OF THE 1960s

Enthusiasm for cricket continued through the 1960s. Though there were many excellent players during these years, those who won the Arjuna Award are:

- 1961: Salim Durani;
- 1964: Mansur Ali Khan, nawab of Pataudi (Junior);
- 1965: V.L. Manjrekar;

---

[13] Zakir Husain, *Blowing Hot, Blowing Cold* (New Delhi: Young Zubaan, 2004).

- 1966: C.G. Borde;
- 1967: Ajit L. Wadekar;
- 1968: E.A. Srinivas Prasanna;
- 1969: Bishen Singh Bedi.

ALSO IN 1969

31 January: Death of Meher Baba (b. 25 February 1894), a spiritual teacher, who still has a large following in India and abroad

28 August: Death of Makhdoom Mohiuddin (b. 1908), Urdu poet. The same year, he wins the Sahitya Akademi Award for his collection of poems *Bisat-e-Raqs*.

24 September: The National Service Scheme (NSS) is inaugurated to involve college and high-school students in programmes of social service and national development.

The Tarapur Atomic Power Station is set up in Maharashtra to use nuclear power for peaceful purposes and to generate electricity from nuclear energy.

Firaq Gorakhpuri (1896–1982), Urdu poet and writer, wins the Jnanpith Award.

Khan Abdul Ghaffar Khan (1890–1988), nicknamed Frontier Gandhi, visits India, and is presented with the Jawaharlal Nehru Award for International Understanding in 1967.

The Dadasaheb Phalke Award, for outstanding contribution to the growth and development of Indian cinema, is presented for the first time. It is introduced by the Government of India in memory of Dadasaheb Phalke (1870–1944), one of the greatest early contributors to Indian cinema. The first award is presented to Devika Rani.

24

1970: THE LOK SABHA IS DISSOLVED

Indira Gandhi had been trying to bring in economic reforms, but her new party, the Congress (R), only had 220 members in the Lok Sabha. She had nationalized banks in 1969, but in February 1970, the Supreme Court ruled that the bank nationalization was not valid. She issued an ordinance for bank nationalization once again. She also wanted to abolish privy purses—the income given to former Indian rulers—but in August 1970, the Rajya Sabha, just by one vote, rejected this bill. She attempted an ordinance for this too, but the Supreme Court did not allow it. In December, therefore, she asked the President to recommend dissolution of the Lok Sabha. This took place on 27 December, and preparations for holding the next elections started.

✤ UTTERLY BUTTERLY DELICIOUS: THE WHITE REVOLUTION

India's White Revolution, or Operation Flood, refers to a plan to increase milk production, which started in July 1970. The National Dairy Development Board, which

The Amul girl

had been set up in 1965 to develop the dairy industry on the Amul (Anand milk) plan, played a big role. It had grouped rural producers together in cooperatives. By March 1985, the project included 136 milk sheds, covering 34,500 cooperative societies. By 1993, there were 64,700 dairy cooperatives; and by 1998, India became the world's largest milk producer. There were many people responsible for this success, but the person who started the programme in Anand, Gujarat, was Verghese Kurien (1921–2012), whose model was then used across the country.

AMUL AND THE AMUL GIRL

The Anand milk cooperative (Amul) was soon known all across India for producing milk powder, butter, cheese and other products. By 2016, Amul was owned by 36 lakh farmer families.

The Amul girl, with the caption 'Utterly Butterly Delicious', used in all Amul advertisements, was created in 1966 by Eustace Fernandez, art director of daCunha Communications. The round-faced young girl wears a polka-dot frock, with her blue hair cheekily tied on top of her head. Nisha Da Cunha thought of the popular caption.

The first Amul girl advertisement was displayed in Bombay in March 1966, during the horse-racing season. It showed her riding a horse, with 'Thoroughbread' written across the top and 'Utterly Butterly Amul' in the corner. A thoroughbred is a race horse, but 'thorough*bread*' indicated bread on which Amul butter could be spread! Such puns became typical of Amul ads. From then till now, the Amul girl has continued to comment on all events of national importance.

● AHMED JAN 'THIRAKWA' IS AWARDED THE PADMA BHUSHAN

Ahmed Jan 'Thirakwa' (1891–1976) was one of India's great tabla players, who received the Padma Bhushan in 1970. He received the Sangeet Natak Akademi Award (1954) too. Born in Moradabad, in present-day Uttar Pradesh, he studied music with Munir Khan, Bher Khan and Faiyaz Khan, and became professor of tabla at Bhatkhande Music Institute, Lucknow.

● KANTHE MAHARAJ DIES

The year saw the death of the great tabla player Kanthe Maharaj (b. 1880) on 1 August. An extraordinary player of the Varanasi gharana, his legacy was continued by his nephew, Kishan Maharaj (1923–2008), and other students. Kishan Maharaj received the Padma Vibhushan in 2002, one among his other awards. A versatile person, he could play other instruments too, and was also a poet, painter and sculptor.

THE TABLA AND OTHER DRUMS

A tabla has two drums: one larger, known as the *bayan* or the *dagga*, and the other, the *dayan*. Both together, or the dayan alone, are known as the tabla. The drums are played with the hands, in various tempos, and primarily accompany Hindustani music.

The dholak is a two-headed drum, which can be of different sizes and with a variety of features. Usually, larger drums are called the dhol or the *dhak*, while the smaller ones are known as dholaks.

The pakhawaj is a long, barrel-shaped drum with a wooden body, which was once popular in Hindustani music but has now been largely replaced by the tabla.

> The mridangam (from '*mirutankam*') is also barrel-shaped and long, but with a wider middle and tapering at the ends. It is played on both sides and is used in Karnatic music.

❋ HAHA HUHU REACHES LONDON

Viswanatha Satyanarayana (10 September 1895–18 October 1976) was a Telugu-language writer, who wrote essays, novels, short stories, plays and poems on a wide range of subjects. Born in Nandamuru, in Krishna district of present-day Andhra Pradesh, he wrote over a hundred works in Telugu, some of which have been translated into English. Among his books are three series of historical novels. He also wrote social novels, and provided an innovative twist to myths and legends of the past. For instance, while Haha and Huhu are the two Gandharva sons of the rishi Kashyapa in the Puranas, in Viswanatha's novel of the same name, Haha Huhu is an eight-foot-tall horse-headed deity, which somehow arrives in London, though in an injured state. The novel begins with, 'One morning in London there were a large number of people gathered in Trafalgar Square. They were looking at a strange animal. It had the head of a horse; the rest of its body was human.'[14]

Satyanarayana received a number of awards, including the Padma Bhushan (1970) as well as the Jnanpith Award, also in 1970, for *Srimad Ramayana Kalpavrikshamu*, the story of Rama in six parts, which he wrote in the years 1955–63.

---

[14] Viswanatha Satyanarayana, *Ha Ha Hu Hu*, trans. Velcheru Narayana Rao, quoted in *Journal of South Asian Literature*, Volume 16, No. 1, Part I: East–West Literary Relations (Asian Studies Center, Michigan State University, 1981), 103–131, http://www.jstor.org/stable/40873625.

🟎 GANDHINAGAR

A new city was constructed to become the capital of Gujarat after the separate state was formed. Gandhinagar, located on the bank of River Sabarmati, is close to the former capital of Ahmadabad. It was designed by H.K. Mewada, associate to the architect Le Corbusier, who had designed Chandigarh. Construction began in 1966, and the first state government offices were moved here in 1970.

🟎 THE ASIAN GAMES

In 1970, the Asian Games were held in Bangkok. India won six golds, nine silvers and ten bronzes. The gold medals were won in athletics, boxing and wrestling.

Kamaljeet Sandhu became the first individual female to win a gold medal for India, finishing first in the 400-metre race.

ALSO IN 1970

24 June: Death of the last ruler of Jaipur State, Sawai Man Singh II (b. 1911)

22 September: Death of Bengali-language writer Sharadindu Bandyopadhyay (b. 30 March 1899), creator of the fictional detective Byomkesh Bakshi

21 November: Death of Nobel Prize–winning physicist C.V. Raman (b. 1951).

The Padma Vibhushan is awarded to Tara Chand, an archaeologist and historian, and to Suranjan Das, a civil servant.

Zeenat Aman (b. 1951), model, actor and second runner-up in the Miss India contest, wins the Femina Miss India Asia Pacific title.

25

1971: BANGLADESH IS BORN

The Lok Sabha was dissolved towards the end of 1970, and fresh elections were held in March 1971. Four parties joined together to form a 'grand alliance' against Indira's party, the Congress (R). These four were the Congress (O), the Bharatiya Jana Sangh, the Swatantra Party and the Samyukta Socialist Party. Their main aim was to remove Indira from power. 'Indira *hatao*' ('Get rid of Indira') became their slogan as they felt that she was the cause of the country's problems. Indira and her party put forward the counter-slogan '*Gareebi* hatao' ('Get rid of poverty'), and said that their aim was to bring about economic progress. The new election symbol for the Congress (R) was a cow-and-calf pair. The old Congress symbol of two bullocks and a plough remained with the Congress (O).

The results showed that the people still trusted Indira. Her party won 352 out of the 518 Lok Sabha seats. The grand alliance together secured forty-nine seats, out of which the Congress (O) only had sixteen.

Meanwhile, across the borders, in West and East Pakistan, there were new developments. Pakistan, which attained independence at the same time as India, had not been able to establish a stable democracy.

Their first direct elections, in which every adult was allowed to vote, were held in 1970. At this time, General Yahya Khan was President of Pakistan. East Pakistan had always resented the dominance of the Punjabis of the west. In the 1970 elections, the Awami League, a political party of East Pakistan, headed by Mujibur Rahman, won 169 out of the 313 seats for the whole of Pakistan. If a government had been formed based on the election results, it would have given East Pakistan a dominant position. To West Pakistan, this was unacceptable. President Yahya Khan imposed martial law, imprisoned Mujibur Rahman and appointed General Tikka Khan as administrator of East Pakistan. Tikka Khan terrorized and attacked the Bengali population there, both Hindu and Muslim. Refugees escaping from Tikka Khan's brutalities crossed the border into India. By November 1971, this total reached 10 million. East Pakistan organized a guerrilla force called the Mukti Bahini to join in the fight against West Pakistan. India decided to support the Mukti Bahini and help East Pakistan gain freedom.

A war between India and Pakistan began on 3 December 1971, when Pakistan attacked eight airfields in Kashmir. By 16 December, the Pakistani commander in the east, Lieutenant General Niazi, surrendered. In the west, a ceasefire was agreed to on the 17th. East Pakistan, renamed Bangladesh, became independent, with Dhaka as the capital. Mujibur Rahman was its first President.

❋ TARASHANKAR BANDYOPADHYAY AND BISHNU DEY

The year saw the death of a great writer in Bengali literature, Tarashankar Bandyopadhyay (23 July 1898–14 September 1971), who had written over a hundred books, including novels, short stories, plays, memoirs, poems and essays. Among his novels is *Ganadebata* (1943), which won him the Jnanpith

Award (1966). *Ganadebata* is set in pre-Independence India, in the small village of Shivkalipur, where people of different castes live together. The story begins with the lower castes not doing their hereditary work of being barbers, carpenters, etc., as they are not earning enough. Instead they want to work in a mill. The plot moves on to the responses to this from the higher castes and to other incidents in the neighbouring villages. Tarashankar wrote several other realistic works based in Bengal. *Hansuli Banker Upakatha* (1951) is about the zamindars of rural Bengal, and was made into a film by Tapan Sinha in 1962. *Ganna Begum* (1965), *Mahanagari* (1966), *Aranyabahni* (1966) and *Janapada* are among his later works. Apart from the Jnanpith, he received the Rabindra Puraskar (1955), the Sahitya Akademi Award (1956), the Padma Shri (1962) and the Padma Bhushan (1969).

Bishnu Dey (1920–82), another Bengali-language writer and poet, won the Jnanpith Award in 1971 for his poetry collection *Smriti Satta Bhabhishyat* (Memory, Being, the Future).

❈ THE FIRST PLANE HIJACK IN INDIA

An Indian Airlines plane was hijacked on 30 January 1971. It was flying from Srinagar to Jammu, and was diverted to Lahore. The hijackers belonged to the Jammu Kashmir Liberation Front. All passengers and crew were released and returned to India. The two hijackers were seventeen-year-old Hashim Qureshi and his cousin Ashraf Qureshi. At first, the hijackers were welcomed in Pakistan, but later, they and others of the JKLF were arrested and tried on the grounds that they were collaborating with India's intelligence agencies. Hashim Qureshi, along with several others, was imprisoned. Most were released after two years, but Hashim remained in prison till 1980.

As a result of this incident, India banned overflights by Pakistan and this helped India during the 1971 war. But was Hashim really an Indian agent? In retrospect, it is most unlikely.

❖ UDAY SHANKAR WINS THE PADMA VIBHUSHAN

Uday Shankar (8 December 1900–26 September 1977), an eminent dancer and choreographer, created new styles in modern Indian dance.

Born in Udaipur, he was the son of Shyamashankar Chowdhury, who was a tutor to the maharaja of Udaipur and later, an official in the state of Jhalawar (Rajasthan). Uday was the elder brother of the sitarist Ravi Shankar. Uday Shankar studied art at Sir J.J. School of Art in Bombay, as well as Indian classical music. Next, he joined the Royal College of Art, London. By then, his father had moved to London, married an Englishwoman and would organize Indian dance and music performances. Uday began to participate in these.

Uday Shankar

After meeting Anna Pavlova, the famous Russian ballet dancer, his interest in dance grew, and he toured with her troupe. He returned to India in 1929 and explored classical Indian dance forms. In 1938, he founded the Uday Shankar India Cultural Centre for dance, drama and music at Simtola, near Almora. World War II was just starting and this centre closed in 1942, reopening in Calcutta in 1965 as the Uday Shankar Centre for Dance.

He created a number of ballets in a fusion style, combining western ballet and Indian classical and modern dance. He formed his own troupe, and his fusion ballets mainly had Indian dancers and instruments, apart from the French dancer and pianist Simone Barbier, known as Simkie. Themes of his ballets included traditional Indian ones, such as Radha–Krishna and Tandava nritya, as well as modern ones, such as labour and machinery, harvest and grass-cutters. He also made a film, *Kalpana* (1948). In 1962, he was awarded the Sangeet Natak Akademi Fellowship for lifetime achievement, and in 1971, he received the Padma Vibhushan. He was presented the Desikottama award by Visva-Bharati University in 1975.

He married Amala, who used to dance with him, and they had a son, Ananda, who became a musician, and a daughter, Mamata, who became a dancer.

Uday Shankar was among the earliest to present modern dance in India, and he was followed by many others. Among them is his daughter, Mamata Shankar; Shobana Jeyasingh, who now lives and works in the UK, and Shiamak Davar (b. 19 October 1961), who has choreographed dances in films and theatre, and has created his own unique style. Today, numerous choreographers for films keep creating new and contemporary dance styles.

❋ RAJESH KHANNA: THE FIRST SUPERSTAR

Rajesh Khanna (29 December 1942–18 July 2012), a Hindi film actor, can be said to be India's first superstar. The first film he acted in was *Aakhri Khat* (1966). He had fifteen hit films between 1969 and 1972 and many more after that, having acted in around 180 films in total. His co-stars include Sharmila Tagore, with whom he appeared in several films, such as *Aradhana* (1969) and *Amar Prem* (1972), both extremely popular, as well as Mumtaz, Asha Parekh, Zeenat Aman, Tina Munim and others.

His popularity possibly exceeded that of any other actor of the time. Music composer R.D. Burman and Kishore Kumar, who sang his songs, worked with Rajesh Khanna in thirty-two films. He won several Filmfare Awards, including the Lifetime Achievement Award in 2005.

SHARMILA ON RAJESH

Sharmila Tagore has described how girls used to chase him, and even marry his photographs! She had seven box office hits paired with Rajesh Khanna.

Sharmila married the cricketer Mansur Ali Khan Pataudi in 1969, and among their children, Saif Ali Khan is a noted actor. She continued to act in Hindi and Bengali films, receiving several awards, including the Filmfare Lifetime Achievement Award in 1998.

ALSO IN 1971

25 January: Himachal Pradesh becomes a state.

29 September: A cyclone in the Bay of Bengal hits Orissa; 10,000 are killed.

31 December: Death of Vikram Sarabhai (b. 12 August 1919), a prominent physicist as well as space and nuclear scientist

The Bharat Ratna is awarded to Indira Gandhi.

The Param Vir Chakra is awarded to Arun Khetarpal, Albert Ekka and Nirmal Jit Singh Sekhon posthumously, and to Hoshiar Singh, for their bravery in the 1971 war.

Air India gets its first Boeing 747 plane, named Emperor Ashoka.

1972: ASSEMBLY ELECTIONS

In March 1972, it was time to hold elections in all except four states (Uttar Pradesh, Orissa, Kerala and Madras). The Congress (R) won victories in every state. Indira Gandhi continued her economic policies with the nationalization of general insurance (in August 1972) and that of the coal industry (1973).

Meanwhile, after the 1971 war, peace had to be worked out between India and Pakistan. The then President of Pakistan, Zulfikar Ali Bhutto, came to Shimla for talks. It was agreed that both countries would settle issues through amicable means and would respect the Line of Control that resulted from the ceasefire of 17 December in Jammu and Kashmir. It was also decided that the 90,000 Pakistani prisoners of war that India had captured would be returned when Pakistan recognized Bangladesh. This transfer took place in 1973–74.

❋ OTHER KEY EVENTS

Among the other main events of the year were changes in India's north-eastern territory.

- ❋ The North-East Frontier Agency became the union territory of Arunachal Pradesh.

- Mizoram was made a union territory with its own legislative assembly.
- Tripura, previously a union territory, became a state.
- Meghalaya became a separate state.
- Manipur, previously a union territory, became a state.

MEENA KUMARI AND PRITHVIRAJ KAPOOR

The year saw the death of two prominent actors, Meena Kumari and Prithviraj Kapoor. Meena Kumari (1 August 1933–31 March 1972) was hardly thirty-nine years old when she died. Her mother, Iqbal Begum, was a dancer, and Meena Kumari, originally called Mahjabeen, was pushed into acting at the age of six with the film *Leather Face* (*Farzande Watan* in Hindi/Urdu). She acted in about a hundred films, among them *Baiju Bawra* (1952), which was a great hit, *Parineeta* (1953), *Daera* (1953), *Chandni Chowk* (1954), *Azaad* (1955), *Bandish* (1955), *Ek Hi Raasta* (1956), *Sharada* (1957), *Sahib, Bibi aur Ghulam* (1962), *Mere Apne* (1971) and *Dushman* (1971).

She married film director and producer Kamal Amrohi in 1952, in a secret ceremony. Their romance had blossomed after Meena was seriously injured in a car accident in 1951. At the time of the wedding, she was only nineteen while he was thirty-four. The marriage was made public a year later, and though the first few years with Kamal were happy ones, she began to feel oppressed by him as he kept watch over her and tried to control everything she did. She left his home in 1964 and continued to act in many more films, but began drinking heavily. For her film *Pakeezah* (1972), she was reconciled with Kamal Amrohi, who produced and directed it, but she died soon after its release. *Gomti ke Kinare* (1972) was another film of her last years, and was released after her death. Meena also wrote poetry under the name Naaz.

She received many awards, including the Filmfare Award, and *Pakeezah* is still considered a classic.

Prithviraj Kapoor (3 November 1906–29 May 1972) was an actor, producer and director. He was born in Lyallpur (now Faisalabad), in present-day Pakistan, moved to Bombay in 1928 and began acting in films, including in India's first talkie, *Alam Ara*. He set up his own company, Prithvi Theatre, in 1944. Prithvi Theatre was a travelling group of 150 members. It produced and staged over 2000 plays, including *Shakuntalam*, *Pathan* and *Deewar*. He later tried to secure a permanent location for the theatre and leased some land in Juhu, Bombay, but by that time, his health was declining. His son Shashi and daughter-in-law Jennifer bought the land after Prithviraj's death, and Prithvi Theatre finally acquired a fixed location on 5 November 1978. Jennifer promoted Hindi theatre and after her death, her daughter, Sanjana, and son Kunal continued to do so.

Prithviraj acted in various films, including *Mughal-e-Azam* and *Sikandar* (1941). *Sikandar* told the story of Alexander the Great and his invasion of India, in which Prithviraj played the lead role. His last major film was *Kal Aaj Aur Kal* (1971). He received a number of awards, including the Sangeet Natak Akademi Fellowship in 1954, the Sangeet Natak Akademi Award in 1956, the Padma Bhushan in 1969 and the Dadasaheb Phalke Award for the year 1971. He was also nominated to the Rajya Sabha twice.

Prithviraj was married to Ramsarni Mehra. Though two of their sons died, all three of his surviving sons, Raj Kapoor, Shammi Kapoor and Shashi Kapoor, became actors and film-makers. His grandchildren and great-grandchildren too are actors. They include Raj Kapoor's sons Randhir Kapoor and Rishi Kapoor; Randhir Kapoor's daughters, Karisma and Kareena Kapoor; Rishi Kapoor's son, Ranbir Kapoor. Karan Kapoor, Kunal Kapoor and Sanjana Kapoor are Shashi Kapoor's children.

The Prithvi Theatre Festival commemorated his birth centenary in 2006.

❋ THE WILDLIFE PROTECTION ACT AND THE CHEETAH

By the Wildlife Protection Act, passed on 9 September 1972, the hunting of all wild animals in India was banned. While later modifications were made to the act, it also led to the creation of more national parks and to attempts to protect and preserve animals and prevent their decline and extinction. Among animals that were already extinct by the time is the Asiatic Cheetah (*Acinonyx jubatus venaticus*).

The cheetah, which looks similar to the leopard, is the fastest land animal. Do you know how fast a cheetah can run? Its speed is 110–120 kilometres per hour, i.e., 2 kilometres in one minute, which is faster than Usain Bolt, the world's fastest man![15] Once, there were many cheetahs in northern India, but now it is extinct in the country. The Mughals and other rulers used to catch the animal, tame it and use it to hunt other animals. Because cheetahs tire easily, the animal would travel to the hunt seated in luxury on a horse or carried in a palanquin. They were fed and treated well, but it was an unnatural life for a wild animal. Others were killed for their skin and fur. The last three known cheetahs in India were shot in 1947 by the maharaja of Surguja, a small state that is now part of Madhya Pradesh. This man also shot more than a thousand tigers.

The cheetah

---

[15] Bolt has a speed of 44.6 kilometres per hour, calculated as per his performance in a 100-metre race.

ALSO IN 1972

8 May: Death of P.V. Kane (b. 7 May 1880), known for his monumental work on the Dharmashastras

29 May: The Dalit Panthers, an anti-caste group, is founded by Namdeo Dhasal and others in Maharashtra.

28 June: Death of Prasanta Chandra Mahalanobis (b. 29 June 1893), eminent scientist and statistician

October: The All India Anna Dravida Munnetra Kazhagam (AIADMK), a political party created by a split in the Dravida Munnetra Kazhagam, is founded by M.G. Ramachandran.

The Indian Council of Historical Research is set up in New Delhi to fund and coordinate research in history.

The Nehru Yuva Kendras (NYKs) are founded to provide non-students and rural youth with opportunities for self-development.

The Madras Snake Park Trust (now the Chennai Snake Park Trust) is founded by herpetologist Romulus Whitaker.

1973: ECONOMIC PROBLEMS

In 1972 and 1973, the monsoon failed. Economic problems further increased due to the rise of crude oil prices in the world in 1973, which had an impact on India too.

A plus point of the year was the resolution of the Telangana situation. An agitation had begun in Andhra Pradesh in 1968–69 for a separate state of Telangana as the people felt that they had inadequate educational and employment opportunities. The state of Andhra Pradesh had been formed in 1956, by joining together two regions: Telangana, which had been under the Nizam of Hyderabad, and Andhra, which had become a state in 1953 and was earlier a part of the Madras Presidency. An agreement was reached in 1973, and the Thirty-Second Constitutional Amendment was passed, giving preference to residents of all districts in the state in the fields of education and employment. Some years passed before the Telangana issue started again.

❖ THE FIRST FIELD MARSHAL

Sam H.F.J. Manekshaw (April 1914–June 2008) became Chief of the Army Staff in 1969 and retired on 15 January 1973. Just before this, he was appointed field marshal for life on 3 January.

Manekshaw had participated in World War II and held many top military posts after Independence. He was in charge during the Indo-Pakistan war of 1971.

Sam Manekshaw received several civil and military awards, including the Padma Vibhushan in 1972.

Sam H.F.J. Manekshaw

✸ KRISHNARAO SHANKAR PANDIT RECEIVES THE PADMA BHUSHAN

Krishnarao Shankar Pandit (26 July 1893–22 August 1989), a Hindustani classical music singer, was considered one of the best exponents of the Gwalior gharana.

He studied with his father, Shankarrao Pandit, as well as with father and son Nathu and Nissar Hussain Khan. He mainly sang khayal, but also the *dhrupad*, *tarana* and tappa. He began giving public performances at the age of eleven, and when he was just eighteen, he founded the Shankar Gandharva Mahavidyalaya in Lashkar, Gwalior State. He wrote books on music, including *Sangeet Sargam Sar* and *Sangeet Alap Sanchari*.

Krishnarao received a number of awards, including the Sangeet Natak Akademi Award for Hindustani vocal music in 1959, the Padma Bhushan in 1973 and the Tansen Samman in 1980. Of his four sons, Narayanrao Pandit and Lakshman Krishnarao Pandit are also musicians.

TYPES OF HINDUSTANI CLASSICAL MUSIC

Two important styles of Hindustani classical music are the dhrupad and the khayal. Dhrupad, which comes from the term *dhruva pada*, is a slow and majestic style used in praise of gods and goddesses, kings and queens and sometimes nature too. Khayal is an imaginative and romantic style, and uses ornamentation, such as *gamaka*s.

Light classical styles include the tappa, tarana, *dadra*, *dhamar*, thumri, ghazal, bhajan and qawwali. Tappa, originally a type of folk song, has a strong rhythm. Tarana uses *sargam*s or scales, and the words are nonsense syllables. Dhamar is related to dhrupad, and thumri to khayal. Thumri consists of a melodic composition. Most khayal recitals end with a thumri. Dadra generally has a faster tempo than thumri. Bhajans are devotional songs, while ghazals, composed in Urdu, are usually romantic. Qawwalis are devotional songs in the Sufi tradition.

❃ THE 1973 JNANPITH AWARDS

Two writers received the Jnanpith Award in 1973: D.R. Bendre, a poet, critic, playwright and translator writing in Kannada, and Gopinath Mohanty, who wrote in Odia.

Dattatreya R. Bendre (31 January 1896–26 October 1981) wrote poetry of various kinds under the name Ambikatanayadatta. The Jnanpith Award was awarded for his collection *Naaku Tanti* (Four Strings, 1964). He published several other collections. As he grew older, Bendre tried to understand life through numbers, and wrote two books on this, one in English, titled *A Theory of Immortality* (1977). Apart from the Jnanpith, he received other awards, including the Padma Shri (1968).

Gopinath Mohanty (1914–91) wrote twenty-four novels, apart from short stories, plays and other works, depicting life in Orissa. He received the Jnanpith Award for his novel *Paraja* (1945). He was also awarded the Sahitya Akademi Award (1955) and the Padma Bhushan (1981). Some of his novels, including *Paraja*, have been translated into English. In this novel, Mohanty describes the life and culture of the Paraja tribe and the tragedy of a Paraja family after a sahukar (moneylender) takes over their land.

❉ DAULAT SINGH KOTHARI IS AWARDED THE PADMA VIBHUSHAN

Daulat Singh Kothari (July 1906–93), an eminent scientist, was awarded the Padma Bhushan in 1962 and the Padma Vibhushan in 1973. Born in Udaipur, Rajasthan, he received a PhD from the University of Cambridge after completing an MSc from the University of Allahabad. He held several important posts, being a faculty member of the department of physics, University of Allahabad, professor of physics at the University of Delhi and scientific adviser to the Ministry of Defence. He was also chairman of the University Grants Commission (1961–73). He wrote the book *Nuclear Explosions and their Effects* as well as several scientific papers. A stamp was issued in his honour in 2011.

ALSO IN 1973

The Directorate of Film Festivals is set up, under the Ministry of Information and Broadcasting, to organize film festivals in India and abroad.

Death of Swami Ramananda Tirtha (b. 1903), nationalist, educationist, social activist and sannyasi

The first national archery championship is held in Lucknow.

1974: TOTAL REVOLUTION— THE JP MOVEMENT

India had achieved a lot since Independence, but issues of poverty, unemployment and food shortages still remained. Corruption had increased and prices in the market were rising. There were agitations in several parts of the country in 1973–74, including Lucknow, Gujarat and Patna. A railway strike was held in April 1974, which was harshly suppressed. In the same month, protesting students in Bihar asked Jayaprakash Narayan to lead their movement. JP, as he was known, had participated in the freedom struggle and had been a member of the Socialist Party. In 1954, he left the party and joined Vinoba Bhave's campaigns. Twenty years passed, and as he became the leader of a new movement, he put forward two unique ideas—of 'partyless democracy' and 'total revolution' (*sampurna kranti*). He aimed to establish a different type of political structure. As the movement grew, JP called for civil disobedience, and asked the police, army and others to join in. JP believed in non-violence and was idealistic, honest and dedicated to the

Jayaprakash Narayan

country, but many different types of people, who had nothing in common with him, joined his movement. Thus, the strikes and agitations increased.

However, Indira Gandhi still seemed to be popular. Elections were held for the states of Uttar Pradesh and Orissa, and the Congress (R) won a majority.

A new President, Fakhruddin Ali Ahmed, was elected, as well as a new vice president, B.D. Jatti.

❋ THE BLACK TORNADO: VIJAY AMRITRAJ

After Ramanathan Krishnan, who won the Junior Wimbledon championship in 1954, some of the prominent tennis players were Jaideep Mukherjee, Premjit Lall, Naresh Kumar and Anand Amritraj, all of whom won the Arjuna Award at different times. But it was Anand's younger brother Vijay (b. 14 December 1953) who was the most famous. In his long tennis career, he won numerous matches, beginning with the junior nationals in 1970 and the senior nationals in 1972, also defeating Jimmy Connors, the then Wimbledon champion, in 1973 at the Volvo International tournament. Throughout his career, Vijay often came close to winning, only to lose at the last minute.

Because of the high speed at which Vijay played, he came to be known as the Black Tornado, though perhaps this name would be politically incorrect today! He retired in 1993, and became an actor, tennis coach and sports commentator.

The Amritraj brothers Vijay and Anand played many doubles matches together. Vijay Amritraj received the Arjuna Award in 1974.

❋ THE ONE-HORNED RHINOCEROS AND KAZIRANGA NATIONAL PARK

The one-horned rhinoceros, known since ancient times, is depicted on the seals of the Harappan civilization, but today its existence is threatened. In 2015, it was estimated that there were 3555 rhinos living in the wild in India. Kaziranga National Park, set up in 1974, has the highest rhino population in the country. It also has wild buffaloes, tigers, elephants, barasinghas, hog deer, wild boar and leopards, as well as other animals, birds and reptiles. Located near River Brahmaputra in Assam, Kaziranga floods every year. And then the animals move to higher ground, though some lose their lives. The floods also enrich the grasslands.

Kaziranga was earlier a wildlife sanctuary, from 1940 onwards, but as a national park, it has more protection. Orang National Park, to the west of Kaziranga, also has a number of rhinos, and so does the nearby Pobitora Wildlife Sanctuary. Some rhinos have been relocated to Dudhwa National Park, in Uttar Pradesh. Jaldapara and Gorumara parks in West Bengal also have some rhinoceros.

SOME RHINO FACTS

- The Indian rhinoceros (*Rhinoceros unicornis*) is one of the four rhino species in the world.
- It is about 1.6 metres tall.
- It weighs about 1820 kilograms.
- A newborn calf weighs 60 kilograms.
- They are usually solitary, but rhinos of an area choose one common space to use as their bathroom!
- They are killed for their horns, which are used in traditional medicine.
- They can run at a speed of 48–50 kilometres per hour.

❈ BEGUM AKHTAR AND AMIR KHAN

The year saw the untimely death of two great singers.

Begum Akhtar Abbasi (b. 1914), a singer of Hindustani classical music, was known as the Ghazal Queen of India. Though ghazals were her speciality, she also sang thumris, dadras and other types of music. There are different accounts of her first performance. According to Rita Ganguly, her disciple and biographer, she began singing in public at the age of eleven, in Calcutta, when the original performers were unavailable. Though trembling with fear, she sang the ghazal 'Deewana Banana Hai Toh' and was a hit. Later she performed at concerts in India and across the world, apart from singing in a few films. Born in Faizabad, she married Ishtiaq Ahmed Abbasi, a lawyer, in 1940, and stopped singing in public for a few years. When she resumed, she focused on the ghazals of Ghalib, Mir and others. A few days after performing at a concert, she died in Ahmadabad of a heart attack on 30 October. She received the Padma Shri in 1968 and was awarded the Padma Bhushan posthumously in 1975.

Amir Khan (b. 1912), another Hindustani classical music singer, specialized in the khayal. He initially studied with his musician father Shahmir Khan and was also influenced by Abdul Waheed Khan, Rajab Ali Khan and Aman Ali Khan. He developed his own singing style, which came to be known as the Indore gharana. He received an award from the Sangeet Natak Akademi in 1967 and the Padma Bhushan in 1971, and had performed at many concerts in India and abroad. He died in a car accident in Calcutta on 13 February.

Among those who died that year were two other noted musicians but, unlike Begum Akhtar and Amir Khan, they were both rather advanced in age: Chembai Vaidyanatha Bhagavathar (b. 1896), one of the best Karnatic musicians, and Anjanibai Malpekar (b. 1883), a Hindustani music vocalist.

● CHIPKO (CLING TO)

What do forests bear?
Soil, water and pure air.

This was one of the songs of the Chipko movement, a campaign for the protection of trees in the Garhwal Himalayas, which started in the early 1970s. It began in the villages of Mandal and Reni, when local women clung to the trees to prevent them from being cut. This concept of preserving trees spread to other villages in the region.

The threat to the trees came from the government, contractors and even the men of the villages, ready to sell the trees for commercial gain. It was the women who saw the value of forest cover and trees in their lives. Gaura Devi, Chandi Prasad Bhatt and Sunderlal Bahuguna initially led the movement. Though it died down by the 1980s, it became an example for ecological conservation.

SATYENDRANATH BOSE

Satyendranath Bose (b. 1894), an eminent Indian physicist, significantly contributed to the formulation with Einstein, known as the Bose–Einstein law of quantum mechanics, which assumes that any number of identical particles can occupy the same quantum state. Since then, such particles have been called bosons, named after him. Bosons are a class of particles, including photons, gluons and others. Of a different class are fermions, which cannot occupy the same quantum space.

Bose died on 4 February 1974.

ALSO IN 1974

18 May: The first underground nuclear experiment intended for peaceful use is conducted in Pokhran, in the Rajasthan desert.

20 July: Death of Kamal Dasgupta (b. 1912), Bengali music director, composer and folk artist

6 October: Death of Vengalil Krishnan Krishna Menon (b. 1896), former defence minister

16 October: Death of Edasseri Govindan Nair (b. 23 December 1906), Malayalam poet

Vishnu Sakharam Khandekar wins the Jnanpith Award for his Marathi novel *Yayati*.

29

1975: THE EMERGENCY

The year 1975 saw an important event in Indian history. While the Congress (R), led by Indira Gandhi, had a large majority in the Lok Sabha and had won all the recent state elections, many continued to oppose her. Jayaprakash Narayan planned a civil disobedience movement against the government starting from 29 June and he was joined by other leaders. Morarji Desai, who was then a senior minister, said, 'We intend to overthrow her, to force her to resign.'[16]

Meanwhile, as Indira Gandhi was looking for a way to counter the opposition, things got worse for her. On 12 June 1975, the Allahabad High Court stated that Indira Gandhi's election to the Lok Sabha was not valid. This was on the basis of some technical details. Indira filed an appeal in the Supreme Court, and received a conditional stay on the judgment. Then she met the President late at night on 25 June and asked him to proclaim an internal emergency. The following morning, the cabinet ministers agreed with the decision. All the major Opposition leaders were woken

---

[16] Morarji Desai to Oriana Fallaci, *New Republic*, quoted in Francine R. Frankel, *India's Political Economy, 1947–1977* (Delhi: Princeton University Press, 1978), 544.

up, arrested and sent to prison under the Maintenance of Internal Security Act (MISA), which had already been passed in 1971. Newspapers and magazines were censored. In the next few days, over 10,000 people were arrested, including students, intellectuals, politicians, journalists and others. Most fundamental rights were suspended by a presidential ordinance.

The Emergency had an effect on all aspects of life. But at the same time, even while people protested and thought of what to do, the cultural life of India continued.

MISA BHARTI

Misa sounds like a pretty name for a girl, but there is a story behind the name of Lalu Prasad Yadav's daughter Misa Bharti. During the Emergency, Lalu was a supporter of Jayaprakash Narayan and was among those jailed under the MISA. His daughter was born at the time in 1976, and he named her Misa—after the Maintenance of Internal Security Act!

❋ OTHER KEY EVENTS

In 1975, Sikkim became a part of India. Since 1950, India had been responsible for Sikkim's defence, communications and external relations.

Sheikh Abdullah, the leader of Jammu and Kashmir, had been in prison for many years and was later exiled from the state. In 1974, an agreement was reached between him and Mrs Gandhi. He became chief minister of the state in 1975.

Bonded labour was abolished across the country on 25 October 1975 through the Bonded Labour System (Abolition) Act, 1976.

ROSHEN DALAL

THREE MUSICIANS: THE FEMALE TRINITY OF KARNATIC MUSIC

Among the Padma Vibhushan awardees that year was M.S. Subbulakshmi (16 September 1916–11 December 2004), one of the three most famous female Karnatic musicians, the other two being D.K. Pattammal and M.L. Vasanthakumari.

Though Subbulakshmi was essentially a Karnatic music vocalist, she also sang Marathi *abhang*s, Hindi bhajans, folk music and light classical. In addition to that, she could also play the veena. She was born in Madurai to Subramaniya Iyer and Shanmuga Vadivu. Shanmuga was a musician herself, and Subbulakshmi learnt from her, accompanying her at recitals. In 1940, she married T. Sadasivam, who supported her in every way.

Apart from the Padma Vibhushan in 1975, she received many awards, including the Padma Bhushan (1954), the Sangeet Natak Akademi Award for Karnatic vocal music (1956), the Ramon Magsaysay Award (1974), the Indira Gandhi Award for National Integration (1990) and the Bharat Ratna (1998). She performed at numerous concerts in India and abroad, including the inaugural concert at the Festival of India, London, in 1982.

D.K. Pattammal (28 March 1919–16 July 2009) was born in Kanchipuram, and studied with Ambi Dikshithar and T.L. Venkatrama Iyer. Her first performance on the radio was at the age of ten. She sang different types of compositions, including bhajans, even for films, the last being for the Tamil film *Hey Ram* (2000), in which she sang 'Vaishnava Janato', one of Mahatma Gandhi's favourite bhajans. She received several awards, including the Padma Bhushan (1971), the Padma Vibhushan (1999) and the Sangeetha Kalanidhi (1970), and was made a fellow of the Sangeet Natak Akademi in 1992.

M.L. Vasanthakumari (3 July 1928–31 October 1990), the youngest of the three musicians, died first. She studied with

G.N. Balasubramaniam, and sang classical ragas, compositions of the Haridasas, particularly of the Bhakti saint Purandaradasa, as well as songs for films. She received the Sangeet Natak Akademi Award in 1970 and the Padma Bhushan in 1967, among others.

❋ LIONS AND DANCING DEER: TWO STATE ANIMALS

The Asiatic lion (*Panthera leo persica*) was once common in Asia, but now its last habitat is the Gir National Park and Wildlife Sanctuary. It is the state animal of Gujarat.

In 2015, there were 523 lions in the area. Located in Junagadh district of Gujarat, the lions were first protected by Nawab Sir Mahabat Khan of the state of Junagadh. He even issued postage stamps depicting the lion in 1929. After Independence, hunting was banned in the area, and a wildlife sanctuary was set up in 1965. The core area of 258 sq. km became a national park in 1975, with the total area being 1412 sq. km.

Gir is a hilly area with streams and light deciduous forests. There are a number of other animals here, including leopards, the rusty-spotted cat, golden jackals, porcupines, blackbucks, as well as numerous birds and reptiles. The lions here have got used to people, and are often seen in the nearby villages.

In a national park, no encroachment of any kind is allowed, while a sanctuary does not have such strict rules.

The dancing deer, sangai or brow-antlered deer (*Rucervus eldii*) are found only in Manipur, in the Keibul Lamjao National Park, which was also founded in 1975. The Keibul Lamjao is a floating swamp on Lake Loktak. People cannot walk on it without sinking, but the deer,

The sangai deer

with their long hooves, take small hops, by way of which they manage to stay on the island (which measures about 40 sq. km). These hops give them the name 'dancing deer'.

There were only fourteen deer in 1975; by 1984, the number increased to fifty and by the year 2000, to 162. The sangai is Manipur's state animal and has a place in local legends. Its soul is said to provide a bridge between humans and nature, but the deer and its habitat are increasingly under threat.

ALSO IN 1975

17 April: Death of Sarvepalli Radhakrishnan (b. 1888), the second President of India (1962–67) and eminent writer on philosophy

2 October: Death of K. Kamaraj (b. 15 July 1903), who had been Congress president and chief minister of Madras State. He opposed Indira Gandhi and was also known for the Kamaraj Plan.

31 October 1975: Death of Sachin Dev Burman (b. 1 October 1906), composer of classical, folk and light music as well as director of films

27 December: A mining disaster in Chasnala, near Dhanbad, leads to the death of 372 miners. The film *Kaala Patthar* (1979) was based on this.

The Bharat Ratna is awarded to V.V. Giri (1894–1980), President of India from 1969 to 1974.

Akilan (1922–88), Tamil-language writer, wins the Jnanpith Award for his novel *Chitra Pavai*.

1976: THE TWENTY POINT PROGRAMME

With the Emergency in place, Indira Gandhi could act like a dictator. She now had the power to do as she liked. In 1976, an amendment to the Constitution was passed by which the words 'secular' and 'socialist' were added to the preamble and the directive principles were made superior to the fundamental rights. The terms of Parliament and the state assemblies were extended from five to six years. Many other basic changes were made. Indira also aimed to improve the economy and introduced the Twenty Point Programme to reduce prices, continue land reforms and improve conditions for workers and the poor. Initially, there were some benefits, but gradually these reduced. Government officials and the police had too much power—to arrest, imprison and torture people. More than 1,40,000 people had been arrested by 1976.

Sanjay, Indira's younger son, started his own programmes, which included family planning and beautifying cities. These ideas were not carried out properly, and houses and shops were destroyed and men were sterilized against their wishes.

Soon, almost everyone in north India was against the Emergency, which is where it had the most impact.

In Tamil Nadu, Karunanidhi of the DMK was chief minister. He too was against the Emergency, and this led to his government being dismissed by Indira Gandhi on 31 January on corruption charges. President's Rule was imposed on the state.

❋ YASHPAL AND KHANDEKAR: TWO NOTED WRITERS

Yashpal (3 December 1903–26 December 1976) has been considered the best writer in Hindi literature since Premchand. He was born in Kangra district, in present-day Himachal Pradesh, and began his studies at Gurukul Kangri, Haridwar. After completing his schooling in Ferozepur, he continued to the National College, Lahore. There, he came in contact with Bhagat Singh and became a revolutionary, even planting a bomb in a train in which Lord Irwin, the then viceroy, was travelling, in December 1929. Lord Irwin was not injured. But Yashpal was arrested in 1931 for his revolutionary activities, and released only in 1938, after the election of the Congress government to the provincial legislatures. He began writing after his release, and his stories and novels reflect his political background as well as his desire to live in a free and equal India.

Some of his major works include his autobiography, *Sinhavalokan*, in three volumes (1951–55); *Jhootha Sach*, a two-volume work on Partition (1958–60); *Dada Kamred* (1941); *Manushya ke Roop* (1949); *Ramrajya ki Katha* and *Marxbad*. He was awarded the Padma Bhushan in 1970 and the Sahitya Akademi Award in 1976 for his novel *Meri Teri Uski Baat* (1974). Some of Yashpal's works have been made into television programmes, such as *Guldasta* (1995) and *Jeevan ke Rang* (2005).

Another great writer who died that year was the Jnanpith Award winner and Marathi-language author Vishnu Sakharam Khandekar (11 January 1898–2 September 1976). He wrote sixteen novels apart from hundreds of short stories and essays. Some of his novels were made into films, including *Pardeshi* (1953).

❋ ASHAPURNA DEVI: THE FIRST WOMAN TO WIN THE JNANPITH

Ashapurna Devi

Ashapurna Devi (8 January 1909–13 July 1995), Bengali-language writer, was the first woman to win the Jnanpith Award, in 1976.

Ashapurna was an extraordinary poet, novelist and short story writer. She wasn't formally educated, but she and her sisters starting reading at an early age. Her mother, Sarola Sundari, loved books, while her father, Harendra Nath Gupta, was an artist. Her first poem was published when she was thirteen and that was the start of her literary career, even though she was soon married at the age of fifteen. Ashapurna took care of her family, but never stopped writing. *Chhoto Thakurdar Kashi Yatra* (1983) was one of her early children's books. She wrote over 150 works, including novels, short story collections and books for children. Her most important work is a three-part series, the first being *Pratham Pratishruti* (The First Promise, 1964), about a young village bride, who overcomes many problems. The second part of the trilogy, *Subarnalata*, was published in 1967 and the third, *Bakul Katha*, in 1974. Other than the Jnanpith Award, she won the Rabindra Puraskar of the West Bengal government in 1965, the Padma Shri in 1976, the Sahitya Natak Akademi Fellowship in 1994, as well as other awards.

❋ VIVAN SUNDARAM FOUNDS THE KASAULI ART CENTRE

Vivan Sundaram is an artist with a political conscience. Born in 1943 in Shimla, Himachal Pradesh, he studied at the M.S. University of Baroda and then at Slade School, London.

He has painted in different styles over the years—having worked in ink and wash, linear drawings, watercolours, installations, photography and video art. His influences include surrealism, Dadaism and the Fluxus (a group of artists who combine different media). He has created art on Pablo Neruda's poem 'Heights of Macchu Picchu', on the Emergency of 1975, the Gulf War of 1991 and, more recently, on social and environmental themes, and has held exhibitions across the world. He is a founder member of the Safdar Hashmi Memorial Trust (founded 1989), has founded the Kasauli Art Centre in 1976 and continues to innovate in art. *Black Gold* (2012), one of his more recent installations, used fragments of 2000-year-old pottery from the archaeological site of Pattanam to create a city.

ALSO IN 1976

July: Parveen Babi (4 April 1949–20 January 2005) becomes the first Indian film star to be depicted on the cover of *Time* magazine.

10 September: An Indian Airlines plane flying from Delhi to Bombay is hijacked and taken to Lahore; all passengers are eventually released.

The Bharat Ratna is posthumously awarded to K. Kamaraj.

1977: A NEW GOVERNMENT—
THE JANATA PARTY

The Emergency continued into 1977, but suddenly, in January, Indira Gandhi announced that elections would take place in March. Had she always planned on holding elections again? Did she think she would win? Her party was supported by the Communist Party of India and the All India Anna Dravida Munnetra Kazhagam. The Opposition had a number of parties on its side. The Bharatiya Jana Sangh, the Bharatiya Lok Dal, the Congress (O) and the Samyukta Socialist Party joined together to form the Janata Party and fight the elections as one group. Some senior Congress leaders, including Jagjivan Ram, formed a new party, Congress for Democracy. They allied with the Janata Party to oppose the Congress (R). The Dravida Munnetra Kazhagam, the Akali Dal and the CPI (M) were also part of the Opposition.

The election results were a shock for Indira and the Congress (R). Both she and her son Sanjay lost. In Uttar Pradesh, Bihar, Punjab, Haryana and Delhi, the Congress did not win even a single seat. In Madhya Pradesh, Rajasthan and Kashmir, they had only one seat each. Other states had not been affected to the same extent by the Emergency, and overall, the Congress (R) got

153 seats. The Janata Party and Congress for Democracy together won 298, and the two parties merged. Along with their allies, they had 330 seats and formed the government on 23 March 1977, with the eighty-one-year-old Morarji Desai as prime minister.

Morarji Desai (29 February 1896–10 April 1995), prime minister from 1977 to 1979, was the first non-Congress prime minister since Independence. He had a long career in politics, including the posts of finance minister and deputy prime minister from 1967. In 1969, he led the Congress (O) in opposition to Indira Gandhi's Congress (R) and was imprisoned for nineteen months during the Emergency. Morarji lived a simple life. He was a vegetarian and believed in naturopathy.

THE CHESS PLAYERS

The year saw a brilliant new film from Satyajit Ray: *Shatranj ke Khilari* (The Chess Players) is set in a significant time in

A reproduction of a scene from *Shatranj ke Khilari*

history, and is about two nawabs of Awadh who loved to play chess and continued playing even as the state was being attacked and taken over by the British. Satyajit Ray himself loved to play chess, but sold his chess books to collect money to make his first film! The film is based on Premchand's story of the same name. Premchand (31 July 1880–8 October 1936) was one of India's best writers. Though he lived and died before Independence, his works continue to be popular today. He wrote a number of novels, among them *Rangbhoomi* (1924), *Godaan* (1936), *Gaban* (1931) and *Premashram* (1922), as well as numerous short stories.

❋ AN UNTIMELY DEATH AND A JNANPITH AWARD: KRISHAN CHANDER AND SHIVARAM KARANTH

Krishan Chander (23 November 1914–8 March 1977), novelist and writer in Hindi/Urdu literature, died suddenly of a heart attack while working at his desk, leaving a sentence unfinished. He wrote over twenty novels, numerous short stories and screenplays for Hindi films. Born in Bharatpur, Rajasthan, he grew up in Poonch, in Jammu and Kashmir, and his novel *Mitti ke Sanam* is about his early memories. Among his notable stories are 'Annadata', 'Galicha', 'Kalu Bhangi' and 'Garjan ki Ek Sham'. His most important novels are *Shikast* and *Jab Khet Jage*. He wrote about the problems of ordinary people, the exploitation of women and the poor, and about life in the villages of Kashmir. He received a number of awards, including the Padma Bhushan in 1969 and the Soviet Land Nehru Award in 1966.

Shivaram Karanth (10 October 1902–9 December 1997), Kannada-language writer, won the Jnanpith Award in 1977 for his book *Mookajjiya Kanasugalu* (Dreams of a Grandmother). He wrote both poems and novels, some of them published before Independence. *Chomana Dudi* (Choma's Drum) is a tragic story about a Dalit; *Bettada Jeeva*, in which a freedom fighter learns the stories of common villagers, was made into an award-winning film. He wrote a number of other books, and also helped to revive the dance form Yakshagana. Apart from the Jnanpith, he received a number of other awards, including the Sahitya Akademi Fellowship in 1985.

❋ SIDDHESHWARI DEVI: AN UNWANTED ORPHAN WHO BECAME A GREAT SINGER

Siddheshwari Devi (1908–77), a vocalist of Hindustani music, was born in a musical family in Varanasi and was the daughter of Shamu Misra. Her parents died young, and her aunt took her into her family. In Siddheshwari's autobiography, written along with her daughter, she recounts how her aunt did not take care of her, but fate enabled her to learn from the great musician Siyaji Maharaj. Then she lived with him and his family. She also trained with Bade Ramdas, Rajab Ali Khan and Inayat Khan. She usually sang khayal, as well as light classical, thumri, dadra, *kajri*, tappa, *hori* and *chait*.

She taught music at Shriram Bharatiya Kala Kendra, New Delhi, from 1965 until her death, and won several awards, including the Sangeet Natak Akademi Award for Hindustani vocal music in 1966, the Padma Shri in 1967, the award of the Uttar Pradesh Sangeet Natak Akademi in 1976 and the Sahitya Kala Parishad Award in 1975. A documentary film was made on her life in 1989.

Her daughter Savita Devi is also a noted musician, and founded a music academy in memory of her mother in 1977.

❋ ALKAZI RETIRES FROM THE NATIONAL SCHOOL OF DRAMA

Ebrahim Alkazi (b. 18 October 1925) is one of the greatest theatre directors and teachers in India. He trained at the Royal Academy of Dramatic Art, in London, and was director of the National School of Drama from 1962 to 1977. He directed numerous plays in his long career, among them Girish Karnad's *Tughlaq*, Dharmvir Bharti's *Andha Yug* and adaptations of Greek and Shakespearean plays. Together with his wife, Roshan Alkazi, he founded the Art Heritage Gallery in New Delhi.

ALSO IN 1977

11 February: Death of Fakhruddin Ali Ahmed (b. 13 May 1905), President of India (1974–77)

June: Jyoti Basu (8 July 1914–17 January 2010) becomes chief minister of West Bengal (1977–2000).

25 July: Sanjiva Reddy becomes President of India.

Ela Bhatt (b. 7 September 1933), founder of SEWA (Self-Employed Women's Association of India), wins the Ramon Magsaysay Award; she also wins the Right Livelihood Award (1984) and the Padma Bhushan (1986).

1978: THE FORTY-FOURTH AMENDMENT

In 1978, the Forty-Fourth Amendment was made to the Constitution. This removed most of the changes made by Mrs Gandhi in the Forty-Second Amendment, and also made it more difficult to impose an emergency in future. Meanwhile, there were further changes in the Congress.

In January 1978, the Congress (R), which had been formed in 1969 after a split in the Congress, further divided into two—the Congress (I), led by Indira, and the Congress (S), led by Swaran Singh. Y.B. Chavan was a part of the second group. In the Lok Sabha, the Congress (I) now had seventy members, while the Congress (S) had seventy-six. Indira Gandhi had been re-elected from Chikmagalur, in Karnataka, with the help of Devaraj Urs. In April 1979, he was expelled from the Congress (I), after which he started another party, the Congress (U).

❀ OTHER KEY EVENTS

The Indian Coast Guard was formed on 1 February 1977, and on 18 August 1978, was declared an armed force.

❋ THE NATIONAL MUSEUM OF NATURAL HISTORY

A number of museums had been set up in India, but in 1972, Indira Gandhi felt that a museum of natural history was required, which would showcase the animals, plants and minerals of India. The museum, located in New Delhi, was finally opened to the public on 5 June 1978. Regional natural history museums were later set up.

❋ THE *GOTUVADYAM*

The gotuvadyam, also known as the *chitra* veena, is a stringed instrument. It is a type of veena with six main strings and additional sympathetic strings. The instrument does not have frets, and is popular in Karnatic music. It gets its name from the *gotu*, a cylindrical piece used to press the strings.

Among its best players was Budalur Krishnamurthy Sastrigal (1894–1978), who began his musical career as a singer. Later, he studied with Gotuvadyam Narayana Iyengar, the disciple of Sakharama Rao, and specialized in playing the gotuvadyam. This is known to be a difficult instrument, but Krishnamurthy became an expert. Rukmini Devi Arundale invited him to join Kalakshetra, and he became its principal. He was responsible for the increased popularity of the instrument. He also taught at the Central College of Karnatic Music in Madras.

The gotuvadyam

Among other exponents of the instrument is Chitravina N. Ravikiran (b. 1967), who invented a new type called the *navachitra* veena. He is the grandson of Gotuvadyam Narayana Iyengar.

P.S. REGE: A MODERN MARATHI POET

Purushottam Shivaram Rege (1910–78) wrote poems and novels, as well as essays, a play and his autobiography. He is particularly known for his poems, of which several volumes have been published. Rege wrote on different themes, including love and the beauty of women, as well as world events and social problems. He also played with words, as indicated in the first verse of a short, two-verse poem titled 'Song':[17]

> The song that the bird sings in the tree
> Has another tree again in the song
> That the bird in the tree sings.

SACHCHIDANANDA VATSYAYAN WINS THE JNANPITH AWARD

Sachchidananda Vatsyayan 'Agyeya' (7 March 1911–4 April 1987), Hindi writer, was primarily a poet but also wrote several novels, stories, travelogues and essays, among other works. He won the Jnanpith for his poem and anthology 'Kitne Naavon mein Kitni Baar' (1967).

His father was an archaeologist, and Sachchidananda was actually born in a tent in Kushinagar district, where his father was excavating. He moved to different places with his family, later completing a BSc degree in industrial science and then joining the revolutionary movement for Indian independence. He was imprisoned between 1930 and 1933, and began writing at that time. During World War II, he sided with the British and the allies against fascism. He continued writing after Independence, and was also an editor and professor.

---

[17] Quoted in *Journal of South Asian Literature, Volume 17* (n.p.: Asian Studies Center, Michigan State University, 1982).

He wrote a vast number of poems. Among his other post-Independence anthologies are *Indradhanu Raunde Hue Ye* (1957), *Ari O Karuna Prabhamaya* (1959), *Kyonki Mein Use Jaanta Hoon* (1969) and *Aisa Koi Ghar Aapne Dekha Hai* (1986). He also wrote in English, though the majority of his work is in Hindi. His poetry was constantly evolving, reflecting new forms and content.

THEATRE IN INDIA

After Independence, Indian theatre took on several different forms. With its roots in India's past, it was influenced by contemporary forms from across the world. The setting up of the Sangeet Natak Akademi and the National School of Drama along with regional state academies definitely helped its growth. There have also been several other theatre groups, such as the Indian People's Theatre Association, formed before Independence and including leftist artists; Anamika in Calcutta (1955); Theatre Unit in Bombay (1954); the Delhi Art Theatre (1951) and the Indraprastha Theatre (1959). Later groups included Om Shivpuri's Dishantar and Rajinder Nath's Abhiyan (1967), founded to produce new plays, and many more. Playwrights have been numerous, among them Badal Sircar, Vijay Tendulkar and Girish Karnad. Habib Tanvir (1 September 1923–8 June 2009) wrote, directed and acted in plays, and won both national and international awards. His play *Charandas Chor* (1975) was his biggest hit. He is known for his Naya Theatre group, founded in 1959, which worked with the tribals of Chhattisgarh.

Folk theatre, once a popular form of entertainment, still exists, though it has declined. Puppet theatre has both traditional and new forms.

ALSO IN 1978

January: The government demonetizes the high-value notes of Rs 10,000, 5000 and 1000.

The minimum marriageable age is raised to twenty-one for men and eighteen for women through the Child Marriage Restraint (Amendment) Act, 1978.

1979: CHARAN SINGH

The Janata government, made up of many different groups, had numerous conflicts. Morarji Desai tried to maintain peace, but he did not succeed. On 11 July 1979, Y.B. Chavan, leader of the Opposition, initiated a vote of no confidence against the government, which resigned on 15 July. Charan Singh briefly became prime minister, as he was offered the support of the Congress (I), led by Indira Gandhi, the Indian Congress (Socialist), led by Y.B. Chavan, the CPI and some socialists. He had to resign on 20 August because Indira Gandhi withdrew support, but remained the caretaker prime minister until the next elections were held in January 1980 and a new government was formed.

● **NEW POLITICAL PARTIES**

The All Assam Students' Union joined with other organizations to form the All Assam Gana Sangram Parishad that year.

The Lok Dal was another political party formed that year, though it had earlier origins. It originated in 1969 as the Bharatiya Kisan Dal (BKD), led by Charan Singh. In 1974, some socialists joined the BKD and formed a new party, the Bharatiya Lok

Dal (BLD). In 1977, the BLD merged with the Janata Party. In 1979, the Janata Party split and part of it became the Lok Dal.

❖ RAMESH KRISHNAN: A RISING TENNIS STAR

Ramesh Krishnan (b. 5 June 1961), son of the tennis player Ramanathan Krishnan, won the Junior Wimbledon singles in 1979 as well as the French Open junior title, and later, the US Open Junior championship. He won the national men's title and was part of the Indian team that participated in the Davis Cup, 1987. He won several other national and international tournaments, including the Manila Grand Prix in 1981, the Stuttgart Grand Prix in 1982, the Grand Prix Metz (France) in 1984, the Japan Open Grand Prix and Hong Kong Grand Prix in 1986, the Wellington Open in 1988, the ATP Auckland Open in 1989 and the Schenectady Open in 1990. He received the Arjuna Award in 1980–81. He retired in 1993 and, along with his father, founded the Krishnan Tennis Centre in Chennai in 1995. He received the Padma Shri in 1998.

❖ DHYAN CHAND DIES AT SEVENTY-FOUR

Dhyan Chand (29 August 1905–3 December 1979), a hockey wizard, was part of the team that won Olympic golds in 1928, 1932 and 1936.

He joined the army at the age of sixteen, and played hockey for the army team from 1921 onwards and for the national team from 1926 to 1948. He retired from the army in 1956 and was awarded the Padma Bhushan the same year.

Dhyan Chand

THE TOP FILMS OF THE 1970S

The 1970s are considered to be the best years of Hindi cinema. Here is a look at the box office hits:

- 1970: *Johny Mera Naam*; *Sachaa Jhutha*; *Aan Milo Sajna*.
- 1971: *Haathi Mere Saathi*; *Mera Gaon Mera Desh*; *Caravan*.
- 1972: *Seeta aur Geeta*; *Pakeezah*; *Raja Jani*.
- 1973: *Bobby*; *Daag: A Poem of Love*.
- 1974: *Roti Kapada aur Makaan*; *Chor Machaye Shor*; *Dost*.
- 1975: *Sholay*; *Pratiggya*; *Jai Santoshi Maa*.
- 1976: *Dus Numbri*; *Laila Majnu*; *Charas*;
- 1977: *Amar Akbar Anthony*; *Chacha Bhatija*; *Dulhan Wahi Jo Piya Man Bhaaye*.
- 1978: *Muqaddar ka Sikandar*; *Trishul*; *Don*.
- 1979: *Suhaag*; *Jaani Dushman*; *Sargam*.

Among these, *Sholay* was an all-time blockbuster and the top grosser of the 1970s, with the teenage romantic drama *Bobby* coming second.

There was also a new wave in Hindi cinema, beginning with *Bhuvan Shome* and *Sara Akash* in 1969. Such films in the 1970s include *Uski Roti* (1970), *Garm Hava* (1973) and *27 Down* (1973), among many more. In 1975, *Nishant*, a film directed by Shyam Benegal won the National Film Award and marked a new era in Hindi films. Directors of these new wave films were Shyam Benegal, Govind Nihalani, Saeed Mirza and Muzaffar Ali, among others. These films were known for their realistic portrayal of serious topics.

Among the best actors of the 1970s were Amitabh Bachchan, Dharmendra, Rajesh Khanna, Rishi Kapoor, Mithun Chakraborty, Shatrughan Sinha, Raj Kapoor, Dev Anand, Naseeruddin Shah, Om Puri, Girish Karnad, Hema Malini, Sharmila Tagore, Rekha, Rakhee, Jaya Bhaduri (Bachchan), Shabana Azmi and Smita Patil.

MOTHER TERESA WINS THE NOBEL PEACE PRIZE

Mother Teresa (1910–97) was the founder of the Missionaries of Charity. Born in Albania, her original name was Agnes Bojaxhiu. She came to India in 1928, and after completing her novitiate in the Loreto order, became a teacher and then principal at St Mary's High School, Calcutta. She believed that in 1946, on her way to a spiritual retreat in Darjeeling, she was sent a divine message from Jesus to care for the homeless and unwanted living in India. She experienced a spiritual call to serve Jesus by going into the slums and helping the poorest of the poor. After receiving permission from Pope Pius XII, she discarded her nun's habit and chose a white sari with a blue border as the new outfit to be worn by all the members of the Missionaries of Charity. This was recognized as a new congregation in Calcutta in October 1950. In 1952, she opened a home for the dying in Calcutta, next to the Kali temple, and soon extended her service to those afflicted with leprosy, orphans and the destitute. In February 1963, a branch for men was started, the Missionaries of Charity Brothers.

After opening several homes across India, her work spread to other countries, including England, Italy, Sri Lanka, Tanzania and Venezuela. She received a number of awards, including the Pope John XXIII Peace Prize presented by Pope Paul VI (1971), the Jawaharlal Nehru Award for International Understanding (1969), the Nobel Peace Prize (1979) and the Bharat Ratna (1980). Some miracles performed by her were reported after her death, and she was canonized as a saint in 2016.

PERSIS KHAMBATTA ACTS IN *STAR TREK*

Persis Khambatta (b. 1948), model and actor, is remembered for her 1979 role in *Star Trek: The Motion Picture*, in which she acted as Lieutenant Ilia and for which she was nominated for the Saturn

Award. This part required her to be bald, and Persis shaved her head even before appearing for the audition—something that contributed to her getting the role. Born in Bombay, she won the Femina Miss India contest in 1965 at the age of seventeen and then participated in the Miss Universe contest.

After *Star Trek*, she acted in other Hollywood films and in a Hindi television series. She also wrote a book, *Pride of India* (1997), on former beauty queens. Persis was injured in a car crash in Germany in 1980, and had a heart problem. She underwent coronary bypass surgery in 1983. She died of a heart attack on 18 August 1998, when she was only forty-nine years old.

ALSO IN 1979

9 February: Death of Bengali-language writer Banaphul (b. 1899)

19 May: Death of Hindi writer Hazari Prasad Dwivedi (b. 1907)

August: The Morvi dam in Gujarat bursts, leading to floods and the death of thousands.

27 August: Death of Lord Louis Mountbatten (b. 25 June 1900), viceroy of India from 26 March 1947 to 15 August 1947 and governor general of independent India from 15 August 1947 to 21 June 1948, by a bomb blast in a fishing boat near County Sligo, on the coast of Ireland. The blast was attributed to the Irish Republican Army.

8 October: Death of Jayaprakash Narayan (b. 11 October 1902), freedom fighter, supporter of the Bhudan movement and organizer of the opposition to Indira Gandhi

1980: THE SEVENTH GENERAL ELECTIONS

The seventh general elections to the Lok Sabha were held in January 1980.

The main parties were the Congress (I), with its new symbol of an open hand, other Congress parties, the Communist parties, the Janata Party and some parties formed by groups that had left the Janata. Among these was the Lok Dal, led by Charan Singh.

The results indicated that the Emergency was forgotten. The Congress (I) won 353 out of the 529 seats. Indira and Sanjay won by large margins. Indira Gandhi became the prime minister again.

But a new tragedy faced her as she lost her son Sanjay on 23 June 1980 in a plane crash. Sanjay had been flying a small aircraft of the Delhi Flying Club.

❈ OTHER KEY EVENTS

The Bharatiya Janata Party (BJP) was a new political party formed that year, after members of the Jana Sangh withdrew from the Janata Party.

INDIA AT 70

❋ THE NANDA DEVI NATIONAL PARK: MOUNTAIN ANIMALS

High in the Himalayan region, the snow leopard (*Panthera uncia*) roams. This beautiful animal has a thick grey coat with black spots and patches, and is about two metres long. It is protected under the Indian Wildlife Protection Act, and one of the places where it is found is the Nanda Devi National Park, located in Chamoli district of Uttarakhand. This park, which covers an area of 630 sq. km, was established in 1980, and declared a wildlife park in 1982. Other animals here include black and brown Himalayan bears, leopards, bharal, musk deer, tahr, wild boar and various birds, including the brightly coloured monal, the state bird of Uttarakhand. The park lies below the mountain Nanda Devi, the second-highest in India and twenty-third in the world, approximately 7816 metres above sea level.

Another beautiful national park founded in 1980, 20 kilometres to the north-west of the Nanda Devi Park, is that of the Valley of Flowers, where meadows of unique alpine flowers bloom.

The red panda (*Ailurus fulgens*), or cat bear, is another unique mountain animal and the only variety of panda found in India, mainly in the eastern Himalayas at altitudes above 1525 metres. It is protected in the Nokrek and Balpakram national parks in Meghalaya, and is the state animal there.

The red panda

❋ *ORU DESATHINTE KATHA*: THE STORY OF A PLACE

Oru Desathinte Katha, an autobiographical novel in Malayalam, won the Jnanpith Award in 1980. It is written by S.K. Pottekkatt

(14 March 1913–6 August 1982), and has a vast canvas. The book portrays the people of the village of Athiranippadam through the first twenty years of the life of the semi-fictional character Sridharan. It looks at Sridharan's relationship with his father, while including the stories of the various village folk. The account continues with Sridharan's departure from the village when his father dies and his eventual return after thirty years. The book was even made into a film.

Pottekkatt wrote a number of novels, short stories, poems, and travelogues. He travelled to numerous countries, including those in Europe and Africa, and his work has been translated into several languages.

● SUNIL GAVASKAR IS NAMED THE *WISDEN* CRICKETER OF THE YEAR

Sunil Gavaskar (b. 10 July 1949), a batsman popularly known as Sunny, began playing for India in Test cricket in 1971. He made 774 runs in four Test matches, averaging 154.80 in the 1970–71 series against the West Indies, the highest made by a test debutant. He continued playing Test cricket till 1987, and also played one-day internationals (ODIs) from 1974 onwards. Overall, he played in 125 Tests and scored thirty-four centuries, and was captain of the Indian team several times in the 1970s and 1980s. He was also the first Test batsman to score 10,000 runs. He won the Arjuna Award in 1975, the Padma Bhushan in 1980 and the C.K. Nayudu Lifetime Achievement Award in 2012. He was named cricketer of the year by *Wisden* in 1980. After retirement he became a commentator and also wrote four books on cricket, including his autobiography, *Sunny Days*. The Border–Gavaskar Trophy, a Test cricket series, was instituted in honour of Sunil Gavaskar and Allan Border.

♦ SPORTS: INTERNATIONAL SUCCESSES

The 1980 Summer Olympics were held in Moscow, USSR, where India won the gold medal in hockey.

In badminton, India finally got a world champion, as Prakash Padukone won the All England Championship.

WHAT IS THAT WHISTLE YOU HEAR?

If it's summer and you are visiting a national park somewhere in India, you may hear a low whistling sound. It is not a person whistling at you—but the chausingha, or four-horned antelope! This is the smallest antelope in Asia, just around 60 centimetres tall and weighing about 16 kilograms. Its top coat is a dull red-brown with white below and it has two pairs of horns. This unique aspect leads to it being threatened by hunters. The animal is protected under the Wildlife Protection Act.

ALSO IN 1980

11 February: Death of R.C. Majumdar (b. 4 December 1888), noted historian, who is known for his work on the history of India

11 April: The National Film Development Corporation (NFDC) is founded by merging the Film Finance Corporation and the Indian Motion Picture Export Corporation. It aims at promoting excellence in Indian cinema in all Indian languages.

24 July: Death of actor Uttam Kumar (b. 1926)

25 October: Death of Sahir Ludhianvi (b. 1921), Urdu poet and lyricist

The first Asian Junior Volleyball Championship is held in 1980, and both the boys' and girls' teams from India come third.

1981: INTERNAL DEVELOPMENTS

Indira Gandhi was devastated by the death of her younger son, Sanjay, and persuaded her elder son, Rajiv, to join politics. He had been a pilot in Indian Airlines, but reluctantly agreed to help his mother and was elected from Amethi in 1981.

By this time, India had begun to change. An integrated programme of rural development had started in 1976, and by 1980, had extended across the country. Though there was still a lot of poverty, there was more awareness of rights and the condition of scheduled castes (Dalits) had started improving. As Dalits and other groups began to assert themselves, they came into conflict with the higher castes and rich landowners.

❋ KHALISTAN

A movement for a separate Sikh state, to be called Khalistan, began in the 1970s, and Jagjit Singh Chauhan declared the formation of the state in May 1980, while he was in London. Baljit Singh Sandhu made the same announcement in Amritsar, but it was ignored by both the state and national governments. Gradually, Sant Jarnail Singh Bhindranwale, a Sikh priest who had started the Dal Khalsa party in 1978, became the leader of the movement. In 1981, Sikh militants hijacked a plane flying from Delhi to Amritsar, taking it to Lahore. They demanded the release of Sikh prisoners and of Sant Bhindranwale, who had been arrested in September, as well as a Rs 45,00,000 fund for the Khalistan movement. The hijackers were overpowered by Pakistani commandos, and the passengers were rescued.

❋ NARGIS DUTT DIES OF CANCER

Nargis Dutt (1 June 1929–3 May 1981), considered to be one of the best Hindi film actors, acted in films from the 1940s to the 1960s. Among her most memorable roles were those in *Awara*, *Shree 420*, *Mother India* (1957)—for which she won the Filmfare Award for the best actress (1958)—and *Raat aur Din* (1967)—for which she won the National Film Award for the best actress. She acted in several films with Raj Kapoor, and married her fellow actor Sunil Dutt in 1958. They had three children, among whom Sanjay Dutt is a well-known actor.

Sanjay Dutt made his acting debut in 1981. He has acted in romance, comedy and gangster films.

❋ SALMAN RUSHDIE WINS THE BOOKER PRIZE

Salman Rushdie was born in Bombay on 19 June 1947 and then moved to England, completing his master's degree in history in 1968 from the University of Cambridge. *Midnight's Children* (1981), his second book, based on India after Independence, won him the Booker Prize, later renamed the Man Booker in 2002. Rushdie also won the Booker of Bookers (1993) and the Best of the Booker (2008). A film based on the book, directed by Deepa Mehta, was released in 2012.

Rushdie has written twelve novels, short stories and four works of non-fiction. His work has been translated into over forty languages and he has won numerous awards. One of his books, *The Satanic Verses* (1988), which has a character similar to Prophet Muhammad, was banned in India, and protests were held against it in several countries. Though a British citizen, a lot of Rushdie's writing has India–Pakistan as its background and he makes frequent visits to India.

AMRITA PRITAM WINS THE JNANPITH AWARD

Amrita Pritam (31 August 1919–31 October 2005), poet, novelist and essayist in Punjabi and Hindi literature, was known for her honest writing and unconventional life. She won the Jnanpith Award in 1981 for her poetry collection *Kagaz te Canvas* (Paper and Canvas, 1973).

Born in Gujranwala, Punjab, in present-day Pakistan, she moved to India after Partition in 1947. She was only eleven when her mother died, and she began writing soon after that. She married Pritam Singh, an editor, at the age of sixteen, but left him in 1960. For the last forty years of her life, she lived with her partner, Imroz, an artist and writer many years younger than her.

Partition was one of the themes in her writing. In *Ajj Aakhaan Waris Shah Nu* (Today I Invoke Waris Shah, 1948), a long poem, she expresses her despair over the Partition riots, calling on the eighteenth-century poet Waris Shah. Another long poem, *Sunehade* (Messages, 1955), brought her the Sahitya Akademi Award in 1955. She received the Padma Shri in 1969, followed by the Padma Vibhushan and the Sahitya Akademi Fellowship in 2004, apart from other awards. Among her notable novels are *Pinjar* (A Cage, 1950), also on Partition and later made into a film in 2003; *Dilli ki Galiyan* and *Yaatri*. She wrote about twenty-eight novels, numerous poems, stories and essays, as well as her autobiography and works on the spiritual leader Osho.

TRIBAL ART

Tribal or adivasi art, with its ancient traditions, has to some extent been brought into the mainstream, and tribal paintings are now sold commercially, used for book illustrations and created in different media. Gond, Warli and Madhubani are among the many different forms of tribal art.

Several artists are now known by name, one of them being Durga Bai Vyam, a modern Gond artist, whose paintings create a story. He has painted Gond deities, participated in exhibitions of adivasi art and created illustrations for children's books. The artist J. Swaminathan, who promoted tribal art, discovered Durga Bai in 1981. Swaminathan was a prominent artist who held exhibitions of his own paintings and also wrote *The Magical Script* (1983), a compilation of the odd, script-like drawings of the Hill Korwas of Raigarh, Madhya Pradesh.

A Mithila (Madhubani) painting by Shashikala Devi

ALSO IN 1981

26 February: Tamil actor Rajinikanth marries Latha Rangachari.

2 July: The company Infosys is founded in Pune.

In the first Commonwealth Volleyball Championship held in Nottingham in 1981, India places third.

Death of Palghat Mani Iyer (b. 1912), one of the best mridangam players of Karnatic music

1982: THE ASIAN GAMES

In 1982, the Asian Games were organized in New Delhi (19 November–4 December) and marked a turning point in India's history. Sports and games received an impetus, as the Indira Gandhi Indoor Stadium, the Asian Games Village, the Jawaharlal Nehru Stadium, the Siri Fort Auditorium and the Karni Singh Shooting Range were all constructed at this time. New roads and flyovers were built in Delhi, and more buses were introduced. There were new phone lines and connections too. And for the first time, colour television was introduced in India. Rajiv Gandhi, who had become a member of Parliament, and Arun Nehru were in charge of organizing the Games. The transformation that took place was largely based on the ideas of Rajiv Gandhi. It was from this point onwards that he began implementing new technology, the effects of which are seen even today.

The theme song for the event, titled 'Swaagatam', was composed by the sitarist Ravi Shankar. Special stamps commemorating the Games were issued as thirty-three countries with 3411 athletes participated. India won thirteen gold medals, nineteen silver medals and twenty-five bronze medals, overall ranking fifth.

The impressive arrangements enhanced India's status in Asia and the world.

❈ OTHER KEY EVENTS

Zail Singh (5 May 1916–25 December 1994) became the new President of India, serving from 25 July 1982 to 25 July 1987.

A new political party, the Telugu Desam, was founded in Andhra Pradesh by N.T. Rama Rao (known as NTR, 28 May 1923–18 January 1996), a well-known film star. The party came to power in the state assembly elections of 1983, with NTR as chief minister.

❈ A TIGER FOR MALGUDI

An old tiger sits in a zoo and writes about his life. Once he was wild, and he lost his mother when he was still a cub. As he grew up, he terrified other animals in the forest. Later, he was captured and treated harshly in a circus. Then he escaped, and, though people wanted to kill him, he was adopted by a sannyasi. The two became good friends, and only when the sannyasi died did the tiger reach the zoo. This book, *A Tiger for Malgudi*, was written by R.K. Narayan in 1982, who is better known for his other works. He said he got the idea for this one when he saw a picture of a tiger following a sannyasi at a Kumbh Mela.

In 1986, a TV serial called *Malgudi Days* was made based on the book *Swami and Friends* (1935), also written by R.K. Narayan. Malgudi is the fictional place where the young boys Swami, Mani, Rajam and others play and study. R.K. Narayan (1906–2001) wrote many other books, among them *The Financial Expert* (1952), *Waiting for the Mahatma* (1955) and *The Guide* (1958).

THE TIGER AND ITS STRIPES

Did you know that each tiger has a unique pattern of stripes and facial markings?

Though the tiger is the national animal of India, its numbers are dwindling. There are eight types of tigers in the world, and of them, the royal Bengal tiger is found in India. Tigers can be seen on seals of the Indus civilization and were used as symbols on coins of some early dynasties, as they were once found across the country. As the numbers declined, Project Tiger was launched and tiger reserves were set up. According to the 1993 tiger census, the number of tigers in India then was 3750. By 2006, this was down to 1411, but by 2016 it had risen to 2500.

Across the world, tiger populations were estimated at around 1,00,000 in 1900, and today there are only 3900 wild tigers in the whole world. Despite being given protection by India and other countries, tigers are illegally killed for their skin and bones, which are sold for high prices.

❋ THREE GREAT WRITERS

R.K Narayan, Mulk Raj Anand (1905–2004) and Raja Rao (1909–2006) are three well-known writers in English literature, who started writing before Independence. All three wrote a number of books. Mulk Raj Anand's *Untouchable* was published in 1935 and his *Private Life of an Indian Prince*, in 1953.

A reproduction of an Indus civilization seal depicting a tiger

Raja Rao's first novel in English, *Kanthapura*, with India's struggle for independence as its background, was published in 1938. His most famous book, *The Serpent and the Rope*, came out in 1960. His other works include *On the Ganga Ghat* (1989) and *The Meaning of India* (1996). All three authors won several awards as well as international acclaim.

❁ MITHUN CHAKRABORTY ACTS IN *DISCO DANCER*

Mithun Chakraborty (b. 16 June 1950), a well-known actor, gained fame worldwide for his role as street dancer Jimmy in the 1982 film *Disco Dancer*. Even before this, he had won the National Film Award for the best actor for *Mrigayaa* (1976), which was his first film. He has also won the National Film Award for *Tahader Katha* (1992) and *Swami Vivekananda* (1998). In his long career, he has acted in over 350 Hindi, Bengali, Odia and Bhojpuri films.

❁ THE ANDAMAN AND NICOBAR ISLANDS

In 1982, the union territory of the Andaman and Nicobar Islands was finally given its own local administration, with a lieutenant governor located in Port Blair.

The territory has an interesting history. It was used by the British as a penal settlement—a colony where prisoners were sent—from 1857 to 1942. The cellular jail there, where many of India's freedom fighters were once held, is now a national memorial. The islands were also under Japanese control for three years (1942–45). It became a union territory in 1956.

❁ GOLF IN INDIA

Golf was introduced in the 1982 Asian Games. The Indian team of Lakshman Singh, Rajeev Mohta, Rishi Narain and Amit Luthra won the gold, with Lakshman Singh also winning the individual gold.

As with several other games, golf was brought to India by the British. The first golf club in the country was the Royal Calcutta Golf Club (established in 1829). A ladies golf club was founded in Calcutta in 1891. The Indian Golf Union was set up in New Delhi in 1955, and its ladies section in 1970.

P.G. 'Billoo' Sethi, R.K. Pitamber, I.S. Malik and his son, Ashok Malik, were among India's top male golfers in the early years. Good female golfers in the 1960s and 1970s included Maureen Wallis, Anjani Desai, Vinita Tripathi, Champika Nanda and Rohini Chowgule, and Nonita Lall in the 1980s.

The 1982 Asian Games promoted golf in India. Some of the top players since then have been Jeev Milkha Singh, who reached the world rank of 29; Gaurav Ghei; Jyoti Randhawa and Arjun Atwal. Some rising players in 2015–16 were Gaganjeet Bhullar, Anirban Lahiri and Shiv Chawrasia among the men, and Aditi Ashok, Gauri Monga, Vani Kapoor and Sharmila Nicollet among the women.

ALSO IN 1982

26 January: Death of Esther Sherman (b. 1896), an American exponent of Indian classical dance, also known as Ragini Devi

3 March: Death of Urdu writer Firaq Gorakhpuri (b. 1896)

20 July: Death of Mirabehn (b. 1892), originally named Madeleine Slade, Gandhi's disciple, who won the Padma Vibhushan (1982)

8 September: Death of Sheikh Abdullah (b. 1905)

15 November: Death of Vinoba Bhave (b. 1895), founder of the Bhudan movement. He was the first Ramon Magsaysay Award winner (1958), also receiving the Bharat Ratna posthumously in 1983.

The Technology Bank at the Centre for Technology Transfer of the National Research Development Corporation starts functioning.

The Malayalam film *Elippathayam* (The Rat Trap, 1981) wins an award from the British Film Institute.

Death of Antonio Piedade da Cruz (b. 1895), noted artist and sculptor from Goa

March–November: The Festival of India is held in Great Britain, showcasing India's heritage, including its art and history.

The Marine National Park is established in the Gulf of Kutch, Gujarat.

1983: THE DEMAND FOR KHALISTAN

Some states, particularly Assam, Jammu and Kashmir and Punjab, faced major problems and were politically unstable. People of Assam did not want Bengali, particularly Bangladeshi, settlers in their state, and started a movement for their removal. In Kashmir, after Sheikh Abdullah's death in 1982, who had become chief minister in 1975, his son, Farooq Abdullah, succeeded him. But even after he won the assembly elections in 1983, Mrs Gandhi replaced him with his brother-in-law, G.M. Shah, leading to unrest. However, the biggest problem was in Punjab. The Dal Khalsa, started in 1978 by Sant Jarnail Singh Bhindranwale, was still leading the movement for a separate state of Khalistan. The group had begun to collect arms and ammunition, storing some of these in the Golden Temple, in Amritsar. Gradually, violence against Hindus and those Sikhs who opposed Bhindranwale grew in Punjab, even spreading to other areas. Efforts to resolve the situation through talks did not succeed.

❋ OTHER KEY EVENTS

After the success of the 1982 Asian Games, Rajiv Gandhi was more involved in politics, and became the general secretary of the Indian National Congress.

🟊 KAPIL DEV AND THE CRICKET WORLD CUP

In 1983, India won the Cricket World Cup (Prudential Cup). The team was led by Kapil Dev (b. 6 January 1959), an all-rounder, being both a batsman and bowler. Kapil Dev began playing Test cricket in 1978–79. By February 1980, he was known as the first and the youngest cricketer to score 1000 runs and take 100 wickets in the shortest span of time—107 days. He continued to make records. After leading India to victory in the World Cup, winning the final against the West Indies, Kapil crossed the 300-wicket mark, and by 1991–92, had taken 400 wickets, later reaching a record of 434 wickets and 5000 runs in Test cricket. He also played ODIs, taking 252 wickets in 224 one-dayers and scoring 3783 runs.

Kapil retired in 1994. He was named *Wisden*'s Indian Cricketer of the Century in 2002, and in 2010, he joined the ICC (International Cricket Council) Cricket Hall of Fame. He has also received a number of awards, including the Arjuna Award (1979–80), the Padma Bhushan (1991) and the C.K. Nayudu Lifetime Achievement Award (2013).

🟊 SUBRAHMANYAN CHANDRASEKHAR WINS THE NOBEL PRIZE

Subrahmanyan Chandrasekhar (19 October 1910–21 August 1995), an Indian-origin astrophysicist and later an American citizen, won the Nobel Prize in Physics along with William A. Fowler for theoretical studies on the structure and evolution of stars. Born in Lahore, he studied in Presidency College, Madras, and then received a scholarship to the University of Cambridge, from where he completed his PhD in 1933. In 1937, he started teaching at the University of Chicago, and in 1952, was appointed the Morton D. Hull professor of astrophysics there. His research included the study of stellar structure, white dwarfs, black holes and radiative transfer. He continued to work at the University of Chicago until his death.

❂ INSAT-1B IS SUCCESSFULLY LAUNCHED

INSAT-1B (Indian National Satellite System), a multipurpose satellite system, was launched in 1983. (INSAT-1A was launched in 1982, but lost in September 1983). After that, INSAT-1C (1988) and INSAT-1D (1990) were sent to space, followed by the INSAT-2 series.

INSAT-1B

❂ AN AWARD AND A DEATH: TWO MUSICIANS

Vishnu Govind Jog (1922–31 January 2004) was one of the best violinists of Hindustani classical music. Son of Govind Gopal, he was born in Wai, Maharashtra. He studied with V. Shastry, S.G. Atharle, G. Purohit and later, S.N. Ratanjankar and Allauddin Khan. He went on concert tours abroad, and was a music producer and composer for All India Radio, Calcutta. He was also a professor of violin at the Bhatkhande Sangit Vidyapith. Vishnu Govind received the Sangeet Natak Akademi Award in 1980 and the Padma Bhushan in 1983, apart from other honours.

Vasantrao Deshpande (b. 1920), another noted Hindustani classical musician, died on 30 July 1983 at the age of sixty-three. He was primarily a vocalist, but also played various instruments, including the tabla and sitar. He was also known for his performance in the Marathi musical *Katyar Kaljat Ghusali*, first staged in 1967, where he played the role of Khansaheb, the head of a musical gharana. Vasantrao acted in some Marathi movies and provided the music for many more. He received the Sangeet

Natak Akademi Award in 1982. Vasantrao's grandson Rahul Deshpande played the role of Khansaheb in a recent release of the play in 2015.

❈ THE JNANPITH AWARD FOR *CHIKKAVEERA RAJENDRA*

Masti Venkatesh Iyengar (6 June 1891–6 June 1986), writer of Kannada literature, won the Jnanpith Award in 1983. He wrote novels, plays and stories, mainly in Kannada but also in English. His Jnanpith was for *Chikkaveera Rajendra*, a historical novel about the last king of Kodagu. Many of his works were inspired by history and the epics. He also wrote an autobiography, *Bhaava*, in three volumes.

ALSO IN 1983

18 February: In Nellie, a village in Morigaon district of Assam, Assamese–Hindu communities kill around 2000 Muslims whose ancestors had migrated to the region before 1947.

11 June: Death of businessman G.D. Birla

February: Phoolan Devi (1963–2001), known as Bandit Queen, surrenders. After a child marriage that failed, Phoolan had joined a band of dacoits and been involved in several murders.

1984: INDIRA IS ASSASSINATED

The key event of the year was the assassination of Indira Gandhi, but a notable event that took place earlier in the year, on 13 April, was India bringing most of Siachen Glacier, on the border between India and Pakistan, under its control.

❋ OPERATION BLUE STAR

Jarnail Singh Bhindranwale had occupied the Golden Temple (Harmandir Sahib) in Amritsar with many of his followers, and stocked it with arms and ammunition. In June 1984, the army was ordered to attack the temple to get them out. This was called Operation Blue Star. A fierce battle took place during which Bhindranwale, his general, Shabeg Singh, and many others were killed. The army too suffered several losses. As a result of the battle, the Akal Takht and other sacred areas of the temple were destroyed. A number of Sikhs were angry at the damage to their holy gurdwara.

❋ INDIRA GANDHI IS SHOT

On 31 October 1984, Indira Gandhi was shot dead as she was walking out of her house towards her office to meet a TV crew.

She had been prime minister of India from 1966 to 1977 and again from 1980 to 1984.

The killers were two of her security guards who were Sikhs, Beant Singh and Satwant Singh. Rajiv Gandhi was in West Bengal at the time but he rushed back to Delhi. He had already been chosen to take her place as prime minister until the next elections were held. An accompanying tragedy that took place was the killing of over 3000 innocent Sikhs in Delhi and other cities by rioting crowds in response to Indira's death. These were controlled only after 3 November.

● RAJIV GANDHI BECOMES PRIME MINISTER

Elections to the Lok Sabha were already due in early 1985, but they were brought forward to the end of December. Out of the 508 seats for which elections were held (they were not held in Punjab and Assam due to unrest), the Congress won 401, the highest ever. After the elections, Rajiv was sworn in as prime minister again on 31 December 1984 for a term of five years.

● OTHER KEY EVENTS

Meanwhile, yet another tragedy took place on 2–3 December, when poisonous gas leaked in a Union Carbide factory in Bhopal. More than 15,000 people died and many more suffered for years to come.

A new political party, the Bahujan Samaj Party, was formed in Uttar Pradesh by Kanshi Ram, a Dalit leader. Later Mayawati became the leader of the party.

● BHUPEN KHAKHAR IS AWARDED THE PADMA SHRI

Bhupen Khakhar (10 March 1934–8 August 2003) was one of India's leading artists. Born in Bombay, he initially qualified as a chartered accountant. He took evening classes at Sir J.J. School of Art, and later obtained a master's degree in art history from the M.S. University of Baroda. He was working as an accountant even as he began his career as an artist, using various styles. He created collages of deities, their pictures cut from popular posters, embellished and painted in Indian miniature style. Following this he painted ordinary artisans, including barbers, tailors, cobblers—even the accountant with whom he worked—in bright colours. Some of his paintings depicted homosexuality, unusual in Indian art in those days. From 1979 onwards, he held exhibitions abroad with great success. In the 1990s, he began using watercolours more than oils.

Salman Rushdie mentioned him in the novel *The Moor's Last Sigh* (1995), and in return, Bhupen painted Rushdie's portrait, titled *The Moor*, which can be seen in the National Portrait Gallery, London. In 1984, he was awarded the Padma Shri, and subsequently other awards, including the Prince Claus Award of the Netherlands in the year 2000.

HUM LOG AND OTHER EARLY TELEVISION SERIALS

Hum Log (We the People) was India's first soap opera in Hindi, first airing on Doordarshan on 7 July 1984, with 154 episodes.[18] Manohar Shyam Joshi wrote the script, P. Kumar Vasudev directed it and Anil Biswas composed the title song. Actor Ashok Kumar provided a summary-cum-discussion narrative at the end and later at the beginning of each episode. The serial was inspired by the Mexican show *Ven Conmigo* (1975), and its scriptwriter, Miguel Sabido, helped create the Indian version. It was re-telecast by Sony TV in 2000, and then remade by Doordarshan. In its

---

[18] For more on the early years of television in independent India, see *The Puffin History of India: Volume 2*, 399–401.

first telecast, *Hum Log* was extremely popular, being the story of a lower-middle-class family and their daily lives.

Buniyaad, also written by Manohar Shyam Joshi, first aired in 1986. The plot dealt with Partition and its consequences. The main characters were the teacher Master Haveliram, his wife and children. *Khandan* (1985), another early tele-serial, was about a rich family, and though well produced, was not as popular. *Rajani* (1985), created by Basu Chatterjee, was greatly appreciated as it portrayed the problems of society, against which Rajani was a fearless crusader.

● SPORTS ROUND-UP

There were some major sporting landmarks in 1984.

The Sports Authority of India was founded on 25 January to promote sports and games and maintain the stadiums constructed for the Asian Games. Other sports institutes were merged with it in 1987.

India participated in the Summer Olympics in Los Angeles, and P.T. Usha emerged as a winner even though she missed the bronze medal in the 400-metres hurdles by one-hundredth of a second. She had already won two silver medals in the 1982 Asian Games, and went on to win many more, including five gold medals in the 1985 Asian Athletics Championships, four in the 1989 edition, four golds and a silver in the 1986 Asian Games in Seoul, three silvers in the Beijing Asian Games in 1990 and one in the 1994 edition in Hiroshima. Born in 1964 in Payyoli, Kerala, P.T. Usha came to be known as

Bachendri Pal

the Payyoli Express. She received the Padma Shri and the Arjuna Award in 1984, as well as several others. She started a training academy in Kerala, and is employed in the railways.

Bachendri Pal (b. 1954) became the first Indian woman to climb Mount Everest, having been selected for an Indian Army expedition. She too received the Padma Shri in 1984, as well as a gold medal from the Indian Mountaineering Foundation, among many other awards. She became chief of the Tata Steel Adventure Foundation in 1984, and continues to be involved in mountaineering and trekking.

ALSO IN 1984

9 February: Death of T. Balasaraswati (b. 13 May 1918), Bharatanatyam dancer

10 March: Death of I.S. Johar (b. 1920), film actor, writer, director and producer

2 April: The first Indian in space, Squadron Leader Rakesh Sharma goes aboard Soyuz T-11.

6 July: An Indian Airlines airbus, carrying 255 passengers, is hijacked and flown to Lahore. The hijackers eventually surrender.

Death of Rajinder Singh Bedi (b. 1 September 1915), Urdu writer, playwright, screenwriter and film director

39

1985: RAJIV GANDHI— A YOUNG PRIME MINISTER

At only forty years of age, Rajiv Gandhi was the country's youngest prime minister, and he brought in new ways of thinking. He did a lot in his five years in office, particularly attempting to resolve the problems of Punjab, Kashmir and northeast India, founding the Navodaya schools and, most importantly, bringing in the use of computers and laying the foundation for the introduction of mobile phones.

To start with, in Punjab, the Sikh political prisoners were released. In July 1985, Rajiv Gandhi signed a pact with Sant Longowal, a moderate Sikh leader, in Punjab. It was agreed to hold elections in the state in order to bring about normality. And elections were held even though Sant Longowal was shot dead in August. Two years of President's Rule in Punjab ended and the Akali Dal came to power in the state, with Surjit Singh Barnala as chief minister. However, the separatists continued their activities.

Assam had also been a troubled state. Rajiv Gandhi held discussions there with Assamese

Rajiv Gandhi

leaders on the status of illegal immigrants in the state. An agreement was reached on 15 August 1985. The same year, a new party, the Asom Gana Parishad, was constituted, and it formed the government in Assam after elections were held in December.

❋ BHIMSEN JOSHI IS AWARDED THE PADMA BHUSHAN

Bhimsen Joshi (14 February 1922–24 January 2011) was one of Hindustani classical music's best singers, who specialized in singing khayal. Even as a child, he used to follow musical bands and groups. He began studying music with various teachers, and then found his guru in Rambhau Kundgolkar (1886–1952), also known as Sawai Gandharva. His first performance was at the age of nineteen. Apart from khayal and thumri, he sang bhajans in Hindi, Kannada and Marathi. He also sang for some films, including *Birbal, My Brother* (1973) along with Pandit Jasraj. With Vasantrao Deshpande, he organized the Sawai Gandharva Mahotsav every year from 1953 onwards.

Bhimsen was known for his rich voice and complex taans, and preferred certain ragas, such as Darbari, Miyan ki Todi and Bhimpalasi. In an interview, he said that to be a good singer, one must listen to different types of singers. Bhimsen performed at concerts in the USA, Europe, Canada and other parts of the world. Apart from the Padma Bhushan in 1985, which followed the Padma Shri in 1972, and the Sangeet Natak Akademi Award in 1975, he received many more honours, including the Padma Vibhushan (1999) and the Bharat Ratna (2008). Upon his death, he was given a state funeral with a twenty-one-gun salute in Pune, where he died. An obituary notice by Shubha Mudgal in *Open* magazine was headed by the words 'Even Gods Must Die'.[19]

---

[19] Shubha Mudgal, 'Even Gods Must Die', *Open*, 29 January 2011, http://www.openthemagazine.com/article/arts-letters/even-gods-must-die.

Bhimsen's music was divine, but he also had a humane side. He loved good food and fast cars. He married twice, and had seven children from his two marriages.

❋ THE SOUTH ASIAN ASSOCIATION FOR REGIONAL COOPERATION (SAARC)

SAARC was formed to promote cooperation, development and cultural and scientific exchanges among the seven South Asian states of Bangladesh, Bhutan, India, the Maldives, Nepal, Pakistan and Sri Lanka. The first summit was held in Dhaka on 8 December 1985. In 2007, Afghanistan was added to the group.

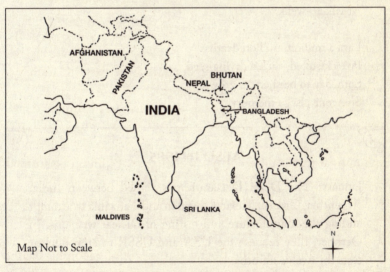

The SAARC countries after 2007

❋ KAMALA DAS WINS THE SAHITYA AKADEMI AWARD

Kamala Das (31 March 1934–31 May 2009), Malayalam and English-language writer and poet, received acclaim for her portrayal of women and their sexuality, and for her openness in her autobiography, *My Story* (also serialized and published in Malayalam as *Ente Katha*). She also wrote newspaper columns. She was married to Madhava Das at the age of fifteen, who encouraged her to write. They had three children. Late in life, Kamala converted to Islam, and was known as Kamala Surayya. She received a number of awards, including the Sahitya Akademi Award in 1985, and was even nominated and shortlisted for the Nobel Prize in Literature in 1984.

Her poem 'Someone Else's Song' begins with the words:[20]

I am a million, million people
Talking all at once, with voices
Raised in clamour, like maids
At village-wells.

I am a million, million deaths
Pox-clustered, each a drying seed
Someday to be shed, to grow for
Someone else, a memory.

ALSO IN 1985

January: The Delhi Declaration is signed between India, Argentina, Greece, Mexico, Sweden and Tanzania to attempt ending the manufacture and testing of nuclear weapons. In October, they request the USA and USSR to stop nuclear tests for twelve months.

---

[20] Quoted in 'Carol Rumens's Poem of the Week: "Someone Else's Song" by Kamala Das', *Guardian*, 3 August 2015, accessed 11 June 2017, https://www.theguardian.com/books/2015/aug/03/poem-of-the-week-someone-elses-song-by-kamala-das.

May 1985: Rajiv Gandhi visits the USSR, and agreements on increasing trade and other mutually beneficial contracts are signed.

15 July–18 August: The Cultural Festival of India is held in London, across 18 acres of the Alexandra Palace. It has over a million visitors from countries around the world.

September: The Indira Gandhi National Open University (IGNOU) is established in New Delhi by an Act of Parliament.

19 November: The Indira Gandhi National Centre for the Arts (IGNCA) is founded in New Delhi.

The Seventh Five-Year Plan (1985–90) is inaugurated, its main aims being to increase foodgrain production and employment and to reduce poverty.

The Anti-Defection Act is passed. This comprises laws on when a legislator can be disqualified on grounds of defection or decamping.

The Ministry of Environment and Forests is established.

1986: PEACE IN MIZORAM

In June 1986, Rajiv Gandhi signed an agreement with tribal leaders in Mizoram, ending their agitation and bringing peace to the state. The Mizo National Front (MNF), led by Laldenga, had started an armed struggle for an independent state, and talks had been going on since 1980 to try and find a solution. The agreement stated that the Congress government in the state would be replaced by a joint Congress–MNF government, with Laldenga as chief minister. This restored stability in the region. Meanwhile, problems continued in Punjab, with the Golden Temple being captured by followers of Bhindranwale. On 30 April, Operation Black Thunder was conducted by the army to get them out.

❖ OTHER KEY EVENTS

Even as Rajiv Gandhi continued to focus on resolving the conflicts in the country, two major happenings of the year that had long-term consequences were the opening of Babri Masjid and the controversial decision on the Shah Bano case.

THE SHAH BANO CASE

Shah Bano, a Muslim woman, filed an appeal in court for maintenance from her ex-husband after divorce (known as alimony). This was granted and the judgment confirmed by the Supreme Court. However, some Muslims protested against this ruling, stating that it was not in conformity with Islamic law. Rajiv Gandhi was initially in favour of the judgment, and upon his request, Arif Mohammad Khan, minister of state, provided a defence of the ruling. But faced with further objections, a new law was passed, The Muslim Women (Protection of Rights on Divorce) Act, 1986, allowing Islamic personal law to prevail unless there was an agreement between husband and wife.

In 2001, the Supreme Court provided an interpretation of the Act that upheld its judgment in the Shah Bano case.

BABRI MASJID

In February 1986, Rajiv Gandhi opened the gates of Babri Masjid in Ayodhya, which had been locked since 1949. Babri Masjid was a disputed site, with Hindus claiming it was the birthplace of the god Rama and that an ancient temple existed there before a mosque had been built in its place. The opening of the mosque led to more turmoil in succeeding years.

● NAVODAYA VIDYALAYAS

The establishment of Jawahar Navodaya Vidyalayas, co-educational residential schools providing free and high-quality instruction, for talented rural children was Rajiv Gandhi's idea. The details were worked out in the National Policy on Education, 1986, and two schools were set up that year. By 2000, there were 423 schools, and by 2016, 660 schools had been sanctioned, though some were not yet ready. Attempts are made to ensure that at least one-third of the students enrolled are girls. Some students are sent to different linguistic areas for a year to promote national integration.

❋ TWO FILM STARS: A DEBUT AND A DEATH

Who wears pink pants, red checked shorts or combinations of yellow, blue and red?

Govinda!

Govind Arun Ahuja (b. 21 December 1963), popularly known as Govinda, appeared in his first film, *Ilzaam*, in 1986. He went on to act in over 150 films and was extremely popular, known for being a comic actor and a good dancer. Govinda is best known, however, for his really colourful and unique clothes! He has been appearing on TV shows since 1999. His films post 2000 did not do well and instead he turned to politics, being elected as a member of Parliament in 2004 after joining the Congress party. (He resigned in 2008 before the end of his term). After a break of a couple of years, he resumed acting in films, but did not regain the same popularity. Govinda is also a singer; he released his music albums in 1998 and 2013. Throughout his career, he received many Filmfare Awards, including those for best actor, best comedian and best villain, as well as the Star Screen, Zee Cine and other awards.

The year saw the death of Smita Patil (17 October 1955–13 December 1986), an actor known for her serious roles, quite the opposite of Govinda. Her first film was Shyam Benegal's *Charandas Chor* (1975). She went on to act in many more mainstream as well as parallel films in Hindi and Marathi.[21]

---

[21] Parallel films are considered more serious and realistic.

Among her best films were *Manthan* (1976), *Bhumika* (1977), *Aakrosh* (1980) and *Mirch Masala* (1987). Smita was married to the actor Raj Babbar, and died after childbirth, at the age of thirty-one. Her son, Prateik Babbar, acted in his first film in 2008. In her short acting career, she received several awards, including two National Film Awards for the best actress and the Padma Shri in 1985. Some of her films, including *Mirch Masala*, were released after her death. In this brilliant film, Smita acts as Sonbai, who works in a mirch (chilli) factory, and resists the subedar's desire for her. She is helped by Abu Mian (Om Puri), who shuts the gates to protect her. After the subedar storms the factory with his men, shooting Abu Mian dead, the women get together to defend her by throwing mirch masala (chilli powder) at the attackers! In 2012, the Smita Patil Documentary and Short Film Festival was initiated, and in 2013, a postage stamp was issued in her honour.

✸ THE BAHA'I LOTUS TEMPLE

The Baha'i Lotus Temple in New Delhi, one of the seven main temples of Baha'i worship in the world, was opened to the public in December 1986. This unique marble temple, which took seven years to build, is constructed like a lotus with two layers of petals.

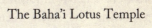
The Baha'i Lotus Temple

The Baha'i religion was founded in the mid-nineteenth century in Iran by Mirza Husain Ali, later known as Baha'ullah. Baha'is believe in one God, and recognize all other prophets or divine beings, including Buddha, Jesus, Krishna and Muhammad, as God's messengers. Its aim is to spread divine love and world unity.

NIKHIL BANERJEE: AN UNTIMELY DEATH

Nikhil Banerjee (14 October 1931–27 January 1986) was a leading sitarist, who studied with Baba Allauddin Khan of Maihar. Nikhil performed at concerts around the world and received several awards, including the Padma Shri (1968), the Sangeet Natak Akademi Award (1974) and the Padma Bhushan (1986). He suffered from heart problems during the 1980s, and eventually succumbed to a heart attack.

THE DAGAR BROTHERS

The Dagar brothers consist of the eight grandsons of the vocalists Zakiruddin Khan and Allabande Khan, who have kept the dhrupad tradition of Hindustani classical music alive. The eight are Nasir Moinuddin Dagar (1919–66), Zia Fariduddin Dagar (1932–2013), Nasir Zahiruddin Dagar (1933–94), Rahim Fahimuddin Dagar (1927–2011), Nasir Aminuddin Dagar (1923–2000), Zia Mohiuddin Dagar (1929–90), Nasir Faiyazuddin Dagar (1934–89) and Hussain Sayeeduddin Dagar (b. 1939).

Of these, Nasir Moinuddin Dagar and Nasir Aminuddin Dagar performed together, and were known as the elder Dagar brothers. Nasir Zahiruddin Dagar and Nasir Faiyazuddin Dagar also performed as a duo, and were known as the younger Dagar brothers. Zia Mohiuddin Dagar, though also a vocalist, specialized in playing the rudra veena. The Dagar brothers represent the nineteenth generation of the Dagar *vani* dhrupad tradition.

After the death of Nasir Moinuddin in 1966, Nasir Aminuddin began performing at concerts on his own. In 1975, he founded the Ustad Nasir Moinuddin Dagar Dhrupad Sangeet Ashram in Calcutta to teach and promote the dhrupad. The main feature of the dhrupad style is the rich and varied alap, which is the introductory portion of the raga.

The brothers received several awards. Among them, Aminuddin Dagar was awarded the Padma Bhushan in 1986. Other members of the Dagar family, as well as sons of these Dagar brothers, continue to promote the dhrupad tradition. Among them is Nasir Faiyazuddin's son, Faiyaz Wasifuddin Dagar (b. 1968), who was awarded the Padma Shri in 2010.

ALSO IN 1986

17 February: Death of philosopher J. Krishnamurti (b. 1895)

16 March: Notorious criminal Charles Sobhraj escapes from Tihar Jail after drugging his guards at his birthday party.

6 July: Death of Jagjivan Ram (b. 1908), nationalist, freedom fighter, Dalit leader and minister in independent India

10 August: General A.S. Vaidya, who led Operation Blue Star, is shot dead.

22 September: The Australia–India Test series in Madras results in a tie.

27 October: The Inland Waterways Authority of India is founded. It is in charge of and supervises transportation along all inland waterways of the country, including rivers, canals and creeks.

16–17 November: The second SAARC summit is held in Bangalore.

November: Operation Brasstacks, a military exercise of the Indian Army in Rajasthan, aimed at testing the readiness of the Indian Armed Forces in case of war, begins.

23 December: The Child Labour (Prohibition and Regulation) Act is passed, banning the employment of

children under the age of fourteen in certain occupations and providing guidelines for working conditions.

23 December: The Bureau of Indian Standards Act is passed. It provides for the establishment of a bureau to standardize processed and natural products and ensure their quality.

24 December: The Consumer Protection Act is passed, facilitating consumer councils and other institutions to protect the interests of consumers.

Sachidananda Routray (1916–2004), Odia-language writer, receives the Jnanpith Award.

1987: SRI LANKA AND THE IPKF

Rajiv Gandhi introduced new schemes in the country, but the year 1987 is otherwise remembered for India's involvement in Sri Lanka. Tamils had been in Sri Lanka since the British rule, when they had been taken there as labour. Over time, conflicts between them and Sri Lankans had grown. By 1987, the Tamil population was concentrated in the northern part of the island, Jaffna. The main political group fighting for the Tamils was the Liberation Tigers of Tamil Eelam (LTTE), founded and led by Prabhakaran, who had started an armed rebellion.

In 1985, when the Sri Lankan Army attacked Jaffna, India came to the rescue of the Tamil people there by dropping food supplies from the air. In 1987, Junius Jayewardene, President of Sri Lanka, asked for Rajiv Gandhi's help in resolving the problem of the Tamil population in Sri Lanka. An agreement was signed on 29 July 1987, to give Tamils some autonomy, on the condition that they surrender their arms. In return, India agreed to stop helping them. However, this agreement was not liked by the Tamils of Sri Lanka. So the Indian Peace Keeping Force (IPKF) was set up, consisting of troops from the Indian Army, who remained in Sri Lanka for two years and fought against the agitating Tamils, who felt betrayed by India. No result was achieved and the Indian troops started withdrawing in 1989.

OTHER KEY EVENTS

Also important were the first steps taken towards the liberalization of the economy. Some import of consumer goods, which had earlier been banned, began. Rajeev Gandhi's desire to bring about development led to the inauguration of six technology missions, conceived and developed with the help of Sam Pitroda, a telecom engineer from the USA. These included programmes to increase the supply of drinking water and the production of milk and oilseed, to improve literacy, increase immunization and bring telephones to every village. All these missions had great benefits. Rajiv Gandhi also encouraged the production and use of computers in India.

V.P. SINGH LEADS AN ANTI-CORRUPTION CAMPAIGN

V.P. Singh was expelled from the Congress (I) in 1987 because of his anti-corruption campaign that targeted several people in positions of power. He returned to Parliament as an independent and organized an opposition party, the Jan Morcha. He later formed the Janata Dal party.

AFFAIRS OF THE STATES

Elections were held in the state of Jammu and Kashmir after Rajiv Gandhi came to an agreement with Farooq Abdullah, leader of the party Jammu and Kashmir National Conference. G.M. Shah had been made chief minister of Kashmir when Indira Gandhi was prime minister. As he was both corrupt and inefficient, he was removed in 1986, and President's Rule was imposed in Kashmir.

An alliance of the Congress and the National Conference led to a joint win in the elections, but they lost popularity as the elections were considered rigged.

In Punjab, President's Rule was imposed again in May as there had been no end to violence in the state.

There were communal riots in Meerut, and 150 people died while property worth Rs 20 crore was destroyed.

❋ ROOP KANWAR: A YOUNG WOMAN IS BURNT TO DEATH

Sati, the custom of a woman being burnt alive on her husband's pyre if he died before her, was an age-old practice, particularly in Rajasthan. In the past, many efforts had been made to stop this tradition, and it was completely banned in India. Even so, on 4 September 1987, an eighteen-year-old widow was burnt to death on her husband's funeral pyre in the village of Deorala, Rajasthan. Was it a voluntary act, as some claimed, or was she forced into it?

Roop Kanwar was hailed as a goddess by thousands of local people, and she was worshipped at the site of her death, though many across the country were horrified. Several people were arrested for causing her death, but finally all were released. The Sati (Prevention) Act was passed by the Government of Rajasthan in 1987, and it became an Act of Parliament in 1988. It seeks to prevent the voluntary or forceful burning or burial of any widow, as well as the glorification of it.

❋ 'MOGAMBO *KHUSH HUA!*'

'Mogambo *khush hua!*' (Mogambo is happy!) is a much-quoted dialogue from *Mr India*, the most popular Hindi film at the box office in 1987. It was directed by Shekhar Kapur, and the lead actors were Anil Kapoor, Sridevi and Amrish Puri. The story

A reproduction of the poster of *Mr India*

centres on Mogambo, who lives on an island and aims to conquer India, and Arun, a violinist, who takes care of orphaned children. Through his dead father, Arun obtains a device that makes him invisible, and finally manages to defeat Mogambo. Sridevi shines in the film, particularly in the dance number 'Hawa Hawai'.

KHWAJA AHMAD ABBAS PASSES AWAY

Khwaja Ahmad Abbas (7 June 1914–1 June 1987) was an important film director, novelist and scriptwriter. Among his films, *Shehar aur Sapna* (1963) won the National Award for the best feature film. As a screenwriter, he was responsible for some of Raj Kapoor's best films, including *Awara*, *Shree 420*, *Mera Naam Joker* and *Bobby*. He wrote over seventy books, including non-fiction, novels and stories. He was also a journalist, writing in Urdu, Hindi and English.

KAMALADEVI CHATTOPADHYAY WINS THE PADMA VIBHUSHAN

Kamaladevi Chattopadhyay (3 April 1903–29 October 1988) was a nationalist who participated in the freedom movement, but is mainly remembered for her efforts to revive Indian handicrafts and promote theatre. She founded the All-India Women's Conference in 1927, and joined Mahatma Gandhi's Dandi March or the Salt Satyagraha of 1930. After Independence, she helped rehabilitate the refugees from Pakistan.

Her most notable actions were those to preserve and revive traditional crafts, and to provide status and honour to craftspeople. She started the National Awards for craftspeople and set up cottage industries, emporia and crafts museums. Kamaladevi received the Padma Bhushan in 1955, the Ramon Magsaysay Award in 1966 for community leadership, a UNESCO award in 1977 and the

Padma Vibhushan in 1987. She also founded theatre institutes and wrote a number of books on handicrafts, theatre, women, social movements and political affairs. Her memoirs, *Inner Recesses, Outer Spaces*, were published in 1986.

> ### HANDICRAFTS IN INDIA
>
> Crafts in India include woollen carpets, shawls and rugs; woven goods; hand-printed textiles; wood- and metalwork; terracotta items, handcrafted jewellery; items made of semi-precious stones, bone or shell; handmade pottery and ceramics; embroidery; basketry; painting; inlay work; lacquer work; dolls and toys; papier mâché, etc.

❊ VISHNU VAMAN SHIRWADKAR WINS THE JNANPITH AWARD

Vishnu Vaman Shirwadkar (27 February 1912–10 March 1999), Marathi-language poet, playwright and novelist, wrote under the name Kusumagraj. He won the Jnanpith in 1987 for his play *Natsamrat*. Other awards received by him include the Sahitya Akademi Award (1974) and the Padma Bhushan (1991).

❊ OPERATION BLACKBOARD

An educational scheme known as Operation Blackboard was started in 1987–88 to improve government-run primary schools by providing quality teachers and teaching equipment. It was a joint venture between the Centre and the states, and had considerable success. By the year 2000, 5,22,902 primary and 1,27,257 upper primary schools had benefited from the scheme.

🟎 A NEW PRESIDENT

Ramaswamy Venkataraman (4 December 1910–27 January 2009) became President of India on 25 July 1987, and his term ended on 25 July 1992.

ALSO IN 1987

20 June: Death of ornithologist Salim Ali (b. 1896), known as the Birdman of India

September: The Nuclear Power Board is reconstituted as the Nuclear Power Corporation of India Limited (NPCIL). Over the years, several atomic power stations begin functioning under the board.

31 October: Death of Raj Chandra Bose (b. 1901), an eminent mathematician and statistician

July: The Festival of India starts in the USSR.

November: The Soviet cultural festival comes to New Delhi in a reciprocal visit.

24 December: Death of M.G. Ramachandran (b. 17 January 1917), chief minister of Tamil Nadu, followed by violence and anarchy in Madras. V.R. Nedunchezhiyan is appointed interim chief minister.

1988: ATTEMPTS TOWARDS PEACE

Rajiv Gandhi attempted to bring peace in the region of South Asia and within the country. He had had a number of meetings with Pakistani President General Zia-ul-Haq. They discussed the signing of a friendship treaty, but before this could take place, Zia died in a plane crash on 17 August 1988. Benazir Bhutto became the prime minister of Pakistan in December 1988.

At the fourth SAARC summit, which took place in Islamabad, Pakistan, at the end of December, three agreements were signed between India and Pakistan to improve relationships. These were aimed at increasing trade and cooperation, and to refrain from attacking each other's nuclear facilities. In the same month, Rajiv visited China. This was an Indian prime minister's first visit to China in thirty-four years.

In internal affairs, Rajiv Gandhi signed a pact in August with the militant group Tripura National Volunteers and their leader Hrangkhawl, by which they agreed to lay down arms. Tripura was also dealing with the problem of illegal immigrants from Bangladesh.

Another accord, signed the previous month, was with Subhash Ghisingh, leader of the Gorkha National Liberation Front, who wanted a separate state of Gorkhaland. As part of the agreement with the West Bengal government, the Darjeeling Gorkha Hill Council would be set up, providing the Gorkhas of the region with some autonomy.

In Punjab, militants had once again occupied the Golden Temple. On 18 May, they were forced to surrender after commandos surrounded them.

❋ OTHER KEY EVENTS

A new political party, the Janata Dal was formed in 1988, as a result of the merger of the Janata Party, the Lok Dal and the Jan Morcha.

❋ VISWANATHAN ANAND BECOMES INDIA'S FIRST CHESS GRAND MASTER

Viswanathan Anand (b. 11 December 1969) became India's first chess grand master at the young age of eighteen. This was the culmination of many tournament wins. Born in Mayiladuthurai, Tamil Nadu, he moved with his family to Madras, and began playing tournament-level chess at a young age. He was the youngest Asian to become an international master, in 1985. In 1986, he became the national champion and in 1987, he won the World Junior Chess Championship in Baguio, Philippines. He became the FIDE (Fédération Internationale des Échecs) world chess champion in 2000, defeating Alexei Shirov, and won the World title again in 2007, 2008, 2010 and 2012.

He has received a number of awards, including the Arjuna Award (1985),

Viswanathan Anand

the Soviet Land Nehru Award (1987), the Padma Shri (1988), the Rajiv Gandhi Khel Ratna Award (1991) and the Padma Vibhushan (2007).

CHESS HIGHLIGHTS

- According to some accounts, chess originated in India. Even before Independence, Mir Sultan Khan, who was illiterate, played in international tournaments and was considered one of the ten best players in the world.
- The All India Chess Federation was formed in 1951, and the first national championship was conducted in 1955. The championship was divided into categories A and B in 1967, with the better players in category A. The first women's nationals were held in 1974.
- Manuel Aaron was the first Indian to become an international master (1961). The second was V. Ravikumar (1978).
- After Viswanathan Anand, Dibyendu Barua, K. Sasikiran, Pravin Thipsay and Abhijit Kunte were the next to become grand masters in India, with many more in succeeding years.
- The Khadilkar sisters, Vasanti, Jayshree and Rohini, dominated women's chess in the 1970s and 1980s. Rohini Khadilkar won the Asian Championship in 1981 and 1983. In 1978, Jayshree Khadilkar became the first Indian woman international master. Other female players at this time were Bhagyashree Sathe Thipsay and Anupama Abhyankar-Gokhale. The latter won the Asian Championship in 1987, at the age of eighteen.

- In 2001, Subbaraman Vijayalakshmi became India's first woman grand master, followed by Koneru Humpy and several others
- Harika Dronavalli has emerged as a promising player in recent times. She became a grand master in 2011 and won the bronze medal in three world championships (2012, 2015 and 2017), apart from other tournaments.
- In 2017, Viswanathan Anand remains India's top player among men, with a world rank of 9 in July 2017, and Koneru Humpy, among women, with a world rank of 4. Ranked second is Pentala Harikrishna among men, and Harika Dronavalli among women.

❋ THE RAMAYANA AND THE MAHABHARATA: TWO TELEVISION SERIALS

The Hindi television serials based on these two epics were extremely popular. Hardly anyone would be out on the streets when they'd be on air. While Ramanand Sagar's *Ramayan* ended in 1988, Ravi Chopra's *Mahabharat* began that year.

Ramayan, with seventy-eight episodes, was telecast on Doordarshan between 25 January 1987 and 31 July 1988. Arun Govil starred as Ram and Deepika Chikhalia as Sita. A remake of the series was aired on NDTV Imagine in 2008.

Mahabharat had ninety-four episodes and was broadcast on DD National from 2 October 1988 to 24 June 1990. The show was produced by B.R. Chopra. Rahi Masoom Raza was responsible for the script, the narrator was Harish Bhimani and the title song was sung by Mahendra Kapoor. The cast was vast; among them, Puneet Issar acted as Duryodhan, Firoz Khan as Arjuna, Nitish

Bharadwaj as the god Krishna. The serial was also telecast by the BBC. It was remade with new actors and broadcast on Star Plus from 16 September 2013 to 16 August 2014. The show has been dubbed in other Indian languages, and also aired in Indonesia, Thailand and Mauritius.

ALSO IN 1988

17 March: The first remote sensing satellite made in India, IRS-1A, is launched.

9 July: The National Housing Bank is established in New Delhi to promote and regulate housing finance companies.

21 August: An earthquake in Nepal affects north Bihar, killing around a thousand people and injuring many.

17 September–2 October: India participates in the Summer Olympics in Seoul, South Korea, but does not win any medals.

C. Narayana Reddy (1931–2017), Telugu-language writer, wins the Jnanpith Award for his long poem *Viswambhara*.

1989: V.P. SINGH—A NEW PRIME MINISTER

In 1989 too, Rajiv Gandhi continued his policies of development and his attempts to improve relations with the country's neighbours. In April, he started the Jawahar Rozgar Yojana by merging two existing schemes, by way of which a minimum of 100 days of employment was provided in rural areas. As part of his foreign policy, he made an official visit to Pakistan in July 1989. In the Maldives, he helped protect President Maumoon Abdul Gayoom, who was being threatened by a coup, by paradropping Indian Army troops. However, Rajiv's popularity was gradually declining. He was accused in a number of corruption cases, though nothing was proved against him.

He had almost completed five years in office when he announced elections. These took place between 22 and 26 November 1989, and the Congress (I) won only 193 seats. They decided not to form the government. V.P. Singh became the prime minister on 2 December.

Vishwanath Pratap Singh (25 June 1931–27 November 2008) had been finance and defence minister in Rajiv Gandhi's government, but he resigned in April 1987 and was also expelled from the Congress. His current party, the Janata Dal, along with the Telugu Desam, DMK, the Asom Gana Parishad and the Congress (S) had formed an alliance known as the National Front, which won 144 seats. It was able to form the government with the support of the Bharatiya Janata Party, with eighty-six seats, and the leftist parties, with fifty-four.

❋ OTHER KEY EVENTS

On 8 December, Rubaiya Sayeed, daughter of the then home minister Mufti Mohammad Sayeed, was kidnapped by members of the Jammu Kashmir Liberation Front. Their demand for the release of five of their members from prison was accepted to ensure her liberation. After this, militancy in Kashmir increased.

In Tamil Nadu, the DMK won the assembly elections held in January, and M. Karunanidhi became chief minister.

Significant international happenings also had an effect on India. That year, the Cold War ended, the Berlin Wall fell and the Tiananmen Square massacre took place.

❋ THE NEHRU CENTENARY

On 14 November 1989, a hundred years after Jawaharlal Nehru's birth, his birth centenary was celebrated. There were many different programmes for the celebration. Fifty thousand schoolchildren prepared a placard display, depicting India's story and successes, while the Nehru Shatabdi Natya Samaroh, organized by the Sangeet Natak Akademi, put up fifteen plays over two weeks. Mahesh Elkunchwar and Bijon Bhattacharya were among the playwrights whose plays were staged. Elkunchwar's *Wada Chirebandi* (Old Stone Mansion), directed by Vijaya Mehta, is a family-cum-social drama. Utpal Dutt's *Kallol* (Sound of the Waves) was also presented. Other plays included *Adhe Adhure*, *Hayavadana*, *Ghashiram Kotwal*,

Urubhangam and *Chakravyuha*. At the same time, Chauraha, the first all-India street theatre festival, took place over three days and included thirteen groups. These plays looked at the problems of superstition, corruption, dowry and communalism.

The Jawaharlal Nehru Cup, a cricket tournament, was launched to celebrate the centenary, while a science and technology seminar series was held.

Even special coins were minted. Four types of proof-set coins and four UNC (uncirculated, not for general use) coins were issued. In the former group, a 100-rupee single-coin set cost Rs 350. A special five-rupee coin too was released on the occasion.

Nehru's birth centenary was also celebrated in Latin American countries.

❋ SAFDAR HASHMI IS KILLED

Safdar Hashmi (b. 12 April 1954), the founder of the theatre group Jana Natya Manch, died on 2 January after he was injured on the 1st while staging a play called *Halla Bol* (Raise Your Voice) in Ghaziabad, near Delhi. He was attacked by the supporters of a municipal election candidate.

Jana Natya Manch was founded in 1973, and staged many socially relevant and controversial plays. Safdar was a member of the Communist Party of India (Marxist), and his plays revealed the problems of the poor and those of women. He also produced documentaries, wrote books and poems, worked as a lecturer and journalist, and was, for some time, press information officer of the West Bengal government. After his death, he became a symbol of resistance to authority. The Safdar Hashmi Memorial Trust was founded in his memory a month after his death. He has inspired films, books and even a painting by M.F. Husain, whose *Tribute to Hashmi* sold for a million dollars.

TWO GREAT MUSICIANS

ALI AKBAR KHAN WINS THE PADMA VIBHUSHAN

Allauddin Khan's son Ali Akbar Khan (14 April 1922–18 June 2009) was another excellent sarod player, who studied with his father and his uncle, Aftabuddin. He was the court musician of Jodhpur, and participated in the activities of Uday Shankar's India Cultural Centre, Simtola. In 1956, he founded the Ali Akbar College of Music in Calcutta, and in 1967, another one in San Rafael, in Marin County, California. By this time, he had performed at numerous concerts around the world, apart from his appearances on All India Radio. He received a number of awards, including the Sangeet Natak Akademi Award (1963), the Padma Bhushan (1967) and the Padma Vibhushan (1989).

Ali Akbar Khan

Ali Akbar was a great composer. He composed music for films, and created a new raga, Chandranandan, by combining elements of four existing ragas. He performed with other musicians, such as Ravi Shankar, Nikhil Banerjee and Alla Rakha, even including western maestros such as George Harrison and Bob Dylan. He spent the last forty years of his life in the USA. Several of his twelve children (from three wives) are musicians.

LATIF AHMED KHAN DIES

Latif Ahmed Khan (1942–89) was an expert tabla player of Hindustani music, who belonged to the Delhi gharana. He was born into a family of musicians and studied with his uncle, Gameh

Khan, and his son Inam Ali Khan. He performed in India and all over Europe with noted musicians, such as Ravi Shankar and Bhimsen Joshi, as well as with dancers such as Birju Maharaj. He also composed a new tala, called the Latif tala, which has five and a quarter beats. He came to be called Allahwale (Blessed by God) because of his virtuosity and the purity of his notes. His two sons, Babar Khan and Akbar Khan, are also noted tabla players. His main disciple was Divyang Vakil.

❖ TRENDS IN BOLLYWOOD

In the late 1980s, love stories became popular, even those that ended in tragedy, like *Qayamat se Qayamat Tak* (1988), popularly known as QSQT. The film is based on Shakespeare's *Romeo and Juliet*. Directed by Mansoor Khan and produced by Nasir Hussain, the lead actors are Aamir Khan and Juhi Chawla. *Maine Pyar Kiya* (1989) was another such hit.

❖ SALMAN KHAN

Salman Khan (b. 27 December 1965), a top Bollywood actor, made his debut in 1988, in the film *Biwi Ho To Aisi*. Salman's second film was *Maine Pyar Kiya*, which won him the Filmfare Award for the best actor. His other notable films include *Hum Aapke Hain Koun..!* (1994), *Kuch Kuch Hota Hai* (1998), *Dabangg* (2010), *Ek Tha Tiger* (2012), *Dabangg 2* (2012), *Bajrangi Bhaijaan* (2015) and *Sultan* (2016). Salman has won a number of other awards, including two National Film Awards, as well as the Star Screen, IIFA and Zee Cine awards. His charitable organization, Being Human, provides education and healthcare for the underprivileged. He launched his own film production company, Salman Khan Being Human Productions, in 2011.

🟅 THE VOTING AGE IS LOWERED

The voting age is lowered from twenty-one to eighteen years by the Sixty-First Amendment to the Constitution, 1989. The bill was passed by the Lok Sabha and the Rajya Sabha in 1988, and then ratified by twenty states, receiving the assent of the President in March 1989.

ALSO IN 1989

22 May: The Agni-I missile is test-fired. With this, India becomes a missile power.

August: The first women's billiards and snooker nationals are held in Bangalore.

5 October: Salman Rushdie's *Satanic Verses* is banned in India.

6 October: M. Fathima Beevi (b. 30 April 1927) becomes the first female judge of the Supreme Court. She later becomes a member of the National Human Rights Commission and Governor of Tamil Nadu (1997–2001).

15 November: Sachin Tendulkar makes his Test debut in international cricket.

The 14th Dalai Lama is awarded the Nobel Peace Prize.

India wins a gold medal in archery in the sixth Asian Archery Championships, held in Beijing. The Indian team consists of Limba Ram, Shyam Lal and Skalzang Dorje.

November: The National Open School, later renamed the National Institute of Open Schooling, is established under the Ministry of Human Resource Development.

Qurratulain Hyder (1927–2007) wins the Jnanpith Award for her Urdu novel *Akhir-e Shab ke Humsafar* (translated as *Fireflies in the Mist*).

1990: ANOTHER GOVERNMENT—CHANDRA SHEKHAR

V.P. Singh and the National Front only remained in power till 10 November 1990. Their government too had to deal with the problems in Punjab, Kashmir and Assam.

State elections held in eight states and the union territory of Pondicherry in February 1990 indicated the changing political scenario. The Indian National Congress won only in Maharashtra and Arunachal Pradesh. The DMK succeeded in Pondicherry, while the remaining states—Orissa, Bihar, Gujarat, Rajasthan, Madhya Pradesh and Himachal Pradesh—were shared between the BJP and the Janata Dal. At the Centre, a political struggle continued among the disparate parties of the National Front that held power together.

Devi Lal, former chief minister of Haryana, was forced to resign on 1 August 1990 after he had ensured that his son, Om Prakash Chautala, succeeded him. In addition to that, he forged a letter to the President, which he claimed had been written by V.P. Singh. The letter made allegations of corruption against Arun Nehru and Arif Mohammad Khan. After his resignation, he threatened to hold a huge farmers' rally on 9 August, to show the extent of his popularity and support. V.P. Singh diverted attention by announcing that part of the Mandal Commission recommendations on reservation would be put into practice. By this, 27 per cent of jobs would be reserved for backward castes, in addition to the 22.5 per cent already reserved for scheduled tribes and castes. This led to protests and chaos across the country.

The BJP too was trying to make political gains. On 25 September 1990, L.K. Advani, BJP leader, led a rath yatra from Somnath to Ayodhya to lay the foundation of a Ram mandir at the Babri Masjid site. This procession was stopped in Samastipur, Bihar, before it could reach its destination. Conflicts between Hindus and Muslims followed. The BJP's eighty-six members in the Lok Sabha withdrew their support for the government. Then, on 5 November, the Janata Dal split. Chandra Shekhar and Devi Lal formed the Janata Dal (Socialist) with fifty-four members of the former Janata Dal. On 7 November, V.P. Singh had to resign after a no-confidence motion. On 10 November, a new government was formed with Chandra Shekhar (1927–2007) as prime minister. He was a socialist and a follower of Acharya Narendra Dev. Shekhar's party was supported by the Congress.

❉ PREMCHAND DEGRA IS AWARDED THE PADMA SHRI

Premchand Degra (b. 1 December 1955) is one of India's best-known bodybuilders, who was declared the most developed bodybuilder in the 1987 Mr Universe contest, held in Sweden. Premchand began his career in bodybuilding by winning Mr Punjab. He won the Mr India title nine times and the Mr Asia contest eight times. Among his many other wins, he came first in the middleweight category of the World Amateur Bodybuilding Championships held in Brisbane in 1988 and was crowned Mr Universe. He received the Arjuna Award in 1986 and the Padma Shri in 1990.

BODYBUILDING IN INDIA

Bodybuilding was initially associated with wrestling and weightlifting, but then became an individual sport. Since 1980, bodybuilding competitions have been divided into height and weight classes.

After Independence, there have been several successful bodybuilders, such as Monotosh Roy, Manohar Aich, Parimal Roy, Raymond D'Souza, Sunil Kumar Patra and T.V. Pauly. A list of India's ten best bodybuilders as of 2014 includes:

- Murali Kumar, who won the Mr India title in 2013 and 2014;
- Sangram Chougule, who won Mr Universe in 2012 and 2014 in the 85 kg category;
- Suhas Khamkar, who has won the Mr India title nine times;
- Rajendran Mani, formerly in the Indian Air Force, who won the 2013 World Bodybuilding and Physique Sports Championship in the 90 kg category, held in Budaörs, Hungary;
- Ankur Sharma, who has won Mr India and world titles;
- Ashish Sakharkar, who is a four-time Mr India champion, and has also won other contests. He was a bronze medal winner in the 2011 Mr Universe contest;
- Hira Lal, who won Mr Universe 2011 in the 65 kg category;
- Varinder Singh Ghuman, who won Mr India 2009 and has also acted in films;
- Amit Chhetri, who won the Federation Cup, 2013;
- Neeraj Kumar, who was Mr India 2013 and bronze medallist at the Mr Universe contest in the same year.

> **WHAT DO BODYBUILDERS EAT?**
>
> Sangram Chougule eats a kilo of fish, half a kilo of chicken, milk and boiled vegetables every day! But some, like Hira Lal and Varinder Singh Ghuman, are vegetarians.

❋ BABA AMTE WINS THE TEMPLETON PRIZE

Baba Amte (26 December 1914–9 February 2008) was a social reformer, who worked for lepers and for the poor. Though he was named Murlidhar Devidas, he was affectionately called Baba by his family. Born into an extremely wealthy *jagirdar* (landlord) family, Baba had a gun to hunt with and drove a sports car in his young days. He qualified as a lawyer and began his legal practice, but then became involved in the freedom movement and came in touch with Mahatma Gandhi. He gave up all luxuries and became a Gandhian, wearing khadi and spinning the charkha. He was shocked by the poverty of the villagers in his family estate in Chandrapur district, and started helping them. Another transformative event took place when he was in his late forties and he saw a person dying of leprosy, whom no one would touch because of the stigma attached to lepers.

Baba Amte opened a leprosy clinic in Warora, Chandrapur, and later constructed a leprosy centre in Anandwan, Maharashtra. He was helped by his wife, Sadhana Guleshastri, who, though also born into a wealthy family, supported his work. Their sons, daughters-in-law and grandsons are also involved in community work. For some time, Baba Amte also joined the Narmada Bachao Andolan, a movement against the Sardar Sarovar Dam. He received innumerable awards, including the Padma Shri (1971), the Padma Vibhushan (1986), the Ramon Magsaysay Award (1985), the

United Nations Prize in the Field of Human Rights (1988), the Templeton Prize (1990) and the Gandhi Peace Prize (1999).

❋ TWO MUSICIANS WIN THE PADMA VIBHUSHAN

Semmangudi Srinivasa Iyer (25 July 1908–31 October 2003) was a renowned vocalist of Karnatic music. After training with Semmangudi Narayanaswamy Iyer, Thiruvadaimaruthur Sakharama Rao and Maharajapuram Viswanatha Iyer, he began performing at concerts from 1926. His singing was technically perfect, and at the same time it had a devotional quality. Semmangudi received numerous awards, including the Sangeet Natak Akademi Award (1953) and the Padma Bhushan (1969), before being awarded the Padma Vibhushan in 1990.

Kumar Gandharva (8 April 1924–12 January 1992), a singer of Hindustani classical music, was another musician who received the Padma Vibhushan in 1990. He was a child prodigy, who sang melodiously since the age of six. He was initially named Shivaputra Siddharamayya Komkali, but was renamed Kumar Gandharva (Young Gandharva) after the divine singers and musicians of myth, the *gandharva*s. He trained with B.R. Deodhar but did not follow any gharana, and developed his own style instead. In his twenties, he suffered from tuberculosis, which affected his voice, but he recovered and began singing again. Apart from classical ragas, Kumar Gandharva sang bhajans and folk songs.

❋ MADHURI DIXIT

Madhuri Dixit (b. 15 May 1967) is a leading Bollywood actor. Her first film was

Madhuri Dixit

Abodh (1984), and she went on to act in many hits in the 1980s, 1990s and 2000s. Among these are *Ram Lakhan* (1989), *Dil* (1990), *Hum Aapke Hain Koun..!* (1994), *Pukar* (2000) and *Devdas* (2002). She is known for her dancing skills, and was artist M.F. Husain's muse. She married Dr Shriram Nene in 1999 and they have two children.

Madhuri took a break after her children were born, but returned to act in *Aaja Nachle* in 2007, followed by other films. She has also been a judge on the reality dance show *Jhalak Dikhhla Jaa*. She is the recipient of several Filmfare and other cinema awards, as well as the Padma Shri (2008).

ALSO IN 1990

19 January: Death of Osho, also known as Rajneesh (b. 11 December 1931), an independent philosopher, who set up ashrams in the USA and India, and wrote over a hundred books. His ashram in Pune is still flourishing.

7 March: Death of Shuddhananda Bharati (b. 11 May 1897), philosopher, who wrote the Tamil *mahakavyam* (epic poem) *Bharata Shakti*, as well as other books and poems

4–10 May: A cyclone in Andhra Pradesh kills about a thousand people and 1,00,000 animals.

2 June: Death of Shriram Sharma Acharya (b. 1911), founder of the Gayatri Pariwar, a spiritual and social organization

21 October: Death of Prabhat Ranjan Sarkar (b. 1921), philosopher and author

1 December: Death of Vijaya Lakshmi Pandit (b. 18 August 1900), sister of Jawaharlal Nehru and participant in the freedom movement, who held important government posts after Independence

The Jnanpith is awarded to Vinayaka Krishna Gokak for his Kannada work *Bharatha Sindhu Rashmi*.

1991: RAJIV GANDHI IS ASSASSINATED

In the beginning of 1991, Chandra Shekhar was still prime minister, with his party being backed by the Congress. However, the Congress withdrew support on 5 March 1991. Elections had to be held again, and these began on 19 May 1991. After just one phase of voting, an event took place that temporarily suspended the elections. Rajiv Gandhi was assassinated.

As Rajiv Gandhi had been campaigning for votes across the country, it had seemed that the Congress had regained its popularity. Perhaps the people were tired of the constant changes in the government. This lack of continuity meant that government policies and development programmes could not be put into practice.

As part of his campaign, Rajiv Gandhi had reached Sriperumbudur, in Tamil Nadu, on 21 May at around 10 p.m., where a crowd had been waiting to greet him. A woman had come forward to garland him, and detonated a bomb she was wearing. Rajiv Gandhi, his killer and others nearby had been blown apart. Later the killer was identified as Dhanu, a member of the LTTE— the group was still angry that the IPKF had been sent to Sri Lanka.

After Rajiv's shocking death, the people of India felt deep sorrow as he was such a young leader. Rajiv was only forty-six years old.

The elections were resumed and completed in June. The Congress won 232 seats and the next highest number, 120 seats, was secured by the Bharatiya Janata Party. The Janata Dal had fifty-six seats. The Congress managed to form the government, and chose P.V. Narasimha Rao as prime minister. Born on 28 June 1921, Narasimha Rao took part in the freedom movement and after Independence, held various important posts. He had been chief minister of Andhra Pradesh and a union minister, as well as a writer and poet.

Soon the Janata Dal had another split, and the Janata Dal (A), led by Ajit Singh, joined the Congress, increasing their number of seats to 266.

❋ M.F. HUSAIN IS AWARDED THE PADMA VIBHUSHAN

Maqbool Fida Husain (29 November 1913 or 17 September 1915–9 June 2011)[22] was perhaps India's greatest artist in the post-Independence period. He was the winner of many awards, including the Padma Vibhushan (1991), and was known as the Picasso of India.

Born in Pandharpur, Maharashtra, Husain was a self-taught artist. He moved to Bombay in 1935 and began painting billboards for Hindi movies, also working in a toy factory. Simultaneously, he created paintings, and held an exhibition in 1947, soon becoming part of the Bombay Progressive Artists' Group. Husain had his own style as a painter, developed from cubism, and in his early years, he was known for his unique paintings of prancing horses. An important early work of his is *Man* (1951). He also painted people, scenes from the Ramayana and the Mahabharata, Hindu deities and more. His innovative series of paintings in the 1970s was titled Passage through Human Space. Later in life, he was

---

[22] Both birthdates are quoted across sources.

entranced by the actor Madhuri Dixit and portrayed her in several artworks. She was also his inspiration for and lead star in his film *Gaja Gamini* (2000).

In 2006, he left India because of threats from some Hindu groups, who objected to his paintings of Hindu goddesses, and in 2010, he became a citizen of Qatar. In 2011, he died in London after a heart attack, and is buried in Brookwood Cemetery, England.

M.F. Husain's six highest-selling paintings are:

* *Battle of Ganga and Jamuna* (sold for Rs 6.5 crore at Christie's South Asian Modern + Contemporary Art sale, held in New York in 2008);
* *Tribute to Hashmi*;
* *The Sixth Seal*;
* *Cinq Sens* (Five Senses);
* *The Puppet Dancers*;
* *The Horse That Looked Back*.

In 2013, Sotheby's celebrated Husain's centenary year.

A reproduction of M.F. Husain's *Sprinkling Horses*

BHARATANATYAM

Bharatanatyam, one of the classical dances of India, is described in Bharata's Natya Shastra, and used to be performed in south India as a temple dance. It was earlier known as Dasi Attam, Sadir Attam and other names, and would be performed by devadasis. In the early nineteenth century, Ponnaiya, Chinnaiya, Sivanandam and Vadivelu, four brothers who lived in the court of the Maratha ruler Serfoji II, in Thanjavur, gave the dance its present form. Rukmini Devi Arundale made further changes to its performance. Bharatanatyam has three broad categories:

- Nritta, or pure dance;
- Nritya, or interpretive dance depicting emotions;
- Natya, or dance that narrates a story.

A typical dance routine begins with Alarippu (literally a flowering bud), an invocatory dance, followed by Jatiswaram, the pure dance that uses a combination of notes, then Shabdam, which uses lyrics and notes, then Varnam, a combination of pure dance and abhinaya (expression), concluding finally with the pure dance or Tillana. Varnams may be substituted by lighter romantic items like Padams and Javalis. Bharatanatyam is always accompanied by music, which includes instruments and vocalists. Rhythm is an important aspect of it.

Apart from Rukmini Devi Arundale, some of the noted Bharatanatyam dancers in the post-Independence period have been: Meenakshi Sundaram Pillai (22 September 1869–1954), teacher of Rukmini Devi and other dancers;

> T. Balasaraswati (1918–84), also a reputed Karnatic music vocalist; Mrinalini Sarabhai (11 May 1918–21 January 2016), dancer and choreographer, who founded the Darpana Academy of Performing Arts; Mallika Sarabhai (b. 9 May 1954), also a Kuchipudi dancer, film-maker and social activist; Sonal Mansingh (b. 30 April 1944), also an Odissi dancer and winner of various awards, including the Padma Vibhushan (2003); Yamini Krishnamurthy (b. 1940), who has trained in Bharatanatyam, Odissi and Kuchipudi, established the Yamini School of Dance, New Delhi, in 1990 and won the Padma Bhushan (2001); Alarmel Valli (b. 1957) and Padma Subrahmanyam (b. 4 February 1943), among others.

❋ DILIP KUMAR

Dilip Kumar (b. 11 December 1922), whose original name was Muhammad Yusuf Khan, is one of India's most influential actors. His first film was *Jwar Bhata* (1944), for which he changed his name to Dilip Kumar. He received the first Filmfare Award for the best actor, in 1954. Among his notable roles are those of Devdas in *Devdas* (1955) and Prince Salim in *Mughal-e-Azam*. His success declined in the 1970s, but in 1986, he had a key role in the hit film *Karma*, and in 1991, in *Saudagar*, which also did well at the box office. Among his many awards is the Filmfare Lifetime Achievement Award (1993).

❋ M. BALAMURALI KRISHNA WINS THE PADMA VIBHUSHAN

M. Balamurali Krishna (1930–22 November 2016) was one of India's most renowned Karnatic classical music vocalists. He too was awarded the Padma Vibhushan in 1991. He was born in Sankaraguptam, in present-day Andhra Pradesh, to a musical family. His mother, a veena player, died when he was a child. The young Balamurali trained with Parupalli Ramakrishnayya Pantulu and began performing at the age of eight. Apart from being a classical singer, he played several instruments, acted and sang in films, and composed music.

Balamurali created new ragas as well as talas, and composed music in all seventy-two basic ragas. His numerous awards include the Padma Shri (1971), the Sangeet Natak Akademi Award (1975), the Sangita Kalanidhi title from the Music Academy, Chennai (1978), the Padma Vibhushan (1991) and the Chevalier de L'Ordre des Arts et des Lettres (Knight of the Order of Arts and Letters), an award from the French government (2005). He also received two National Awards: for the best playback singer for the film *Hamsageethe* (1975) and for the best music director for the film *Madhvacharya* (1986). Balamurali performed at more than 25,000 concerts around the world.

❋ THE 1991 CENSUS OF INDIA

The census results of 1991 indicated an increase in population and in the number of cities. There were now 300 cities with a population of over a lakh, and twenty-three cities with a population of over a million. The total population had risen to 83,85,83,988.

ALSO IN 1991

22 September: Death of actor Durga Khote, who acted in several Hindi films from the 1930s to the 1970s

The Cultural Festival of India is organized in New Jersey, USA. The thirty-one-day event, held in Middlesex County College, Edison, has over a million visitors.

Rajiv Gandhi is posthumously awarded the Bharat Ratna.

Shanno Khurana (b. 1927), Hindustani music vocalist, is awarded the Padma Shri.

Star TV is launched in India.

The Jnanpith Award is presented to Bengali-language poet Subhash Mukhopadhyay for his poetry collection *Padatik* (The Foot Soldier, 1940).

1992: NARASIMHA RAO— ECONOMIC REFORMS

In 1991, when Narasimha Rao became prime minister, India faced a financial crisis, with a huge debt and low foreign exchange reserves. Though some economic reforms were implemented in the 1980s, the International Monetary Fund (IMF) insisted that more were required. Narasimha Rao appointed Manmohan Singh as finance minister and put in place a series of new policies. These led to economic growth, accompanied by the rise of new consumer goods. The reforms had long-lasting effects and changed India, ushering in a new era of modernization.

Narasimha Rao

❋ OTHER KEY EVENTS

Another incident took place in 1992 that has had a long-term impact. On 6 December 1992, *kar sevak*s (voluntary workers), led by leaders of the Bharatiya Janata Party, the Vishva Hindu

Parishad and other groups, destroyed Babri Masjid, the disputed site in Ayodhya. This led to increased conflict between Hindus and Muslims.

The Panchayati Raj Bill, which was formulated by Rajiv Gandhi, was passed in 1992 and enacted in 1993, along with the Nagar Palika Bill, to regulate elections to municipal corporations. These respectively became the Seventy-Third and Seventy-Fourth Amendments to the Constitution. This is because the panchayati raj system that had been functioning since 1958–59 had no uniformity or regularity, and adequate finances were not available.

The Mandal proposals were finally passed. These had earlier caused nationwide unrest, but now did not attract much attention.

A new political party, the Samajwadi Party, was founded in Lucknow, Uttar Pradesh, and led by Mulayam Singh Yadav. Its members were mainly from the Janata Dal.

Among the country's new foreign policy initiatives was India's establishment of diplomatic relations with Israel for the first time, even while continuing to support Palestine.

● KARUNA SRI DIES

Karuna Sri (4 August 1912–21 June 1992), Jandhyala Papayya Sastry's alias, was a noted Telugu-language poet. Born in Kommuru, a village in Guntur district, he wrote a number of poems, including 'Pushpa Vilapamu' and 'Kunthi Kumari'. He was known as Karuna Sri because of the *karuna* (compassion) in his works.

In 'Pushpa Vilapamu' (Lament of the Flowers), he indicates how he was going to pluck flowers for his daily worship when the flowers began to speak to him, and asked him why he was killing them and why even others treated them so badly. Here are two verses of this composition from K. Godavari Sarma's 1944 translation:[23]

> You are born in the land of the Buddha,
> Why is natural love just dead in you?
> O murderer, murdering beauty,
> Tainted indeed is your human birth.
> For God's sake leave your worship,
> Don't cut our innocent throats!
> Oh! What grace can you earn
> Killing us with your own hands?

❈ DHARAMVIR BHARATI: *SURAJ KA SATVAN GHODA*

Suraj ka Satvan Ghoda (The Seventh Horse of the Sun) won the 1992 National Award for the best feature film in Hindi, with Shyam Benegal as the director. The story is based on Dharamvir Bharati's novel of the same name. Dharamvir (1926–97) was a poet and writer as well as editor of the Hindi magazine *Dharmayug* from 1960 to 1987.

❈ RAHI MASOOM RAZA PASSES AWAY

Rahi Masoom Raza (1 September 1927–15 March 1992), an Urdu poet, novelist and screenwriter, wrote scripts for television serials and for a number of Hindi films.

Raza was born in the village of Gangauli, in Ghazipur district of Uttar Pradesh, studied at Aligarh Muslim University and obtained a PhD in Urdu literature. He worked as a lecturer at AMU for some time. Among his novels, *Aadha Gaon* depicts the tragedies

---

[23] Quoted in *Modern Indian Literature: An Anthology; Surveys and Poems*, ed. K.M. George (Delhi: Sahitya Akademi, 1992).

accompanying Partition while *Neem ka Ped* is the story of a tenant labourer, which was made into a TV serial. He is best known for his script for Ravi Chopra's popular tele-serial *Mahabharat*.

❋ MALLIKARJUN MANSUR IS AWARDED THE PADMA VIBHUSHAN

Mallikarjun Mansur (1 January 1911–12 September 1992) was a singer of Hindustani classical music, who mostly sang khayal. Born in Mansur, near Dharwad, in present-day Karnataka, his father apprenticed him to a Yakshagana theatre group, where he was encouraged to sing. He began learning Karnatic music with Pandit Appaya Swamy, and then Hindustani music under Nilkanth Bua Alurmath, who introduced him to Alladiya Khan. He then trained under Alladiya's son Manji Khan, and after his death, with Manji's brother, Bhurji Khan. Mallikarjun gave numerous performances, and was known for singing rare ragas, such as Adambari Kedar and Asa Jogiya. He received several awards, including the Padma Vibhushan.

ALSO IN 1992

The tenth conference of the Non-Aligned Movement takes place in Jakarta, Indonesia.

The Festival of China is held in India, and the performers tour across eleven cities.

29 May: Indo-US joint naval exercises are held with American troops.

The Children's Film Society, India, which was set up in 1955, is renamed the National Centre of Films for Children And Young People (NCYP) and its scope is expanded.

17 May: The National Commission for Minorities is set up by an Act of Parliament, replacing the earlier commission set up in January 1978. The organization safeguards the interests of minority communities.

Satyajit Ray receives the honorary Academy Award.

The Jnanpith is awarded to Hindi writer Naresh Mehta (1922–2000).

1993: NARASIMHA RAO CONTINUES AS PRIME MINISTER

Narasimha Rao stayed on as prime minister, though he faced a vote of no confidence that year. He did not have a clear majority, but four members of the Jharkhand Mukti Morcha voted in his favour and saved the government. Later, in 1996, he was accused of having bribed them to vote for him.

❋ OTHER KEY EVENTS

Across India, there are many ethnic groups. Among them is the Bodo community of the North-east, who include a number of tribes, among them the Cutiya, the Kachari, the Rabha, the Garo, the Mech, the Koch, the Dhimal, the Jaijong, the Dimasa, the Galang, the Hojai, the Lalung, the Tippera and the Morah. These tribes of the plains of Assam, led by the All Bodo Students' Union, had started an agitation in 1987 for a separate state. This was accompanied by considerable violence. An agreement was signed in 1993 to set up the Bodoland Autonomous Council, under which they'd have some authority within the state. However, Bodos continued to demand full statehood.

❋ KELUCHARAN MOHAPATRA ESTABLISHES SRJAN

Among the great Odissi dancers was Kelucharan Mohapatra (1926–2004), who gave several performances and also played the pakhawaj. In 1993, he set up his dance institute, Srjan, in Bhubaneswar. Kelucharan received a number of awards, such as the Sangeet Natak Akademi Award (1966), the Padma Shri (1974), the Padma Bhushan (1988), the Kalidas Samman (1988–89), the Sangeet Natak Akademi Ratna Sadasya (1991) and the Padma Vibhushan (2000). His notable students include Sanjukta Panigrahi, Gangadhar Pradhan, Nandita Behera, Sonal Mansingh, Kumkum Mohanty, Madhavi Mudgal and Aditi Bandyopadhyay.

Sanjukta Panigrahi (1944–97) was responsible for popularizing the dance style.

An Odissi dancer

ODISSI

Odissi is the classical dance style of Odisha, which used to be performed in temples, initially by women and later by boys, known as *gotipua*s, who were dressed as girls. The dance features *bhangi*s, which are stylized postures, and *karana*s, which are fluid. The karanas are the basic dance units.

The dance begins with an invocation and an offering of flowers, followed by Bhumi Pranam (salutation to Mother Earth), then Batu (pure dance) and then Pallavi (lyrical and graceful dance), concluding finally with nritya, conveying a story, and natya, a dance drama. The dance sequence ends in Moksha, which is similar to the Tillana of Bharatanatyam. An Odissi performance is accompanied by music.

Among other noted Odissi dancers are Surendranath Jena, Jhelum Paranjape, Mayadhar Raut and Kiran Segal, who started studying dance with her mother, Zohra Segal, and then trained in Bharatanatyam, after which she learnt Odissi with Mayadhar Raut. Kiran is both a dancer and a choreographer, and has an individual style.

❋ A SUITABLE BOY

Vikram Seth (b. 20 June 1952), one of India's greatest writers, had his epic novel *A Suitable Boy* published in 1993. The novel, set in independent India, is over 1300 pages long. It sold over a million copies, won the WH Smith Literary Award and made the author famous.

Born in Calcutta, and educated at The Doon School, Dehradun, and then at the universities of Oxford and Stanford, Vikram Seth had already written a number of books by 1993, including *Mappings* (1980), a volume of poems; *From Heaven's Lake* (1983), a description of his travels as a hitch-hiker from China through Tibet to India, which won the Thomas Cook Travel Book Award; *The Humble Administrator's Garden* (1985) and *The Golden Gate* (1986), a novel in rhyming verse. After his return to India in 1987, *All You Who Sleep Tonight*, another volume of poems, was published in 1990, and *Beastly Tales from Here and There* in 1992.

Since *A Suitable Boy*, Seth has written more works: *An Equal Music* (1999), followed by *Two Lives* (2005). He is currently writing *A Suitable Girl*. He has received several awards, including the title of Commander of the Order of the British Empire (CBE), in 2001, for his services to literature.

● UTPAL DUTT PASSES AWAY

Utpal Dutt (29 March 1929–19 August 1993) was a multitalented actor, director, producer, writer and theatre personality. Born in Shillong, he was the son of G.R. Dutt and Sailo, and studied in Shillong and Calcutta. Initially, he worked in theatre, establishing a Shakespeare theatre group in 1947 and acting in the Bard's plays. He renamed it the Little Theatre Group in 1949, which at first, performed Western plays and later, plays translated into Bengali as well as original Bengali plays. For some time, he also worked as a journalist with *Statesman*. The first film he acted in was *Michael Madhusudan* (1950). He acted in a number of films thereafter, including *Bhuvan Shome* (1969), *The Guru* (1969), *Hirak Rajar Deshe* (1980), *Agantuk* (1991), *Jana Aranya* (1976), *Guddi* (1971) and several others.

Dutt wrote and produced a number of plays and directed some films. As he was a Marxist, the themes of his plays were often not appreciated by the government, and some were banned. His actors also faced assault. His play *Dushapner Nagari* (City of Nightmares) was banned by the Congress government in 1975. *Ebar Rajar Pala* (Now It's the King's Turn) was a play about the Emergency. Both were extremely popular in Bengal. His books include *Chayer Dhoya* and *Shakespeare Samaj Chetana*, the latter on theatre. Utpal Dutt also directed and acted in many plays, among them *Titas Ekti Nadir Naam* (an adaptation of Adwaita Mallabarman's novel of the same name) and *Jallianwala Bagh*.

Utpal Dutt received a number of awards, including the Sangeet Natak Akademi Fellowship for lifetime achievement in theatre (1990); the National Film Award for the best actor, for *Bhuvan Shome* (1970); the Filmfare Best Comedian Award (1980, 1982, 1987) for three of his films: *Gol Maal*, *Naram Garam* and

Rang Birangi. His comic roles were indicative of his versatility, as most of his work had serious themes.

● SOUND SCAPES

Music that is close to nature is often referred to as soundscapes. A series of recordings called Sound Scapes include compositions by Hariprasad Chaurasia.

Music of the Rivers (1993), composed by Chaurasia, begins with 'Water Poems' and ends with 'Delta: Journey to the Sea'. Two others in the Sound Scape series are *Music of the Mountains* (1993), composed by Shivkumar Sharma, and *Music of the Deserts* (1993), by Zakir Hussain.

Another series was called The Elements, in which Chaurasia composed *Wind*, and Zakir Hussain, *Space*, both in 1995.

ALSO IN 1993

16 July: Death of Nissar Hussain Khan (b. 12 December 1906), Hindustani music vocalist

24 August: Death of D.B. Deodhar (b. 14 January 1892), Indian cricketer. The Deodhar Trophy is named after him.

1 November: Death of Naina Devi (b. 1918), Hindustani music vocalist

The Jnanpith is awarded to Odia-language poet Sitakant Mahapatra (b. 1937) 'for his outstanding contribution to the enrichment of Indian literature during the period 1973–92'.[24]

---

[24] The Bharatiya Jnanpith 1993 Citation, quoted in *The Text and the Context: An Encounter with Jnanpith Laureates* (New Delhi: Bharatiya Jnanpith, 1994).

1994: ECONOMIC GROWTH

Narasimha Rao's precarious government continued into 1994. In fact, the number of Congress members in Parliament had risen to 266. Meanwhile, a new political party, the Samata Party, was founded by George Fernandes and Nitish Kumar, who had previously been part of the Janata Dal.

A health crisis took hold of the country as a plague breakout was reported in the city of Surat, Gujarat, and between August and October, spread to other states after people left the city in fear. A total of fifty-six deaths were reported across India. A positive result was that following this, the city of Surat was renovated and disinfected, and remains the cleanest city in India today.

In foreign affairs, the fourth G-15 summit was held in New Delhi. The Group of Fifteen originally included fifteen countries from Asia, Latin America and Africa, its aim being to increase prosperity among the nations through cooperation, trade, technology and investment. The number of member countries rose to nineteen, but currently there are seventeen, though the name remains the same.

ROSHEN DALAL

❖ MRINALINI MUKHERJEE HOLDS A SOLO EXHIBITION

Mrinalini Mukherjee (1949–2 February 2015), a Bombay-born artist, was the daughter of artists Benode Behari and Leela Mukherjee. She studied art at the M.S. University of Baroda, and began using natural fibres as a medium under her mentor, K.G. Subramanyan. She received a scholarship to study sculpture at the West Surrey College of Art and Design in the UK, and there she developed her unique style. Initially she used hemp and sisal ropes, dyed in rich colours, to create her sculptures. Her figures of women seem to emerge from the world of vegetation. She held several exhibitions abroad, and in 1994, had her first international solo show at the Museum of Modern Art, Oxford. Mrinalini eventually moved from fibre to ceramics, and later to bronze. Her largest fibre mural, a 14 x 70 ft installation, is displayed at the Gandhi Memorial Institute in Mauritius.

A retrospective of her work, titled *Transfigurations*, opened towards the end of January 2015 at the National Gallery of Modern Art, New Delhi, but Mrinalini was unable to attend. She died of lung problems in early February. Ninety of her works, including fibre, ceramic and bronze sculptures, were displayed at the exhibition. Some of the fibre sculptures, *Pakshi*, *Devi* and *Vanshree*, resemble nature spirits. *Palmscape IX* is one of her last bronze works.

A reproduction of *Palmscape IX*

❖ VISHWA MOHAN BHATT RECEIVES THE GRAMMY AWARD

Vishwa Mohan Bhatt (b. 27 July 1950), a musician who plays Hindustani classical and fusion music, was born to musician parents Manmohan Bhatt and Chandrakala Bhatt. He initially learnt music from his parents, and then with Ravi Shankar. His innovations include two new instruments, the Mohan veena, an Indianized Hawaiian guitar with fourteen extra strings, and the Vishwa veena, a traditional veena with some elements of a harp.

Bhatt received the Grammy Award in 1994, for his album *A Meeting by the River*, in collaboration with Ry Cooder. The same year, he won a state award from the Government of Rajasthan. He was awarded the Sangeet Natak Akademi Award in 1998, the Padma Shri in 2002 and the Padma Bhushan in 2017. Bhatt has produced numerous albums, and has performed in countries around the world. His son Salil Bhatt also plays the Mohan veena.

> **FILMS IN REGIONAL LANGUAGES**
>
> In 1994, 153 Telugu, 135 Tamil, 69 Malayalam and 62 Kannada films were produced.

● MISS WORLD AND MISS UNIVERSE

That year, India saw success in beauty pageants, with Aishwarya Rai being crowned Miss World, and Sushmita Sen, Miss Universe.

Aishwarya Rai (b. 1 November 1973) went on to become an extremely successful film star. Her first two films were Mani Ratnam's *Iruvar*, in Tamil, and *Aur Pyar Ho Gaya*, in Hindi, both released in 1997. *Hum Dil De Chuke Sanam* (1999), *Devdas* (2002), *Chokher Bali* (2003), *Raincoat* (2004), *Guru* (2007), *Jodhaa Akbar* (2008) and *Enthiran* (2010) are among her many films. She also starred in the British film *Bride & Prejudice* (2004), an adaptation of Jane Austen's *Pride and Prejudice*, which was a commercial success and also received critical acclaim. She married actor Abhishek Bachchan in 2007 and they have a daughter. Aishwarya has been called the most beautiful woman in the world. Her awards include two Filmfare Awards for the best actress (2000, 2003), the Padma Shri (2009) and the Ordre des Arts et des Lettres (2012) of the French government.

Sushmita Sen (b. 19 November 1975) won the Femina Miss India competition and the Miss Universe title in 1994. She also went on to become a successful actor. *Dastak* (1996) was her first film, while *Main Hoon Na* (2004) has been her biggest success. She has received several awards for the best supporting actress, the Rajiv Gandhi Award for her achievements in Bollywood (2006) and the Mother Teresa Memorial International Award for Social Justice (2013). Sushmita Sen has adopted two girls, Renée and Alisah.

❋ THE TOP FILMS

A Bollywood romantic hit of 1994, *Hum Aapke Hain Koun...!*, written and directed by Sooraj R. Barjatya, starring Salman Khan, Madhuri Dixit and others, was a family film with fourteen songs. It is one of the biggest box office grossers till date.

Kadhalan, a Tamil film, dubbed in Hindi as *Humse Hai Muqabla*, was another great hit of the year, as well as an award winner. Prabhu Deva and Nagma were the lead actors, and the music was by A.R. Rahman.

Shekhar Kapur's *Bandit Queen*, released the same year, narrated the true story of Phoolan Devi. It received the National Film Award for the best feature film in Hindi.

'MADE IN INDIA'

Alisha Chinai started a new trend in Indipop (Indian pop music) with the song 'Made in India', which became a major sensation. This was followed by several other singers and bands, composing new music as well as remixes. Notable among the singers was Daler Mehndi, while bands included Silk Route, Colonial Cousins and others.

Indipop flourished with the launch of music channels Channel [V] and MTV.

ALSO IN 1994

1 March: Air India is converted into a public limited company.

29 August: Death of Tushar Kanti Ghosh (b. 1899), journalist, editor and prominent Bengali-language writer

Narasimha Rao visits the US for the second time, marking the start of improved ties between India and the US, as well as the strengthening of business relationships.

The Jnanpith is awarded to U.R. Ananthamurthy (1932–2014) for his contribution to Kannada literature.

1995: THE EIGHTH SAARC SUMMIT, NEW DELHI

The year saw no major changes in the central government as Narasimha Rao remained prime minister.

Among changes in the states, Chandrababu Naidu became chief minister of Andhra Pradesh after taking over leadership of the Telugu Desam Party. In Maharashtra, the Shiv Sena gained power and in Uttar Pradesh, Mayawati of the Bahujan Samaj Party became chief minister. The same year, Bombay was renamed Mumbai. In a continued attempt to promote peace in South Asia, the eighth SAARC summit was held in New Delhi. It included a cultural programme, and a trade zone for South Asia was proposed.

A Kathakali dancer

❋ KATHAKALI ON OTHER SHORES

In 1995, Kalamandalam Vijayakumar and his Kala Chethena Kathakali Company (founded in 1987 with the artist Barbara Vijayakumar) worked with other artists to create the dance drama *Hima*

Sundari, based on 'Snow White'. The performers toured the UK with their show titled *Oppression of the Innocent*. Since then, they have held workshops and performed at numerous events across the UK. The adaptation of 'Snow White' was one of the many experimental Kathakali performances taking place in the 1990s.

In 1995, the Kerala Kalamandalam (founded in 1930) toured the US. The traditional dance form thus became better known in other parts of the world.

CLASSICAL DANCE FORMS OF KERALA

Kerala has a number of classical dance forms, including Kathakali, Krishnanattam, Mohiniattam, Chakiarkoothu, Koodiyattam and Ottanthullal. Kathakali (from katha, meaning 'story', and *kali*, meaning 'play') is one of the main classical forms, presented as a dance drama, of which every movement is set by tradition. It is extremely stylized, with elaborate costumes and make-up. Both are colourful, and each colour has a meaning. The facial colours applied on dancers are made of rice paste and vegetable dye. A predominantly green face indicates a god, or a noble or heroic person. If there is a red patch in the green, the dancer represents an anti-hero. If the face is mainly black, a demon is being embodied. On the other hand, a black beard signifies a hunter or forest dweller. A white beard is for divine beings, while a yellow face represents ascetics and women. Emotions are expressed through facial and finger movements. Instruments such as drums accompany the dance, and singers deliver the story or dialogue. Kathakali probably evolved from folk dramas, and used to be performed in the courts of kings.

Attakatha is a type of play specially composed in Malayalam for Kathakali, usually based on stories from the Ramayana, the Mahabharata and the Puranas. The Kerala Kalamandalam in Cheruthuruthy, founded by the poet Vallathol, is one of the best training institutes for Kathakali. Kalamandalam Krishnan Nair (1914–90) and Kalamandalam Gopi (b. 1937) are among the leading exponents of Kathakali. Kottakkal Sivaraman (1936–2010) made a name for himself performing strong female roles. Until recently, most female roles in Kathakali were performed by male dancers.

Krishnanattam originated in the second half of the seventeenth century. Early performances were based on the Krishnagiti, a Sanskrit work on Krishna's life, composed by Manaveda (1585–1658 CE), the Zamorin of Calicut. This form of dance was confined to temples, and continues to be performed at Guruvayur Temple, in Kerala.

Chakiarkoothu and Koodiyattam are other types of dance dramas, traditionally performed in temples by members of the Chakiar caste. Chakiarkoothu is a solo performance, narrating myths and legends while relating them to current and local events. Female roles are played by Nangyaramma, women of the Ambalavasi Nambiar caste. Mani Madhava Chakyar (15 February 1899–14 January 1990) is considered the best twentieth-century performer of both Chakiarkoothu and Koodiyattam. Another great Koodiyattam performer was Ammannur Madhava Chakyar (12 May 1917–2 July 2008), who even performed in Europe and Japan.

Mohiniattam is usually a solo dance by female performers, and also originated in temples. The name comes from Mohini, the female form adopted by the god Vishnu. It has similarities in style with Bharatanatyam and Odissi.

> Ottanthullal is another solo dance form, developed by Kunchan Nambiar. Kunchan, a Malayalam poet, lived in the eighteenth century. His innovations in dance included the use of background music, and he wrote several *thullal* compositions himself. Ottanthullal has dialogues in simple Malayalam, and many of the routines depict the issue of social inequality.
>
> All these traditional dance forms have now led to new and innovative forms.

● KANNADA FILMS: DID HE EAT THE RABBIT?

America! America!! is a Kannada film released in 1995 that won the National Film Award in the Kannada regional category. Written and directed by Nagathihalli Chandrashekhar, the three main actors are Ramesh Aravind (as Surya), Akshay Anand (as Shashank) and Hema Panchamukhi (as Bhoomi). The film shows a love triangle. Of the three childhood friends—Surya, Shashank and Bhoomi—Shashank goes to the US for further studies and upon a return visit, his marriage is arranged with Bhoomi, whom Surya loves. Later, Surya starts a business that flourishes and for which he visits the US. There he meets Shashank and Bhoomi, and gifts them a rabbit. As the relationship between Shashank and Bhoomi deteriorates, Shashank gives away her beloved rabbit to a humane society, but initially pretends that he has eaten it! Naturally Bhoomi leaves Shashank, who, after a series of incidents, dies in an accident.

The film was a box office hit, as well as widely acclaimed. It ran in theatres for a whole year in Karnataka, was the first Kannada film to be released in the US and was dubbed in Telugu, Hindi and Tamil. The film was largely shot in San Francisco, and the music was composed by Mano Murthy.

Chandrashekhar had another award-winning film, *Kotreshi Kanasu* (The Dreams of Kotreshi, 1994), centring on a Dalit boy's desire for an English education. Other interesting Kannada films released around the same time were *Amruthavarshini* (1997), about unrequited love; *Nammoora Mandara Hoove* (The Mandara Flower from My Village, 1997) and the intriguing *Beladingala Baale* (Daughter of the Moonlight, 1995). *Beladingala Baale* is the story of a chess player—the world champion and only grand master from India—and a mystery woman whom he falls in love with and has to identify by clues given to him over the phone.

Among earlier landmarks in Kannada cinema was *Bedara Kannappa* (1954), which tells the story of Kannappa, devotee of the god Shiva, and was directed by H.L.N. Simha. It marked the debut of the actor Rajkumar. In 1970, Pattabhirama Reddy's *Samskara* won the President's Gold Medal for the best feature film. Several good films followed, with directors such as Girish Karnad, B.V. Karanth and M.S. Sathyu.

❋ THE TOP FILMS

Dilwale Dulhania Le Jayenge (popularly known as DDLJ), a Bollywood hit of the year, was written and directed by Aditya Chopra and produced by Yash Chopra. A romantic film, the lead actors were Shah Rukh Khan and Kajol. The film won the National Film Award and ten Filmfare Awards, and its box office collections exceeded even those of *Hum Aapke Hain Koun...!*, of the previous year.

Mani Ratnam's *Bombay*, a Tamil film about the love story between Shekhar (played by Arvind Swamy), a Hindu man, and Shaila Banu (played by Manisha Koirala), a Muslim woman, was another top grosser. It shows the initial opposition from their families, their reconciliation and the problems faced during the Bombay riots after the demolition of Babri Masjid. The film's message is communal harmony. The music, by A.R. Rahman, contributed to its popularity. The film won several national and international awards.

🟊 MOBILE PHONES AND THE INTERNET

Mobile phones were introduced in India. At that time, usage charges were extremely high.

While the Internet had reached India in 1994, the first commercial internet service was introduced in 1995 and private participation in internet services started in 1997.

🟊 A SOLAR ECLIPSE

The last eclipse of this century was visible over northern India on 24 October 1995. Three other eclipses visible from India after Independence include those on 30 June 1954, 15 February 1961 and 16 February 1980.

ALSO IN 1995

11 May: The whole town of Charar-e-Sharif in Kashmir, including its holy shrine, is burnt down during a battle between Indian troops and militants.

7 July: Death of Rajan Pillai (b. 1947), the Biscuit Baron, in custody, just three days after his arrest. Jail reforms follow.

21 September: Across India, Ganesha idols are believed to be drinking the milk offered to them! Scientists explain this through capillary action, but the exact reason behind this so-called Milk Miracle is not clear.

The Jnanpith is awarded to Malayalam writer M.T. Vasudevan Nair for *Randamoozham* (Second Chance, 1984).

1996: THE ELEVENTH GENERAL ELECTIONS

Narasimha Rao and his Congress government had completed five years in power. The eleventh general elections for the Lok Sabha were held in April–May 1996. No party had a clear majority, but for the very first time, the BJP had the highest number of seats—161. Their allies, the Shiv Sena, the Haryana Vikas Party and the Samata Party, together had another twenty-six seats. The Congress was the second-largest party, with 140 seats. On 16 May, the BJP formed the government with Atal Bihari Vajpayee as prime minister, but they did not get enough support and so he had to resign on 28 May. Many different parties now joined together to form the government, supported by the Congress. They were the Janata Dal, the two communist parties, two Tamil Nadu parties—the DMK and the Tamil Maanila Congress—the Telugu Desam, the Samajwadi Party and the Asom Gana Parishad. This group called themselves the United Front and chose H.D. Deve Gowda of the Janata Dal as prime minister. Narasimha Rao, who had remained leader of the Congress party even after the elections, resigned in September 1996 because of corruption cases against him. Sitaram Kesri became the next Congress president.

State elections were held in Jammu and Kashmir for the first time since 1987. The National Conference won the elections, and Farooq Abdullah became chief minister. The National Conference then joined the United Front.

❀ N. RAMANI IS AWARDED THE PADMA SHRI

N. Ramani (15 October 1934–9 October 2015) was one of the best flute players of Karnatic music. He was born in Thiruvarur, in present-day Tamil Nadu, from where the three great Karnatic music composers of the eighteenth century, Tyagaraja, Muthuswami Dikshitar and Syama Sastri, originated. Ramani began learning music from his grandfather, Shri A. Narayanaswami Iyer, who was also a flautist as well as a singer. He continued his training with T.R. Mahalingam (6 November 1926–31 May 1986), and played with him at a concert when he was just eleven years old. Mahalingam, popularly known as Mali, devised a new kind of flute and flute-playing in Karnatic music. Ramani followed this style. Later, he played for All India Radio, and performed at concerts in India and abroad. He also established Ramani's Academy of Flute in Madras in 1982.

Ramani received a number of awards, including the Sangeet Natak Akademi Award in 1984, the Padma Shri in 1987, the Sangeetha Kalanidhi in 1996 and the Sangeetha Kalasikhamani in 2007, posthumously.

❀ THE OLYMPICS: A TENNIS WIN

In the 1996 Summer Olympics, held in Atlanta, United States, India competed in thirteen sports. Leander Paes (b. 1973) won a bronze medal in tennis, India's second individual Olympic medal after Independence.

🟤 MCDONALD'S COMES TO INDIA

With the onset of liberalization, international restaurant chains began to open in India. McDonald's opened its first restaurant in India in 1996, changing its menu to suit Indian tastes by introducing vegetarian items, such as the McAloo Tikki burger and the McSpicy Paneer burger, and eliminating beef and pork. Pizza Hut also started operating in India in 1996.

Other fast-food chains in India are Domino's Pizza (opened in 1996), KFC (opened in 1995), Dunkin' Donuts (opened in 2012), Subway (opened in 2001) and Burger King (opened 2014). All, including KFC, offer vegetarian options.

🟤 N.T. RAMA RAO PASSES AWAY

The year saw the death of N.T. Rama Rao, actor and politician, on 18 January. NTR, as he was popularly known, was not only chief minister of Andhra Pradesh from 1983 to 1989 and from 1994 to 1995, but also a top film star in Telugu cinema. He even produced some films and acted in a few Tamil ones, but his popularity in Telugu movies was unparalleled. His first film was *Mana Desam* (1949), a social drama, and he went on to act in over 300 films. Often he portrayed characters such as Rama and Krishna, adding to his popularity. Some of his characters also reflected the problems of the common person. His last film was *Srinatha Kavi Sarvabhowmudu* (1993), based on the life of the poet Srinatha. One among his remarkable films was *Daana Veera Soora Karna* (1977), produced and directed by him, in which he played the three roles of Karna, Duryodhana and Krishna. The film was a box office hit, even in its reruns. NTR

N.T. Rama Rao

wrote scripts for some films and set up the production company National Art Theatre in Madras, as well as Ramakrishna Studios in Hyderabad.

NTR married Basava Tarakam in 1943, and they had eight sons and four daughters. Basava died of cancer in 1985. Some of NTR's sons and grandsons also acted in films. Among them, his grandson Jr NTR is a top actor. NTR married Lakshmi Parvathi in 1993, though the marriage created a family crisis. Lakshmi Parvathi wrote a two-volume biography of NTR, published in 2004. NTR received several awards, including the Padma Shri in 1968.

AKKINENI NAGESWARA RAO WINS THE NTR NATIONAL AWARD

Akkineni Nageswara Rao (20 September 1924–22 January 2014), was another well-known actor in and producer of Telugu films, and the first recipient of the NTR National Award (1996), awarded in honour of N.T. Rama Rao. He was responsible for setting up Annapurna Studios, in Hyderabad, in 1975, and contributing towards making Hyderabad the centre of Telugu film production, instead of Madras. He acted in many historical and biographical films, as well as in romantic ones. His son Akkineni Nagarjuna is also an actor. Nageswara Rao received numerous awards, including the Padma Vibhushan (2011), the Dadasaheb Phalke Award (1991) and several Filmfare Awards (South).

SILK SMITHA DIES

Vijayalakshmi Vadlapati (2 December 1960–23 September 1996) acted in more than 400 films, mainly in south India. Born in Eluru, Andhra Pradesh, she came to be known as Silk Smitha after she acted as Silk in the Tamil film *Vandichakkaram* (1980). She was celebrated for her beauty and was hugely popular. She died at the young age of thirty-six.

ALSO IN 1996

May: Nemi Chand (1948–23 May 2017), or Chandraswami, a god-man involved in politics, is arrested and sent to jail.

1 June: Death of Neelam Sanjiva Reddy (b. 1913), a nationalist, participant in the freedom movement and President of India (1977–82)

6–7 November: A cyclone hits Andhra Pradesh, resulting in over a thousand deaths.

November: President Jiang Zemin of China visits India; agreements are signed.

12 December: India and Bangladesh reach an agreement on sharing the waters of River Ganga.

30 December: A bomb hits the Brahmaputra Mail, a passenger train, travelling through Assam; around thirty people are declared dead.

The Jnanpith is awarded to Bengali-language writer Mahasweta Devi (1926–28 July 2016) for her novel *Hajar Churashir Ma* (Mother of 1084, 1974). Mahasweta, one of Bengal's greatest writers, has over a hundred novels and numerous short stories to her credit. She was also a social activist. She won other awards, including the Ramon Magsaysay Award (1997), the Padma Shri (1986) and the Padma Vibhushan (2006).

1997: I.K. GUJRAL—
A NEW PRIME MINISTER

Deve Gowda could not remain prime minister for long. The Congress, led by Sitaram Kesri, withdrew their support for the government in March 1997. The Congress would have liked to form the government, but did not have the numbers. Instead, they agreed to support the United Front again if they chose a new prime minister. And so I.K. Gujral (4 December 1919–30 November 2012), also of the Janata Dal, became prime minister in April. In September, though, the Congress withdrew support once again, and elections had to be held. Gujral remained the caretaker prime minister until the vote could take place in 1998.

Though the United Front government had diverse groups, it worked out a basic programme that they all agreed to. This included the continuation of economic reforms, more autonomy for states, a commitment to secularism and a focus on improving the status of women and members of lower castes.

❈ OTHER KEY EVENTS

There were other developments in the states, as well as the formation of some new parties.

A ceasefire was signed with the National Socialist Council of Nagaland (IM), bringing some peace to the state. Another agreement was signed with Bangladesh, for the return of Chakma refugees, who had been living in Tripura. They began to return to Bangladesh in March 1997.

Three new parties were formed that year. Two were offshoots of the Janata Dal: the Rashtriya Janata Dal in Bihar, led by Lalu Prasad Yadav, who had been president of the Janata Dal (1990–97); and the Biju Janata Dal in Orissa. The party Lok Shakti was founded by Ramakrishna Hegde in February 1997.

In July, a new President, Kocheril Raman Narayanan (4 February 1921–9 November 2005), was elected. He had been vice president from 1992 to 1997.

● PUPUL JAYAKAR DIES

The year saw the death of Pupul Jayakar (11 September 1915–29 March 1997), who wrote on Indian culture and promoted indigenous arts and crafts. She was chairperson of the All India Handicrafts Board, established the Handloom and Handicraft Export Corporation, led the initiative behind the Festivals of India held in various countries, along with holding other posts related to heritage and culture. She set up the Indian National Trust for Art and Cultural Heritage (INTACH) in 1984. She was also associated with the philosopher J. Krishnamurti and the Krishnamurti Foundation.

Among her books are *The Earthen Drum* (1980), *The Earth Mother* (1989), *J. Krishnamurti: A Biography* (1986), *Indira Gandhi: An Intimate Biography* (1992) and *The Buddha: A Book for the Young* (1982), as well as stories, essays and accounts of her dialogues with J. Krishnamurti.

✤ THE GOD OF SMALL THINGS

Arundhati Roy (b. 24 November 1961), a writer and social activist, won the Booker Prize in 1997 for her novel *The God of Small Things*. This semi-autobiographical novel looks at forbidden love, class conflicts and complex relationships.

Her second novel, *The Ministry of Utmost Happiness*, was published in June 2017. She has also written screenplays, a television serial and contributed several articles to leading magazines and newspapers. She has received many awards, including the Sydney Peace Prize in 2004 and the Norman Mailer Prize for Distinguished Writing in 2011.

Arundhati Roy

✤ ANITA RATNAM: *A MAP TO THE NEXT WORLD*

In 1997, Anita Ratnam, classical and contemporary Indian dancer and choreographer, created and performed *A Map to the Next World*, based on Native American poet Joy Harjo's poems on the shared colonial legacy of Native Americans and Indians. Here is an extract from a poem:[25]

> We were thinking about each other.
> I was making a song to fit between a heron and the waving grass.

---

[25] Quoted in 'A Map to the Next World: A Collision of Colonization (Synopsis)', *Arangham*, accessed 11 June 2017, http://www.arangham.com/intcol/amap/amap.html.

You were engraving rhythm with your feet beneath the banyan
    tree who was teaching you to dance by standing still.
We were countries away, oceans, elephants, sea monster, deer
    and stars away.
I was thinking of you. You were thinking of me.
I was thinking of you. You were thinking of me.

Anita Ratnam trained in Bharatanatyam, Mohiniattam and Kathakali, and developed new forms in dance, including what she refers to as neo-Bharatanatyam.

Born in Ambala on 21 May 1954, Anita grew up in Madras. She initially trained with Adyar K. Lakshman, a Bharatanatyam dancer, and later at Kalakshetra. After receiving an MA in theatre and television, she worked as a television producer in the US. In 1992, she set up the Arangham Trust in Madras, and then the Arangham Dance Theatre. *A Map to the Next World* is among her choreographed shows, succeeded by several others, including *Seven Graces*, which was performed in New York in 2007. *Seven Graces* is a tribute to the Buddhist deity Tara, with the music composed by Tibetan monks. Anita has given over 1500 performances in twenty-seven countries around the world. In 1998, she started the Other India Festival in Chennai, an alternative to traditional festivals.

❀ SHUBHA MUDGAL AND *DANCE OF THE WIND*

Shubha Mudgal (b. 1959) is a noted singer of Hindustani classical music, who also sings pop and folk music, as well as songs for films. She was born in Allahabad and both her parents, professors of English at the University of Allahabad, had an interest in music and dance. Shubha initially trained in music with Ramashreya Jha, and later with Vinay Chandra Maudgalya and Vasant Thakar, with inputs from Kumar Gandharva, Jitendra Abhisheki and Naina

Devi. She married Maudgalya's son Mukul Mudgal, though the two were later divorced.

Shubha started giving performances in her early twenties, specializing in khayal, thumri and dadra, and also began to sing and compose other types of music. Among the films she has composed music for are *Dance of the Wind* (also known as *Swara Mandal*), a 1997 film that premiered at the Venice Film Festival. Shubha was awarded the Padma Shri in 2000.

❉ SACHIN TENDULKAR IS AWARDED THE RAJIV GANDHI KHEL RATNA AWARD

Sachin Tendulkar (b. 24 April 1973), one of India's best and most popular cricketers, began playing Test cricket at the age of sixteen and continued to play in national and international tournaments for the next twenty-four years. He has scored over 30,000 runs in international cricket, including Tests, ODIs and Twenty20 cricket, and has scored the highest number of centuries. He has received numerous awards, including the Arjuna Award (1994), the Padma Shri (1999), the Padma Vibhushan (2008) and the Bharat Ratna (2014). He retired from international cricket in 2013 and was nominated to the Rajya Sabha in 2012. *Sachin: A Billion Dreams* is a biographical film based on his life, starring Tendulkar himself, directed by James Erskine and released in 2017.

ALSO IN 1997

6 June: The Bangladesh, India, Sri Lanka and Thailand Economic Cooperation (BIST-EC) is formed. Myanmar joins in December 1997 and the organization is renamed BIMST-EC. In 2004, it is renamed the Bay of Bengal

Initiative for Multi-Sectoral Technical and Economic Cooperation (BIMSTEC), after Nepal and Bhutan are admitted.

23 June: A joint press statement is released by India and Pakistan on matters of peace and security.

15 September: The Prasar Bharati (Broadcasting Corporation of India) Act is passed, making Doordarshan and All India Radio autonomous bodies.

6–7 March: India joins the Indian Ocean Rim Association for Regional Cooperation (IOR-ARC). The first meeting takes place in Mauritius. It is now known as the Indian Ocean Rim Association (IORA).

The Jnanpith is awarded to Urdu writer Ali Sardar Jafri.

1998: A BJP-LED GOVERNMENT

With I.K. Gujral as the caretaker prime minister, the twelfth general elections took place in February 1998. The Bharatiya Janata Party got the highest number of seats—182. It had entered into an alliance with a number of other parties, and together they were known as the National Democratic Alliance (NDA). The NDA formed the government with A.B. Vajpayee of the BJP as prime minister. The Congress won 141 seats and was the leading opposition party. Sonia Gandhi, Rajiv Gandhi's widow, had refrained from joining politics until then, but she participated in the election campaign to try and revive the Congress. In April 1998, she became the Congress party president and chairperson of the Congress Parliamentary Committee.

❋ AMARTYA SEN WINS THE NOBEL PRIZE

Amartya Sen (b. 3 November 1933) was born in Santiniketan, where he studied before he went to Presidency College, in present-day Kolkata, and then to the University of Cambridge, where he received a PhD in 1959. He has taught economics in universities in India and those of Oxford, Cambridge and Harvard, among others.

He became interested in welfare economics even while he was doing his PhD, and later continued to work in this field.

In 1998, he was awarded the Sveriges Riksbank Prize in Economic Sciences in Memory of Alfred Nobel, commonly known as the Nobel Prize in Economics. In recognition of this honour, he received the Bharat Ratna in 1999. He has written a number of books and articles on welfare economics, poverty, famine, inequality and related issues. Amartya Sen is still an Indian citizen, despite his many years working and living abroad.

BHAICHUNG BHUTIA WINS THE ARJUNA AWARD

Bhaichung Bhutia

Bhaichung Bhutia (b. 1976), considered one of India's best footballers, became the nineteenth footballer to receive the Arjuna Award, in 1998. The first footballer to receive it was P.K. Banerjee, in 1961. Bhaichung has also received other awards, including the Padma Shri in 2008.

FOOTBALL IN INDIA

India had its own variants of football, but the Western, or British, type was introduced in the late nineteenth century. Sir Mortimer Durand, the foreign secretary, founded the first national trophy tournament (Durand Cup) in 1888. The Rovers Cup was first held in Bombay in 1891, and the IFA Shield was started in 1893. Among the oldest football clubs in India, Mohun Bagan was inaugurated in 1889 and Mohammedan Sporting Club in 1891.

The All India Football Federation, affiliated to the Fédération Internationale de Football Association (FIFA), organizes competitive tournaments in India.

The first men's football nationals were held in 1941, and the first women's nationals, well after Independence, in 1975. India began to participate in international tournaments in the 1940s, and the Indian team played in the Olympics from 1948 to 1960, but did not win any medals. Among the international wins, India won the gold medal in the Asian Games in 1951 and 1962, and a bronze in 1970; and gold medals in the SAF Games (South Asian Federation Games) in 1985 and 1987, with a silver in 1993. They also won the South Asian Football Federation Championship in 1993, 1997, 1999, 2005, 2009, 2011 and 2015. In 2007, India won the Nehru Cup, and in 2008, the AFC Challenge Cup.

There are several football tournaments today, including the Durand Cup, the Subroto Cup, the Santosh Trophy and the Nehru Gold Cup. The first Indian women's football league was established in Calcutta at the centenary celebrations of the Indian Football Association (IFA) in August 1993.

League football began to be played in 1996, and the Indian Super League was founded in 2013 in an attempt to make football more popular. Football academies have been set up to improve India's standing in the game. In January 2017, India was ranked 129 in the world. By July, this rose to rank 96. In women's football, India was ranked 60 in June 2017.

✱ RAJAN AND SAJAN MISHRA WIN THE SANGEET NATAK AKADEMI AWARD

Rajan (b. 1951) and Sajan (b. 1956) are brothers who are Hindustani classical music singers. Born into a musical family, they grew up in Varanasi and initially trained with Bade Ramdasji, their grandfather's brother; their father, Hanuman Mishra; and their uncle, Gopal Mishra, a sarangi player. They started performing together at a young age, specializing in khayal and tarana, and have performed at concerts in India and several other countries. The duo moved to Delhi in 1977, and went on to receive several awards, including the Sanskriti Award (1979), the jointly won Sangeet Natak Akademi Award (1998), the Padma Bhushan (2007) and the National Tansen Samman (2011–12).

✱ *SARHAD*

Ali Sardar Jafri (1913–1 August 2000) was an Urdu writer and editor, primarily known for his poetry, though he also wrote short stories and plays. There are several collections of his poems, including *Parvaz* (1944), *Nai Duniya Ko Salaam* (1948), *Khoon ki Lakeer* (1949), *Asia Jaag Utha* (1951), *Patthar ki Deevar* (1953), *Ek Khwab Aur* (1964), *Mera Safar* and *Sarhad*. This last collection of poems, against war and promoting peace, was released as a music album in October 1998 by Dr Karan Singh in New Delhi. The album, sung by Seema Anil Sehgal and produced by Squadron Leader Anil Sehgal, was among the gifts presented by Prime Minister Vajpayee to Nawaz Sharif, prime minister of Pakistan, in 1999. In February, Vajpayee visited Lahore, participating in the inaugural run of the Delhi–Lahore bus service.

Jafri (born in Balrampur, Uttar Pradesh) moved to Bombay in 1942. He was part of the Progressive Writers' Movement and Association, writing against colonialism and class oppression.

He also edited collections of the works of Ghalib, Kabir, Mir and Meera. His close friends included the Urdu poet Faiz Ahmad Faiz, as well as Nazim Hikmet, the renowned Turkish poet, and the Chilean poet Pablo Neruda. Jafri received many awards, including the Uttar Pradesh Urdu Akademi Award (1979), the Iqbal Gold Medal presented by the Pakistan government (1978), the Padma Shri (1967), the Iqbal Samman (1986) and the Jnanpith Award (1997). He married Sultana in 1948, and they had two sons.

Here are two lines from his poem 'Subh-e-Farda':[26]

Isi sarhad pe kal dooba tha suraj ho ke do tukde
Isi sarhad par kal zakhmi hui thi subh-e-azadi.

(On this border yesterday the setting sun split into two
On this very border, freedom's dawn was wounded.)

Jafri produced two TV shows: *Kahkashan*, an eighteen-part series on the lives of Urdu poets, and *Mehfil-i-Yaaran*, consisting of interviews.

Among other contemporary noted Urdu writers and poets are Sahir Ludhianvi, Kaifi Azmi (1919–2002), Majrooh Sultanpuri (1919–2000), Hameed Akhtar (1924–2011), Faiz Ahmad Faiz (1911–84), Saadat Hasan Manto, Ismat Chughtai (1915–91) and Ahmad Nadeem Qasmi (1916–2006).

❋ GIRISH KARNAD WINS THE JNANPITH AWARD

Girish Karnad (b. 19 May 1938) is well known as an actor, director and playwright. In 1998, he won the Jnanpith Award for his contribution to Kannada literature and theatre. His play *Yayati*

---

[26] Quoted in *Ali Sardar Jafri: The Youthful Boatman of Joy*, ed. Anil Sehgal (New Delhi: Bharatiya Jnanpith, 2001).

(1961), based on the character in the Mahabharata, was a great success. He has acted in Hindi and Kannada films, as well as in television. His directorial debut, along with B.V. Karanth, was the Kannada film *Vamsha Vriksha* (1972). Karnad has won innumerable other awards, and stands up for free speech and multiculturalism.

ALSO IN 1998

15 January: Death of Gulzarilal Nanda (b. 4 July 1898), nationalist, politician and recipient of the Bharat Ratna (1997).

14–15 February: Car bombs kill several people in Coimbatore.

19 March: Death of E.M.S. Namboodiripad (b. 1909), writer, chief minister of Kerala (1957–59, 1967–69) and general secretary of the CPI (M) (1978–92)

11 and 13 May: Underground nuclear tests are successfully conducted at the Pokhran Test Range, Rajasthan. These include a thermonuclear device, a fission device and three sub-kiloton nuclear devices.

9 June: A tropical cyclone hits Gujarat; over a thousand people die.

27 June: Death of Nikhil Chakravarti (b. 3 November 1913), journalist and the first chairman of Prasar Bharati

16 September: Death of Mazhar Khan (b. 1955), actor, producer and director

26 November: A train accident near Khanna, in Punjab, occurs when the Amritsar-bound Frontier Mail train collides with the derailed coaches of the Sealdah Express; kills over 200 passengers.

28 December: The India–Sri Lanka Free Trade Agreement is signed.

1999: THE BJP AGAIN

The National Democratic Alliance was still in power at the beginning of the year. In February, A.B. Vajpayee made a historic visit to Pakistan and signed the Lahore Declaration. After India's nuclear tests in May 1998, Pakistan too had conducted tests, and there had been tension between the two countries. The strained relations had been somewhat eased by September 1998, when both nations had agreed to resolve conflicts and work towards peace. However, the Lahore Declaration marked a new step towards friendship. A.B. Vajpayee, along with other noted Indians, including film stars and cricketers, travelled to Lahore from Delhi, availing the inaugural bus service between the two countries. The declaration, signed on 21 February, reasserted both nations' commitment to peace. While the declaration was welcomed by the people of both India and Pakistan, it was not liked by Pakistani military leaders.

Suddenly, in May, conditions changed as Pakistani troops crossed the Line of Control. Battles were fought in Kargil, Dras and other areas along the border. Though India was eventually the victor, about 475 Indian Army officers and soldiers were killed, more than 1000 were injured and the financial loss was around Rs 5000 crore.

THE KARGIL WAR IN FILMS

This war too was reflected in Hindi films, particularly *LOC Kargil* (2003), directed and produced by J.P. Dutta. Sanjay Dutt, Ayub Khan and Ajay Devgn were among the large cast of actors. The film ends with India's success after several tense battles.

🟎 OTHER KEY EVENTS

In April, the NDA government faced a problem as J. Jayalalithaa of the AIADMK withdrew support, along with eighteen party members. A vote of no confidence on 17 April 1999 led to the fall of the government. After this, the Congress attempted but did not succeed in forming the government. Elections were fixed for September; meanwhile, Vajpayee and his ministers continued as the caretaker government.

Despite the Kargil War, elections to the Lok Sabha were held as planned in September. The BJP was the leading party with 181 seats, and the NDA was able to form the government again with A.B. Vajpayee as prime minister. Congress numbers fell to 114 seats, and Sonia Gandhi became the leader of the Opposition in the Lok Sabha.

🟎 SHABANA AZMI IN *GODMOTHER*

Godmother, a 1999 Hindi film, won the National Award for the best feature film. It is based on a real-life 'godmother', Santokben Jadeja (d. 31 March 2011), who controlled the underworld for several years in Porbandar, Gujarat. Santokben's intriguing and tragic story is narrated in this film, which won several other awards. The title role was well portrayed by Shabana Azmi, who won the

A reproduction of the poster of *Godmother*

National Film Award for the best actress. It was one of Shabana's best works, indicative of the effort she puts into every role.

> ### SHABANA AZMI
>
> Born on 18 September 1950, Shabana is the daughter of poet Kaifi Azmi and stage actor Shaukat Azmi. She debuted with *Ankur* (1974), directed by Shyam Benegal, after which she went on to act in over a hundred films, in Hindi and Bengali, both in mainstream and parallel cinema. *Nishant* (1975), *Shatranj ke Khilari* (1977), *Khandhar* (1984), *Arth* (1982), *Makdee* (2002), *Umrao Jaan* (2006) and *Midnight's Children* (2012) are among her many notable films. Shabana has also acted in foreign films, as well as in television and theatre.
>
> She is a social activist, and was nominated to the Rajya Sabha in 1997. She has received the National Film Award for the best actress five times, as well as five Filmfare Awards, the Padma Shri (1988) and the Padma Bhushan (2012), among other honours.

❋ THE TOP BOLLYWOOD ACTORS OF THE 1990s

While older stars continued to act in successful films, many young actors gained prominence in the 1990s. Among them, Salman Khan, Shah Rukh Khan, Ajay Devgn, Akshay Kumar and Aamir Khan were the top male actors. Sunny Deol, Govinda, Anil Kapoor, Sanjay Dutt, Bobby Deol, Jackie Shroff and Sunil Shetty were also extremely popular. Among the women were Madhuri Dixit, Sridevi, Juhi Chawla, Raveena Tandon, Manisha Koirala, Pooja Bhatt, Karisma Kapoor, Preity Zinta, Rani Mukerji, Kajol, Tabu and many more.

SATISH GUJRAL RECEIVES THE PADMA VIBHUSHAN

Satish Gujral (b. 25 December 1925) is an architect, artist, sculptor and designer, who specializes in murals. At the age of eight, an illness left him deaf. In 1939, he joined the Mayo School of Industrial Art (now the National College of Arts), Lahore, for a course in applied art, and in 1944, the Sir J.J. School of Art, Bombay, where he studied painting. He left Bombay in 1947 because he had fallen sick, and in 1952, received a scholarship to Mexico, where he trained with the artists Diego Rivera and David Siqueiros. Soon he began holding exhibitions in Mexico, India and other parts of the world, seeking different kinds of media that could help him express the trauma of Partition. He has created murals for several buildings in India and abroad, and in 1977, also started designing buildings. His murals incorporate mosaic, ceramic tiles and steel.

Throughout his long career, Satish Gujral has created art of various kinds. He has made oil paintings, murals, paper collages and acrylic paintings. In sculpture, he has used steel, copper, glass, junk and later, burnt wood.

Satish Gujral is married to Kiran, and they have three children. He is the younger brother of former prime minister I.K. Gujral. After sixty-five years of silence, he tried a cochlear implant that enabled him to hear. But he could not cope with the cacophonous sounds around him, and had it removed. Several documentaries have been made on his life, and he has received numerous awards in addition to the Padma Vibhushan in 1999.

ANOTHER PLANE HIJACK

On 24 December, an Indian Airlines plane flying from Kathmandu to Delhi was hijacked and diverted to Kandahar, in Afghanistan. One passenger was killed, while the others were released in exchange for the hijackers being granted the release of three militants imprisoned in India, as well as safe passage out of Afghanistan.

❋ AMJAD ALI KHAN: *STRINGS FOR FREEDOM*

Amjad Ali Khan (b. 9 October 1945), an acclaimed sarod player, started studying and training under his father, Hafiz Ali Khan, a court musician in Gwalior State. His family belongs to the Bangash lineage of musicians. When his family moved from Gwalior to Delhi, he attended Modern School there, though he continued his sarod training. Extremely talented, he started giving performances at the age of ten, and began composing new ragas in 1960. Chandra Dhwani was a 1968 composition, and he went on to create as well as discover many more ragas. He has said, 'Every raga has a soul, and every musical note is the sound of God.'[27]

Amjad Ali Khan has received innumerable awards, including the Padma Shri (1975), the Tansen Samman (1989) the Sangeet Natak Akademi Award (1989), the Padma Bhushan (1991) and the Padma Vibhushan (2001). Several documentaries have been made on him, one of the latest being *Strings for Freedom*, screened in 1996. Amjad Ali married dancer Subhalakshmi Borooah, and even composed a new raga named after her. Their two sons, Amaan and Ayaan, are also noted sarod players. Amjad Ali, his sons and Elmira Darvarova, a classical violinist of Western music, came together to create two albums, *Soul Strings* (2015) and *Amalgam* (2016), the latest of Amjad's many performances with Western musicians. Amjad Ali has performed at prestigious

---

[27] Reagan Gavin Rasquinha, 'Ustad Amjad Ali Khan: Like Cosmic Divinity, Music Knows Few Barriers or Boundaries', *Times of India*, 16 January 2017, http://timesofindia.indiatimes.com/entertainment/hindi/music/news/Ustad-Amjad-Ali-Khan-Like-cosmic-divinity-music-knows-few-barriers-or-boundaries/articleshow/50837752.cms.

events all over the world and, though a classical musician, does not differentiate between classical and other kinds of music. 'Music is music,' he says.[28]

> **ALSO IN 1999**
>
> 16 March: Regular services of the Delhi–Lahore bus begin; it is known as Sadbhavana Express in India and Sada-e-Sarhad in Pakistan.
>
> 1 April: The Swarnajayanti Gram Swarozgar Yojana, an initiative for self-employment, replaces earlier programmes, providing training and assistance in starting small businesses.
>
> 19 June: The Kolkata–Dhaka bus service is launched.
>
> 1 August: Death of Nirad C. Chaudhuri (b. 1897), renowned writer, who wrote *The Autobiography of an Unknown Indian* (1951) and other books
>
> 29 October: A cyclone hits the eastern coast of India, mainly affecting Orissa. Thousands die and property worth crores is damaged.
>
> The Ministry of Tribal Affairs is founded. Tribal affairs were previously under different ministries, and the aim of the new department is to promote the welfare and interests of the country's tribal groups.
>
> Nirmal Verma (Hindi writer) and Gurdial Singh (Punjabi-language writer) jointly win the Jnanpith Award.

---

[28] Amjad Ali Khan, *Master on Masters* (Gurgaon: Penguin Random House India, 2017).

2000: THREE NEW STATES

In November, the three new states of Jharkhand, Chhattisgarh and Uttaranchal, later renamed Uttarakhand, were created. Jharkhand was earlier a part of Bihar, Chhattisgarh, of Madhya Pradesh, and Uttaranchal, of Uttar Pradesh.

❖ RAVI SHANKAR PLAYS AT CARNEGIE HALL

Ravi Shankar (7 April 1920–11 December 2012), India's best-known sitarist of Hindustani classical music, performed live at Carnegie Hall, New York, in October 2000. This was recorded on the album *Full Circle: Carnegie Hall 2000*, which won him the Grammy Award in 2002 for the best world music album. He was eighty years old at the time.

Born in Varanasi, he was the younger brother of the dancer Uday Shankar. At the age of ten, he went to Paris with his mother and brothers, later becoming part of Uday Shankar's dance troupe and gaining exposure to a wide variety of music. Allauddin Khan also came on board as a soloist for

Ravi Shankar

Shankar's tour of Europe, and in 1938, Ravi Shankar joined him in Maihar to become his student. After completing his training in 1944, Ravi began composing and playing music, performing at concerts in India and abroad. He also played ragas from Karnatic music, and explained Indian classical music to his international audiences. He also composed music for films, including Satyajit Ray's Apu trilogy and *Gandhi* (1982).

Though Ravi Shankar was already well known and had collaborated with the great violinist Yehudi Menuhin, he gained even more fame when George Harrison and the Beatles came to learn from him in 1968. Shankar's orchestral compositions have been conducted by André Previn and Zubin Mehta. He received numerous awards, including the Sangeet Natak Akademi Award (1962), the Padma Bhushan (1967), the Padma Vibhushan (1981), the Bharat Ratna (1999) and the Tagore Award for Cultural Harmony posthumously (2012). He was nominated to the Rajya Sabha and was a member from 1986 to 1992.

Ravi Shankar wrote two autobiographies. In his book *My Music, My Life* (1968), he writes this revealing sentence: 'Over the years, with the help of my guru, I have tried very hard to create and build up within me a kind of beauty and spiritual strength, so that I always have this to turn to when the harshness of the world becomes too depressing.'[29] Though the city of Varanasi was always close to his heart, in his last years he lived in Encinitas, California.

Ravi Shankar had liberal views and married twice: Annapurna Devi in 1941 (divorced in 1982) and Sukanya Rajan in 1989. He also had two serious relationships: with Kamala Shastri, a dancer, and with Sue Jones. His children are Shubhendra (1942–92), from Annapurna; the Grammy Award–winning singer Norah Jones (b. 1979), from Sue and the multitalented classical sitarist Anoushka (b. 1981), from Sukanya.

---

[29] Ravi Shankar, *My Music, My Life* (San Rafael: Mandala Publishing, 2007).

ANNAPURNA DEVI AND HER SISTERS

Allauddin Khan had three daughters, Jahanara, Sharija and Roshanara. While Sharija died young, Jahanara learnt music from her father. But after marrying into a traditional family, she was not able to continue her training. Her mother-in-law threatened to burn her tanpura, and locked her in a dark room for singing a bhajan! Ten months after her wedding, Jahanara returned home and died soon in her mother's lap. In light of this, Allauddin then decided not to teach his younger daughter, but Roshanara had picked up music on her own and, seeing her talent, he relented. She learnt vocal music and played the sitar and surbahar, specializing in the latter, a very difficult instrument. Roshanara had a second name, Annapurna, given to her by the maharaja of Maihar, and when she married Ravi Shankar, she became better known as Annapurna Devi. Annapurna stayed away from the limelight, but it is said she was more talented and a better player than Ravi Shankar. Her biography, *An Unheard Melody* (2005), gives an account of her life.

She too received a number of honours, including the Padma Bhushan (1977), the Sangeet Natak Akademi Award (1991), the Desikottama (1999) and the Sangeet Natak Akademi Fellowship (2004).

❋ ALLA RAKHA QURESHI DIES

Alla Rakha Qureshi (1919–2000), a renowned tabla player of Hindustani classical music, was the main accompanist for the sitarist Ravi Shankar from 1962 onwards. He studied with Kader Baksh of the Punjab gharana and later with Ashiq Ali Khan of the Patiala gharana. He began accompanying musicians in 1940, worked for some time with All India Radio and composed music for films. He accompanied both Hindustani and Karnatic classical musicians, and his concert tours with Ravi Shankar brought him international fame. He also played with the jazz drummer Buddy Rich, leading to the release of their 1968 album *Rich à la Rakha*. He had three sons and two daughters, and his son Zakir Hussain is also a noted tabla player. Of his other sons, Fazal Qureshi is a tabla player and Taufiq Qureshi is a percussionist, playing a variety of instruments.

Alla Rakha received the Padma Shri in 1977 and the Sangeet Natak Akademi Award in 1982. He died of a heart attack on 3 February, a day after he heard about the death of his daughter Razia.

Chatur Lal (1925–October 1965), another excellent tabla player, was also Ravi Shankar's accompanist.

❖ THE GREAT KHALI

Dalip Singh Rana (b. 27 August 1972) is a professional wrestler, known in India and around the world as The Great Khali. He became a professional wrestler in the USA in October 2000, and won the World Heavyweight Championship of the World Wrestling Entertainment (WWE) in 2007. At 2.16 metres (7 feet, 1 inch), he is among the tallest wrestlers in the world. He has appeared in both Hollywood and Bollywood films, as well as on television.

❖ KAUN BANEGA CROREPATI

A game show based on the American *Who Wants to Be a Millionaire?* aired on Indian television on 3 July 2000, with Amitabh Bachchan as the host: *Kaun Banega Crorepati*. The popular show has had eight sessions up to 2016, with the ninth scheduled for 2017. The prize money has increased from Rs 1 crore to Rs 7 crore.

ALSO IN 2000

March: American President Bill Clinton visits India. This is a US President's first trip to India in twenty-two years.

1 April: The fiftieth anniversary of establishing diplomatic relations is celebrated by India and China.

12 June: Death of Purushottam Lakshman Deshpande (b. 1919), Marathi-language writer

September: Prime Minister A.B. Vajpayee visits the US.

Indira Goswami (1942–2011), popularly known as Mamoni Raisom, wins the Jnanpith Award for her literary works in Assamese.

The Pradhan Mantri Gramodaya Yojana is implemented for rural development.

30 November: Priyanka Chopra wins the Miss World title. In the same year, Lara Dutta wins Miss Universe and Dia Mirza wins Miss Asia Pacific.

2001: THREE TRADEGIES

Several unfortunate events took place during the course of the year.

On 26 January, a major earthquake shook Gujarat, causing widespread devastation. The quake, with its epicentre near Chobari village in Kutch district, had a moment magnitude of 7.7 and lasted for about two minutes. Estimated deaths were between 14,000 and 20,000, with many more injured and property destroyed. The city of Bhuj was left in ruins, hundreds of surrounding villages were affected and in Ahmadabad, several high-rise buildings collapsed. Reconstruction was achieved with the help of Indian and international organizations, and Bhuj was rebuilt with a new city plan.

A mishap took place across the border too, in Nepal. On 1 June, King Birendra of Nepal and several members of his family were shot dead, probably by his son Dipendra, who then shot himself. Dipendra had allegedly been unhappy because his parents did not approve of the girl he loved. After the massacre, Gyanendra, brother of Dipendra, became king. India supported the new government as it was in India's interests to preserve peace, because of the 1751-kilometre-long common border.

Crossing another shared border, President Musharraf of Pakistan visited India in July, and discussions were held. It was believed that relations between the two countries were improving, but the third tragedy that year took place on 13 December 2001, when terrorists attacked the Parliament. This strained Indo-Pak relations again, and train and bus services between India and Pakistan were suspended early the following year.

In June, two other tragic incidents occurred. On 22 June, a train accident in Kerala led to sixty-four deaths when a Chennai-bound train derailed from a bridge over River Kadalundi and coaches fell into the waters, while the very next day, 23 June, an overcrowded boat capsized in River Ganga in West Bengal's Malda district, causing around fifty deaths.

❋ OTHER KEY EVENTS

In April there was a conflict along the Indo-Bangladesh border, resulting in the death of a deputy commandant and fifteen members of India's Border Security Force. India believed the Bangladesh government was not involved, and therefore the matter was resolved through dialogue. Bangladesh promised that Bodo militants who had crossed into the country from Assam would not be allowed to set up bases there.

In July, a Dhaka–Agartala bus service was announced, connecting Bangladesh and the Indian state of Tripura. The two governments also agreed to restart passenger train services. This took several years, but meanwhile, the Petrapole–Benapole international rail link between the two countries, closed in 1976, was resumed in January 2001, carrying freight.

The ceasefire signed with the National Socialist Council of Nagaland (IM) (1997) was extended.

A new political party was formed: the Telangana Rashtra Samithi, which started another movement for the creation of Telangana. At the Centre, the NDA stayed in power.

❖ LATA MANGESHKAR: THE MELODY QUEEN RECEIVES THE BHARAT RATNA

Lata Mangeshkar (b. 28 September 1929), a brilliant singer of Hindustani classical and light music, is primarily a playback vocalist for films. She sings romantic songs and bhajans, as well as classical music. She was born in Indore and initially learnt music from her father, Deenanath Mangeshkar, who was a Hindustani classical vocalist and a performer in Marathi Natya Sangeet (musical plays). His influence was such that the entire family became singers! While her sister Asha Bhosle is well known too, her other sisters, Meena Mangeshkar and Usha Mangeshkar, are also singers, as well as her brother, Hridaynath Mangeshkar. Lata continued her musical training with Aman Ali Khan and Amanat Ali Khan, and over the years, has sung for more than a thousand movies, mainly in Hindi but also in regional languages. Among her greatest hits are 'Lag Jaa Gale' from the film *Woh Kaun Thi?* (1964), 'Ek Tu Hi Bharosa' from *Pukar* (2000), 'Tere Liye' from *Veer-Zaara* (2004) and 'Pyar Kiya Toh Darna Kya' from *Mughal-e-Azam*. She has received numerous awards, including the Bharat Ratna in 2001.

ASHA BHOSLE

Asha Bhosle (b. 8 September 1933) is also a playback singer, and has contributed to over a thousand Bollywood movies. She has sung other types of music as well, including remixes, Indipop, qawwalis and folk songs. Her best hits include 'Aaiye Meharbaan' from the film *Howrah Bridge* (1958), 'Piya Tu Ab Toh Aaja' from *Caravan* (1971), 'Dum Maro Dum' from *Hare Rama Hare Krishna* (1971) and 'Zara Sa Jhoom

Loon Main' from *Dilwale Dulhania Le Jayenge*. She won the Dadasaheb Phalke Award in 2000 and the Padma Vibhushan in 2008. In 2013, she acted for the first time, in the film *Mai*.

❈ DEV ANAND: ROMANCING WITH LIFE

Dev Anand (26 September 1923–3 December 2011) was a popular actor, as well as director and producer.

Along with his brother Chetan Anand, he founded Navketan Films, a production house, in 1949. Dev Anand acted in over a hundred films and became known as a romantic actor. Among his hits are *Guide* (1965), *Jewel Thief* (1967), *Johny Mera Naam* (1970), *Banarasi Babu* (1973), *Tere Mere Sapne* (1971) and many more. He continued to act in the 1990s and 2000s, his last film being *Chargesheet* (2011). One among the films he directed is *Hare Rama Hare Krishna*, which was a great success.

Dev Anand

Dev Anand received numerous awards and vast recognition, including the Padma Bhushan (2001), the National Film Award for the best feature film for *Guide* (1965), the Dadasaheb Phalke Award (2002) and four Filmfare Awards. His autobiography, *Romancing with Life*, was published in 2007.

❈ THE SANTOOR AND SHIVKUMAR SHARMA

The santoor is a stringed instrument that is laid flat and played with small hammers or mallets. Shivkumar Sharma (b. 1938), his son Rahul Sharma, Bhajan Sopori, Tarun Bhattacharya,

R. Visweswaran and Ulhas Bapat are among its noted players. The instrument is native to Kashmir, but began to be used for classical music only in the 1950s.

At that time, Uma Dutt Sharma, a vocalist and father to Shivkumar, studied the instrument and started teaching his young son to play it. The Kashmiri santoor, believed to have developed from the *shatatantri* veena mentioned in early texts, has 100 strings. Shivkumar modified this instrument, creating one with ninety-one strings and thirty-one bridges. The Kashmiri santoor is kept on a wooden stand but, to play fast passages better, Shivkumar started keeping it on his lap. Other santoor players now use this improved instrument and method.

Shivkumar Sharma, India's best-known santoor player, has performed at concerts in India and several parts of the world. He received the Sangeet Natak Akademi Award for instrumental music in 1986, the Padma Shri in 1991 and the Padma Vibhushan in 2001.

✸ L. SUBRAMANIAM RECEIVES THE PADMA BHUSHAN

L. Subramaniam (b. 23 July 1947), called the God of Indian Violin, is a violinist and composer in both Karnatic and Western music, and is also a qualified doctor. He is particularly known for his works for orchestra. Born into a family of musicians, he initially learnt from his father, V. Lakshminarayana. Later, he studied Western music at the California Institute of the Arts, USA. He has created Indian and Western, as well as fusion music, and has played with world musicians. His arrangements have been played by top orchestras, including the New York Philharmonic, conducted by Zubin Mehta. Though it was his album *Global Fusion*, released in 1999, that brought him worldwide fame, he has numerous others to his credit.

Among his other notable contributions are his sound concepts for Peter Brook's *Mahabharata* (1989) and the scores for some films, both in Hollywood and India. He was awarded the Padma Shri in 1989, the Sangeet Natak Akademi Award in 1990 and the Padma Bhushan in 2001, among many other awards.

He founded the Lakshminarayana Global Music Festival in 1992, in memory of his father.

❋ THE RADIO AND FM CHANNELS

Just after Independence, All India Radio had six radio stations and eighteen transmitters. By 2001, there were 208 radio stations, 149 medium-wave, fifty shortwave and fifty-five FM transmitters.

FM broadcasting started in 1977, but only expanded during the 1990s, when private radio stations also started operating.

ALSO IN 2001

1 January: Calcutta is renamed Kolkata.

March: Pullela Gopichand wins the All England Open Badminton Championship.

21 July: Death of Sivaji Ganesan (b. 1927), Tamil actor with more than 300 Tamil films to his credit and recipient of the Dadasaheb Phalke Award (1996)

25 July: Former bandit Phoolan Devi is shot dead.

10 August: Death of V.S. Gaitonde (b. 1924), noted abstract painter

29 August: Koneru Humpy wins the World Junior Chess Championship, held in Athens.

30 September: Death of Congress leader Madhavrao Scindia and seven others in a plane crash

26 October: Japan lifts economic sanctions imposed on India.

10 December: Death of veteran actor Ashok Kumar (b. 1911), popularly called Dadamoni

December: The Indian embassy is reopened in Kabul after several years. It was closed on 26 September 1996, just before the Taliban entered the area.

December: A.B. Vajpayee visits Japan; a number of agreements are signed.

The Jnanpith is awarded to Gujarati-language poet Rajendra Keshavlal Shah.

2002: A NEW PRESIDENT—
A.P.J. ABDUL KALAM

A.B. Vajpayee was still prime minister, but it was time to elect a new President. A.P.J. Abdul Kalam was chosen and elected unopposed in July. He was a scientist and not a politician, but was acceptable to both the BJP and the Congress. In August, Bhairon Singh Shekhawat was elected as vice president.

The BJP was in power in Gujarat, Himachal Pradesh, Jharkhand and Goa, and formed coalition governments in Uttar Pradesh and Orissa. The number of seats of the Congress had decreased at the Centre but its performance in the states improved. While in 1998, it held power in five states, by 2002, it held power in fourteen states.

Meanwhile, the liberalization of the economy continued. Part of this process was disinvestment—allowing private investment in industries that had previously been owned by the government. Industries had been divided into strategic and non-strategic ones, and the latter could be disinvested. By May 2002, forty-eight public sector units and some of their subsidiaries were disinvested, earning the government substantial money.

❈ OTHER KEY EVENTS

An unfortunate incident took place in Gujarat. On 27 February, over fifty kar sevaks returning from Ayodhya were burnt alive on the Sabarmati Express at Godhra station. This led to riots and attacks on Muslims, with many innocent people killed.

In September–October, elections were held in Jammu and Kashmir, and a coalition government of the People's Democratic Party (PDP) and the Congress was formed. Mufti Mohammad Sayeed of the PDP became chief minister.

❈ KISHORI AMONKAR IS AWARDED THE PADMA VIBHUSHAN

Kishori Amonkar (10 April 1932–3 April 2017), vocalist of Hindustani classical music, sang classical light music across many gharanas. She began studying music with her mother, Mogubai Kurdikar, who had trained with Alladiya Khan. She also studied with Balakrishnabuva Parvatkar and Mohanrao Palekar, and started singing publicly in 1947. She received the Padma Bhushan in 1987 and the Padma Vibhushan in 2002, as well as other awards, including the Hariprasad Chaurasia Puraskar (2014). Her devotional album *Mharo Pranam* (1998), based on Meera Bai's songs, is her most popular one. Kishori remained rather reclusive. In a rare interview, she shared her view on music competitions, saying, 'Little children are made to believe that vocal acrobatics is what music is about.'[30]

---

[30] Yogesh Pawar, 'The Kishori Amonkar Interview: "I prefer majestic isolation to squandering a way of life and saadhana"', *DNA India*, 4 April 2017, http://www.dnaindia.com/lifestyle/interview-the-kishori-amonkar-interview-i-prefer-majestic-isolation-to-squandering-a-way-of-life-and-saadhana-1949403.

❋ MARIO MIRANDA: MISS NIMBUPANI

Mario Miranda (2 May 1926–11 December 2011), noted artist and cartoonist, was awarded the Padma Shri in 1988. He received the Padma Bhushan in 2002 and the Padma Vibhushan, posthumously, in 2012.

By 1988, he was at the height of his career. Self-taught and naturally gifted, Mario was born in Daman, then under the Portuguese. After working in an advertising agency, he began drawing cartoons for *Illustrated Weekly of India*, and later for other magazines and journals. As his fame grew, he held exhibitions all over the world, and received awards not only from India, but also from the Government of Portugal. He also painted murals, wrote books and illustrated books by other authors. Mario settled in Loutolim, his ancestral village in Goa.

One of his most iconic creations is the character Miss Rajni Nimbupani, a curvaceous and charming heroine. His other famous characters include Balraj Balram, Bulbul Brandy and Miss Fonseca.

Mario even illustrated textbooks for the Bal Bharati schools and, for once, children loved their texts!

❋ KULOTHUNGAN RECEIVES THE PADMA BHUSHAN

Kulothungan (1929–10 December 2016), whose real name was V.C. Kulandaiswamy, was a Tamil-language writer, as well as a scientist and educationist. Born in Vangalampalayam village in Tamil Nadu, he completed a PhD in hydrology and water resources from the University of Illinois, USA, and worked in several government departments of India. He was vice chancellor of Madurai Kamaraj University, Anna University and IGNOU, and wrote both prose and poems.

Kulothungan published his first poem at the age of twenty. His collection of essays *Vazhum Valluvam* won him the Sahitya

Akademi Award in 1988. In his poem 'Vayil Tirakkattum' (Let the Door Be Opened, 1958, translated by Hephzibah Jesudasan), he wrote of the achievements of scientists, who worked hard to unveil the mysteries of the universe. The collection of his poems *Manuda Yathirai* (Journey of Man) looks at society, science and spiritualism. He believed that literature had a role in providing a vision for the future, and must lead to action. He received the Padma Shri in 1992 for his contribution to science, education and engineering, followed by the Padma Bhushan in 2002.

In his poem 'Let's Forge a New World', translated by himself, he wrote:[31]

> I ask for nothing from those who
> gaze upwards for a paradise beyond;
> I come to welcome the architects
> with a mind to create a heaven on earth.

MANI KRISHNASWAMI PASSES AWAY

Mani Krishnaswami (3 February 1930–12 July 2002) was a Karnatic music singer and theoretician. Born in Vellore, she initially studied music with Ellaya and Murugan, and later at Kalakshetra. She then gave numerous concerts in India and abroad, and was known for her devotional music, particularly her rendition of the Sanskrit verses Soundarya Lahari. She received a number of awards, including the Sangeet Natak Akademi Award (1987), the Kalaimamani of the Tamil Nadu government (1991), the title of Sapthagiri Sangeetha Vidwan Mani by the Sri Tyagaraja Trust, Tirupati (8 August 1993) and the Padma Shri (2002).

---

[31] Kulothungan, *Earth is Paradise: Poems in Tamil, Translated by the Author* (n.p.: Allied Publishers Limited, 1993).

SHAH RUKH KHAN: THE *BADSHAH* OF BOLLYWOOD

Shah Rukh (b. 2 November 1965) is one of the biggest names in Indian cinema, also called King Khan and the King of Romance. He has acted in over seventy-five Hindi films, has eight Filmfare Awards for the best actor and altogether fifteen Filmfare Awards. He received the Padma Shri in 2005. In 2008, *Newsweek* listed him as one of the most powerful people in the world. In 2011, *Los Angeles Times* called him 'the world's biggest movie star'.

Shah Rukh started acting with television, but then moved to films, his first being *Deewana* (1992). He went on to act in many more, and in 1995, seven of his films were released, of which the most significant were *Dilwale Dulhania Le Jayenge* and *Karan Arjun*. Among his many other notable films are *Kuch Kuch Hota Hai* (1998), *Mohabbatein* (2000), *Kabhi Khushi Kabhie Gham* (2001), *Devdas* (2002), *Kal Ho Naa Ho* (2003), *Veer–Zaara*, *Chak De! India* (2007), *Om Shanti Om* (2007), *My Name Is Khan* (2010), *Happy New Year* (2014) and *Raees* (2017).

Shah Rukh Khan

He married Gauri Chibber (now Khan) in 1991, and they have three children.

Red Chillies Entertainment, a film production and distribution company, was founded by Shah Rukh Khan and Gauri Khan in 2002. This replaced the earlier company, Dreamz Unlimited.

FRANCIS NEWTON SOUZA DIES

Francis Newton Souza (12 April 1924–28 March 2002), an artist, was one of the founders of the Bombay Progressive Artists'

Group. He was born in Saligao, Goa, but moved with his family to Bombay in 1929. An episode of smallpox in his childhood, from which he recovered, left a deep impression on him. Originally named Newton, Francis was added to his name by his mother, in gratitude for his recovery. He later studied at Sir J. J. School of Art, but in 1945, was expelled for nationalist activities. He joined the Communist Party in 1947, and in 1949, moved to London. By then, he had already held one exhibition, and carried on painting while working as a journalist. After an exhibition in 1955, his success grew, and he held shows in India and in cities around the world. He settled in New York in 1967.

Souza's wide variety of paintings include nudes, landscapes and Christian themes. His works now sell at steep prices. In 2015, his 1955 painting *Birth* was resold at a Christie's auction for over $4 million dollars. Though he returned to Mumbai before his death, he felt he was not appreciated in his own country. In his book *Words and Lines* (1959), when writing about the episode of smallpox, he says it would have been better had he died, that it would have saved him a lot of trouble—'I would not have had to bear an artist's tormented soul, create art in a country that despises her artists and is ignorant of her heritage.'[32]

ALSO IN 2002

1 January: The Delhi–Lahore train and bus services are discontinued.

3 January: Death of Satish Dhawan (b. 1920), scientist, Padma Vibhushan winner (1981), director of Indian

---

[32] F.N. Souza, *Words and Lines* (London: Villiers, 1959).

Institute of Science, Bangalore, chairman of the Indian Space Research Organization (ISRO)

6 January: Britain and India sign the New Delhi Declaration to come together to promote peace, security and development.

March: The 1996 trade treaty between India and Nepal is extended till 2007.

14 May: During the Kaluchak Massacre, a terrorist attack in Kashmir, militants open fire at passengers of a tourist bus and members of the Indian Army.

6 July: Death of industrialist Dhirubhai Ambani (b. 1932)

27 July: Death of Krishna Kant (b. 1927), vice president of India (1997–2002)

9 September: The Rajdhani Express travelling from Kolkata to New Delhi derails from a bridge; around 120 people are killed.

24 September: In an armed attack on Akshardham Temple in Gujarat, many pilgrims are murdered.

30 September: The Indian National Scientific Documentation Centre (INSDOC, founded in 1952) and the National Institute of Science Communication (NISCOM, founded in 1951) are merged to form the National Institute of Science Communication and Information Resources (NISCAIR).

11 October: Death of Dina Pathak (b. 1922), veteran film actor

October: Troops massed at the Pakistan border start withdrawing after a ten-month-long standoff. The cost borne by India is Rs 8000 crore, and some soldiers and civilians had died.

The Jnanpith is awarded to Tamil-language writer Jayakanthan.

2003: IMPROVING RELATIONS WITH PAKISTAN

In May, Prime Minister Vajpayee made attempts to resume relations with Pakistan and President Musharraf responded favourably. The Delhi–Lahore bus service, stopped in 2002, was restarted.

However, on 25 August, bomb blasts at several locations in Mumbai led to the death of around fifty civilians.

❋ MOHANLAL COMPLETES TWENTY-FIVE YEARS IN FILMS

Celebrations were held that year, when Mohanlal (b. 21 May 1960), the highest-paid actor in Malayalam films, completed twenty-five years in the profession. By then, he had acted in 255 Malayalam films and went on to act in many more. He has also acted in Hindi, Telugu, Kannada and Tamil films.

> **THE MALAYALAM FILM INDUSTRY**
>
> Other top actors of Malayalam films include Mammootty (Muhammad Kutty); Nivin Pauly, whose films include

Bangalore Days (2014), *Om Shanthi Oshana* (2014), *Premam* (2015); Jayaram, popular in the 1990s; Fahadh Fazil, son of the director Fazil and the highest paid among the young actors, with roles such as that of the anti-hero in the 2012 film *22 Female Kottayam*; Dileep, a character actor; Prithviraj Sukumaran, who has also acted in some Bollywood films and has founded August Cinema, a film production and distribution company; Kunchacko Boban, who acted in *How Old Are You?* (2014) and *Cousins* (2014); Jayasurya, who has acted in films such as *Punyalan Agarbattis* (2013), *Classmates* (2006), *Chocolate* (2007), *Iyobinte Pusthakam* (2014) and *Apothecary* (2014); Dulquer Salmaan, son of Mammootty, a star kid who could become a superstar.

Among the many good directors in the Malayalam film industry, Adoor Gopalakrishnan (b. 3 July 1941) stands out. He has won several awards, including multiple National Film Awards, the Dadasaheb Phalke Award (2004), the Padma Shri (1984) and the Padma Vibhushan (2006). His films include *Swayamvaram* (1972), *Kodiyettam* (1977), *Elippathayam* (1981), *Mukhamukham* (1984, winner of the International Federation of Film Critics Prize), *Anantaram* (1987), *Mathilukal* (1990), *Nizhalkuthu* (2002) and *Naalu Pennungal* (2007), as well as a number of short and documentary films. He has also written plays, essays and books.

Among other well-known directors are Fazil, whose 1993 film *Manichitrathazhu*, a psychological thriller, won several awards, P. Padmarajan, Lal Jose, Bharathan, Alphonse Puthren, K.G. George, Ranjith, Sreenivasan, M.T. Vasudevan Nair, Sibi Malayil, Sathyan Anthikad, Blessy, Sidharth Siva, Kamal, G. Aravindan, Joshi, Anwar

Rasheed, Shafi, Johny Antony, Shaji Kailas, Rafi–Mecartin and T.V. Chandran.

Some Malayalam hit films include *1983* (2014), directed by Abrid Shine; *Thoovanathumbikal* (1987), directed by P. Padmarajan, based on his own novel; *Kilukkam* (1991), directed by Priyadarshan, a blockbuster and cult film; *Ustad Hotel* (2012); *Sandesam* (1991), a political satire; *Oru Vadakkan Veeragatha* (1989), about Chekavar warriors, directed by Hariharan; *Kerala Varma Pazhassi Raja* (2009), a historical film; *Chaappa Kurishu* (2011) and *Drishyam* (2013).

A new wave of Malayalam films started in 2010.

❋ HRITHIK ROSHAN: *KOI MIL GAYA*

Hrithik Roshan (b. 10 January 1974), a top Bollywood actor, has portrayed a variety of roles, including ones in romantic films. *Kaho Naa . . . Pyaar Hai* (2000), the family drama *Kabhi Khushi Kabhie Gham*, his highly successful science fiction films, *Koi . . . Mil Gaya* (2003), *Krrish* (2006) and *Krrish 3* (2013), *Zindagi Na Milegi Dobara* (2011), *Jodhaa Akbar*, *Agneepath* (2012), *Bang Bang!* (2014) and *Kaabil* (2017) are among his hits.

Hrithik married Sussanne Khan in 2000, but they divorced in 2014. They have two sons, Hrehaan and Hridhaan.

❋ BIKASH BHATTACHARJEE IS AWARDED THE LALIT KALA AKADEMI FELLOWSHIP

Bikash Bhattacharjee (21 June 1940–18 December 2006), an artist from Kolkata, received the Lalit Kala Akademi Fellowship in 2003, adding to his many other awards. He used watercolours, oils and other media to make realistic paintings that depict regular people and their lives. He also painted portraits, animals and urban scenes.

❋ KALAVATI DEVI

Kalavati Devi, celebrated Manipuri dancer, trained under the legendary dance teacher Bipin Singh. Kalavati has toured all over India and the world and was head of the Manipuri dance department at Rabindra Bharati University, Kolkata. She received the Sangeet Natak Akademi Award in 2003.

Manipuri dancers

KHAMBA, THOIBI AND MANIPURI DANCE

Who were Khamba and Thoibi? Their story is famous in the traditions of Manipur.

Living in the town of Moirang, Thoibi was a beautiful princess, the daughter of King Chingkhuba's brother, while Khamba was an orphan, taken care of by his elder sister, Khammu. Thoibi and Khamba met by chance and fell in love. Kongyamba, son of a court official, was also in love with Thoibi, though she did not care for him. After several adventures, mishaps and the defeat of Kongyamba, Thoibi and Khamba got married. But not satisfied with this happy ending, Khamba decided to test Thoibi's chastity by entering the house at night, disguised. Fearing that a stranger was trespassing, Thoibi killed him with a spear. When she realized she had killed her husband and not a stranger, she killed herself. Thoibi and Khamba are considered incarnations of deities, earlier of local ones, and later of Shiva and Parvati.

The story has different versions and has evolved over time. It used to be narrated by *pana* singers, and is now performed in Manipuri dances, particularly the dance Lai Haraoba. The pana is an instrument that accompanies a Manipuri performance.

Manipuri dance is the traditional dance style of Manipur. Female dancers take small, gliding steps and wear a special costume known as Kumil, which has a decorated and stiffened floor-length skirt. Male dancers, dressed in dhotis, perform vigorous leaps and movements, and often dance while playing the *pung*, a barrel-shaped drum. This form of dance is known as Pung Cholom.

Manipuri dances present dance dramas in different styles. Lai Haraoba revolves around a festival of the same name, which invokes early deities and has ancient roots. At this festival, the *maiba*s and *maibi*s (priests and priestesses) of the temple re-enact the creation of the world. The legendary love of Khamba and Thoibi is also depicted. Rasa Lila dances are of different types. Many depict the love between Radha and Krishna. New dance dramas, with contemporary topics, are also performed in the Manipuri style.

Rajkumar Singhajit Singh, and his wife, Charu Sija Mathur, are among the leading Manipuri dancers, and have won several awards. Singhajit won the Sangeet Natak Ratna Sadasya in 2011, the Sangeet Natak Akademi Award in 1984 and the Padma Shri in 1986. The two have started a Manipuri dance school in Delhi, Manipur Nrityashram.

ALSO IN 2003

18 January: Death of Harivansh Rai Bachchan (b. 27 November 1907), father of Amitabh Bachchan, who was known for his poetry, particularly the collection of verses *Madhushala*

22 April: Death of Balwant Gargi (b. 4 December 1916), Punjabi writer, who was a Sahitya Akademi Award winner

14 July: Death of actress Leela Chitnis (b. 1909)

24 October–1 November: The first Afro-Asian Games are held in Hyderabad.

9 November: Death of Maithili writer Binod Bihari Verma (b. 1937)

G.N. Devy, researcher of tribal groups, writer and literary critic, receives the Prince Claus Award from the Netherlands.

The Jnanpith is awarded to Marathi-language writer Vinda Karandikar for his poetry collection *Ashtadarshana*.

2004: A NEW GOVERNMENT—THE UPA

The National Democratic Alliance, led by A.B. Vajpayee as prime minister, would complete five years in September. However, they decided to hold elections earlier, between 20 April and 10 May. This time, the number of BJP seats fell to 138 and the NDA altogether had 181. The Congress had also formed an alliance with other parties, known as the United Progressive Alliance (UPA). The Congress won 145 seats, and along with its allies, had 218. The UPA was able to form the government because it also had the support of the leftist parties, the Bahujan Samaj Party and the Samajwadi Party.

As the leader of the Congress party, Sonia Gandhi could have become prime minister, but some were unhappy with the idea because of her Italian background. Instead, she selected Manmohan Singh, an academician and economist, as prime minister. He had been finance minister, initiating economic reforms, when Narasimha Rao was prime minister (1991–96).

In this election, Electronic Voting Machines (EVMs), introduced in India in 1999, were used across the country.

❋ KARNAM MALLESWARI RETIRES

Karnam Malleswari, a female weightlifter, won a bronze medal in the 69 kg category of the Sydney Olympics in 2000.

Born in Srikakulam, Andhra Pradesh, Karnam began training in 1989, and won a number of medals and titles before the Olympic bronze, including two golds and two silvers in Asian competitions. In the 1992 Asian Weightlifting Championships, she won three silver medals. In the 1993 world championships, she won a bronze, and in 1994, two golds and a bronze in Istanbul, when she was just nineteen years old. She won the world title in 1994 and 1995 in the 54 kg category. Karnam retired after participating in the 2004 Olympics. Meanwhile, she married Rajesh Tyagi, another weightlifter, in 1997.

Karnam Malleswari

WEIGHTLIFTING IN INDIA

Among other female weightlifters, Khumukcham Sanjita Chanu won a gold medal in the 48 kg category of the 2014 Commonwealth Games in Glasgow, while Mirabai Chanu won the silver. N. Kunjarani Devi has won twelve silver medals in the world championships, in 1989, 1991, 1992 and 1994, and bronze medals in the Asian Games in 1990 and 1994. Chhaya Adak won bronze medals in the 1990 Asian Games and in the 1989 and 1992 world championships. Bharti Singh won a bronze medal in 1992.

Women have done well in the Asian Weightlifting Championships too. N. Kunjarani Devi has won four silver medals, in 1989, 1991, 1992 and 1993. Silver medals were won by Chhaya Adak (1991, 1993), Bharti Singh (1993) and Karnam Malleswari (1992). Bronze medals were won by L. Anita Chanu (1992) and Neelam Setti Laxmi (1993).

Male Indian weightlifters have performed well in the Commonwealth and Asian Games as well. One among the top performers, E. Karunakaran won a gold medal at the 1978 Commonwealth Games in Edmonton and at the 1980 and 1981 Commonwealth Championships held in Cardiff and Auckland respectively. Male gold medallists in the 2014 Commonwealth Games were Sukhen Dey and Sathish Sivalingam.

❖ THE 2004 SUMMER OLYMPICS

In the 2004 Games, held in Athens, Rajyavardhan Singh Rathore won a silver medal in shooting, in the men's double trap category.

❉ REHMAN RAHI WINS THE JNANPITH AWARD

That year, Rehman Rahi (b. 6 May 1925) became the first writer in Kashmiri literature to be awarded the Jnanpith. He taught Persian at the then University of Jammu and Kashmir, and wrote poetry and essays. He was also a translator.

He composed poetry in Urdu at first, and later in Kashmiri. *Subhuk Soda*, *Kalam-e-Rahi* and *Siyah Rode Jaren Manz* (In a Downpour of Black Rain) are some of his poetry collections. Rahi was influenced by the progressive Kashmiri poet Dinanath Nadim (1916–88). Rahi also received the Sahitya Akademi Award (1961) and the Padma Shri (2000).

❉ THE INDIAN POSTAL SERVICE

The year 2004 marked 150 years of India Post. Commemorative coins were issued to mark this occasion.

India's postal service has both grown and changed with the times. Consisting of 26,130 post offices at the time of Independence, by 2002, there were 1,54,919 post offices. Even with the growth of email, mobile phones and courier services, the postal department maintained its relevance by introducing new services, including the delivery and collection of bills, railway reservations (at certain post offices) and the sale of gold coins.

❉ CHETAN BHAGAT: NEW TRENDS IN INDIAN WRITING IN ENGLISH

Chetan Bhagat (b. 22 April 1974) has been called 'the biggest-selling English-language novelist in India's history'.[33] There may

---

[33] Donald Greenlees, 'An Investment Banker Finds Fame Off the Books', *New York Times*, 26 March 2008, http://www.nytimes.com/2008/03/26/books/26bhagat.html.

now be novelists who have outsold him, but he could be said to have started a new trend in Indian writing that both makes a point and has mass appeal for a younger audience. Beginning with *Five Point Someone* in 2004, a fictionalized account of life in an IIT, Chetan has written seven novels as of 2017, the latest being *One Indian Girl* (2016). Each is a bestseller, and several have been made into films. He has also written screenplays, non-fiction and newspaper columns. Chetan Bhagat began his career as an investment banker, but quit in 2009 to write full-time.

ALSO IN 2004

May: Kiran Bedi (b. 1949), the first woman to become an IPS (Indian Police Service) officer, in 1972, wins the United Nations Medal for outstanding service. She received the Ramon Magsaysay Award in 1994.

September: The Communist Party of India (Marxist–Leninist), or the People's War Group, merges with the Maoist Communist Centre of India to form the Communist Party of India (Maoist).

26 December: An undersea earthquake near Sumatra leads to a tsunami, devastating several countries. India is affected too, and 13,000 people die while more than 4,00,000 have to relocate.

2005: THE RIGHT TO INFORMATION ACT IS PASSED

One of the main achievements of the government that year was the passing of the Right to Information Act on 15 June, which allows citizens to ask for information from any government authority. This act helped change society and end corruption.

❋ OTHER KEY EVENTS

In April, the first bus service in sixty years started between Muzaffarabad, in Pakistan-controlled Kashmir, and Srinagar, in Jammu and Kashmir.

India's relations with China improved as, in April, the countries formed a Strategic and Cooperative Partnership for Peace and Prosperity, and jointly signed a document on a Shared Vision for the Twenty-First Century.

❋ SHYAM BENEGAL WINS THE DADASAHEB PHALKE AWARD

Shyam Benegal (b. 14 December 1934), film director and screenwriter, has made several notable films, starting with *Ankur* in the early 1970s, followed by *Manthan, Nishant, Bhumika, Junoon* (1978), *Kalyug* (1981), *Trikal* (1985), *Mandi* (1983) and others. These films have been called Middle Cinema or New Cinema, as they are realistic portrayals of social themes. In the 1990s, he directed different types of films, including *Suraj ka Satvan Ghoda* and a trilogy of stories about Muslim women: *Mammo* (1994), *Sardari Begum* (1996) and *Zubeidaa* (2001). The last one had music by A.R. Rahman, and Karisma Kapoor starred in the lead role. Among Benegal's other films are *The Making of the Mahatma* (1996) and *Netaji Subhash Chandra Bose: The Forgotten Hero* (2004). He has also written books based on his films.

In addition to the Dadasaheb Phalke Award in 2005, Shyam Benegal has won several others, including the Padma Shri in 1976, the Padma Bhushan in 1991 and seven National Awards for the best feature film in Hindi.

❋ H.D. SHOURIE PASSES AWAY

H.D. Shourie (b. 3 May 1912), a civil servant, died on 28 June 2005 after many years of fighting for the rights of ordinary people.

'The voice of the common man must rise,' he'd say,[34] having founded the Common Cause movement in 1980 after he retired.

The first cause he took up was the rights of pensioners who had retired before 1979, and the Supreme Court verdict was in their favour, helping over 4 million people. There were many other causes he stood for, and seventy writ petitions were filed over twenty-five years. Common Cause continues its struggle even after Shourie's death. In 2014, coal block allocations were cancelled by the Supreme Court through a public interest litigation (PIL) filed by Common Cause.

---

[34] 'Our Founder', *Common Cause*, accessed 11 June 2017, http://commoncause.in/our-founder.php.

R.K. LAXMAN RECEIVES THE PADMA VIBHUSHAN

No one can forget R.K. Laxman's Common Man—always there in the background commenting on every change as the years passed and politicians rose and fell.

Born on 24 October 1921, Laxman created this character for the daily cartoon strip *You Said It* in *Times of India*, first appearing in 1951. He once said that politicians have forgotten the common man, and so his numerous cartoons depict prime ministers, political leaders, as well as various events, even while sympathizing with the ordinary person. The Common Man has a personality that people can identify with.

Laxman's cartoons have been collected and published in numerous books. He also wrote an autobiography, *The Tunnel of Time* (1998). In his last years, he suffered from several strokes and died on 26 January 2015. Laxman received numerous awards, including the Padma Vibhushan in 2005. His elder brother was the well-known writer R.K. Narayan. Laxman was the sketch artist for the television adaptation of Narayan's *Malgudi Days*, which was created in 1986.

R.K. Laxman's Common Man

Cartoonists inspired by him include Harish Chandra Shukla, Sudhir Dhar, Abu Abraham and many more.

THE TOP INDIAN CRICKETERS SINCE INDEPENDENCE

As everyone knows, cricket is India's favourite sport. Though we have looked at some of the country's great cricketers earlier, here are some of the best bowlers, batsmen and all-rounders since Independence:

Ajit Wadekar, Anil Kumble, B.S. Chandrasekhar, Bishen Singh Bedi, Dilip N. Sardesai, Dilip Vengsarkar, E.D. Solkar, Erapalli Prasanna, Farokh M. Engineer, Gundappa Vishwanath, Harbhajan Singh, Javagal Srinath, Kapil Dev, Mansur Ali Khan, Mohammad Azharuddin, Mohinder Amarnath, M.S. Dhoni, Mushtaq Ali, Nari Contractor, Polly Umrigar, Rahul Dravid, Ravi Shastri, Rohit Sharma, S. Venkataraghavan, Sunil Gavaskar, Sachin Tendulkar, Sourav Ganguly, Subhash Gupte, Vijay Hazare, Vijay Merchant, Vinoo Mankad, Virat Kohli, Virender Sehwag, V.V.S. Laxman and Yuvraj Singh.

Among women, the best players include Shantha Rangaswamy, Anjum Chopra, Diana Edulji, Mithali Raj, Jhulan Goswami, Harmanpreet Kaur, Neetu David, Nooshin Al Khadeer, Shubhangi Kulkarni, Purnima Rau and Anju Jain.

In the 2005 ICC Awards ceremony held in Australia on 11 October, two Indian players were honoured: Virender Sehwag, as part of the World Test XI series, and Rahul Dravid, as part of the World One-Day XI.

ALSO IN 2005

25 January: A stampede at Mandher Devi Temple near Wai, Maharashtra, leads to over 200 deaths.

February: *Sholay* is named the best film of fifty years at the fiftieth Filmfare Awards.

26–27 July: Floods bring Mumbai to a standstill.

29 October: The Delta Fast Passenger train derails off a collapsed bridge near the town of Valigonda, Andhra Pradesh, causing over a hundred deaths.

29 October: Bomb blasts take place in three crowded markets of Delhi ahead of Diwali; over sixty people are declared dead.

December: Cricketer M.S. Dhoni (b. 1981) makes his Test debut.

The Jnanpith is awarded to Hindi poet Kunwar Narayan.

2006: THE TWENTY POINT PROGRAMME IS RESTRUCTURED

As Manmohan Singh stayed on as prime minister, the Twenty Point Programme was reviewed and restructured to bring about more development. The National Rural Employment Guarantee Act was initiated to provide employment in rural areas, and achieved some success. And the National e-Governance Plan was approved in May.

Among other events, on 18 February, the Thar Express was inaugurated. This train links Karachi, in Pakistan, to Bhagat ki Kothi near Jodhpur, in Rajasthan.

❋ KIRAN DESAI WINS THE BOOKER PRIZE

Kiran Desai (b. 3 September 1971) won the Man Booker Prize in 2006 for her novel *The Inheritance of Loss*. Born in Chandigarh, she is the daughter of the well-known novelist Anita Desai.

The Inheritance of Loss, her second novel, looks at the life of Biju, an illegal immigrant living in the USA, and Sai, a girl in Kalimpong, India. Sai lives with her maternal grandfather, for whom Biju's father works as a cook. The novel examines colonialism, the legacy of the past in the present, class differences in India and the Gorkhaland movement. This book also won Kiran the 2006 Vodafone Crossword Book Award and the 2007 National Book Critics Circle Award for fiction.

❉ SABRI KHAN IS AWARDED THE PADMA BHUSHAN

Sabri Khan (21 May 1927–1 December 2015), a Hindustani classical sarangi player, was awarded the Padma Bhushan in 2006. Of the Senia gharana, he received a number of other honours, and played in countries all over the world. Audiences in Europe and America became familiar with the sarangi because of him. His son Kamal Sabri and his grandson Suhail Yusuf Khan also play the sarangi. Suhail plays and sings with the fusion group Advaita.

THE SARANGI

The sarangi, a stringed instrument, has three main strings and thirty-five to forty sympathetic strings. It is played with a bow and has a unique sound. Usually the sarangi is made of red cedar wood and is about 60 centimetres long. It was once used as an accompaniment by wandering singers, but during the Mughal period it was incorporated into classical music. It can even be made to sound like a human voice, but it is difficult to tune and play. So in modern times, a harmonium is preferred, though the sarangi is still used to accompany vocal music and as a solo instrument.

Some outstanding sarangi players are:

- Abdul Latif Khan (1934–2002): Born into a family of musicians in Gohad village near Gwalior, he began learning the sarangi from his father. Khan was a staff

artist with All India Radio, Bhopal. He played both Hindustani and rare Karnatic music ragas.
- Bundu Khan (1886–1955): Of the Delhi gharana, he was one of the best sarangi players. He had been a court musician of Indore State and was the first to use metal strings instead of gut ones. At times he used a sarangi smaller than usual, made of bamboo. There are many curious stories about him: Once, invited to a gathering, he could not be seen anywhere and then was found playing his sarangi to the flowers! On another occasion, he took a vow of silence—he would go to the market along with his sarangi and the tune he played would indicate which vegetables he wanted to buy! His best-known students were Abdul Majeed Khan and Sagiruddin Khan.
- Shakoor Khan (1905–75): He belonged to the Kirana gharana.
- Gopal Mishra (1921–77): He studied with his elder brother, Hanuman Prasad Mishra, his father, Sur Sahai Mishra, and the vocalist Bade Ramdas. He lived in Delhi, and played the sarangi both solo and as an accompanist.
- Ram Narayan (b. 1927): From Udaipur, Rajasthan, he has given several solo concerts.
- Sultan Khan (1941–27 November 2011): From the city of Jodhpur, he was also a singer, and received the Padma Bhushan (2010) as well as other awards. He studied with Ghulam Khan of Jodhpur, and with his own uncle, the sarangi player Azim Khan.
- Laddan Khan (b. 1934): He was an excellent sarangi player, though his skill was later affected by a degenerative disease.

- Munir Khan (1926–2011): He studied with his father, Nazir Khan.
- Two noted female sarangi players are Aruna Narayan, daughter of Ram Narayan, and Archana Yadav, a student of Bhagwan Das Mishra.

SARANGI MELAS

Sarangi melas are organized from time to time. At the Bhopal Sarangi Mela of 1989, there was a gathering of over a hundred sarangi players.

ASHTA MAHISHI: BHAMA NRITYAM

Shanta Rao (1930–28 December 2007) was a noted dancer who created the classical dance style Bhama Nrityam, based on the rituals of the cult Bhama Sutram.

Born in Mangalore, she did not come from a line of dancers, but insisted on studying dance. Her father finally relented. She was the very first girl to train in Kathakali at Kerala Kalamandalam, where Guru P. Ramunni Menon accepted her only on the suggestion of Narayana Menon Vallathol, the founder. There she also studied Mohiniattam with the great guru Krishna Panicker. On visits to the village Pandanallur, she learnt Bharatanatyam from Meenakshi Sundaram Pillai. She even went on to study Kuchipudi, which, she felt, should acknowledge its development from the dance form Bhagavata Mela Nataka. Next, she studied with Venkata Chalapathy Shastry, a priest specializing in Bhama

Sutram rituals, which used to be performed in secret within the temple. The mystery is that he asked Shanta to go there, yet asked her not to reveal what she had learnt. So she retreated into a three-year-long meditation.

Then, with the blessings of her guru and in a form that he approved, she performed Bhama Nrityam, which she said was 'the gods' gift to [her].'[35] Her last performance, in 2006, was a Bhama Nrityam composition, *Ashta Mahishi*, depicting the eight wives of the god Krishna. Shanta was much acclaimed, yet she has been called a forgotten legend as she never received the prominence of other dancers. She did not seek publicity and, though applauded by critics, was distressed by the commercialization and decline of pure dance.

She was awarded the Sangeet Natak Akademi Award in 1970 and the Padma Shri in 1971.

Shanta Rao performing Bhama Nrityam

NEW STYLES IN CLASSICAL DANCE

There have been many changes in the presentation of classical dances. While some have continued with traditions,

---

[35] Sunil Janah and Ashoke Chatterjee, *Dances of the Golden Hall*, quoted in Ashoke Chatterjee, 'A Perfect Stillness: The Art of Shanta Rao' (symposium, 'Why Dance?', December 2015), accessed 11 June 2017, http://www.india-seminar.com/2015/676/676_ashoke_chatterjee.htm.

others have innovated, such as using new styles in dress—including leotards, body-hugging suits, shifts and saris. New postures and movements are introduced from yoga, martial arts and other such forms. Many have crossed the boundaries of traditional dance.

Chandralekha Patel (6 December 1928–30 December 2006) was one of the innovators, borrowing sequences and poses from other art forms, along with using special lighting and experimental music. Her production *Sharira*, which premiered in March 2001, was groundbreaking and her dances have been called postmodern. She was awarded the Sangeet Natak Akademi Ratna Sadasya in 2004. Her work has been recorded by Sadanand Menon in his book *Chandralekha, Choreographic Works: Anigka to Sharira 1985–2003*.

Geeta Chandran (b. 14 January 1962) is a Bharatanatyam dancer, whose dance performances reflect her personal vision. She founded Natya Vriksha, an organization to promote dance, and has choreographed new dances as well as worked in television, video, film and theatre. She has been involved in several creative collaborations. Among them are *Her Voice*, a dance and puppetry performance, for which she worked with Anurupa Roy and her puppet theatre company Katkatha. *Her Voice*, based on the Mahabharata, has the theme 'Women and War'.

❋ FACEBOOK

Facebook, a social media and networking site, was founded in 2004, but opened to all users over the age of thirteen in 2006. By June 2015, there were 125 million Facebook users in India, and by

May 2016, India had over 195 million users, the highest number from any country in the world. The US, in second place, had a little over 191 million.

ALSO IN 2006

2–5 March: US President George W. Bush visits India.

28 March: Death of Bansi Lal (b. 1927), former Haryana chief minister

10 April: A fire at the Brand India Fair in Meerut leads to around sixty-five deaths.

12 April: Death of Kannada film actor Rajkumar (b. 1929)

27 August: Death of veteran film director Hrishikesh Mukherjee (b. 1922)

29 August: A meteorite lands in Kanvarpura village, Rajasthan.

9 October: Death of Kanshi Ram (b. 1934), founder of the Bahujan Samaj Party

Zeenat Aman wins the Filmfare Lifetime Achievement Award.

The Jnanpith awardees are Konkani-language writer Ravindra Kelekar and Sanskrit scholar and poet Satya Vrat Shastri.

2007: PRATIBHA PATIL—THE FIRST FEMALE PRESIDENT

The year saw the election of a new President and vice president. In July, Pratibha Devisingh Patil (b. 1934) became the first female President of the country. She has had a long career in politics, having been a member of the Legislative Assembly (MLA) in Maharashtra and later, the Governor of Rajasthan. Mohammad Hamid Ansari (b. 1937) was elected vice president.

❋ OTHER KEY EVENTS

An agreement was signed between India and Pakistan in February to reduce the accidental risk of nuclear war.

In the same month, sixty-eight passengers, mostly from Pakistan, were killed in a terror attack on the Samjhauta Express, a train connecting Lahore and Delhi.

❋ DHARMENDRA: *LIFE IN A ... METRO*

Dharmendra (b. 8 December 1935), an actor in Hindi and Punjabi films, has had many early hits, but among his later films is the contemporary *Life in a . . . Metro* (2007), the story of nine people living in the metropolitan city of Mumbai, directed by Anurag Basu. The popular soundtrack of the film was composed by Pritam, while the lyrics were by Sayeed Quadri, Amitabh Verma and Sandeep Srivastava. The movie won three Filmfare Awards, among other prizes.

Among Dharmendra's noted films are *Phool aur Pathar* (1966), *Mera Gaon Mera Desh* (1971) and the blockbuster *Sholay*. He entered politics and was a member of the Lok Sabha from 2004 to 2009. His later films include *Apne* (2007), *Yamla Pagla Deewana* (2011) and *Yamla Pagla Deewana 2* (2013). He received the Filmfare Lifetime Achievement Award in 1997 and the Padma Bhushan in 2012.

Dharmendra married Parkash Kaur in 1954, and had four children, including his sons Sunny and Bobby. His second marriage was to Hema Malini, and they have two daughters, Esha and Ahana. In 1983, Dharmendra set up the production company Vijayta Films, and launched his sons Sunny and Bobby Deol in films.

Sunny Deol (b. 19 October 1956) starred in numerous films in the 1980s and 1990s. One of his most successful films was *Gadar: Ek Prem Katha* (2001), a period drama set in the time of Partition. Bobby Deol (b. 27 January 1969) has also acted in several films. The films *Barsaat* (1995), *Gupt* (1997) and *Yamla Pagla Deewana* are among his most popular ones.

● AMITAV GHOSH IS AWARDED THE PADMA SHRI

Amitav Ghosh (b. 11 July 1956), well-known writer in English literature, has written several books with a historical background. Among his books are *The Circle of Reason* (1986), his first novel, and the Ibis trilogy, dealing with colonial history: *Sea of Poppies* (2008), *River of Smoke* (2011) and *Flood of Fire* (2015). He also has several non-fiction books to his credit, the latest being *The Great Derangement: Climate Change and the Unthinkable* (2016). He has won a number of prestigious awards, including the Prix Médicis Étranger of France for *The Circle of Reason* (1990). He was co-winner of the Vodafone Crossword Book Award (2009) and co-winner of the Israeli Dan David Prize (2010), both for *Sea of Poppies*. He has also won the Sahitya Akademi Award (1989).

Palace of Assembly, Chandigarh

ARCHITECTURE

Architecture in India after Independence has been largely individualistic, most buildings being built without any notable style. However, there have been some renowned architects, who have designed significant buildings, and even entire cities. Among them was Laurie Baker, who died in 2007.

Architects have to keep in mind the building laws of the area while creating designs. There are two main types of structures: modern and postmodern; and those that use traditional and heritage elements. Modern architecture has minimal decoration, and often uses materials like steel and glass. Le Corbusier, the Swiss–French architect, designed the city of Chandigarh in this style. Some architects use ancient Vastu shastra principles. India's top architects include:

- Achyut Kanvinde (1916–2002): A modernist, he worked with Walter Gropius, founder of the German art school Bauhaus. He used steel and reinforced concrete and created functional yet well-designed buildings. One among the buildings he designed is IIT Kanpur.
- Charles Correa (1930–2015): He was awarded the Padma Shri in 1972 and the Padma Vibhushan in 2006, having received other awards as well. His famous buildings include the Gandhi Smarak Sangrahalya in Ahmadabad, the Jawahar Kala Kendra in Jaipur, and the British Council and Jeevan Bharati buildings in New Delhi. He was chief architect for Navi Mumbai, a planned township of Mumbai, from 1970 to 1975.
- B.V. Doshi (b. 1927): He worked with Le Corbusier and American architect Louis Kahn, and founded several architectural institutes. He received the Padma Shri in 1976 and the French Ordre des Arts et des Lettres in 2011.
- Laurie Baker (b. 1917): He focused on low-cost and environmentally friendly structures, using local and traditional materials and techniques.

❈ INDIA AT 70 ❈

- Joseph Allen Stein (1912–2001): An American, he moved to India in 1952 and was head of the department of architecture, town and regional planning at the Bengal Engineering College (now the Indian Institute of Engineering Science and Technology, Shibpur), Calcutta. He helped in the development and planning of villages in Kashmir and Himachal in the 1960s. He designed a number of famous buildings, including the Triveni Kala Sangam, the India International Centre and the India Habitat Centre in New Delhi. Joseph Stein Lane is a road named after him in New Delhi. He was awarded the Padma Shri in 1992.
- Raj Rewal (b. 1934): He merges tradition with modernity. He has designed the Asian Games Village and the Hall of Nations in New Delhi.

❈ NASEERUDDIN SHAH

Naseeruddin Shah (b. 20 July 1949 or 16 August 1950)[36] is one of the most influential actors of parallel cinema, as well as a theatre actor and director. In 2007, he staged and acted in the Urdu play *Ismat Apa ke Naam*, which focused on three female-oriented stories of Ismat Chughtai. He has acted in numerous New Cinema films, including *Nishant*, *Aakrosh*, *Ardh Satya* (1983), *Masoom* (1983), *A Wednesday!* (2008) and others, as well as in mainstream Bollywood and international films. Most of Naseeruddin's work has received critical acclaim. Naseeruddin has been married twice, the first time to Manara Sikri when he was just nineteen years old. Their

---

[36] Both birthdates are quoted across sources.

daughter, Heeba Shah, is a theatre actor. He married theatre and film actor Ratna Pathak in 1982. He has received several awards, including the Filmfare and National awards, as well as the Padma Shri (1987) and the Padma Bhushan (2003). He has written an autobiography, *And Then One Day: A Memoir* (2014).

❋ KAMLESHWAR AND THE NAYI KAHANI GROUP

The year saw the death of Kamleshwar (6 January 1932–27 January 2007), well-known Hindi writer, as well as scriptwriter for films and television. He was part of the Nayi Kahani (New Story) group of writers that made a break with pre-Independence traditions. Others in this group included Mohan Rakesh, Nirmal Verma, Amarkant, Rajendra Yadav and Bhisham Sahni. Kamleshwar wrote a number of novels and essays, and won the Sahitya Akademi Award in 2003 for his novel *Kitne Pakistan* (2000). He was also awarded the Padma Bhushan in 2005.

Mohan Rakesh (8 January 1925–3 December 1972) wrote a number of novels, stories and plays, winning the Sangeet Natak Akademi Award in 1968. His story 'Uski Roti' was made into a film in 1970, directed by Mani Kaul.

Nirmal Verma (1929–2005) wrote short stories, novels and, after living in Prague for ten years, accounts of some of his travels. He won numerous awards, including the Jnanpith (1999), as well as the Padma Bhushan (2002). His first collection of short stories, *Parinde* (Birds), was published in 1959, and his first novel, *Ve Din* (Those Days), set in Prague, in 1964. Many of his works have been translated into English and various European languages, and he also translated world classics into Hindi.

Bhisham Sahni (8 August 1915–11 July 2003) is best known for his novel *Tamas* (Darkness, 1974), based on Partition. It was made into a television film by Govind Nihalani in 1988. His stories 'Pali' and 'Amritsar Aa Gaya Hai' are also based on Partition.

Among his many awards are the Padma Bhushan (1998) and the Sahitya Akademi Award (2001).

These and other Nayi Kahani writers explored human emotions with great sensitivity.

ALSO IN 2007

28 January: Death of O.P. Nayyar (b. 1926), music director and composer

4 March: Member of Parliament Sunil Kumar Mahato is killed by Maoists while attending a football match near Ghatshila in Jharkhand.

13 June: Death of Ramchandra Gandhi (b. 1937), grandson of Mahatma Gandhi, and a philosopher and writer

8 July: Death of Chandra Shekhar, former prime minister

25 December: Death of G.P. Sippy (b. 1914), film producer and director

Ela Gandhi (b. 1940), granddaughter of Mahatma Gandhi, who worked against apartheid in South Africa, is awarded the Padma Bhushan.

Air India and Indian Airlines merge as Air India Limited, and the airline gets its first Boeing 777 aircraft.

Daya Bai (b. 1940), originally named Mercy Mathew, social activist, wins the Vanitha Woman of the Year Award.

The Jnanpith is awarded to Malayalam poet O.N.V. Kurup.

The artist Jeram Patel (1930–2016) receives the Lalit Kala Akademi Fellowship.

2008: A TERRORIST ATTACK IN MUMBAI

The year 2008 had some unforgettable moments.

Floods are not uncommon in the monsoon season, but in August that year, the floods in Bihar were exceptionally severe. River Kosi changed course, and over 2.3 million people were affected.

In October, the Indo-US Civil Nuclear Agreement was signed and was considered a landmark treaty. According to this, the US would provide India with nuclear fuel and technology for peaceful use.

On 26 November, disaster struck. Terrorists attacked Mumbai. Over 150 people were killed, and more than 300 were injured. The places attacked were Chhatrapati Shivaji Maharaj Railway Terminus, Oberoi Trident Hotel, Taj Mahal Palace Hotel, Leopold Cafe, Nariman House and Cama Hospital. Showing great bravery, police official Hemant Karkare of the Mumbai Anti-Terrorist Squad, Vijay Salaskar, senior police inspector, and Ashok Kamte, additional commissioner of Mumbai Police, tried to stop the terrorists, but lost their lives in the process. Major Sandeep Unnikrishnan of the National Security Guard was also killed. In response to these attacks, the National Investigation Agency was set up in December as a counterterrorism body.

INDIA AT 70

❖ THE 2008 SUMMER OLYMPICS

In the 2008 Olympics, held in Beijing, Abhinav Bindra won a gold medal in shooting, in the men's 10 m air rifle event. Vijender Singh won a bronze medal in boxing, in the middleweight category, and Sushil Kumar won a bronze medal in wrestling, in the 66 kg freestyle category.

> **WRESTLING IN INDIA**
>
> Sushil Kumar's bronze at the 2008 Beijing Olympics was India's second Olympic medal in wrestling, and not the last. Wrestling is a traditional sport in the country. Following K.D. Jadhav's 1952 Olympic bronze and Sushil Kumar's 2008 bronze, Kumar clinched a silver medal in the 2012 London Olympics, in the 66 kg freestyle category, while Yogeshwar Dutt won a bronze in the 60 kg freestyle event. The 2016 Rio Olympics saw the first female medal winner from India, with Sakshi Malik winning a bronze.
>
> Male Indian wrestlers have won several medals in the Asian Games, the Commonwealth Games and in world championships. Indian women have gradually begun participating and winning medals as well. Gold medal winners among female wrestlers are Anita Sheoran, Geeta Phogat and Alka Tomar in the 2010 Commonwealth Games, and Vinesh Phogat and Babita Kumari in the 2014 Commonwealth Games. The rise of female wrestlers in a traditionally male sport has been best depicted in the film *Dangal* (2016). *Dangal* is based on the true story of the Phogat sisters, Geeta and Babita. The Salman Khan starrer *Sultan* also depicts a female wrestler, Aarfa, and shows how

Sultan learns wrestling to win her over, though her pregnancy prevents her from participating in the Olympic Games.

To promote wrestling, the Pro Wrestling League was founded in 2015 by ProSportify and the Wrestling Federation of India, with six city-based franchisee teams. Each team has nine players, five Indian and four foreign. Out of the nine, five are men and four women. A huge amount of money is invested in the initiative.

A WRESTLER'S LIFESTYLE

Indian wrestlers train in an akhara under the guidance of a guru. Wrestlers worship the god Hanuman, and most eat only vegetarian food. Milk, ghee and almonds form an essential part of their diet. Some wrestlers consume 0.5–1 litre of ghee, 2 litres of milk and almonds ground to a paste per day. Sprouted chana is another important food. They also eat fruit, vegetables and cereals. Spicy and hot-and-sour foods are reduced in their diet. Wrestlers are meant to stay off alcohol, tobacco and paan. They are not even supposed to marry, so that nothing distracts them from their sport. Some wrestlers do eat eggs and meat, but this is not the norm in India. Some north Indian akharas hold special functions on Naga Panchami.

❖ SLUMDOG MILLIONAIRE

Slumdog Millionaire, a 2008 British film directed by Danny Boyle, is based on the novel *Q & A* (2005) by Vikas Swarup, an Indian diplomat. It tells the story of Jamal Malik, an eighteen-year-old from the Mumbai slums, who wins the Indian version of *Who Wants to Be a Millionaire?* by answering every question correctly. He is arrested and accused of cheating, but through flashbacks, he explains how he came to know each answer. The film won eight Academy Awards and seven BAFTA Awards. The lead actors were Dev Patel, Freida Pinto, Madhur Mittal, Anil Kapoor and Irrfan Khan.

The music, by A.R. Rahman, was a great hit, particularly the song 'Jai Ho'. Rahman won the Golden Globe Award in 2009 for the best original score and two Academy Awards—for the best original score and the best original song ('Jai Ho'). Resul Pookutty, along with Richard Pryke and Ian Tapp, won the Academy Award for the best sound mixing.

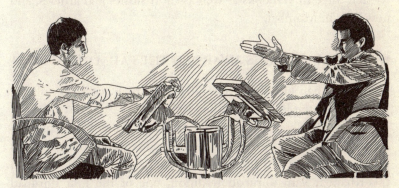

A reproduction of a scene from *Slumdog Millionaire*

❋ ANIL KAPOOR

Anil Kapoor (b. 24 December 1956) has acted in several Bollywood and other films before playing the role of a game show host in the film *Slumdog Millionaire*. Among his many films are *Mr India*, *Tezaab* (1988), *Ghar Ho To Aisa* (1990), *Beta* (1992), *Biwi No. 1*

(1999), *Pukar* (2000), *Calcutta Mail* (2003) and *No Entry* (2005). He has also acted in the action series *24* (first aired in 2013) and in the 2011 Hollywood film *Mission: Impossible, Ghost Protocol*. Anil has been awarded numerous Filmfare and other awards, and is among the most successful Indian actors.

ARAVIND ADIGA: *THE WHITE TIGER*

The White Tiger, Aravind Adiga's (b. 23 October 1974) first novel, won the Man Booker Prize in 2008. This novel provides a critique of the inequalities in Indian society. Aravind spent his early years in India before emigrating to Sydney, Australia, with his family. He began his career as a financial journalist and then worked for *Time* magazine, finally becoming a freelance writer. He has written three more books as well as short stories and articles, and now lives in Mumbai.

ASAD ALI KHAN IS AWARDED THE PADMA BHUSHAN

Asad Ali Khan (1937–14 June 2011), an eminent veena player, was awarded the Padma Bhushan in 2008.

Asad Ali Khan came from a family of rudra veena players. Born in Alwar, his father, Sadiq Khan, was a court musician for the raja of Alwar and the nawab of Rampur. Asad Ali played in the Khandar vani dhrupad tradition, one of the four dhrupad styles, and is considered the best rudra veena player. His nephew, whom he adopted, Ali Zaki Haidar, carries on the tradition. Asad received the Sangeet Natak Akademi Award in 1977.

Other good veena players include Sundaram Balachander (1927–90), E. Gayathri (b. 1959), Jayanthi Kumaresh, Doraiswamy Iyengar (1920–97), Rajhesh Vaidhya, Chitti Babu (1936–96), Emani Sankara Sastry (1922–87), Aswathi Thirunal Rama Verma (b. 1968), Poly Varghese (b. 1970), Nirmala Rajasekar and D. Balakrishna (b. 1955).

● BALIKA VADHU

As television soaps multiplied, some gained a huge amount of popularity. *Balika Vadhu* (Child Bride) is one example. This tele-serial, which aired on the TV channel Colors TV, had over 2000 episodes, beginning on 21 July 2008 and ending on 31 July 2016. *Balika Vadhu* took up several social issues through the story of Anandi, a child bride in Rajasthan. As she grew into an adult, she became a crusader for women's rights despite all odds. The serial found popularity in several other countries, including Vietnam, Indonesia, Croatia and Kazakhstan, and won a number of awards.

Colors TV was launched in 2008, a joint venture between Viacom and the Network 18 group.

ALSO IN 2008

12 February: The festival Year of Russia in India is inaugurated.

14 March: Inauguration of the Hyderabad International Airport, later renamed Rajiv Gandhi International Airport

19 May: Death of playwright Vijay Tendulkar (b. 1928)

23 May: Prithvi II, a nuclear-capable missile, is test-fired off the coast of Orissa.

3 August: A stampede at Naina Devi Temple in Himachal Pradesh kills over 150 people.

12 October: Sister Alphonsa Muttathupadathu, a woman of Indian origin, is canonized by the pope.

October: Barter trade across the Line of Control begins.

29 December: Death of artist Manjit Bawa (b. 1941)

Bhutan becomes a democracy.

The Jnanpith is awarded to Urdu-language poet and academic Akhlaq Mohammed Khan 'Shahryar'.

The Prince Claus Award of the Netherlands goes to Indira Goswami (principal awardee), writer and poet, and photographer Dayanita Singh.

2009: THE UPA GOVERNMENT AGAIN

The UPA government completed five years in office and elections were due in 2009. These were held from 16 April to 13 May. The Congress won 206 seats and the UPA together had 262. The NDA allies had 159 seats, of which the BJP won 116. Once again, the UPA formed the government with Manmohan Singh as prime minister.

In 2009, electoral constituencies had been redefined on the basis of the 2001 census. Out of the 543 constituencies, the boundaries of 499 were redrawn. A total of 13,68,430 EVMs had been used across the country and the Elector's Photo Identity Card (EPIC) had been issued to 82 per cent of the population.

Changes continued to be made to the Twenty Point Programme. The Sampoorna Grameen Rozgar Yojana was merged with the National Rural Employment Guarantee Act on 1 April 2008, and from 31 December 2009, was known as the Mahatma Gandhi National Rural Employment Guarantee Act.

❀ AKSHAY KUMAR IS AWARDED THE PADMA SHRI

Akshay Kumar (b. 1967), originally named Rajiv Bhatia, has acted in over 125 films, and is one of Bollywood's most successful actors. He once worked as a waiter in Bangkok and then as an instructor in martial arts. He took up modelling and then entered films. His acting career began in the 1990s and, though he has specialized in action films, he has played all types of roles. He was noticed after the film *Khiladi* (1992), and went on to achieve great popularity. In 1994, several of his films were hits, particularly *Yeh Dillagi*. Among his many other films are *Hera Pheri* (2000), *Khakee* (2004), *Aitraaz* (2004), *Namastey London* (2007), *Welcome* (2007), *Singh is Kinng* (2008) and *Housefull* (2010). He has won two Filmfare Awards and been nominated many times.

✹ ORIJIT SEN AND THE PAO COLLECTIVE

Orijit Sen (b. 1963) wrote and illustrated *River of Stories* (1994), which is considered to be India's first graphic novel. A graphic artist and designer, he is also one of the five founders of the Pao Collective (2009), which '[supports] comics as a medium and a culture in India.'[37] He has created many artworks and comics. *A Place in Punjab*, conceived by him and completed in collaboration with other artists, is a walk through a seven-storey-high mural that depicts life in Punjab. He has also written and illustrated the graphic story 'Portrait of the Artist as an Old Dog' in *Dogs! An Anthology* (2014), in which all the people are drawn as dogs and he muses on travelling by the Delhi Metro, greying facial hair and other topics. Orijit takes up social issues in his work, as seen in his comic *A Travancore Tale* (2017), dealing with the story of Nangeli, a nineteenth-century Dalit woman who refused to pay the caste-based breast tax imposed upon her.

---

[37] Jeremy Stoll, 'Bread and Comics: A History of the Pao Collective', *International Journal of Comic Art*, Volume 15, No. 2 (n.p.: 2013).

> ### COMICS IN INDIA
>
> Indian comics have a long history, including the famous Amar Chitra Katha series, depicting history and mythology, as well as several other series developed over the years. There is even an Indian version of Batman, while among indigenous superheroes was the Bengali comic character Bantul the Great. From around 2000 onwards, webcomics have been numerous, many of which provide a social message or a commentary on public affairs.
>
> India held its first comics convention, the Delhi Comic Con, in February 2011.

AMITABH BACHCHAN ACTS IN *PAA*

Paa may not be Amitabh Bachchan's best-known film, but it is certainly a unique role, and a most challenging one for any actor. In this film, Amitabh acts as Auro, a twelve-year-old boy with the genetic disorder progeria, which makes him look five times older. Amitabh was sixty-seven years old at the time, and to turn him into the pre-teen Auro for the film required four to five hours of make-up every day—and two hours to remove it! Eight layers of clay were used, and while the make-up was being put on, he was not able to drink, eat or talk. Bachchan also wore special dentures to change his voice to that of a child. After the make-up was applied, he was unrecognizable as his usual self.

Amitabh Bachchan (b. 11 October 1942) is among India's top actors. Born in Allahabad, son of the noted poet Harivansh Rai Bachchan and of Teji Bachchan, he began his acting career with *Saat Hindustani* in 1969, followed by *Anand* (1971) and several others. His image as an angry young man was established in 1973 with *Zanjeer*, which made him a star. The year 1975 was another landmark year for him, when he acted in *Deewaar*—considered to be one of the top twenty-five Bollywood films of all time—and even more importantly, in the blockbuster *Sholay*. Many more films followed, including *Kabhi Kabhie* (1976), *Amar Akbar Anthony* (1977), *Suhaag* (1979) and *Silsila* (1981). He became so popular that in 1982, when he was injured while filming *Coolie*, the whole country prayed for his recovery.

Amitabh Bachchan

In 1984, he entered politics, contesting elections from Allahabad, and was elected to the Lok Sabha, but resigned within three years. He founded ABCL (Amitabh Bachchan Corporation Ltd), an entertainment company, but this venture soon failed. Amitabh made a comeback in films, and from 2000 has again been a superstar with numerous hits, such as *Kabhi Khushi Kabhie Gham*, *Baghban* (2003), *Black* (2005) and several more. Among his latest Bollywood hits are *Piku* (2015) and *Pink* (2016). He has also appeared in the Hollywood movie *The Great Gatsby* (2013). Amitabh has hosted the television show *Kaun Banega Crorepati*. He is known for his support of social causes, including clearing the debts of farmers and supporting animal welfare and the upliftment of the girl child. He has received numerous awards, such as National Film Awards, Filmfare Awards and the Padma awards, including the Padma Vibhushan (2015).

Amitabh is married to Jaya Bhaduri (Bachchan) and they have two children, Abhishek and Shweta. Abhishek Bachchan is also an actor, married to Aishwarya Rai. Abhishek has acted in a range of films, including playing the role of Auro's father in *Paa*.

❋ *WAKE UP SID*: RANBIR KAPOOR

Ranbir Kapoor (b. 28 September 1982), son of actors Rishi Kapoor and Neetu Singh and grandson of Raj Kapoor, has made his mark in films. His successful films include *Wake Up Sid* (2009), *Ajab Prem ki Ghazab Kahani* (2009), *Rocket Singh: Salesman of the Year* (2009), *Rockstar* (2011), *Barfi!* (2012), *Yeh Jawaani Hai Deewani* (2013) and *Ae Dil Hai Mushkil* (2016).

ALSO IN 2009

2 January: The ICC Cricket Hall of Fame is inaugurated with the inclusion of fifty-five players.

25 May: The severe cyclone Aila hits India's east coast, causing mass destruction and death.

May: The LTTE is finally defeated by the Sri Lankan Army.

3 June: Meira Kumar becomes the first female Speaker of the Lok Sabha.

11 August: An earthquake takes place in the Andaman Islands.

Shamshad Begum (1919–2013), Hindi playback singer, receives the O.P. Nayyar Award and the Padma Bhushan.

Sunderlal Bahuguna (b. 1927), involved in the Chipko movement against the Tehri Dam, is awarded the Padma Vibhushan.

The Jnanpith awardees are Hindi writers Amarkant and Shrilal Shukla.

The sixtieth anniversary of the Commonwealth is celebrated.

2010: MAOIST ATTACKS IN WEST BENGAL AND CHHATTISGARH

Even as the country continued on the path of development, many problems remained unsolved. Among these was the Maoist problem. In 2006, Prime Minister Manmohan Singh had said that they posed 'the single biggest internal security challenge ever faced by our country'.[38] In 2009, an Integrated Action Plan had been launched by the government to tackle the issue, yet it persisted.

On 15 February, there was an attack on an army camp in West Bengal, resulting in twenty-four soldiers being killed. Later that year, a train accident in West Bengal, leaving 100 dead, is believed to have been caused by Maoists. Then on 6 April, over seventy soldiers were killed in an ambush in Dantewada district, Chhattisgarh. Chhattisgarh saw at least three more attacks in May, which killed CRPF (Central Reserve Police Force) men, others in the police and paramilitary forces and villagers. In June, twenty-six more policemen were killed in a Maoist attack in Narayanpur district, Chhattisgarh. Some Maoists had already been arrested and a Maoist leader, Umakant Mahato, was shot dead in a police

---

[38] 'India's Deadly Maoists', *The Economist*, 26 July 2006, http://www.economist.com/node/7215431.

encounter in August, but the police did not have much success in stopping their activities.

Maoists aim to create a more equal society and to work for the poorest people. However, their violent methods have not led to anything positive. The Integrated Action Plan tried to introduce more development schemes in Maoist areas, at the same time increasing funds for the police. This programme had some success, and in 2010, Karnataka was removed from the list of Maoist-affected states.

❋ ARTIST RAM KUMAR WINS THE PADMA BHUSHAN

Ram Kumar (b. 1924) paints abstract landscapes, mostly in oil or acrylic paints. His painting *Vagabond* (1956), sold for over $1 million at a Christie's auction. He is the brother of the writer Nirmal Verma, and has received many awards, including the Padma Bhushan in 2010 and the Lalit Kala Akademi Fellowship in 2011.

INDIAN ARTISTS

Among the numerous other artists in independent India, some of the notable ones are given below:

Krishen Khanna (b. 1925), one of India's best artists, was born in Lyallpur and after completing his education, joined Grindlays Bank in 1946. He had little formal training in art, though he attended evening classes at the Mayo School of Industrial Art in Lahore. He had been painting since childhood, and after he moved to Bombay, one of his early paintings, *News of Gandhiji's Death* (1948), showing people reading a newspaper after his assassination, was chosen for the Progressive Artists' Group exhibition in 1949. Since 1961, he has been a full-time painter, and has painted different themes, depicting various characters from myth and from real life, in his own unique way. For instance, his painting *The Last Bite* (2004) shows eleven painters dressed as labourers, sitting in a dhaba. He has held numerous exhibitions in India and abroad, and has received several awards, including the Padma Bhushan in 2011. A documentary on him, *A Far Afternoon: A Painted Saga by Krishen Khanna*, was released in 2015.

Paritosh Sen (18 October 1918–22 October 2008) was a founder member of the Calcutta Group of artists. His art evolved through several phases, from stylized figures to a Picasso-like approach. His honours include the Lalit Kala Akademi Fellowship in 1986.

Jogen Chowdhury (b. 16 February 1939) studied in Calcutta and Paris, and became a professor at Kala Bhavana, Santiniketan. He is also a member of the Rajya Sabha from the party Trinamool Congress. Jogen's art has a political conscience. For instance, his painting *Tiger in the Moonlight* (1978/1979) is a statement against the Emergency while a six-foot-long drawing, *Abu Ghraib* (2004), is a form of protest against the torture of prisoners that took place in Abu Ghraib, Baghdad. Jogen's art is inspired by everyday life, and he also writes about art. He is also a photographer, textile designer and poet.

Sayed Haider Raza (22 February 1922–23 July 2016) was one of the founder artists of the Progressive Artists' Group. He studied art in Nagpur and then at Sir J.J. School of Art in Bombay, and in 1950, received a scholarship to continue his studies in Paris. Raza began with expressionist paintings and moved on to symbolic and abstract work, the *bindu* (dot) forming the focal point of many of his paintings. His French wife died in 2002, and Raza thought of returning to India, but finally came back in 2011. His paintings sell for high prices and he received numerous awards, including the Lalit Kala Akademi Fellowship (1984), the Padma Bhushan (2007) and the Padma Vibhushan (2013).

Ganesh Pyne (11 June 1937–12 March 2013) belonged to the Bengal school of art, but developed his own style based on folk stories and myths. He used watercolours, gouache and tempera, and his work included abstract and surrealistic paintings. In the 1970s, M.F. Husain referred to him as India's best painter. His paintings sold for vast sums, but he was against the commercialization of art, and kept to himself in later years.

Sarbari Roy Choudhury (21 January 1933–21 February 2012) was one of India's great sculptors, who created portraits and bronzes.

❋ AMISH TRIPATHI: *THE IMMORTALS OF MELUHA*

Amish Tripathi (b. 18 October 1974) is one of India's bestselling authors, writing in English on mythological themes. His first three books, beginning with *The Immortals of Meluha* (2010), comprise the Shiva trilogy, a fantasy on the god Shiva's life. His Ram Chandra series begins with *Scion of Ikshvaku* (2015). Tripathi's books have been translated into Indian and foreign languages,

A reproduction of Sayed Haider Raza's *Bindu* (2001)

and *The Immortals of Meluha* is being made into a film. Tripathi began his career in the financial services industry and his unique marketing skills have helped promote his books.

After him, several others have started writing mythology-based novels, among them Kavita Kane, who weaves her stories around female characters, Christopher Doyle and Anand Neelakantan. The retelling of epic stories has been prevalent in regional languages from very early days. Two prominent recent writers in English who focus on retellings of epic myths and stories are Ashok Banker and Devdutt Pattanaik.

❈ AAMIR KHAN IS AWARDED THE PADMA BHUSHAN

Aamir Khan (b. 14 March 1965) has acted in and produced numerous films, many with a socially relevant theme. Among them are *Taare Zameen Par* (2007), on autism, *3 Idiots* (2009), based on Chetan Bhagat's *Five Point Someone*, and *Dangal*, on female wrestlers Geeta and Babita Phogat. His historical films include *Lagaan* (2001) and *Rang de Basanti* (2006).

Khan also created a TV series, *Satyamev Jayate* (first aired in 2012), on pressing social issues. He has received numerous awards: nine National Film Awards, eight Filmfare Awards and two Padma awards, including the Padma Bhushan in 2010.

❈ THE 2010 COMMONWEALTH GAMES

In October 2010, the Commonwealth Games were held in New Delhi. India won 101 medals, including thirty-eight golds, and came second overall, behind Australia. The gold medals were won in shooting (fourteen), wrestling (ten), archery (three), boxing (three), athletics (two), weightlifting (two), badminton (two), table tennis (one) and tennis (one). Two prominent gold medallists were Krishna Poonia in the women's discus throw and Geeta Phogat in women's wrestling. Ashish Kumar won India's very first medals in gymnastics—a silver and a bronze.

ALSO IN 2010

13 February: A bomb blast in the German Bakery in Pune kills seventeen people and injures many.

27 February: Death of Nanaji Deshmukh (b. 1916), social activist

30 March: Somali pirates capture Indian ships and take sailors hostage

14 June: Death of renowned English-language author Manohar Malgonkar (b. 1913)

6 August: Ladakh is hit by a flood. Leh and at least seventy other towns and villages are affected, and over 250 people die.

5 September: Death of Homi Sethna, nuclear scientist (b. 1923)

4 December: Nicole Faria, Femina Miss India, wins Miss Earth 2010.

23 December: Death of K. Karunakaran (b. 1918), former chief minister of Kerala

S.R. Srinivasa Varadhan (b. 1940), mathematician, is awarded the National Medal of Science by the President of the United States. He received the Padma Bhushan in 2008.

The Jnanpith is awarded to Chandrashekhara Kambara for his contribution to Kannada literature.

The year marks sixty years of diplomatic exchanges with China.

2011: ANNA HAZARE AGAINST CORRUPTION

One of the highlights of 2011 was a movement against corruption started by Anna Hazare (b. 1937), a social activist. He demanded the creation of a strong *lokpal* (literally 'protector of the people'), an anti-corruption authority who could look into cases of corruption against members of Parliament and central government employees. The idea of a lokpal was actually first put forward in the 1960s. Lokpal bills were introduced in Parliament several times, but never passed. In response to Anna Hazare's campaign, the Lokpal (for the union) and Lokayuktas (for the states) Act was finally passed in 2013.

❖ OTHER KEY EVENTS

Legislative assembly elections, held in Assam, Kerala, Tamil Nadu, West Bengal and Puducherry, indicated both continuity and change. In Assam, the Indian National Congress retained power, and chief minister Tarun Gogoi was sworn in for the third time. In Kerala, the United Democratic Front, led by the Congress, had a narrow win, while in Tamil Nadu, the AIADMK won, with J. Jayalalithaa becoming chief minister for the third time. In West

Bengal, the long thirty-four-year rule of the Communist Party ended with the Trinamool Congress coming to power for the first time, with Mamata Banerjee as chief minister.

NEW TRENDS IN ART: THE INSTAGRAM GENERATION

In 2011, the app Instagram launched a hashtag feature, so that users could tag their photos with relevant descriptors. And keeping pace with the rest of the world, artists in India have also moved forward to use experimental styles and digital and mixed media. A few of the main trends are:

- Crossover Art: A term for artistic creation that merges different forms such as painting, dance, music, photography and new media. For instance, in this form, C. Krishnaswamy creates abstract designs by performing yoga asanas on painted canvases.
- Multimedia Art: Combines various types of media in creating art
- Digital Art: Digital artists use software such as Corel Painter and PostworkShop (now PhotoDonut). Such artists include photographers, film-makers and illustrators who combine messages with still and moving images.
- Video Art: Started in India in the mid-1990s. Early video artists include Ayisha Abraham, Ranbir Kaleka, Sonia Khurana and Shilpi Gupta.
- Concept Art: Uses different media to convey an idea, and has gradually developed in India in the 2000s.
- Animation: Has always been used in comics, but is now digitized and also influenced by Japanese manga
- Art is also created for the gaming industry.
- Countless Instagram artists use smartphones to create art, such as Ashwin Gurbuxani, who develops scenes with a textured background and superimposed messages.

There are numerous new artists trying their hand at unique styles. For example, Devajyoti Ray (b. 1974) refers to his work as 'pseudorealism'. Using abstract techniques, unusual colours and geometric shapes, he creates paintings that depict reality. *Pseudorealist Renderings* was the title of his 2008 art exhibition in Mumbai. On the other hand, Gigi Scaria (b. 1973) creates entire stories through video and multimedia art. *Lost City* (2005), *Amusement Park* (2009) and *Prisms of Perception* (2010) are among these works. Other new media artists include Oli Ghosh, Jaishri Abichandani, Aharon Rothschild, Akash Anand and Archan Nair.

❈ SATHYA SAI BABA PASSES AWAY

Sathya Sai Baba (b. 23 November 1926) died on 24 April. A spiritual guru with a vast following, he established his ashram, Prasanthi Nilayam, in Puttaparthi, Andhra Pradesh, and is often considered a reincarnation of Shirdi Sai Baba. Sathya Sai centres have been set up in over 125 countries, along with free hospitals, schools and other facilities.

❈ THE SUFI GOSPEL PROJECT

Singer and composer Sonam Kalra started the Sufi Gospel Project in 2011. It puts forward the message of peace and oneness through prayer, poetry and music. Sonam is trained in Indian and Western music, and has performed with her group around the world. 'God has no religion,' she says,[39] and her multireligious group sings songs from all religions and in many languages. Amir Khusrau's

---

[39] 'Religion isn't God and God has no Religion | Sonam Kalra | TEDxGateway,' YouTube video, 4:52, from a talk given at a TEDx event using the TEDx conference format (n.d.), posted by 'TEDx Talks', 22 September 2015, https://www.youtube.com/watch?v=PIRo8rVcuJE.

and Kabir's verses, Christian hymns, Sufi songs, Gaelic texts—all form part of the repertoire.

❋ RABINDRANATH TAGORE'S 150TH BIRTH ANNIVERSARY

The year 2011 marked the 150th birth anniversary of Rabindranath Tagore (1861–1941). India, Bangladesh, and even China, celebrated his life and works in a grand way.

Rabindranath, a great poet, writer and artist, has always held a special place in the hearts of Indians. His mystical poems are still recited, his song is still the national anthem and he was India's first Nobel Prize winner, in 1913. Bangladesh's national anthem is also composed by Tagore. And in China too, Rabindranath is both remembered and appreciated. His writings had been popular there even before he first visited the country in 1924 for a lecture tour. At his sixty-third birthday celebrations in China, he was given the Chinese name Zhu Zhendan. An admirer of the Chinese civilization, Rabindranath wrote a touching verse shortly before his death:[40]

Rabindranath Tagore

> Once I went to the land of China,
> Those whom I had not met
> Put the mark of friendship on my forehead
> Calling me their own.

---

[40] Quoted in *Tagore and China*, ed. Tan Chung, Amiya Dev, Wang Bangwei, Wei Liming (New Delhi: Sage Publications, 2011).

The year 2011 was named the Year of India–China Exchanges, and one of the main programmes was the celebration of Rabindranath's legacy, both by the Indian embassy in Beijing and by the Chinese consulate in Kolkata.

ALSO IN 2011

14 January: A stampede near Sabarimala in Kerala leaves over a hundred dead.

24 February: Death of Anant Pai (b. 1929), creator of Amar Chitra Katha

21 March: Badminton player Saina Nehwal (b. 1990) wins the Swiss Open Grand Prix Gold.

2 April: India wins the 2011 Cricket World Cup. The final is played between India and Sri Lanka at the Wankhede Stadium, Mumbai. The Indian team is led by M.S. Dhoni.

12 April: Death of screenwriter Sachin Bhowmick (b. 1930)

24 April: Death of mountaineer Nawang Gombu (b. 1936), who climbed Mount Everest twice and was the first Indian to reach the summit of Nanda Devi, in 1964

6 July: Death of distinguished film director Mani Kaul (b. 1944)

14 August: Death of award-winning actor Shammi Kapoor (b. 1931)

The Jnanpith is awarded to academic and writer Pratibha Ray for the work *Yajnaseni* (Odia).

2012: SIXTY YEARS OF THE INDIAN PARLIAMENT

By 2012, Parliament had been functioning for sixty years. There had been many changes in Indian politics, but democracy was still flourishing—perhaps India's greatest achievement. A new President, Pranab Mukherjee (b. 1935), was elected in 2012. He had been part of the Indian National Congress and had held several cabinet posts in the central government, including those of foreign minister, defence minister and finance minister.

Among other events this year was the formation of a new political party, the Aam Aadmi Party (AAP), on 26 November 2012 by Arvind Kejriwal, ex-income-tax officer and supporter of Anna Hazare.

❁ YASH CHOPRA DIES

The year saw the death of Yash Chopra (b. 1932), film director and producer, on 21 October. He had great success directing films, his early ventures being *Dhool ka Phool* (1959), *Dharmputra* (1961) and *Waqt* (1965). He went on to found his own company,

Yash Raj Films (1970), and continued to direct successful films in the 1970s, including *Deewaar*, *Kabhi Kabhie* and *Trishul*. He had numerous hits in the 1990s and 2000s, including *Lamhe* (1991), *Darr* (1993), *Dil to Pagal Hai* (1997), *Veer–Zaara* and *Jab Tak Hai Jaan* (2012), his last. He announced his retirement after this, and died soon after. He received a number of film awards, as well as the Padma Bhushan in 2005.

Among the many other great Bollywood directors of the past and present are Bimal Roy (1909–66), Mehboob Khan (1907–64), V. Shantaram (1901–90), Manmohan Desai (1937–94), Mani Kaul, G.P. Sippy, Hrishikesh Mukherjee, Sanjay Leela Bhansali (b. 1963), Anurag Basu (b. 1974), Rajkumar Hirani (b. 1962), Vishal Bhardwaj (b. 1965), Ashutosh Gowariker (b. 1964), Anurag Kashyap (b. 1972) and Govind Nihalani (b. 1940). There are several more brilliant directors, but as India produces over a thousand feature films per year, apart from documentaries, short films and films on new media outlets like YouTube, this list remains incomplete.

❖ THE EAST INDIA COMEDY

In the new India, there are new forms of entertainment. The East India Comedy, founded in 2012 by Sorabh Pant and others, is one of them. They are a group of comedians performing shows, both live and on YouTube, with satirical commentary on politics, films and religion, among other topics. They also organize comedy workshops, television shows and short films. There are several other popular comedy start-ups. Comedians, individuals as well as groups, are often called for corporate events, brand development and weddings, and they also feature in magazine columns. Comedy shows are popular in regional languages too; the Gujarat-based Comedy Factory performs in Hindi and Gujarati.

🏵 PHOTOGRAPHERS: REMEMBERING HOMAI VYARAWALLA

Homai Vyarawalla (1913–2012) was one of India's best photographers and the first female photojournalist, who captured historic images of the freedom struggle and other key events, such as Jawaharlal Nehru's and Mahatma Gandhi's cremations.

Since then, India has had many unique photographers. One of them, Dayanita Singh links a photograph with other images, creating a series. She also makes portable exhibits—wooden structures that open like accordions, holding and displaying a number of photographs. *Go Away Closer* was a retrospective exhibition of her photographs, held in December 2013 in London. Raghu Rai, another well-known photographer, has published innumerable photographs of India in all its aspects. Pablo Bartholomew is known particularly for his photographs of the Bhopal gas tragedy. Other prominent photographers are Raghubir Singh (1942–99), Benu Sen (1932–2011), Robin Banerjee (1908–2003), B.S. Ranga (1917–2010), Prabuddha Dasgupta (1956–2012), Bharat Sikka (b. 1973), Avinash Pasricha (b. 1936), Anita Khemka and many more. Photographers now use new media to give a different twist to their shots.

Homai Vyarawalla

🏵 THE 2012 SUMMER OLYMPICS

In the 2012 Olympics, held in London, India performed relatively well. Vijay Kumar won a silver medal in shooting, in the men's 25 m rapid-fire pistol event; Sushil Kumar won a silver in wrestling, in the men's 66 kg freestyle category; Saina Nehwal won a bronze in badminton, in the women's singles; Mary Kom won a bronze in boxing, in the women's flyweight category; Gagan Narang won a bronze in shooting, in the men's 10 m air rifle event; Yogeshwar Dutt won a bronze medal in wrestling, in the men's 60 kg freestyle division.

FILMS ON BOXING

Mary Kom's Olympic boxing medal brought the sport into the limelight. The film *Mary Kom* was based on her life. It was released in 2014 and Priyanka Chopra starred as the protagonist. There have been other Bollywood films on boxing, including *Main Intaquam Loonga* (1982), *Boxer* (1984), *Ghulam* (1998) and *Apne* (2007).

✽ THE ADVENTURES OF KAKABABU AND OTHER DETECTIVES

Sunil Gangopadhyay (b. 7 September 1934) was a Bengali poet and novelist who died on 23 October 2012. He was the author of over 200 books, including *Prathama Alo* (First Light, 2001). He also wrote children's books, creating the fictional character Kakababu. Starting in the 1970s and first published in *Anandamela* magazine, thirty-six Kakababu adventure books were written until the death of the author. Kakababu has also figured in comics, films and television.

Kakababu, a middle-aged former director of the Archaeological Survey of India, helps the Central Bureau of Investigation (CBI) solve criminal cases, even though he has lost a leg and walks with a crutch. Shontu, Kakababu's college-going nephew, is his main helper. There are several other characters, including Jojo, Shontu's best friend. Two of the Kakababu books have now been translated into English: *The Dreadful Beauty* (2010, *Bhoyonkor Shundor*), set in Kashmir, and *The King of the Verdant Island* (2010, *Shobuj Dwiper Raja*), set in the Andamans.

Byomkesh Bakshi and Feluda are other great detectives in Bengali fiction for youngsters. Byomkesh was created by Sharadindu Bandopadhyay, and Feluda by Satyajit Ray.

Shirshendu Mukhopadhyay (b. 2 November 1935) featured the detective Fatik in some of his books and the detective Shabar Dasgupta in others. Mukhopadhyay wrote for both adults and children. His books and stories have been made into comics, among them *Bipinbabur Bipod*, and others into movies, such as *Patalghar* (2003) and *Goynar Baksho* (2013). His first children's book, *Manojder Adbhut Baari* (1978), is about Manoj, a teenage boy with a strange family. Shirshendu received the Vidyasagar Award in 1985 for his contribution to children's literature.

🟣 INDIAN MUSIC BANDS

There are numerous Indian bands, some of which started performing in the 1990s and many more in the 2000s. These bands indicate that music in India is not confined to Bollywood and Indian classical, but continues to redefine itself. Many of the bands play a fusion of folk and rock; there are some heavy metal bands and some that play pure rock. Though most compose songs in English, others use languages such as Hindi, Bengali and Malayalam. Some Indian contemporary bands are:

- 🟣 Raghu Dixit Project: Plays a mixture of Indian folk music and rock and roll

- Thermal and a Quarter: A rock band based in Bangalore, with three members—Bruce Lee Mani, Rajeev Rajagopal and Leslie Charles
- Tetseo Sisters: A folk band from Nagaland
- Indus Creed: Based in Mumbai, they have given several performances and have four albums.
- Swarathma: A Bangalore-based folk–rock band
- Soulmate: A blues band from Shillong
- Papon and the East India Company: They play fusion and folk music.
- Parikrama: Among the country's oldest rock bands
- Indian Ocean: Pioneers of rock–fusion music in India
- Bhayanak Maut: A metal band from Mumbai
- Kailasa: Founded by singer Kailash Kher, they blend Indian classical, rock, western and Sufi music.
- Coshish: Formed in 2006, this rock band has compositions in Hindi.
- Cassini's Division: From Kolkata, a rock band with songs that have meaningful lyrics
- Still Waters: A rock band from Gangtok, formed in 2001
- Thaikkudam Bridge: Formed in 2013, a rock band with Malayalam songs
- Fiddler's Green: They play folk music from South Asia.

RAVURI BHARADHWAJA WINS THE JNANPITH AWARD

Ravuri Bharadhwaja (d. 18 October 2013), a Telugu-language writer, was the winner of the Jnanpith Award in 2012, for his book *Paakudu Raallu*, which describes life behind the scenes in the film industry. He has written seventeen novels, numerous short stories, children's books and plays. He is the third writer in Telugu literature to win the Jnanpith Award, and has received several other honours. *Kadambari* and *Jeevan Samaram* are his other works.

ALSO IN 2012

24 January: Death of Sukumar Azhikode (b. 1926), Malayalam-language scholar and writer

9 March: Death of actor and director Joy Mukherjee (b. 1939)

12 July: Death of wrestler and actor Dara Singh (b. 1928)

26 August: Death of actor A.K. Hangal (b. 1914)

17 November: Death of Shiv Sena founder Bal Thackeray (b. 1926)

29 December: Death of Delhi gang-rape victim, dubbed 'Nirbhaya' (literally 'fearless'). The attack on this young woman creates national outrage, and leads to protests and vigils across the country. Subsequently, changes are made in Indian criminal law to make punishment more stringent in such cases.

67

2013: THE MARS ORBITER MISSION IS LAUNCHED

On 5 November, Indian space research took a step forward when Mangalyaan, the Mars Orbiter Mission by ISRO, was launched from the Shriharikota High Altitude Range using a Polar Satellite Launch Vehicle. After 298 days, it reached the Mars orbit on 24 September 2014. With that, ISRO became the fourth space agency in the world to reach Mars, the first to succeed at the first attempt and at the lowest cost.

Mangalyaan, the Mars Orbiter Mission

✤ OTHER KEY EVENTS

Rahul Gandhi, son of former prime minister Rajiv Gandhi, began to take on a greater role in the Indian National Congress. He had been a member of Parliament from Amethi since 2004,

NSUI (National Students' Union of India) chairman since 2007, chairman of the Indian Youth Congress since 2007, as well as general secretary of the Indian National Congress (2007–13). In 2013, he was elected vice president of the Congress party, after which he became their main strategist.

In June 2013, incessant rains caused widespread floods and destruction in the mountain state of Uttarakhand. Many people, mules and other animals were killed, and more than a thousand roads and bridges were washed away. Some of the major temples, including that of Kedarnath, were also severely affected. Army helicopters were used to rescue pilgrims on the *char dham* yatra (pilgrimage to four holy sites).

❋ NUNGSHI AND TASHI: THE CLIMBING TWINS

Nungshi and Tashi Malik (b. 21 June 1991), twin sisters, are also known as the Everest Twins. They are the first female twins to reach the summit of Mount Everest, the first twins and siblings to climb the Seven Summits[41] and the youngest to complete the Explorers Grand Slam and the Three Poles Challenge. These records include reaching the highest peaks in each of the seven continents, as well as the North and South Poles. In December 2016, they became the first twins to scale Mount Cook, the highest peak in New Zealand, and one that is very difficult to climb.

So how did the twins become climbers? Born in the village of Anwali in Haryana, they are daughters of a retired army officer, Colonel Virendra Singh Malik. They began training at the Nehru Institute of Mountaineering in Uttarkashi, Uttarakhand,

---

[41] Nungshi and Tashi have climbed Mt Kilimanjaro (Africa), Mt Everest (Asia), Mt Elbrus (Europe), Mt Aconcagua (South America), Mt Carstensz Pyramid (Oceania), Mt McKinley (North America) and Mt Vinson Massif (Antarctica).

and after their ascent of Mount Everest on 19 May 2013, there was no looking back. On that special occasion, Samina Baig of Pakistan also reached the summit, and all three planted the flags of both countries in a gesture of peace. Nungshi and Tashi live in Dehradun in between their climbs and adventures, and are brand ambassadors for the empowerment of the girl child.

ZUBIN MEHTA PERFORMS IN KASHMIR

Western music, including classical, jazz and pop, has also had its proponents in India. The most renowned Western classical musician to emerge from India is the conductor Zubin Mehta. His father, Mehli Mehta (1908–2002), a trained accountant, was also a musician, violinist and conductor, who founded the Bombay Symphony Orchestra in 1935 and the Bombay String Quartet in 1940. Mehli conducted several orchestras around the world.

Zubin Mehta (b. 29 April 1936), growing up in musical surroundings, started studying medicine, but dropped out to join the then Imperial Academy of Music and the Performing Arts, in Vienna, in 1954. He began conducting orchestras at a young age. His notable appointments have been music director of the Montreal Symphony Orchestra (1961–67), music director of the Los Angeles Philharmonic orchestra (1962–78), music adviser to the Israel Philharmonic Orchestra (appointed 1969) and music director of the same since 1977. In 1981, he became music director for life of the Israel Philharmonic Orchestra, and will end his tenure in 2019. He became music director of the New York Philharmonic in 1978, continuing in the post for thirteen years. Since 1985, he has been chief conductor of the Orchestra del Maggio Musicale Fiorentino in Florence, and will continue till 2017. He has also been an opera conductor since 1963, and has conducted numerous arrangements.

Zubin Mehta has won several honours and awards. He is an honorary citizen of Florence and Tel Aviv, and honorary conductor of a number of international orchestras. In September 2013, he performed with the Bavarian State Orchestra in Srinagar, Kashmir. In the same month, he received the Tagore Award for Cultural Harmony from the Government of India. In 1966, he was awarded the Padma Bhushan and in 2001, the Padma Vibhushan.

Zubin Mehta married the movie and TV actress Nancy Kovack in 1969. This is his second marriage, the first being to Carmen Lasky, a Canadian soprano, in 1958. They have two children, and after their divorce, Carmen married his brother, Zarin Mehta. With Zarin, Zubin runs the Mehli Mehta Music Foundation in Mumbai, training youngsters in Western classical music. Another couple of his ventures are the Buchmann–Mehta School of Music in Tel Aviv and the project Mifneh (established 2009), to teach music to young Israeli Arabs. Though he lives mainly in the USA, Zubin remains an Indian citizen.

● SRIDEVI ACTS IN *ENGLISH VINGLISH*

Sridevi (b. 13 August 1963) is an actor who has worked in Tamil, Telugu, Malayalam, Kannada and Hindi films. She entered the industry as a child actor, when she was only four years old, with the Tamil film *Thunaivan* (1969), appearing in her first Bollywood film, *Julie* (1975), a few years later. Recognized as a leading actress in Tamil and Telugu films, she has also made a mark in Bollywood, with *Himmatwala* (1983), *Mr India* and other films. She took a break after her film *Judaai* in 1997, returning to the screen in 2012 with the much-appreciated *English Vinglish*. She has also appeared in television and in fashion shows, and has even gained recognition as a painter. Sridevi has won a number of Filmfare and other awards, including the Padma Shri, the Stardust

Award for the best actress, for *English Vinglish*, and the NDTV Entertainer of the Year—all in 2013.

❋ THE LAST TELEGRAM

The last telegram in India was sent on 14 July, before telegrams passed into history. By this time, a Web-based telegraph mailing service had been developed, but even this was hardly being used

Before mobile phones, telegrams used to bring good news and bad. Exam results, interview calls, deaths—all were announced by express telegram. Greetings telegrams were a different, and colourful, category, and each standard greeting had a specific number. Phonograms were a method of sending telegrams by phone. The country's first telegraph line, between Calcutta and Diamond Harbour, using Morse code, was opened in 1851. By March 1884, telegraph messages could be sent from Agra to Calcutta. In 1947, there were 3324 telegraph offices with 2.7 crore telegrams already sent. In 1986, over 6.086 crore telegrams had been sent. And in 1991, India had more than 40,000 telegraph offices. But by the end of the 1990s, the decline of the telegram had begun.

ALSO IN 2013

14 January: The first season of the Hockey India League begins.

7–10 February: The first Golf Premier League tournament is held, and won by the Uttarakhand Lions.

21 April: Death of Shakuntala Devi (b. 1929), a genius in mental mathematics

30 May: Death of Rituparno Ghosh (b. 1963), renowned Bengali film director

12 July: Death of veteran actor Pran (b. 1920)

14 August: The first season of Indian Badminton League (later renamed Premier Badminton League) starts.

24 October: Death of great playback singer Manna Dey (b. 1919)

27 December: Death of notable actor Farooq Sheikh (b. 1948)

The Jnanpith is awarded to Hindi poet Kedarnath Singh for his collection *Akaal Mein Saras*.

68

2014: NARENDRA MODI BECOMES PRIME MINISTER

Narendra Modi

Another round of general elections was held from 7 April to 12 May, with the results being declared on 16 May. Narendra Modi had been projected during the election campaign as the BJP's prime-ministerial candidate. The campaign succeeded, with the BJP winning 282 seats and the NDA together securing 336. The Congress suffered a severe defeat, winning its lowest-ever number of seats—forty-four, while the UPA together had sixty seats. On 26 May, a new BJP government was sworn in, with Narendra Modi as prime minister.

❋ A NEW STATE

A major event that year was the creation of the state of Telangana, formerly part of Andhra Pradesh, in June, raising the number of Indian states to twenty-nine.

❋ RINA SHAH AND POLO IN INDIA

Not many women in India play polo, but Rina Shah is one of them. She became interested in the game in 2010, and then trained in Argentina, the UK, the USA and Rajasthan, after which she started her own team, named Rinaldi Polo, in 2014. Rina also designs equestrian clothing and accessories.

Polo is said to have originated in India, and was played by the sultans of Delhi, Mughals and Indian princes. The first-known polo club in India was set up in Silchar in 1834. This was followed by the Calcutta Polo Club, founded in 1862–63. The Indian Polo Association was established in 1892. International rules for playing the game were introduced after the First World War. In 1957, India won the World Cup in France.

The Indian Polo Association marked its centenary in 1992. Polo is now played by army and private teams, and sponsored by corporations. The country has over thirty-three polo clubs, and there are several domestic matches held every year.

❋ KAMAL HAASAN RECEIVES THE PADMA BHUSHAN

Kamal Haasan (b. 7 November 1954), an actor as well as a director, producer and singer, has won several awards, including four National Awards and a total of nineteen Filmfare Awards and Filmfare Awards (South) as well as the Padma Shri (1990), the Padma Bhushan (2014) and the French Chevalier de L'Ordre des Arts et des Lettres (2016).

He began acting as a child, and won the President's Gold Medal for his role in the Tamil film *Kalathur Kannamma* (1960) when he was only six years old. This film tells the story of a landlord's son, Rajalingam, who marries Kannamma, a farmer's daughter. Through a series of events, their child, Selvam—

played by Kamal Haasan—grows up in an orphanage. Kamal has gone on to act in Tamil, Malayalam and Telugu films, as well as the Hindi remakes—and even a Bengali one—of his films.

❊ KABADDI: THE PINK PANTHERS, THE PATNA PIRATES AND MANY MORE

Kabaddi is among India's indigenous sports, dating back to ancient times. Gradually, Kabaddi has gained popularity in different countries, and become a world sport. The All India Kabaddi Federation was formed in 1950, bringing standardized rules into the game. The first kabaddi nationals (men's) were held in 1951, while the first National Kabaddi Championship for women was held in 1955. Junior nationals for boys and girls were introduced in 1974 and 1976 respectively. The All India Kabaddi Federation was reconstituted in 1972 and renamed the Amateur Kabaddi Federation of India.

Kabaddi was introduced in the eleventh Asian Games, held in Beijing in 1990. India won the gold medal, and continued to win the gold in subsequent Asian Games, in 1994, 1998, 2002, 2006, 2010 and 2014. The Kabaddi World Cup was introduced in 2004, and India won all three World Cup matches played up to 2016. Runners-up have included Iran, Pakistan and Canada. In a parallel World Cup series conducted by the Government of Punjab, India won all six men's tournaments held from 2010 to 2016, and all four women's tournaments held from 2012 to 2016. India has also won most of the matches in the SAF Games.

The Pro Kabaddi league was introduced in 2014, with eight teams. In the first league tournament, the Jaipur Pink Panthers, owned by Abhishek Bachchan, emerged as the winner. Rakesh Kumar was the player bought for the highest bid, by the Patna Pirates, at a cost of Rs 12.80 lakhs.

The World Kabaddi League too was introduced in 2014.

❖ PRIVATE INDIA

Private India, a thriller, was written by Ashwin Sanghi and James Patterson, and released in 2014. Ashwin Sanghi (b. 25 January 1969) has written several other thrillers based on semi-historical myths and legends. He became a bestselling author with his first book, *The Rozabal Line* (2007), while his latest, *The Sialkot Saga*, was published in 2016. *The Rozabal Line* revolves around the legendary account of Jesus living the last years of his life in Kashmir. His other books include *Chanakya's Chant* (2010), for which he won the 2010 Vodafone Crossword Popular Award.

❖ RUSKIN BOND IS AWARDED THE PADMA BHUSHAN

Ruskin Bond (b. 19 May 1934) is India's best-known writer for children in English, though he also writes for adults. Born in Kasauli, Ruskin had a difficult childhood, as his mother left his father and remarried when he was eight, and his father died when he was just ten. His interest in writing developed while he was in school, and has continued throughout his life. His first novel, *The Room on the Roof* (1956), received the John Llewellyn Rhys Prize in 1957. This semi-autobiographical novel is about a boy named Rusty, an orphan from an Anglo-Indian family.

Ruskin has written over fifty books for children, apart from short stories, novels, essays and newspaper columns. His book *A Flight of Pigeons* was made into the Hindi film *Junoon* in 1978, while *The Blue Umbrella* (1980), a novel for children, was also turned into an award-winning film of the same name. His story 'Susanna's Seven Husbands' became the film *7 Khoon Maaf* (2011). Since 1963, he lives in Mussoorie, along with his adopted family that has expanded over the years.

He received the Sahitya Akademi Award in 1992, the Padma Shri in 1999 and the Padma Bhushan in 2014.

🟊 FLASH FICTION: DRIBBLES AND DRABBLES

With new media, there are new forms of fiction. These include flash fiction, which has various types. It can be a very short story of six words; a dribble, which has fifty words; or a drabble, which has 100 words. Also part of flash fiction is sudden fiction i.e., longer stories of 750 words. Then there are Twitter stories of 140 characters.

Among Twitter fiction, Chindu Sreedharan, an Indian academic at a British university, narrated the Mahabharata from Bhima's point of view in 2628 tweets over 1065 days. This unique retelling was put together as *Epic Retold*, and published by HarperCollins in 2014.

TWITTER

Twitter was founded in 2006. The number of Twitter users in India in 2013 was 11.5 million. By 2015, it rose to 22.2 million.

ALSO IN 2014

13 January: Death of Anjali Devi (b. 1927), Telugu and Tamil actor and producer, known for her role as Sita in the film *Lava Kusha* (1963)

25 May: Malavath Purna (b. 10 June 2000) reaches the summit of Mount Everest, becoming the youngest girl to do so.

10 July: Death of noted actor Zohra Segal (b. 1912) at age 102

20 August: Death of yoga expert B.K.S. Iyengar (b. 1918)

22 August: Death of Kannada-language writer U.R. Ananthamurthy

28 August: The Pradhan Mantri Jan-Dhan Yojana is launched, providing a simple method to open basic savings accounts in banks, with zero balance.

September: Heavy rainfall floods Kashmir. More than 450 people die and over 2500 villages are affected.

The Jnanpith is awarded to Marathi-language writer Bhalchandra Nemade for *Hindu: Jagnyachi Samrudhha Adgal*.

2015: THE AAM AADMI PARTY WINS IN DELHI

While the BJP government, headed by Prime Minister Modi, was well established with its large majority in the Lok Sabha, two state elections indicated different trends. In February, the Aam Aadmi Party won sixty-seven out of the seventy seats in the Delhi assembly elections. One could say that they had a clean sweep, particularly as their election symbol is the broom! In November, the BJP–NDA alliance faced another defeat, when an alliance of the Janata Dal (U) (formed in 2003), the Rashtriya Janata Dal and the Congress won the state assembly elections in Bihar. Nitish Kumar of the Janata Dal (U) was re-elected as chief minister.

Meanwhile, changes were being brought about in the structure of the government. The Planning Commission, which had existed since 1950, was dissolved on 17 August 2014. In 2015, it was replaced by a new organization, the NITI (National Institution for Transforming India) Aayog.

❈ NEK CHAND'S ROCK GARDEN

Nek Chand Saini (15 December 1924–12 June 2015), a self-taught artist, created a wonderful complex near Lake Sukhna in

Chandigarh—a landscaped rock garden, with sculptures of people, dancers, musicians and animals. A road inspector of the Public Works Department (PWD), Nek Chand began constructing his garden in the 1960s. He used unusually shaped rocks, cement, sand and waste materials, such as pieces of broken glass, pottery, bits of steel and tin, iron slag, old sanitary fittings and other items. His constructions on this land were illegal, and the authorities finally became aware of it in 1975. By this time, there were hundreds of sculptures in the courtyards linked by pathways, covering an area of 5.3 hectares. As Nek Chand had used forest land, officials wanted to destroy his creation. But public opinion saved it, and its value was recognized. Finally, in 1976, the garden was given official recognition and opened to the public. Nek Chand was even given a salary and fifty workers to help him, and he continued to add to it until his death in 2015.

Nek Chand's Rock Garden

The rock garden now covers 25 acres. There is even a miniature village, waterfalls, a canal and an open-air theatre. The garden has over 5000 visitors every day, and is popular among tourists. His sculptures have been displayed in the USA, England and Switzerland, and books have been written about him and his art. He received the Padma Shri in 1984. In 1997, the Nek Chand Foundation was set up to support his work.

❋ PRIYANKA CHOPRA STARS IN *QUANTICO*

Priyanka Chopra (b. 18 July 1982), one of India's top actors, secured the lead role in the American television series *Quantico* that year.

After winning the Miss World pageant in 2000, Priyanka became a Hindi film actor, her first Bollywood film being *The Hero* (2003). Before this, she acted in a Tamil film, *Thamizhan* (2002). Many other films followed, among them *Krrish*, *Fashion* (2008), *7 Khoon Maaf*, *Barfi!*, *Mary Kom* and *Bajirao Mastani* (2015). She has also sung for films and released music albums. Priyanka has won several awards, including the National Film Award for the best actress, for *Fashion*, five Filmfare Awards and the Padma Shri (2016).

Deepika Padukone and Kareena Kapoor are equally well-known film actors.

❋ SANIA MIRZA IS AWARDED THE RAJIV GANDHI KHEL RATNA AWARD

Sania Mirza (b. 15 November 1986) is the best women's tennis player India has ever seen. She was born in Bombay, but moved with her family to Hyderabad soon after and started learning tennis at the age of six. She began playing international matches in 2001, but retired from singles in 2013. Till then, she had been India's top-ranking female tennis player since 2003. In 2007, she was world no. 27 in singles and in the first place in doubles.

Sania has won numerous medals and matches, and had a WTA (Women's Tennis Association) number one ranking in doubles in 2015 and 2016. Other than the Rajiv Gandhi Khel Ratna Award in 2015, the Padma Bhushan in 2016 is among her many awards. In 2010, she married Pakistani cricketer Shoaib Malik. Sania has set up a tennis academy in Hyderabad, and is the brand ambassador of the state of Telangana.

Early female tennis players include Nirupama Vaidyanathan (now Nirupama Sanjeev), Shikha Uberoi and Sanaa Bhambri. At present, Ankita Raina, Rishika Sunkara, Prerna Bhambri and Prarthana Thombare are good players, but none have reached Sania's level of success. Ankita Raina reached a singles world ranking of 222 in 2015.

India's best male tennis players include Leander Paes, Mahesh Bhupathi, Yuki Bhambri, Somdev Devvarman, Rohan Bopanna, Akhtar Ali and his son, Zeeshan Ali. Cotah Ramaswami (1896–1990), an early player, represented India in both cricket and tennis.

NAMDEO DHASAL'S LEGACY

Namdeo Dhasal (15 February 1949–15 January 2014), a Buddhist Dalit, was one of the founders of the Dalit Panthers, who were in revolt against upper-caste society. However, he became a fan of Indira Gandhi when she pardoned all cases against him during the Emergency, and later allied with the Shiv Sena.

He is remembered as a powerful Marathi poet, whose first poetry collection, *Golpitha* (1973), is named after the area in Bombay where he grew up. Many other poetry collections followed. Dilip Chitre, who has translated some of his work, feels *Golpitha* can be compared to T.S. Eliot's *Waste Land* (1922), and that he deserved the Nobel Prize. Namdeo did not receive the Nobel, though several others came his way, including the Padma Shri (1999) and the Sahitya Akademi's Golden Jubilee Lifetime

Achievement Award (2004). On his death anniversary in 2015, a function, Sarv Kahi Samishtisathi (Everything for Equality), was organized by the Namdeo Dhasal Felicitation Committee in Mumbai, with films, poetry readings, ballads and discussions on his work and life. He remains a Dalit icon, and his work is classified as Dalit literature.

> ### DALIT LITERATURE
>
> Dalit literature was first written in the 1960s and 1970s in Marathi, and then in other languages—Hindi, Tamil and Telugu. There are several other writers in this category, including Baburao Bagul, Raja Dhale, Arjun Dangle, J.V. Pawar, Bama, Om Prakash Valmiki, Narendra Jadhav, Baby Kamble and Ajay Navaria, among others. At the same time, one can question this category: Is Dalit literature only written by Dalits? Or is it only that which narrates the atrocities and oppression that Dalits face?

● KHUSHWANT SINGH'S 100TH BIRTH ANNIVERSARY

Khushwant Singh (2 February 1915–20 March 2014), one of India's best-known journalists and writers, known as the Grand Old Man of Indian literature, was awarded the Padma Vibhushan in 2007.

Khushwant Singh began his career as a lawyer, but went on to become an editor. In his nine years as editor of *Illustrated Weekly of India*, its readership multiplied. However, he is remembered for his books, including novels, short stories and non-fiction, and for his love of jokes, which he collected from everywhere. His classic novel *Train to Pakistan* (1956), set in the time of Partition, was made into a film of the same name and is still widely read. Khushwant was a nominated member of the Rajya Sabha from 1980–86.

ALSO IN 2015

19 January: Death of Rajni Kothari (b. 1928), political scientist

26 January: US President Barack Obama is chief guest at the Republic Day parade.

20 February: Govind Pansare (b. 1933), author, activist and CPI leader, dies after being shot by assailants.

8 March: Death of editor and writer Vinod Mehta (b. 1942)

25 April: A major earthquake in Nepal affects India.

21 June: The first International Yoga Day is observed.

1 July: The Digital India programme is launched by Prime Minister Narendra Modi, which aims to increase digital platforms and connectivity, leading to the transformation of India.

27 July: A.P.J. Abdul Kalam, former President, dies of a heart attack while speaking to students in Shillong.

30 August: M.M. Kalburgi (b. 1938), vice chancellor of Kannada University, Hampi, is shot dead.

November–December: Severe floods affect Chennai and other parts of Tamil Nadu. More than 500 die and over 18 lakh people have to be relocated.

Anirban Lahiri, one of India's top golfers, wins two tournaments.

27 September: Pankaj Advani wins the IBSF (International Billiards & Snooker Federation) World Billiards Championship.

The Jnanpith is awarded to Raghuveer Chaudhari for his contributions to Gujarati literature.

2016: DEMONETIZATION

On 8 November, Prime Minister Narendra Modi announced that all 500- and 1000-rupee notes were to be withdrawn from circulation at midnight. This amounted to 86 per cent of the cash in circulation. The aim behind this note ban was to curb black money, remove counterfeit notes and provide an impetus to a digital economy. As new notes, in denominations of Rs 500 and Rs 2000, were few and cash withdrawals were limited, many faced hardships, though most hoped the withdrawal of the old notes would bring long-term positive results.

Meanwhile, the central government remained stable, with Narendra Modi as prime minister. Five state elections, held in April–May, showed varied results. In Assam, the BJP came to power, while in West Bengal, the Trinamool Congress gained a majority for the second time and Mamata Banerjee was re-elected chief minister. In Tamil Nadu, the AIADMK (led by Jayalalithaa) won, while in Puducherry, it was a victory for the Congress. In Kerala, the Left Democratic Front, a coalition of leftist parties, came to power.

✸ IROM SHARMILA: THE IRON LADY OF MANIPUR

Irom Sharmila (b. 14 March 1972), a human rights activist in Manipur, finally ended her fast after sixteen years, on 9 August.

The Malom massacre—in which ten civilians were killed by the paramilitary force Assam Rifles in Malom, a village near Imphal—led to her fast. This incident took place in November 2000. Since then, Irom vowed to not eat or drink anything, nor comb her hair or look in a mirror until the Armed Forces (Special Powers) Act (AFSPA) was repealed. This act grants special powers to the Indian Armed Forces to deal with internal security issues in disturbed areas.

Irom Sharmila

Irom was arrested and tube-fed on multiple occasions, but continued her fast, even while gaining support from many in India and around the world. The AFSPA was not repealed, and finally, after the longest hunger strike in history, Irom decided to change tactics—stop fasting and instead contest elections. Many did not want her to end her fast, even though none had fasted with her. She ended her fast with a lick of honey, and started a new political party, Peoples' Resurgence and Justice Alliance, in October.

During her long years fasting, Irom spent time writing. She wrote *Rebirth*, a poem in 1010 lines, in 2007, which starts with, 'Today is Tuesday, the day on which I was born.'[42] In 2007, a seven-poem collection was published under the title *Ima* (Mother), while another poetry collection, *Fragrance of Peace*, was published in 2010. Her poem 'Wake Up' begins with the lines:[43]

---

[42] Quoted in Deepti Priya Mehrotra, *Burning Bright: Irom Sharmila and the Struggle for Peace in Manipur* (New Delhi: Penguin Books, 2009).

[43] Quoted in Rosheena Zehra, 'Wait for Me, My Love: Excerpts From Irom Sharmila's Poetry', *Quint*, 9 August 2016, https://www.thequint.com/books/2016/08/09/irom-sharmilas-poetry-the-ideas-behind-a-16-yr-old-hunger-strike.

Wake up, brothers and sisters
The saviour of the nation
We have come out all the way
Knowing we all will die.

She has written more than a hundred poems, though most are yet to be translated. Irom has received several awards and vast recognition for her peaceful protest. Books have been written about her too.

> **WHAT IROM EATS**
>
> Sagem Pomba, a Manipuri dish made with fermented soya bean, roots and water vegetables, is Irom's favourite dish.

❈ CONFLUENCE: THE FESTIVAL OF INDIA IN AUSTRALIA

A special Festival of India, titled Confluence, took place in Australia in August–September. It was celebrated across seven cities, including Sydney, Melbourne and Brisbane. Different Indian dance forms, music, puppet shows, art installations and plays were part of the festival. There were fusion performances too—in which Aboriginal dancers of Australia joined Manipuri dancers and Western a cappella singers sang with Indian classical vocalists. Workshops of many kinds were held, and Cricket Connect, a multimedia exhibition, reflected the two countries' shared passion for the sport. The festival created long-lasting cultural connections and relationships.

❈ MARTIAL ARTS AT SEVENTY-FOUR

Meenakshi Gurukkal gained prominence that year, when a video of the seventy-four-year-old martial arts teacher became popular.

She has her own school, Kadathanadan Kalari Sangam, in Vadakara, near Kozhikode, Kerala, where she teaches the ancient martial art Kalaripayattu. Over a third of her students are girls. The school was set up by her husband, Raghavan Master, in 1949, and later taken over by Meenakshi.

There are legends of medieval female warriors proficient in Kalaripayattu. Unniyarcha is one, and is believed to have lived in north Malabar (Kerala) in the sixteenth century. Several films and a television serial have been based on her. The Unniyarcha story forms part of Vadakkan Pattukal, the ballads of north Kerala. An expert at using the *urumi*, a flexible sword, Unniyarcha is said to have defeated the bandits in Nadapuram market, who used to disturb local women. She also avenged the death of her brother.

❈ SHAHID KAPOOR

Shahid Kapoor (b. 25 February 1981) has made his mark in Indian cinema, having acted in different types of roles, from romantic comedies *Ishq Vishk* (2003) and *Jab We Met* (2007) to serious roles in *Haider* (2014) and *Udta Punjab* (2016).

❈ INSTAGRAM AND OTHER PHOTOGRAPHY WINNERS OF THE YEAR

Instagram, the mobile photo-sharing app, was launched in October 2010, with over 300 million users by December 2014. There are many brilliant photographers on Instagram. Among them, Ronny Sen of India won the Getty Images Instagram Grant in 2016 for his project on the struggle of people living in Jharia, a coal-rich area.

Three other young photographers won prizes that year. Among them, Nayan Khanolkar, a Mumbai-based photographer, won the Natural History Museum's Wildlife Photographer of the Year award in the Urban category, for his photograph *Alley Cat*, which captured a leopard in Mumbai's lanes. Ganesh H. Shankar won the Wildlife Photographer of the Year title in the Birds category. His photograph, called *Eviction Attempt*, shows a parakeet biting the tail of a lizard attacking its nest. Varun Aditya, a photographer from Tamil Nadu, won *National Geographic*'s Photographer of the Year contest, in the Animal Portraits category, for his photograph of a snake titled *Dragging You Deep into the Woods*.

❋ SPORTS ROUND-UP

In the 2016 Summer Olympics held in Rio de Janeiro, P.V. Sindhu won a silver medal in badminton, in women's singles, while Sakshi Malik won a bronze in women's freestyle 58 kg wrestling.

BADMINTON HIGHLIGHTS

In March 2015, Saina Nehwal was ranked world number one in women's singles. Ashwini Ponnappa and Jwala Gutta are among other good female badminton players. However, in 2016, P.V. Sindhu had the highest ranking after winning her Olympic silver.

❋ FROM BUS CONDUCTOR TO SUPERSTAR

Kabali, a Tamil film in which Rajinikanth plays the lead role, was released in 2016. The film explores the life of Kabaleeswaran, aka Kabali, a gang leader in Kuala Lumpur who is released after spending twenty-five years in prison. Imprisoned on false charges, he resumes control of his gang after his release. The film was dubbed in Hindi and Telugu, and also released in Malay. *Kabali* is considered to be one of star Rajinikanth's best.

Rajinikanth (b. 12 December 1950) was born in Bangalore in a Marathi family, and was originally named Shivaji Rao Gaekwad. He spoke Marathi and Kannada, and later learnt Tamil. He acted in plays even as he worked as a bus conductor in the Bangalore Transport Service. He joined the Adyar Film Institute (now the M.G.R. Government Film and TV Institute) in 1973, and after acting in his first film, *Apoorva Raagangal* (1975), there has been no looking back. He soon became a top star, winning several awards, including the Padma Vibhushan in 2016.

❁ GINNI MAHI BECOMES AN INTERNET SENSATION

An eighteen-year-old pop icon from Punjab has become a singing sensation, with over 1,00,000 subscribers on YouTube. Young Ginni (aka Gurkanwal Bharti) is a Dalit and sings about Dalit problems and leaders, as well as about various saints. She has songs about Guru Nanak, Bulleh Shah, Sant Ravidas and Ambedkar. Earlier Dalit singers from Punjab include Chamkila, Roop Lal Dhir and Rani Armaan, but none had such a huge following. Ginni started singing at the age of eight and now studies at Hans Raj Mahila Maha Vidyalaya in Jalandhar, and has a team of writers to help her compose the lyrics of her songs. Despite many of her songs, such as 'Danger Chamar', being about Dalits, she tries to move beyond caste-based compositions, saying that an artist has no caste. Her aim, she says, is to unite and empower everyone.

ALSO IN 2016

April: Women activists attempt to enter temples as well as Haji Ali Dargah, where they are banned.

29 June: Death of Veena Sahasrabuddhe (b. 14 September 1948), Hindustani music vocalist

14 August: Death of Na. Muthukumar, Tamil-language writer, poet and lyricist

5 September: Reliance Jio, mobile telecom operator, launches its free services.

22 November: Death of Karnatic music vocalist Balamurali Krishna

5 December: Death of J. Jayalalithaa, chief minister of Tamil Nadu

December: Manipur creates seven new districts, making a total of sixteen districts. In opposition, the United Naga Council (UNC) calls for an economic blockade, closing off national highways 2 and 37. Naga groups are unhappy as they want to include some hill districts of Manipur in their territory. The creation of the new districts in Manipur makes this unlikely.

December: India wins the Hockey Junior World Cup title.

2017: INDIA AT SEVENTY

Elections were held in February–March 2017 in five states, with the results being announced on 11 March. Though these were state elections, they were, to some extent, considered to be a referendum on the BJP government at the Centre and Prime Minister Narendra Modi at midterm.

In the largest and most important state, Uttar Pradesh, the BJP won a massive victory with 312 out of the 403 seats in the legislative assembly. Yogi Adityanath was appointed chief minister. The Samajwadi Party–Indian National Congress alliance came a poor second with just fifty-four seats. In Uttarakhand too, the BJP was victorious with fifty-seven out of the seventy seats. However, in Punjab, the Congress formed the government with Amarinder Singh as chief minister, winning seventy-seven out of the 117 seats. In Manipur, the Congress won twenty-eight out of the sixty seats and the BJP, twenty-one. Despite this, the latter formed the government with the support of other parties. The defeat of Irom Sharmila, who polled only ninety votes, was another significant aspect of the Manipur elections. The results in Goa were similar to Manipur's. The Congress won seventeen seats and the BJP, eleven, but the latter gained the support of other parties to form the government.

🌸 OM PURI PASSES AWAY

The beginning of the year saw the death of the actor Om Puri (18 October 1950–6 January 2017), who acted in mainstream Bollywood and alternative films, as well as in international productions. Among the many films in which he played a role are *Bhumika*, *Ardh Satya*, *City of Joy* (1992), *Hey Ram* (2000), *Rang de Basanti*, *Agneepath* (2012) and *Bajrangi Bhaijaan*. He received several film awards, as well as the Padma Shri (1990).

🌸 THE ISHARA INTERNATIONAL PUPPET FESTIVAL

A reproduction of the poster of the 2017 Ishara International Puppet Festival

The Ishara Puppet Theatre Trust, founded in 1986 by Dadi Pudumjee, is among India's leading contemporary puppet theatre groups. From 3–10 February this year, it celebrated its thirtieth anniversary with the fifteenth Ishara International Puppet Festival, held in New Delhi, Gurgaon and Chandigarh. All types of puppets and puppet theatre, both traditional as well as modern, were showcased with participants from India and around the world. Among the puppet theatre programmes were *The Lantern Festival*, presented by artists from Taiwan; *The Merchant and the Parrot*, presented by artists from Berlin; *The Theft of Sita*, a modern reinterpretation of a Ramayana theme, presented by artists from Bali; *Special Creatures*, showcasing the magic of puppets made from ordinary objects, presented by artists from Spain; and many more.

🟅 A WEDDING CELEBRATED WITH A MARATHON

Poonam R. Chikane and Navnath J. Dighe, a bride and groom from Kaloshi village in Maharashtra, decided to inaugurate their wedding ceremony in early February in a unique way. Instead of the sacred fire, priests and the wedding horse, the couple ran 25 kilometres to the registrar's office! There they finally exchanged vows and garlands. The *baraati*s too had to run that distance. Dighe, a member of the Marathon Association Satara, which supported and hosted the marriage, said this was a message to promote health and fitness. India hosts several marathons and half-marathons every year.

> **MARATHONS IN FILMS**
>
> *Ethir Neechal* (2013), a Tamil sports drama, shows the hero gaining confidence by winning a marathon, and later opening a marathon training academy.

🟅 SQUASH WINS

India won the gold, silver and bronze medals in January this year in the U-19 British Junior Open Squash, a prestigious tournament. The winners were Velavan Senthilkumar, Abhay Singh and Adhitya Raghavan, who have been training in the Indian Squash Academy in Chennai with their coach Cyrus Poncha (b. 1976). Also in January, India's top U-13 player, Shreyas Mehta, won the Scottish Junior Open. These wins indicate how far squash has progressed in India.

A HISTORY OF SQUASH IN INDIA

The first national championship for squash was held in 1953, and was won by Rajkumar Narpat Singh, who went on to win the championship for the next two years. A great pre-Independence player was Hashim Khan. Other good players after 1947 have been Anil Nayar, who won both national and international championships; Adrian Ezra; the Pandole family, including Dinshaw Pandole and Darius and Farokh Pandole; and some army officers, particularly Major K.S. Jain and Colonel R.K. Manchanda.

Among women, Bhuvaneshwari Kumari (b. 1960) won the national title sixteen times (1977–92). Misha Grewal (b. 1970) was another top squash player, who went on to become a television actor.

After the founding of the Squash Rackets Federation of India and the Indian Squash Academy, both in Chennai, India has produced many good squash players. In August 2016, Indian squash players won three medals at the WSF World Doubles Squash Championships in Australia—one silver and two bronzes. The silver and the bronze were won in the mixed doubles, and the other bronze in the women's doubles. The winners were Saurav Ghosal, Dipika Pallikal, Harinder Pal Sandhu and Joshna Chinappa.

Top-ranking male Indian players as of January 2017 are:

- Saurav Ghosal: World No. 23;
- Vikram Malhotra: World No. 64;
- Mahesh Mangaonkar: World No. 69;
- Harinder Pal Sandhu: World No. 104;
- Kush Kumar: World No. 152.

Top-ranking female Indian players as of January 2017 are:

- Joshna Chinappa: World No. 13;
- Dipika Pallikal: World No. 26;
- Sachika Ingale: World No. 74;
- Janet Vidhi: World No. 107;
- Akanksha Salunkhe: World No. 139.

ALSO IN 2017

15 February: ISRO launches 104 satellites from a single rocket, creating a world record.

February: Chess grand master Harika Dronavalli wins a bronze medal in the World Women's Chess Championship, held in Tehran, for the third time.

6 March: *INS Viraat*, the Indian Navy's oldest aircraft carrier, is decommissioned.

1 July: The Goods and Services Tax (GST) is initiated. This creates a single indirect taxation system across India, replacing multiple taxes.

20 July: Ram Nath Kovind of the BJP, previously Governor of Bihar, is elected as President of India.

UK/India 2017, a culture festival, is celebrated to strengthen bilateral ties. The festival is being organized by the British Council in India, and the Government of India in the UK.

CONCLUSION: A CULTURAL REVOLUTION BEGINS

As this book shows, India has made great progress since Independence seventy years ago. The most significant achievement has been that India has remained a stable, functioning democracy, having followed the Constitution that was created soon after Independence. Though many amendments have been made to the Constitution since it was inaugurated, its basic structure has remained the same.

Some other examples of progress made by India are that though the country has not achieved total literacy, the literacy rate has risen to 74 per cent (as of 2011). Schools and educational institutions have multiplied, with the number of university-level institutions reaching 291 by the year 2000. Indian Institutes of Technology and Indian Institutes of Management have been set up, along with other scientific and technological institutes. Government schemes for education are numerous and private institutions also work towards the same end. Hospitals and health centres have proliferated, and the results are clear—with the infant mortality rate going down from 146 per thousand in 1951 to 47 in 2011, and the death rate reducing from 27.4 per thousand in 1951 to 8 in 2011 (equivalent to the USA). As for economic growth, it has been considerable—with the national income increasing from Rs 8710 crore in 1948–49 to Rs 64,66,860 crore in 2010–11.

Conclusion

Installed power generation capacity rose from 1400 MW in 1947 to 2,09,276 MW in 2012. In 1956, only 7294 villages had been provided with electricity. By 2011, 6,40,867 were electrified. There has been immense growth in industry, transport and communication too. Digital television, mobile phones and the Internet have spread across India.

Culture—the main focus of this book—while retaining its roots in tradition, is in a continuous process of transformation. China, one of the other great civilizations of Asia, attempted to initiate a new culture by destroying its past. This enforced change, known as the Cultural Revolution, took place between 1966 and 1976, leading to the death of around 1.5 million people and causing a setback in most spheres of Chinese society. In India, however, one can see a gradual cultural revolution taking place, with the use of new media and new types of literature, art, music, dance, food and more. India's politics may see many ups and downs in the coming years, but for India's varied culture, there is no looking back as it continues its progress. Jawaharlal Nehru's words describing India as ancient, eternal and ever-new are an apt statement that can be particularly applied to its culture.

ACKNOWLEDGEMENTS

This book owes a lot to a number of people at Penguin Random House India. Particularly, I would like to thank Sohini Mitra for suggesting this book; Kankana Basu for enhancing the text with her expert editing; Meena Rajasekaran and her design team for the beautiful cover; the artist Sayan Mukherjee for the attractive illustrations and all others involved in its production.

Several friends also shared their ideas, among whom I would like to thank Chanda Rani Akhouri.

INDEX

Note: Page numbers in bold+italics denote the entries that are part of trivia boxes, while those in italics are part of the timelines at the end of each chapter.

Aam Aadmi Party (AAP), 367, 386
Aan, 33
Aaron, Manuel, ***226***
Abbas, Khwaja Ahmad, ***86***, 221
Abbasi, Ishtiaq Ahmed, 153
Abdul Kalam, A.P.J., 306, 391
Abdullah, Farooq, 36, 196, 218, 271
Abdullah, Sheikh, 31, 36, 72, 157, 194, 196
Abhisheki, Jitendra, 278
Abraham, Abu, 327
Acharya, Debendra Nath, 82
Acharya, Shriram Sharma, *241*
Adak, Chhaya, ***322***
Adhikari, H.R., 61
Adiga, Aravind, 348
Adityanath, Yogi, 399
Advani, L.K., 237
Advani, Pankaj, *391*
Adyar Film Institute (M.G.R Government Film and TV Institute), 397
Aftabuddin, 232
Agni-I (missile), *234*
agriculture, xiv, 84, 106, 109, 112, 122
Ahana, 338

Ahmad, Iftikhar, 17
Ahmed, Fakhruddin Ali, 151, 169
Ahmed, Ghulam, ***61***
Ahuja, Govind Arun (Govinda), 212
Aich, Manohar, ***238***
Air Corporations Act, *41*
Air India Limited, *343*; Air India, *41*, *94*, *140*; Air India International, *41*, *94*; as a public limited company, *263*
Ajmer, 13
Akali Dal, 165, 205
Akbar, Ali, 232
Akhtar, Hameed, 285
Akilan, *160*
Ali, Ahmed, 32
Ali, Akhtar, 389
Ali, Aruna Asaf (Aruna Ganguly), 71
Ali, Mirza Husain (Baha'ullah), 213
Ali, Mushtaq, ***61***
Ali, Muzaffar, 177
Ali, Naushad, 23, 33, 65
Ali, Salim, *223*
Ali, Wazir, 61
Ali, Zeeshan, 389
Alkazi, Roshan, 169

INDEX

Alkazi, Ebrahim, 168–69
All Assam Gana Sangram Parishad, 175
All Assam Students' Union, 175
All Bodo Students' Union, 254
All India Anna Dravida Munnetra Kazhagam (AIADMK), *145*, 165, 288, 362, 392, *see also* Dravida Munnetra Kazhagam (DMK)
All India Chess Federation, *226*
All India Football Federation, *283*
All India Institute of Medical Sciences (AIIMS), *62*
All-India Women's Conference, 221
Alurmath, Nilkanth Bua, 252
Alvares, Peter, 85
Amaan, 292
Aman, Zeenat, *134*, 139, *336*
Amarnath, *61*, *328*
Ambani, Dhirubhai, 312
Ambedkar, Bhimrao Ramji, 56–58
Ameeta, 98
America! America!!, 267
Amitabh Bachchan Corporation Ltd (ABCL), 354
Amonkar, Kishori, 307
Amritraj, Anand, 151
Amritraj, Vijay, 151
Amrohi, Kamal, 142
Amte, Baba, 239
Amul (Anand milk cooperative), 131
Amul girl, *131*
Anand, Akshay, 267
Anand, Dev, 61, 177, 302
Anand, Mulk Raj, 192
Anand, Viswanathan, 225–27
Ananthamurthy, U.R., *263*
Andaman and Nicobar Islands, 13, 56, 193; earthquake in, *355*
Andhra Pradesh, 37, 56, 118, 146, 191, 241, 243, 264, 272; agitation in, 146; cyclone in, 274
Angaarey, 32

Animal Rights Day, 113
Anita Chanu, L., *322*
Anjali Devi, *384*
Annadurai, C.N., 18, 126
Annapurna Devi (Roshanara), 80, 97, 295–96; and sisters, *296*
Annapurna Studios, 273
Anthikad, Sathyan, *314*
Anti-Defection Act, *209*
Antony, Johny, *315*
Apsara (nuclear reactor), *62*
Apte, Narayan, *18*
Ara, K.H., 15
Arangham Dance Theatre, 278
Aravind, Ramesh, 267
Aravindan, G., *314*
architecture, *339–341*
Armed Forces Medical College, *12*
Armed Forces, 15, 91, 93
Art Heritage Gallery, 169
artists, of India *357–59*, *see also under separate names*
Arunachal Pradesh, 25, 88; North-East Frontier Agency becoming, 141
Arundale, George, 58
Arundale, Rukmini Devi 58–59, 171, *245*
Asan, Kumaran, 72
Ashapurna Devi, 163
Ashok, Aditi, 194
Asian Archery Championships, *234*
Asian Athletics Federation, 28
Asian Games Federation (earlier Asian Athletics Federation), 28
Asian Games, 28–29, 70–71, 94, 134, 190, 193–94, 196, 203, 283
Asian Junior Volleyball Championship, *184*
Asiatic lion, 159
Asif, K., 81
Asom Gana Parishad, 206, 230, 270
Assam, 13, 24, 56, 124, 196, 201, 205–06, 236, 254, 274

Index

Assamese literature, 82
Assam–Tibet earthquake, *24*
assembly elections, 141, 196, 230, 362, 386
Atal Bihari Vajpayee Institute of Mountaineering and Allied Sports, 87
Atharle, S.G., 198
Atomic Energy Commission, 9
Atomic Energy Establishment, *68*
attakatha, *266*
Atwal, Arjun, 194
August Cinema, *314*
Aurobindo, Sri, 21–22
Auroville, 122
Awami League, 136
Ayaan, 292
Azad, Maulana Abul Kalam, *72*
Azhikode, Sukumar, *373*
Azmi, Kaifi, 285
Azmi, Shabana, 177, 288–*90*; in *Godmother*, 288

Baba, Meher, *129*
Babbar, Prateik, 213
Babbar, Raj, 213
Babi, Parveen, *164*
Babita Kumari, *345*
Babri Masjid, 210–11, 237, 250, 268
Babu, Chitti, 348
Bachchan, Abhishek, 354, 382
Bachchan, Amitabh, *86*, 177, 297, 353–54
Bachchan, Harivansh Rai, *318*, 353
Bachchan, Shweta, 354
Bachchan, Teji, 353
Badal Utsav, 120
Badayuni, Shakeel, 33
badminton, 304, 360, 366, 370, 379, *396*
Bagul, Baburao, *390*
Baha'i Lotus Temple, 213
Bahuguna, Sunderlal, 154, *355*

Bahujan Samaj Party, 201, 264, 320, 336
Bai, Anusuya (Sushila Devi), 34
Bai, Daya, *343*
Baij, Ramkinkar, 43, ***112***
Baker, Laurie, ***340***
Bakre, S.K., 15
Baksh, Ali, 94
Baksh, Kader, 296
Bakshi, Byomkesh, 371
Balachander, K., 126
Balachander, Sundaram, 348
Balakrishna, D., 348
Balamurali Krishna, M., 246–47, *398*
Balasaraswati, T., *204*, 246
Balasubramaniam, G.N., 159
Balasundaram, Pavalar, 126
Balika Vadhu, 349
Balwant Rai Mehta Committee (1957), 69
Bama, ***390***
Banaphul, *179*
Bandopadhyay, Ajitesh, ***120***
Bandyopadhyay, Aditi, 255
Bandyopadhyay, Bibhutibhushan, 53
Bandyopadhyay, Sharadindu, *134*
Bandyopadhyay, Tarashankar, *115*, 136–37
Banerjee, Mamata, 363, 392
Banerjee, Nikhil, 97, 214
Banerjee, P.K., 282
Banerjee, Robin, 369
Banerjee, Shute, 61
Bangkok Asian Games, *115*
Bapat, Ulhas, 303
Barjatya, Sooraj R., 262
Barnes, Malcolm, 38
Barodekar, Hirabai, 127
Bartholomew, Pablo, 369
Barua, Dibyendu, ***226***
Basu, Anurag, 338, 368
Basu, Jyoti, *169*
Basu, Rajshekhar, 82
Bawa, Manjit, 43, 349

Index

Bedi, Bishen Singh, 129
Bedi, Kiran, *324*
Bedi, Rajinder Singh, *204*
Begum Akhtar Abbasi, 152–53
Begum, Shamshad, 33
Begum, Waheeda, 31
Behera, Nandita, 255
Being Human Productions, 233
Bendre, Dattatreya R., 148
Benegal, Shyam, 86, 177, 212, 251, 325–26
Bengal famine, xiv
Bengali literature, 136; *Ganadebata*, 136–37
Bengali theatre, 119
Besant, Annie, 17
Bhabha, Homi, *115*
Bhagat, Chetan, 323–24, 360
Bhagat, Dhanraj, 43
Bhakra Dam, *98*
Bhama Nrityam, 333–34
Bhambri, Prerna, 389
Bhambri, Sanaa, 389
Bhambri, Yuki, 389
Bhansali, Sanjay Leela, 368
Bharat Ratna, 47
Bharatanatyam (Sadirnatyam), 38, 58, 245–46, 256, 278, ***245–46***
Bharathan, *314*
Bharathidasan, 103
Bharati, Dharamvir, 251
Bharati, Shuddhananda, *241*
Bharatiya Jana Sangh, 29, 31, 36, 135, 165
Bharatiya Janata Party (BJP), 180, 230, 243, 249, 281, 306, 351, 380, 392, 399; and NDA alliance, 386
Bharatiya Kisan Dal (BKD), 175
Bharatiya Lok Dal, 165, 175
Bharadhwaja, Ravuri, 372
Bhardwaj, Vishal, 368
Bhate, Rohini, *40*
Bhatnagar, Shanti Swarup, *54*

Bhatt, Chandi Prasad, 154
Bhatt, Chandrakala, 260
Bhatt, Ela, *169*
Bhatt, Pooja, 290
Bhatt, Salil, 261
Bhatt, Vijay, 33
Bhatt, Vishwa Mohan, 260
Bhattacharjee, Bikash, 315
Bhattacharya, Bijon, 230
Bhattacharya, Birendra Kumar, 82
Bhattacharya, Tarun, 302
Bhave, Vinoba, 26, 150, *195*
Bhembre, Laxmikant, 85
Bhindranwale, Jarnail Singh, 185, 196, 200
Bhopal, 13, 201; gas leak in, 201
Bhosle, Asha, ***301–02***
Bhowmick, Sachin, *366*
Bhudan movement, 26, *179*, *195*
Bhullar, Gaganjeet, 194
Bhupathi, Mahesh, 389
Bhutia, Baichung, 282
Bhutto, Zulfikar Ali, 141
Bhuvaneshwari Kumari, ***402***
Bidyutprabha Devi, 64–65
Bihar, 3, 13, 56, 116, 150, 165, 236–37, 294
Biju Janata Dal, 276
Bilaspur, 13
'Billoo' Sethi, P.G., 194
Bindra, Abhinav, 345
Birendra (king), family mishap in, 299
Birla, G.D., *199*
Biswas, Anil, 23, 202
Blessy, *314*
Bodoland Autonomous Council, 254
bodybuilding, ***238–39***
Bohurupee theatre group, ***120***, *see also* Little Theatre Group; Yakshagana theatre group
Bollywood, 233; actors in, 290, *see also under separate names*

Bolt, Usain, 144
Bombay Progressive Artists' Group, 15, 243, 310, see also Progressive Writers' Association; Progressive Writers' Movement and Association
Bombay, 13, 15, 23, 25, 35, 51, 56, 60–61, 79, 85, 143; division of, 79
Bond, Ruskin, 383
Bonded Labour System (Abolition) Act, 1976, 157
bonded labour, xiv; abolishment of, 157
Bopanna, Rohan, 389
Bora, Lakshminandan, 82
Borde, C.G., 129
Border Security Force, *109*
Border, Allan, 182
Border–Gavaskar Trophy, 182
Bordoloi, Gopinath, *24*
Borgohain, Homen, 82
Borlaug, Norman, 121
Bose, Dilip, 17
Bose, Nandalal, 28, 43, *112*–13
Bose, Raj Chandra, *223*
Bose, Satyen, 104
Bose, Satyendranath (physicist), 154
Brahmaputra Mail bomb blast, 274
British rule, xi, 11–13, 102, 217, see also independence
Brook, Peter, 303
Bucher, Roy (General Sir), 15
Burger King, 272
Burman, R.D., 139
Burman, S.D., 23, 77, 98, *160*
Bush, George W., *336*

Calcutta, 10, 18, 22–23, 25, 138, 153, 178, 194, 198, 214, 232; becomes Kolkata, 304
Cariappa, K.M. (General), 15
Census of India, 25, 247
Central Potato Research Institute, 59

Chakiarkoothu, 38, **265–66**
Chakma refugees, 276
Chakraborty, Mithun, 177, 193
Chakravarti, Nikhil, *286*
Chakyar, Ammannur Madhava, *266*
Chakyar, Mani Madhava, *266*
Chand, Dhyan, 10, 176
Chanda, A.K., *55*
Chander, Krishan, 167
Chandran, Geeta, *335*
Chandran, T.V., *315*
Chandrasekhar, Subrahmanyan, 197
Chandrashekhar, Nagathihalli, 267–68
Chandraswami (Nemi Chand), *274*
Channel [V], *263*
Chanu, Khumukcham Sanjita, *322*
Charandas Chor, *173*, 212
Chattopadhyay, Kamaladevi, 221
Chaudhari, Raghuveer, *391*
Chaudhuri, Nirad C., *293*
Chaudhuri, Sankho, 43
Chauhan, Jagjit Singh, 185
Chaurasia, Hariprasad, *80–81*, 258
Chaurasia, Rajeev, *81*
chausingha (four-horned antelope), *183*
Chautala, Om Prakash, 236
Chavan, Y.B., 170, 175
Chawla, Juhi, 233, 290
Chawla, P.M., 60
Chawrasia, Shiv, 194
cheetah, 144
Chemmeen, 106–07
Chennai train derailing, 300; floods, *391*
chess players, 166, 268, see also under separate names
Chhetri, Amit, *238*
Chibber (now Khan), Gauri, 310
Chikane, Poonam R., 401
Chikkaveera Rajendra, 199
Child Labour (Prohibition and Regulation) Act, *215*

Index

Child Marriage Restraint (Amendment) Act, 1978, 174
Children's Day, 32–33
Children's Film Society, *252*
Chinai, Alisha, **262–63**
Chinappa, Joshna, **402–03**
Chinese invasion, 90
Chipko movement, 154
Chitnis, Leela, *318*
Chocolate production, **59**
Chopra, Aditya, 268
Chopra, Priyanka, 298; in *Quantico*, *388*
Chopra, Yash, 268, 367
Choudhury, Malay Roy, 88–89
Choudhury, Sarbari Roy, *359*
Chougule, Sangram, **238–39**
Chowdhury, Jogen, *358*
Chowdhury, Salil, 77, 107
Chowdhury, Shyamashankar, 138
Chowgule, Rohini, 194
Chughtai, Ismat, 32, 285
classical dance: **334–35**; forms in Kerala, *265*
classical music, *5*, *see also* Hindustani music; Karnatic/Carnatic music
Clinton, Bill visits India, *298*
Coimbatore car bombs, *286*
Cold War, 49, 230
comics, *353*
Commonwealth Games, 70–71, 322, 345, 360–61, *see also* Asian Games
Commonwealth of Nations, 18
communal riots in Meerut, 219
communication, xv
Communist Party of India (Marxist), 104, 231, 117, 165, 286
Communist Party of India (Marxist–Leninist), 117
Communist Party of India, 63, 90, 104, 117, 165, 231
Congress (I), 170, 175, 180, 218, 229
Congress (O), 126, 135, 165–66

Congress (R), 125, 130, 135, 141, 151, 156, 165–66, 170
Congress (S), 170, 230
Congress Socialist Party, 9
Connors, Jimmy, 151
Constituent Assembly, xiii, 2–3, 19, 57
Constitution of India, xiii; first amendment to, *29*
Consumer Protection Act, *216*
Coorg, 13
Corbusier, Le, 134
Correa, Charles, **340**, *see also* architecture
corruption, 325, 362
Cousins, Colonial, *263*
cricket, **60–61**
Cricketers, *328*, *see also under separate names*
cultural festivals, *209*, *247*, *403*
cyclone Aila, *355*

D'Souza, Raymond, *238*
Dadasaheb Phalke Award, 11, 129, 273
Dadra and Nagar Haveli, 14, 42, 84
Dagar, Faiyaz Wasifuddin, 215
Dagar, Hussain Sayeeduddin, 214
Dagar, Nasir Aminuddin, 214, 215
Dagar, Nasir Faiyazuddin, 214
Dagar, Nasir Moinuddin, 214
Dagar, Nasir Zahiruddin, 214
Dagar, Rahim Fahimuddin, 214
Dagar, Zia Fariduddin, 214
Dagar, Zia Mohiuddin, 214
Daji, Yasmin, 114
Dal Khalsa, 185, 196
Dalit literature, **390**
Dalit Panthers, *145*, 389
Dalits, 56, 124, 167, 201, 215, 268; attacks on, *124*
dance, xv, 22, 38–40, 58, 138, 241, 245–46, 256, 265–67, 278–79; Kathak, *39*
Dangle, Arjun, **390**

Index

Dani, Shashikala, 108
Darius, *402*
Darjeeling Gorkha Hill Council, 225
Darvarova, Elmira, 292
Das, Bhagwan, 55, *73*
Das, Jibanananda, *48*
Das, Jogesh, 82
Das, Kamala, 207–08
Das, Suranjan, *134*
Dasgupta, Buddhadeb, 54
Dasgupta, Kamal, *155*
Dasgupta, Prabuddha, 369
Davar, Shiamak, 139
Dayal, Girvar, *40*
de Braganza Cunha, Tristao, 85
de Fonseca, Angelo, 119
de Mascarenhas, Telo, 85
Degra, Premchand, 237
Deka, Hitesh, 82
Delhi Declaration, *208*
Delhi Public Library, *29*
Delhi Zoo, *78*
Delhi, 1, 7, 13, 19, 25, 29, 56, 71, 164–65, 201, 291–92
Delhi–Lahore bus service, 284, 293, *see also* Indo-Pakistan Bus Service
democracy, xv, 101, 165–66
demonetization, *174*, 392
Deodhar, B.R., 240
Deodhar, D.B., *258*
Deol, Bobby, 290, 338
Deol, Sunny, 290, 338
Department of Atomic Energy, *48*
Desai, Anita, 330
Desai, Anjani, 194
Desai, Kiran, 330
Desai, Manmohan, 368
Desai, Morarji, 59, 111, 125, 156, 166, 175
Deshmukh, Nanaji, *361*
Deshpande, Purushottam Lakshman, *298*
Deshpande, Rahul, 199

Deshpande, Vasantrao, 198, 206
Dev, Kapil, 197
Deve Gowda, H.D., 270, 275
Devgn, Ajay, 288, 290
Devika Rani, 34, 129
Devvarman, Somdev, 389
Devy, G.N., *319*
Dey, Bishnu, 136–37
Dey, Manna, 76, 98, 107, *379*
Dey, Sukhen, *322*
Dhaka–Agartala bus service, 300
Dhale, Raja, *390*
Dhar, Sudhir, 327
Dharamshala, 74
Dharmendra, 91, 98, 177, 337–38
Dhasal, Namdeo, *145*, 389
Dhawan, Satish, *311*
Dhoni, M.S., *328*, *329*, *366*
Dhwani, Chandra, 292
Dighe, Navnath J., 401
Dikshithar, Ambi, 158
Dilip Kumar, 33, 76, 81, 246
Dilwale Dulhania Le Jayenge (DDLJ), *268*, 302, 310
Directorate of Film Festivals, *149*
Disco Dancer, 193
Diu, 14
Dixit, Madhuri, 240, 244, 262, 290
Domino's Pizza, 272
Doraiswamy, Seetha, 108
Doshi, B.V., *340*
Doyle, Christopher, 360
Dravida Kazhagam, 18, 126
Dravida Munnetra Kazhagam (DMK), 18, 116, 126, 162, 165, 230, 236, 270
Dreamz Unlimited, 310
Dronavalli, Harika, *227*, *403*
Dunkin' Donuts, 272
Durrani, G.M., 22
Dutt, G.R., 257
Dutt, Geeta, 67
Dutt, Guru (Vasanth Kumar Shivashankar Padukone), 65, 67

Index

Dutt, Sanjay, 186, 290
Dutt, Sunil, 61, 65, 186
Dutt, Utpal, 230, 257
Dutt, Yogeshwar, *345*, 370
Dutta, J.P., 288
Dwivedi, Hazari Prasad, 64, *179*
Dylan, Bob, 232

earthquake in Bihar, *228*; in Nepal, 228, *391*
East India Comedy, 368
East Pakistan, xi, 6, 135–36
economic problems, 146; reforms, 130, 249, 275
Ekka, Albert, *140*
elections, 30–31, 63, 90, 116–17, 135–36, 165, 201, 205–06, 218–19, 242–43, 270–71; in Jammu and Kashmir, 271; symbols in, 31, 135
electricity, xv, 129
Electronic Voting Machines (EVMs), 320, 351, *see also* elections
Elkunchwar, Mahesh, 230
Elwin, Verrier, *104*
Emergency, 156–57, 161–62, 164–66, 180, 257
English Vinglish, 377–78
Enlai, Zhou, 90
Erskine, James, 279
Esha, 338
Essential Commodities (Amendment) Ordinance, *104*

Facebook, 335, *see also* Instagram
Faiz, Faiz Ahmad, 32, 285
Faria, Nicole, *361*
Faria, Reita, 114
Fathima Beevi, M., *234*
Fazil, *314*
feature films, 29
Fernandes, George, 259
Fernandez, Eustace, 131
Festival of China, *252*

Festival of India, 158, 195, *223*, 278; in Australia, 394
Films Division of India, 11
films, 10–11, 61, 65–66, 76, 81–82, 98, 103–04, *177*, 212–13, 262, 268–69; actors of 1990s, 290; on boxing, *370*; Goan struggles in, *86*; in Kannada, 267; in Malayalam, 313, 315; of 1970s, 177; in regional languages, *261*; singers of, 22–23; women in 33–34
Five-Year Plan, 111; First, *35*; Third, 84; Fourth, *109*, 111; Seventh, *209*
flash fiction, 384
flute players, 79–80
folk theatre, *173*
Food Corporation of India, *109*
food items, xv, 59
football, *282*
Forty-Fourth Amendment, 170
Fowler, William A., 197
freedom movement, 9, 12, 16, 20, 22, 24, 89, 101, 109, 221, 239
French territories, 14, 56, 90

G-15 summit, 259
Gade, H.A., 15
Gaitonde, Pundalik, 86
Gaitonde, V.S., 15, *304*
Gandharva Vidyalayas, 50–51
Gandhi, Ela, *343*
Gandhi, Indira, 101, 110–11, 125, 130, 135, 141, 151, 156–57, 161–62, 170–71, 175, 180, 200; assassination of, 200; Bharat Ratna for, *140*; Twenty Point Programme of, 161
Gandhi, Mahatma, 1, 7, 20, 60, 72, 113, 158, 239; association with Nehru, 101; shot by Godse, 8
Gandhi, Rahul, 374–75

INDEX

Gandhi, Rajiv, 185, 190, 196, 201, 205, 209–11, 217–18, 224, 229, 242, 248; assassination of, 242; as youngest prime minister, 205
Gandhi, Ramchandra, *343*
Gandhi, Sanjay, 161, 180, 185; death of, 180
Gandhi, Sonia, 320
Ganesan, Anayampatti S., 108
Ganesan, Gemini, 126
Ganesan, Sivaji, *304*
Ganesha idols drinking milk, *269*
Ganga, boat capsized in, 300
Gangani, Guru Kundanlal, **40**
Gangopadhyay, Sunil, 370
Ganguly, Rita, 153
Ganguly, Suren, 28
Gargi, Balwant, *318*
Gaura Devi, 154
Gavaskar, Sunil (Sunny), 182
Gayathri, E., 348
Gayoom, Maumoon Abdul, 229
general elections, 90, 116–17, 180, 270, 281
George, Evagrio, 85
George, K.G., *314*
German Bakery blast in Pune, *361*
gharana, **39–40**, 50–**51**, 96, 147, 198, 240; Delhi, 232, 332; Etawah, 123; Gwalior, 50, 147; Indore, 153; Jaipur, 40; Jaipur–Atrauli, 127; Kirana, 127; Lucknow, 39, 123; Maihar, 96; Patiala, 297; Punjab, 296; Senia, 51, 96; Varanasi, 132
Ghatak, Ritwik, 54
Ghei, Gaurav, 194
Ghisingh, Subhash, accord with, 224
Ghosal, Saurav, **402**
Ghosh, Amitav, 338–39
Ghosh, Pannalal, 80, 97
Ghosh, Rituparno, *379*
Ghosh, Tushar Kanti, *263*
Ghuman, Varinder Singh, **238–39**

Gir National Park and Wildlife Sanctuary, 159
Giri, V.V., 125, *160*
Glimpses of World History, 101
Goa, 14, 84–86, 119, 126–27, 195
Goan freedom fighters, 85
Godhra incident, 307
Godse, Nathuram, 8, **18**
Goel, Suresh, 60
Goetz, Hermann, 43
Gokak, Vinayaka Krishna, *241*
Golf Premier League tournament, *378*
golf, xv, 193–94
Gombu, Nawang, *366*
Goods and Services Tax (GST), *403*
Gopalakrishnan, Adoor, **314**
Gopalan, M.J., **61**
Gopi, Kalamandalam, **266**
Gopichand, Pullela, *304*
Gorakhpuri, Firaq, *129*, *194*
Gorkha National Liberation Front, 224
Gorkhaland, 225
Goswami, Indira, 298, *350*
Goswami, Prafulla Datta, 82
gotuvadyam, 171
Gowarikar, Ashutosh, 368
green revolution, 121, see also agriculture
Grewal, Misha, **402**
Guha, Manoj, 60
Gujarat, cyclone, *286*; earthquake, 299
Gujral, I.K., 275, 281, 291
Gujral, Kiran, 291
Gujral, Satish, 291
Gulab Bai (Kamala Devi), **34**
Guleshastri, Sadhana, 239
Gupt, Maithili Sharan, 102
Gupta, Harendra Nath, 163
Gupta, Pradosh Das, 28
Guruji, Sane, 44

Gurukkal, Meenakshi, 394
Gutta, Jwala, 396

Haasan, Kamal, 381–82
Haidar, Ali Zaki, 348
Haji Ali Dargah, and women's entry, 397
Haldar, Asit Kumar, 28
Hamid, Abdul, *109*
handicrafts, 122, *222*
Handloom and Handicraft Export Corporation, 276
Hangal, A.K., *373*
Hangal, Gangubai, 127
Haqeeqat, 91–92
Harjo, Joy, 277
Harrison, George, 108, 232, 295
Haryana, 111, 165, 236
Hashim Qureshi, 137
Hashmi, Safdar, 231
Hazare, Anna, 362, 367
Hazare, V.S., **61**
Hegde, Ramakrishna, 276
hijacking, *164*, 137, *186*, *204*, 291
Himachal Pradesh, 13, 56, 87, 98, *140*, 163
Himalayan Mountaineering Institute in Darjeeling, 38, 87
Hindi, xii, 10, 16, 29, 58, 63, 80, 95–96, 102, 107, 261–62; films in, 23, 33, 54, 61, 76, 91, 167, 177, 247, 288
Hindu Marriage Act, 49
Hindu–Muslim conflict, 250
Hindustani music, 5, 24, 81, ***147–48***, 153, 198, 206, 214, 240, 252, 296–97
Hiralalji, Guru, **40**
Hirani, Rajkumar, 368
Hockey India League, *378*
Holley, Robert W., 123
Hrangkhawl, 224
Hull, Morton D., 197
Hum Log, 202–03

Humpy, Koneru, *304*
Hungry Generation, 88
Husain, M.F., 15, 43, 231, 241, 243–44, ***359***
Husain, Zakir (President), *99*, 116; Magic Key series of 127–28; death of 125
Hussain, Zakir, 258, 297
Hussain, Nasir, 98, 233
Hyder, Qurratulain, *235*
Hyderabad, 2, 8, 13, 17, 25–26, 28, 94, 117–18, 273; International Airport of, *349*

Imperial Bank of India (later State Bank of India), *54*
Independence Day, 10, 19
Independence, xi, 1–2
India and Bangladesh Ganga waters agreement, *274*
India and China, 42
India and Nepal trade treaty, 312
India and Pakistan, xii, 2, 121, 136, 141, 200, 224, 287; agreement on nuclear war, 337; war (1971), 136
India Hockey Federation, 10
Indian Agricultural Research Institute, 121
Indian Air Force Museum, *120*
Indian Badminton League, *379*
Indian Coast Guard, 170
Indian Coinage (Amendment) Act of 1955, 68
Indian Council for Cultural Relations, 23
Indian Council of Historical Research, *145*
Indian embassy, Kabul, *305*
Indian Football Association (IFA), ***283***
Indian Foreign Service, 9
Indian Forest Service, *115*
Indian Institute of Skiing and Mountaineering, 87

INDEX

Indian Institute of Technology (IIT), 29, 405
Indian literature, *16*
Indian Mountaineering Foundation, 86, 204
Indian music bands, 371–72
Indian National Congress, 9, 17, 20, 31, 109, 125–26, 196, 236, 362, 367, 374–75
Indian National Scientific Documentation Centre (INSDOC), *312*
Indian National Trust for Art and Cultural Heritage (INTACH), 276
Indian Ocean Rim Association for Regional Cooperation (IOR-ARC), *280*
Indian Oil Corporation Ltd, *104*
Indian Peace Keeping Force (IPKF), 217, 242
Indian People's Theatre Association, 31, *173*
Indian Polo Association, 381
Indian Postal Service, 323, *see also* telegram
Indian Squash Academy in Chennai, 401, *402*
Indian Standards Act, *216*
Indian states, xiii, 13, 17, 20, 61; as princely states, xi, *see also* British Rule
India–Sri Lanka Free Trade Agreement, *286*
Indira Gandhi National Centre for the Arts (IGNCA), *209*
Indira Gandhi National Open University (IGNOU), *209*
Indo-Bangladesh border conflict, 300
Indo-China war, 90
Indo-Nepal Treaty of Peace and Friendship, *24*
Indo-Pakistan bus services, 325; war, 147

Indo-US: Civil Nuclear Agreement, 344; joint naval exercises, *252*
Infosys, *189*
Ingale, Sachika, *403*
Inland Waterways Authority of India, *215*
INSAT-1B, 198
Instagram, 363–64, 395
Institutes of Management, 405
Integrated Photo Unit, 77
integration of the states, 2, 8, 13
International Film Festival, *35*
International Yoga Day, *391*
Internet, 269
Ishara International Puppet Festival, 400
ISRO, *403*
Ivory, James, 123
Iyengar, B.K.S., *385*
Iyengar, Doraiswamy, 348

Jadhav, K.D., 32, ***345***
Jadhav, Narendra, 390
Jafri, Ali Sardar, *280*, 284–85
Jahan, Rashid, 31
Jain, K.S., *402*
Jain, Rama, 108
Jaipuri, Hasrat, 76
jal tarang, 108
Jammu and Kashmir, 13, 25, 56, 105, 157, 167, 218, 271
Jammu Kashmir Liberation Front, 137, 230
Jan Morcha, 218, 225
Jan, Ahmed 'Thirakwa', 132
'Jana Gana Mana' as national anthem, 20
Jana Natya Manch, 231
Janata Dal (U), 386
Janata Dal, 218, 225, 229, 236–37, 243, 250, 259, 270, 275–76
Janata Party, 165–66, 176, 180, 225, 230, 243, 249, 281; Bharatiya Lok Dal merges with, 176

Jasraj, Pandit, 206
Jatti, B.D., 151
Jawahar Institute of Mountaineering and Winter Sports, 87
Jawahar Navodaya Vidyalayas, 211–12
Jawahar Rozgar Yojana, 229
Jawaharlal Nehru Award for International Understanding, 109, 129, 178
Jawaharlal Nehru Cup, 231
Jaya Bhaduri (Bachchan), 177, 354
Jayakanthan, *312*
Jayakar, Pupul, 276
Jayalalithaa, J., 126, 288, 362, 392, *398*
Jena, Surendranath, 256
Jeyasingh, Shobana, 139
Jha, Ramashreya, 278
Jharkhand Mukti Morcha, 254
Jiang Zemin of China, *274*
Jinnah, Muhammad Ali, xi; death of, *12*
Jnanpith Award, **108**
Jog, Vishnu Govind, 198
Johar, I.S., *204*
Jose, Lal, *314*
Joshi (film director), *314*
Joshi, Bhimsen, 206–07, 233
Joshi, Manohar Shyam, 202–03
Joshi, Umashankar, 118
JP Movement, 150
Jr NTR, 273
Junagadh, 2, *12*, 159; nawab of, 8
Jung III, Salar, 28

kabaddi, 382, *see also* World Kabaddi League
Kabra, Brij Bhushan, 81
Kadathanadan Kalari Sangam, 395
Kailas, Shaji, *315*
Kairon, Partap Singh, *109*
Kajol, 268, 290
Kakababu, 370–71
Kakodkar, Purushottam, 86

Kala Chethena Kathakali Company, 264
Kalakshetra, 58, 171, 278
Kalavati Devi, 316
Kalburgi, M.M., *391*
Kallianpurkar, Mohanrao, **40**
Kamal (film director), **314**
Kamaraj, K., 160, *164*
Kambara, Chandrashekhara, *361*
Kamble, Baby, **390**
Kamleshwar, 342
Kanchanprabha Devi (queen), 18
Kane, P.V., *99*, *145*
Kant, Krishna, 312
Kanvinde, Achyut, **340**
Kanwar, Roop, 219
Kapoor, Anil, 219, 290, 347–48
Kapoor, Jennifer, 143
Kapoor, Karan, 143
Kapoor, Kareena, 143
Kapoor, Karisma, 143, 290, 326
Kapoor, Kunal, 143
Kapoor, Prithviraj, 11, 81, 142–43
Kapoor, Raj, 10–**11**, 33, *35*, 54, 61, 76–77, 103, 143, 177, 186, 221
Kapoor, Ranbir, 143, 355
Kapoor, Randhir, 143
Kapoor, Rishi, 143, 177
Kapoor, Sanjana, 143
Kapoor, Shahid, 395
Kapoor, Shammi, 143, *366*
Kapoor, Shashi, 10, 143
Kapoor, Shekhar, 262
Kapoor, Vani, 194
Kapur, Shekhar, 219
Karaikal, 90
Karandikar, Vinda, *319*
Karanth, B.V., 268, 286
Karanth, Shivaram, 167
Kargil war, 287–88; films on, **288**, *see also* films
Kariat, Ramu, 106
Karikal, 14

Index

Karnad, Girish, 169, *173*, 177, 268, 285;
Karnatic/Carnatic music, 5, 76, 78, 80, 108, 133, 153, 158, 171, 189, 271, *see also* Hindustani music
Karuna Sri (Jandhyala Papayya Sastry), 250–51
Karunakaran, E., *322*, *361*
Karunanidhi, M., 126, 162, 230
Karve, Dhondo Keshav (Maharishi Karve), 73
Kasauli Art Centre, 163–64
Kashmir National Conference, 218
Kashmir, 2, 7–8, 36, 105, 136, 165, 167, 196, 205, 218, 230; Charar-e-Sharif in, 269; literature, 323; Pakistan and invasion of, 2; war in, 2, 7–8
Kashyap, Anurag, 368
Katari, Ram Dass (vice admiral), 15
Kathakali, 38, 264, 278
Kaul, Mani, 342, *366*, 368
Kaun Banega Crorepati, 297
Kaur, Parkash, 338
Kaur, Rajkumari Amrit, *104*
Kaur, Rani Raj, 63–64
Kaur, Sundar, 64
Kaziranga National Park, 151–52
Kaziranga, 152
Keibul Lamjao National Park, 159
Kejriwal, Arvind, 367
Kelekar, Ravindra, *336*
Kerala Kalamandalam, 265
Kerala Sahitya Akademi, *62*
Kerala, 56, 63, 72, 107, 116, 141, 204, 265–66, 286; train accident in, 300
Kerkar, Kesarbai, 126
Kesarilal, Shankardas, 76
KFC, 272
Khadilkar sisters, *226*
Khakhar, Bhupen, 201
Khalistan, 185–86, 196
Khamba, *317–18*

Khambatta, Persis, 178–79
Khamkar, Suhas, *238*
Khan Pataudi, Mansur Ali, *140*
Khan, Aamir (actor), 233, 290, 360
Khan, Abdul Latif, *331*
Khan, Abdul Majeed, *332*
Khan, Abdul Waheed, 153
Khan, Akhlaq Mohammed 'Shahryar', *350*
Khan, Ali Akbar, 97, 232
Khan, Ali Baksh, 3
Khan, Allabande, 214
Khan, Alladiya (Sangeet Samrat), 126–27, 252
Khan, Allauddin, 55, 80, 96–97, 198, 214, 232, 294
Khan, Aman Ali, 94, 153, 301
Khan, Amanat Ali, 301
Khan, Amir (Hindustani singer), 50, 152–53
Khan, Amjad Ali, 292
Khan, Arif Mohammad, 211, 236
Khan, Asad Ali, 348
Khan, Ashiq Ali, 296
Khan, Ayub, 70, 110
Khan, Baba Allauddin, *55*
Khan, Bade Ghulam Ali, 81, 94
Khan, Barkat Ali, 94
Khan, Bher, 132
Khan, Bhurji, 252
Khan, Bismillah, 2–5, 20
Khan, Bundu, *332*
Khan, Faiyaz, *24*, 132
Khan, Gameh, 232–33
Khan, Ghaus Mohammad, 17
Khan, Hafiz Ali, 292
Khan, Hashim, *402*
Khan, Iftikhar Ali (nawab of Pataudi), *61*
Khan, Ilyas, 123
Khan, Inam Ali, 233
Khan, Inayat, 123, 168
Khan, Irrfan, 347

Index

Khan, Khan Abdul Ghaffar (Frontier Gandhi), *129*
Khan, Laddan, ***332***
Khan, Latif Ahmed, 232
Khan, Mazhar, *286*
Khan, Mehboob, 33, 65, 368
Khan, Mir Osman Ali, (Nizam), 117–18
Khan, Mir Sultan, ***226***
Khan, Mubarak Ali, 94
Khan, Mugalu, 75
Khan, Muhammad Yusuf, 246
Khan, Munir, 132, ***333***
Khan, Nathu, 147
Khan, Nawab Sir Mahabat, 159
Khan, Nissar Hussain, 147, *258*
Khan, Nizam Mir Osman Ali, 8
Khan, Rajab Ali, 75, 153, 168
Khan, Sabri, 331
Khan, Sagiruddin, *332*
Khan, Saif Ali, ***140***
Khan, Salman, 233, 290
Khan, Shah Rukh, 268, 290; Badshah, 310
Khan, Shakoor, 332
Khan, Sindhi, 94
Khan, Suhail Yusuf, 331
Khan, Sultan, ***332***
Khan, Sussanne, 315
Khan, Tikka, 136
Khan, Vilayat, 122–23
Khan, Wazir, 96
Khan, Yahya, 136
Khan, Yousuf Ali, 28
Khan, Zakiruddin, 214
Khandekar, Vishnu Sakharam, *155*, 162
Khanna, Krishen, 15, 43, ***357–58***
Khanna, Rajesh, 139–***40***, 177
Khanolka, Nayan, 395
Khemka, Anita, 369
Khetarpal, Arun, *140*
Khorana, Har Gobind, 123
Khote, Durga, 34, 81, 247
Khurana, Shanno, *248*
Khusrau, Amir, 122
Koi Mil Gaya, 315
Koirala, Manisha, 268, 290
Kolkata–Dhaka bus service, *293*
Kom, Mary, 370
Koodiyattam, ***266***
Kosygin, Alexei, 110
Kothari, Daulat Singh, 149
Kothari, Rajni, *391*
Kovack, Nancy, 377
Kovind, Ram Nath, *403*
Kripalani, Krishna, 47
Krishna Iyer, E., 58
Krishna Menon, V.K., *89*
Krishnamurthy Sastrigal, Budalur, 171
Krishnamurthy, Yamini, ***246***
Krishnamurti, J., *215*, 276
Krishnan Nair, Kalamandalam, ***266***
Krishnan, N.S., *68*
Krishnan, Ramanathan, 83, 151
Krishnan, Ramesh, 176
Krishnanattam, 38, ***265–66***
Krishnashastry, A.R., *124*
Krishnaswami, Mani, 309
Kulkarni, Dhondutai, 127
Kulothungan (V.C. Kulandaiswamy), 308–09
Kumar Vasudev, P., 202
Kumar, Akshay (Rajiv Bhatia), 10, 290, 351
Kumar, Ashish, 361
Kumar, Ashok, 61, 98, 202, *305*
Kumar, Gandharva (Shivaputra Siddharamayya Komkali), 240
Kumar, Kishore, 139
Kumar, Kush, ***402***
Kumar, Meira, *355*
Kumar, Mohan, 103
Kumar, Murali, ***238***
Kumar, Naresh, 17, 151
Kumar, Neeraj, ***238***
Kumar, Nitish, 259, 386
Kumar, Raaj, 76

Index

Kumar, Rajendra, 65
Kumar, Ram, 43
Kumar, Sushil, *345*, 370
Kumar, Uttam, *184*
Kumar, Vijay, 369
Kumaresh, Jayanthi, 348
Kundgolkar, Rambhau, 206
Kunjarani Devi, N., *322*
Kunte, Abhijit, *226*
Kurdikar, Mogubai, 307
Kurien, Verghese, 131
Kurup, O.N.V., *343*
Kutch, 13
Kuvempu, 118

Laccadive, 56
Ladakh, *361*
Lahiri, Anirban, 194, *391*
Lakshman, Adyar K., 278
Lal, Bansi, *336*
Lal, Chatur, 297
Lal, Devi, 236
Lal, Hira, **238–39**
Lalit Kala Akademi, 44, 113
Lall, Nonita, 194
Lall, Premjit, 151
Lama, Dalai, 74–**75**, *234*
languages, **16**
Lasky, Carmen, 377
Laxman, R.K., 327
Laxmi, Neelam Setti, **322**
Laxmikant–Pyarelal, 23
Leela, P., 107
Liaquat–Nehru Pact, *23*
Liberation Tigers of Tamil Eelam (LTTE), 217, 242, *355*
libraries, xiv, 28, 41, 47, 118
Line of Control, 141, 287
literacy rate, xiv
Little Theatre Group, 257
Lohia, Ram Manohar, 49, *120*
Lok Dal, 175–76, 180, 225
Lok Sabha, 30–31, 63, 130, 135, 156, 170, 180, 201, 234, 237, 288

Longowal, Sant, 205
Ludhianvi, Sahir, 184, 285

'Made in India' by Chinai, **262**
Madhubala, **33**, 81
Madhya Bharat, 13
Madhya Pradesh, (Central Provinces and Berar), 13, 56–57, 96, 144, 165, 188, 294
Madras Snake Park Trust, *145*
Madras, 9, 13, 18, 25, 36–37, 56, 58, 61, 116, 141, 273; National Volleyball Championship in, 32
Mahalanobis, Prasanta Chandra, *145*
Mahalingam, T.R., 80, 271
Mahapatra, Sitakant, *258*
Maharaj, Acchan, **39**
Maharaj, Birju, **39–40**, 233
Maharaj, Kanthe, 132
Maharaj, Kishan, 132
Maharaj, Lachhu, **39–40**
Maharaj, Shambhu, **39**–40
Maharishi Mahesh Yogi, 108–9
Maharshi, Ramana, 21–22
Mahasweta Devi, *274*
Mahato, Sunil Kumar, *343*
Mahé, 14, 90
Mahi, Ginni (Gurkanwal Bharti), 397
Mahjoor, Ghulam Ahmad, 31–32
Mahmood, Talat, 22–23
Mahmud-uz-Zafar, 32
Maintenance of Internal Security Act (MISA), 157
Majumdar, Kshitin, 28
Majumdar, R.C., *183*
Majumdar, Tarun, 54
Malayalam film industry, 313, **314–15**
Malayil, Sibi, **314**
Malgonkar, Manohar, *361*
Malgudi Days, 191, 327
Malhotra, Vikram, **402**
Malik, Ashok, 194
Malik, I.S., 194
Malik, Nungshi, 375

Index

Malik, Sakshi, *345*, 396
Malik, Syed Abdul, 82
Malik, Tashi, 375
Malik, Virendra Singh, 375
Malini, Hema, 177, 338
Malleswari, Karnam, 321–*22*
Malpekar, Anjanibai, 153
Mammootty (Muhammad Kutty), *313*
Man Singh II, Sawai, *134*
Manavadar, state of, 8, *12*
Manaveda, *266*
Manchanda, R.K., *402*
Mandal Commission, 237, 250
Mane, Saraswati, 127
Mane, Sureshbabu, 127
Manekshaw, Sam H.F.J., 146–47
Mangalyaan, xi, 374
Mangaonkar, Mahesh, *402*
Mangeshkar, Deenanath, 301
Mangeshkar, Hridaynath, 301
Mangeshkar, Lata, 23, 33, 76, 81, 98, 301
Mangeshkar, Usha, 301
Mani Iyer, Palghat, *189*
Mani, Rajendran, *238*
Manipur, 13, 56, 142, 159; dance of, *317–18*
Mankad, Nirupama, 83
Mankad, V., *61*
Mansingh, Sonal, *246*, 255
Mansur, Mallikarjun, 252
Manto, Saadat Hasan, 32, 51, 53, 285
Manto, Safia, 53
Maoists, 117, 324, 343, 356–57
Marathon Association Satara, 401
Mardhekar, B.S., *61*
Marshall, John (Sir), *73*
martial arts, 394
massacres, in Kaluchak, 312; in Malom, 393; in Tiananmen Square, 230
Mathur, Charu Sija, *318*
Maudgalya, Vinay Chandra, 278

Mayawati, 201, 264
Mazumdar, Charu, 117
Mazumdar, Nirode, 28
McDonald's, 272
Meatless Day, 113
Meena Kumari (Mahjabeen), 61, 142, 301
Meghalaya, 181; becoming a state, 142
Meherhomji, K.R., *61*
Mehli Mehta Music Foundation in Mumbai, 377
Mehndi, Daler, *263*
Mehra, Harish Chandra, 67
Mehra, Ramsarni, 143
Mehta, Jimmy, 17
Mehta, Mehli, 376
Mehta, Shreyas, 401
Mehta, Tyeb, 43
Mehta, Vijaya, 230
Mehta, Vinod, *391*
Mehta, Zarin, 377
Mehta, Zubin, 295, 303, 376–77
Menon, Anjolie Ela, 43
Menon, Sadanand, *335*
Menon, V.P., 13, 20
Menon, Vengalil Krishnan Krishna, 155
Merchant, Vijay, *61*
Mewada, H.K., 134
Minicoy and Amindivi Islands, 56
minimum marriageable age, 49, *174*
Ministry of Environment and Forests, 209
Ministry of Tribal Affairs, 293
Ministry of Utmost Happiness, The, 277
Mira Movement, 113
Mirabehn, *194*
Miranda, Mario, 308
Mirza, Saeed, 177
Mirza, Sania, 388–89
Misa Bharti, *157*
Mishra, Bhagwan Das, *333*

Mishra, Gopal, 284, *332*
Mishra, Rajan, 284
Mishra, Samina, 128
Mishra, Sumant, 17–18
Miss World and Miss Universe, 261–62
Missionaries of Charity Brothers, 178
Missionaries of Charity, 178
Mistri, Colonel, *61*
Mittal, Madhur, 347
Mizo National Front (MNF), 210
Mizoram, 142, 210
mobile phones, 205, 269
Modi, Narendra, 380, 386, 391–92, 399
Mohammad, Bakshi Ghulam, 36
Mohan, Madan, 23
Mohanlal, 313
Mohanty, Gopinath, 148
Mohanty, Kumkum, 255
Mohapatra, Kelucharan, 255
Mohiniattam, 38, 265–*66*, 278
Mohiuddin, Makhdoom, *129*
money, 68
Monga, Gauri, 194
Morvi dam in Gujarat bursts, *179*
Motilal, 76
mountaineering, 86–87, 204
Mountbatten, Louis (Lord), 3, 9, *179*
Mr India, 219–21
Mudgal, Madhavi, 255
Mudgal, Mukul, 279
Mudgal, Shubha, 206, 278
Mukerjee, Subroto (air marshal), 15, 47
Mukerji, Rani, 290
Mukesh, 22–23, 76, 98
Mukherjee, Benode Behari, 43
Mukherjee, Hrishikesh, 76, 82, *336*, 338
Mukherjee, Jaideep, 151
Mukherjee, Joy, *373*
Mukherjee, Mrinalini, 260
Mukherjee, Pranab, 367
Mukherjee, Sailoz, 43
Mukherjee, Shyama Prasad, *29*, 36
Mukhopadhyay, Shirshendu, 371
Mukhopadhyay, Subhash, *248*
Mukti Bahini, 136
Multi-Sectoral Technical and Economic Cooperation (BIMSTEC), *280*
Mumbai, terrorist attack in, 344
Mumtaz, 139
Munim, Tina, 139
Murthy, Mano, 267
Musharraf, 313; visiting India, 299
music, 258, *see also* Hindustani; Karnatic/Carnatic, *see also under artists' names*
musical clock, 27–28
Muslim League, xi
Muslim Women (Protection of Rights on Divorce) Act, 1986, 211
Muthukumar, Na., *398*
Muttathupadathu, Alphonsa (Sister), canonization of, 349
Myanmar, Union of Burma as, *11*
Mysore, 13, 56

Naaz, 142, *see also* Meena Kumari
Nadim, Dinanath, 323
Nadira, Florence Ezekiel, *33*
Nagar Palika Bill, 250
Nagarjuna, Akkineni, 273
Nageswara Rao, Akkineni, 273
Naidu, Chandrababu, 264
Naidu, Leela, 82
Naidu, Sarojini (Nightingale of India), 16–17
Naina Devi, *258*, 278–79; temple stampede, 349
Nair, Edasseri Govindan, *155*
Nambiar, Kunchan, *267*
Namboodiripad, E.M.S., 63, 286
Nanda Devi National Park, 181
Nanda, Champika, 194

Index

Nanda, Gulzarilal, 286
Nangyaramma, *266*
Narang, Gagan, 370
Narasimha Rao, P.V., 243, 249, 254, 259, 263–64, 270, 320
Narayan, Jayaprakash, 150, 156–*57*, *179*, *see also* JP Movement
Narayan, Kunwar, *329*
Narayan, R.K., 191–92, 327
Narayan, Ram, *332*–33
Narayan, Shovana, *40*
Narayana Iyengar, Gotuvadyam, 171
Narayana Reddy, C., *228*
Narayanan, Kocheril Raman, 276
Narayanaswami Iyer, A., 271
Narayanaswamy Iyer, Semmangudi, 240
Naresh (Hindi-language writer), *253*
Nargis, 10, *34*, 54, 61, 186
Narmada Bachao Andolan, 239
Natekar, Nandu, 60
National Archery Championship, *149*
National Award for teachers, *73*
National Bal Bhavan, *73*
National Book Trust, *68*
National Bravery Award, 67
National Cadet Corps, *12*
National Children's Museum, *73*
National Commission for Minorities, *253*
National Conference, 271
National Council of Educational Research and Training (NCERT), *89*
National Crafts Museum, *62*
National Dairy Development Board, *109*, 130
National Defence Academy, *54*
National Defence College, *83*
National Democratic Alliance (NDA), 281, 287–88, 300, 320
National Doctors' Day, 88
national emblem, 20–21
National Film Archive of India, *104*
National Film Awards, 11, 44, 53, 97, 177, 186, 193, 213, 233, 257, 267–68
National Film Development Corporation (NFDC), *183*
national flag, 1, 3, 20
National Foundation for Teachers' Welfare, 93
National Gallery of Modern Art, 43
National Housing Bank, *228*
National Institute of Science Communication and Information Resources (NISCAIR), *312*
National Institution for Transforming India Aayog (NITI), 386
National Library in Kolkata, 41
National Museum of Natural History, 171
National Museum, *18*
National Open School, *234*
National Orchidarium, 77
national pledge, 93–94
National Research Development Corporation, *41*, 195
National Rural Employment Guarantee Act (Mahatma Gandhi National Rural Employment Guarantee Act), 351
National School of Drama, 77, 169, *173*
National Service Scheme (NSS), *129*
National Socialist Council of Nagaland (IM) ceasefire agreement, 300
National Socialist Council of Nagaland (IM), 276
national symbols, 20–21
Navaria, Ajay, *390*
Navketan Films, 302
Navle, J.G., *61*
Navodaya Vidyalayas, 211
Naxalites, 117, 119

Index

Nayi Kahani Group, 342
Nayudu, C.K., *60*, 182, 197
Nayyar, O.P., 23, *343*
Nedunchezhiyan, V.R., *223*
Neelakantan, Anand, 360
Nehru's centenary, 230
Nehru Institute of Mountaineering, 87, *88*
Nehru Shatabdi Natya Samaroh, 230
Nehru Yuva Kendras (NYKs), *145*
Nehru, Arun, 190, 236
Nehru, Indira Priyadarshini, see Gandhi, Indira
Nehru, Jawaharlal, 1–3, 8, 20, 27, 33, 49, 55, 67, 70, 79, 100–01, 109, 111, 406; death of, 100; as first prime minister, 3; in freedom movement, 101; Independence Day speech of, 2
Nehru, Kamala, 101
Nehru, Motilal, 101
Nehwal, Saina, *366*, 370, 396
Nellie incident, *199*
Nemade, Bhalchandra, *385*
Nene, Shriram, 241
Neruda, Pablo, 164, 285
New Delhi Declaration, *312*
Niazi (Lt Gen.), 136
Nicollet, Sharmila, 194
Nihalani, Govind, 177, 342, 368
Nimmi, 10, 33
Nirbhaya, *373*
Nirenberg, Marshall W., 123
Nobel Prize, 46, 123
Nokrek and Balpakram national parks, 181
Non-Aligned Movement, *252*
Norgay, Tenzing, 37–38, 87
North-East Frontier Agency (NEFA), 25, 91, 141
Nrityabharati Kathak Dance Academy, Pune, *40*
nuclear experiment, Pokhran, *154*

Nuclear Power Corporation of India Limited (NPCIL), *223*
Nutan, 76, 98

Obama, Barack visits India, *391*
Odakkuzhal, 106–7
Odissi, 38, 246, ***255–56***, 266
Olympics, 9, 32, 70, 271, 283
Operation Blackboard, 222
Operation Blue Star, 200, 215
Operation Brasstacks, *215*
Operation Flood, 130
Orient Cricket Club, *60*
Orissa cyclone, 293
Orissa, 13, 56, 116, 140–41, 149, 151, 236, 293
Oru Desathinte Katha, 181–82
Osho, *241*
Ottanthullal, 38, ***265***, 267

Paa, 253–54
Padukone, Prakash, 183
Paes, Leander, 389
Pai, Anant, *366*
Pakistan, xi, xiii, 2, 7–8, 70–71, 105, 110–11, 135–38, 141, 224, 287; parts of, xi; relations with, 313; war with, 105, 110
Pal, Bachendri, 203–04
palaeobotany, 15–16
Palekar, Mohanrao, 307
Pallikal, Dipika, ***402–03***
Paluskar, Dattatreya Vishnu, 50
Paluskar, Vishnu Digambar, 50
Panchamukhi, Hema, 267
panchayat system, 69
Panchayati Raj Bill, 250
Pandit, Krishnarao Shankar, 147
Pandit, Lakshman Krishnarao, 147
Pandit, Narayanrao, 147
Pandit, Shankarrao, 147
Pandit, Vijayalakshmi, 70, *241*
Pandole, Dinshaw, ***402***
Pandole, Farokh, ***402***

INDEX

Panicker, Krishna, 333
Panigrahi, Sanjukta, 255
Pansare, Govind, *391*
Pant, G.B., *68*, *89*
Pant, Sumitranandan, 123
Pantulu, Parupalli Ramakrishnayya, 247
Pao Collective, 352
Param Vir Chakra, 93, *109*, 140
Parameswara Iyer, Ulloor, 72
Paranjape, Jhelum, 256
Parekh, Asha, 139
Parliament, 3, 30, 35, 161, 190, 209, 212, 218–19, 253, 300, 362, 367, 374; Council House as, 3
Partition, xii, 10, 42, 51, 53, 70, 91, 94, 113, 162, 187
Parvathi, Lakshmi, 273
Parvatkar, Balakrishnabuva, 307
Pasricha, Avinash, 369
Patel, Chandralekha, *335*
Patel, Dev, 347
Patel, Jeram, *343*
Patel, Sardar, 13, 20
Patel, Vallabhbhai Jhaverbhai, 20
Pathak, Dina, *312*
Pather Panchali, 53, 70–71
Patiala and East Punjab States Union (PEPSU), 13
Patil, Pratibha Devisingh, 337
Patil, Smita, 177, 212–13
Patra, Sunil Kumar, *238*
Pattammal, D.K., 158
Patwardhan, Vinayakrao, 50
Pauly, T.V., 238
Pavlova, Anna, 58, 138
Pawar, J.V., *390*
Pawar, Lalita, 76
peacock, 21, *99*
peasant movements, 117
People's Democratic Party (PDP), 307
People's War Group, *324*
Peoples' Resurgence and Justice Alliance, 393

Persons of Indian Origin, Agreement on, 102
'Perumthachan', 107
Petrapole–Benapole international rail link, 300
Phalke, Dadasaheb, 129
Phizo, Angami Zapu, 84
Phogat, Geeta, 345, 360
Phogat, Vinesh, *345*
Phoolan Devi, *199*, *262*, *304*
photography, 395
Piedade, Antonio, *195*
Pillai, Meenakshi Sundaram, 58, *245*, 333
Pillai, Rajan, *269*
Pillai, Thakazhi Sivasankara, 106
Pinto, Freida, 347
Pitamber, R.K., 194
Pitroda, Sam, 218
Planning Commission, 116
Pobitora Wildlife Sanctuary, 152
Pokhran Test Range, 286
Pondicherry, 56, 85, 90, 103, 236; Aurobindo ashram in, 22
Ponnappa, Ashwini, 396
Pookutty, Resul, 347
population, xvi, 25
Pottekkatt, S.K., 181–82
Powell, David, 114
Pradhan Mantri Gramodaya Yojana, *298*
Pradhan Mantri Jan-Dhan Yojana, *385*
Pradhan, Gangadhar, 255
Praja Socialist Party (PSP), *34*, 49, 94, 106
Pran, *379*
Prasad, Jaishankar, 123
Prasad, Rajendra, 19, 94, *98*
Prasad, Sunder, 40
Prasar Bharati (Broadcasting Corporation of India) Act, *280*
Premchand, 32, 162, 167, 237
Premnath, 33

INDEX

President's Rule, 162, 205, 218–19, see also Emergency
Previn, André, 295
Pritam, Amrita, 187
Pritchard, Norman, 9
Prithvi II, *349*
Prithvi Theatre, 143; Festival of, 144
Private India, 383
Progressive Writers' Association, 31–32, see also Bombay Progressive Artists' Group
Progressive Writers' Movement and Association, 284
Pryke, Richard, 347
Pudumjee, Dadi, 400
Punjab, xi, xiii, 13, 56, 109, 111, 116, 165, 196, 205, 236–37
Puppet theatre, **173**
Puraskar, Hariprasad Chaurasia, 307
Puri, Amrish, 219
Puri, Om, 177, 213, 400
Purna, Malavath, *384*
Purohit, G., 198
Puthren, Alphonse, *314*
Puttappa, Kuppali Venkatappa (Kuvempu), 119
Pyne, Ganesh, *359*

Qasmi, Ahmad Nadeem, 285
qawwalis, 23, **148**
Quadri, Sayeed, 338
Quantico, 388
Qureshi, Alla Rakha, 296
Qureshi, Ashraf, 137
Qureshi, Hashim, 137

Raaj Kumar, 65, 76
Radhakrishnan, Sarvepalli, 19, 47, 93, *160*
Rafi, Mohammed, 22–23, 33
Rafi–Mecartin, *315*
Raghavan, Adhitya, 401
Rahi, Rehman, 323
Rahman, A.R., 262, 268, 326, 347

Rahman, Mujibur, 136
Rai, Aishwarya (Bachchan) 354, 261
Rai, Raghu, 369, see also photography
railways, xii, 204; merger of Central and Western, *29*
Raina, Ankita, 389
Raj Kumar, *336*
Rajagopalachari, Chakravarti (Rajaji), 9, 19, 47, 74
Rajasekar, Nirmala, 348
Rajasthan, 13, 27, 56, 116, 149, 165, 167, 219, 236, 261, 286
Rajendra Kumar, 65, 98, 103
Rajinikanth (Shivaji Rao Gaekwad), *189*, 396–97
Rajkumari Amrit Kaur Coaching Scheme, *41*, see also sports
rajpramukh, 8, 13, 117; abolishment of, 56
Rakesh, Mohan, 342
Rakha, Alla, 297
Rakhee, 177
Ram Kumar, 357
Ram, Jagjivan, 165, 215
Ram, Kanshi, *336*
Ram, Lila, 71
Rama Rao, N.T. (NTR), 191, 272–73
Ramachandra Reddy, Vedre, 26
Ramachandran, M.G., 126, *145*, 223
Raman, C.V., 46–47, 134
Ramananda Tirtha, Swami, *149*
Ramani, N., 80, 271
Ramaswami, Cotah (cricketer), **61**, 389
Ramavarma, Vayalar, 107
Ramchand, G.S., **61**
Ramdas, Bade, 168, 284
Ramuni Menon, Guru P., 333
Rana, Dalip Singh (Khali), 297
Randhawa, Gurbachan Singh, 103
Randhawa, Jyoti, 194
Ranga, B.S., 369
Rani, Devika, *34*
Rani, Sharan, 97

Ranji Trophy, *61*
Ranjitsinhji, K.S. (Ranji), *61*
Rao, Palladam Sanjeeva, 80
Rao, Raja, 192–93
Rasheed, Anwar, *314–15*
Rashtrapati Bhavan, 3, 18
Rashtriya Janata Dal, 276, 386
Rashtriya Lalit Kala Kendras, 44
Ratanjankar, S.N., 198
Rathore, Rajyavardhan Singh, 322
Ratnam, Anita, 278
Ratnam, Mani, 261, 268
Raut, Mayadhar, 256
Ravikiran, N., 171
Rawat, Nain Singh, 87
Ray, Devajyoti, 364
Ray, Pratibha, *366*
Ray, Satyajit, 53–54, 76, 82, 104, 166–67, 253, 295
Raza, Rahi Masoom, 227, 251
Raza, Sayed Haider, 15, *358*
Red Chillies Entertainment, 310
red panda, 181
refugees, 8, 15, 23, 54, 74, 221
Rege, Purushottam Shivaram, 172
Rekha, 177
Reliance Jio, *398*
remote sensing satellite, *228*
Republic Day, 3, 9, 19, 67
Reserve Bank of India, *18*,111–22
Rewal, Raj, *341*
rhinoceros, one-horned, 151; facts about, *152*
Richard, Mirra Alfassa, 122
Right to Information Act, 325
Rock Garden, Chandigarh, 386–88
Roerich, Nicholas (Nikolai), 5, 43
Roshan, Hrithik, 315
Routray, Sachidananda, *216*
Roy Chowdhury, Devi Prasad, 43
Roy, Arundhati, 277
Roy, Bidhan Chandra, 88
Roy, Bimal, 44, 98, 368
Roy, Debi, 88

Roy, Jamini, 43, 51
Roy, Monotosh, *238*
Roy, Pankaj, *61*
Roy, Parimal, *238*
Royal Calcutta Golf Club, 194
Roychoudhury, Samir, 88
Rushdie, Salman, 186–87, 202; *Satanic Verses* by, *234*

SAARC summit, second, *215*; fourth, *224*; eighth, 264
Sabarimala stampede, *366*
Sabri, Kamal, 331
Sachchidananda Vatsyayan 'Agyeya', 172–73
Sadasivam, T., 158
Sadhana, 98
Sadhu Vaswani Mission, 113
Sadiq, M., 98
Safdar Hashmi Memorial Trust, 164, 231
Sagar, Ramanand, *124*
Sahasrabuddhe, Veena, 397
Sahib, Kale Khan, 94
Sahitya Akademi, 47
Sahnan, Joginder Singh, 93
Sahni, Balraj, 82, 91
Sahni, Bhisham, 342–43
Sahni, Birbal, 15–16
Sai Baba, Sathya, 364
Saigal, K.L., *6*, 22
Sailo, 257
Saini, Nek Chand, 386–87
Sainik Schools, *89*
Sakharama Rao, Thiruvadaimaruthur, 240
Sakharkar, Ashish, *238*
Salunkhe, Akanksha, *403*
Sam H.F.J. Manekshaw, 146–47
Samajwadi Party, 320
Samajwadi Party–Indian National Congress alliance, 399
Samata Party, 259
Samman, Kalidas, *40*, 255

Index

Sampoorna Grameen Rozgar Yojana, 351
Samyukta Socialist Party (SSP), *94*, 106, 135, 165
Sandhu, Baljit Singh, 185
Sandhu, Harinderpal, *402*
Sandhu, Kamaljeet, 134
sangai (brow-antlered deer), 159–60
Sangeet Natak Akademi, 38–*39*, 153, 158, 173, 230
Sanghi, Ashwin, 360, 383
Sanjiva Reddy, Neelam, 125, *169*, 274
Sankara Kurup, G., 107
Sankrityayan, Rahul (Baba Ram Udar Das), 95–96
santoor, 302
Sanyal, Bhabesh, 43
Sapru, Tej Bahadur, *18*
Sarabhai, Mallika, *246*
Sarabhai, Mrinalini, *246*
Sarabhai, Vikram, *140*
sarangi melas, *333*
sarangi, *331–32*
Sarkar, Jadunath, *73*
Sarkar, Prabhat Ranjan, *241*
sarod, *97*
Sasikiran, K., *226*
Sastry, Emani Sankara, 348
Sati, 219
Sati (Prevention) Act, 219
Satyanarayana, Viswanatha, 133
Savita Devi, 168
Sawai Gandharva Mahotsav, 206
Sayeed, Mufti Mohammad, 230, 307
Sayeed, Rubaiya, 230
Scientific Policy Resolution, 69
Scindia, Madhavrao, *304*
Segal, Kiran, 256
Segal, Zohra, 256, *385*
Sehgal, Anil, 284
Sehgal, Seema Anil, 284
Sekhon, Nirmal Jit Singh, *140*
Sen, Amartya, 281–82
Sen, Benu, 369
Sen, Mrinal, 54
Sen, Orijit, 352
Sen, Paritosh, 28, *358*
Sen, Sukumar, *23*
Sen, Sushmita, 262
Senthilkumar, Velavan, 401
Seth, T.N., 60
Seth, Vikram, 256
Sethna, Homi, *361*
Seventy-Third Amendment Act of 1992, 69
Shafi, *315*
Shah Bano case, 210–11
Shah, G.M., 196, 218
Shah, Naseeruddin, 177, 341–42
Shah, Rajendra Keshavlal, *305*
Shah, Rina, 381
Shailendra, 76–77, 82, 98
Shakila, 61
Shakuntala Devi, *378*
Shamshad, Begum, 355
Shankar, Amala, 139
Shankar, Ananda, 139
Shankar, Ganesh H., 396
Shankar-Jaikishan, 23, 76–77
Shankar, Mamata, 139
Shankar, Ravi, 77, 82, 97, 138, 190, 232–33, 261, 294–97
Shankar, Uday, 97, 138–39, 232, 294
Shantaram, V., 368
Sharma, Ankur, *238*
Sharma, Dinanath, 82
Sharma, Rahul, 302
Sharma, Rakesh, *204*
Sharma, Shivkumar, *81*, 302–3
Sharma, Uma Dutt, 303
Sharma, Uma, *40*
Sharmila, Irom, 392–93, 399
Shastri, Acharya Chatursen, *83*
Shastri, Lal Bahadur, 101, 105, 110–11, 115
Shastry, V., 198
Shastry, Venkata Chalapathy, 333
shehnai, 2–5, 20

Index

Sheikh, Farooq (actor), *379*
Shekhar, Chandra, 236–37, 242, *343*
Shekhawat, Bhairon Singh, 306
Sheoran, Anita, *345*
Sher-Gil, Amrita, 43
Sherman, Esther, *194*
Shetty, Sunil, 290
Shilpi Chakra, 15
Shirali, Vishnudas, 51
Shirodkar, Pandurang Purushottam, 85–86
Shirov, Alexei, 225
Shirwadkar, Vishnu Vaman (Kusumagraj), 222
Shiv Sena, 111, 270
Sholay, *328*
Shourie, H.D., 326
Shroff, Jackie, 290
Shukla, Harish Chandra, 327
Shukla, Shrilal, *355*
Shyamchi Aai, 44–46
Siddheshwari Devi, 168
Sikhs, xii, 53, 63–64, 185, 196, 200–1, 205; attack on, 201
Sikka, Bharat, 369
Sikkim, 88, 157
Silk Smitha (Vijayalakshmi Vadlapati), 273–74
Sindhu, P.V., 396
Singh, Abhay, 401
Singh, Ajit, 243
Singh, Amarinder, 399
Singh, Arjan, *47*
Singh, Balbir, *68*
Singh, Beant, 201
Singh, Bhai Vir, 63
Singh, Bharati, *322*
Singh, Charan, 175, 180
Singh, Dara, *373*
Singh, Dayanita, *350*, 369
Singh, Gurnam, 10
Singh, Hari (Maharaja of Kashmir), 2, 36, 71
Singh, Hoshiar, *140*
Singh, Jeev Milkha, 194
Singh, Karan, 36, 284
Singh, Kedarnath, *379*
Singh, Keshav Prasad (Maharaja), 3
Singh, Khushwant, 390
Singh, Manmohan, 320, 330, 351, 356
Singh, Milkha, 70–71, 79; Ayub Khan on, 70
Singh, Pritam, 187
Singh, Raghubir, 369
Singh, Rajkumar Narpat, *402*
Singh, Rajkumar Singhajit, *318*
Singh, Ramdhari, 124
Singh, Satwant, 201
Singh, Shabeg, 200
Singh, Shaitan, 93
Singh, Swaran, 170
Singh, V.P., 218, 229, 236–37
Singh, Vijender, 345
Singh, Vir, 63
Singh, Zail, 191
Sinha, Shatrughan, 177
Sinha, Tapan, 54, 137
Sippy, G.P., *343*, 368
Sir J. J. School of Art, 311
Sircar, Badal, 119–20, *173*
Sirima–Shastri Pact, 102
Siva, Sidharth, *314*
Sivalingam, Sathish, *322*
Sivaraman, Kottakkal, *266*
Smita Patil Documentary and Short Film Festival, 213
Soares, Mario, 86
Sobhraj, Charles, *215*
Socialist Party, 9, 34, 49, 94, 106, 120, 150
Solar eclipse, 269
Somali pirates, *361*
Somayajulu, Nemani, 108
Sonam Gyatso Mountaineering Institute, 88
Sopori, Bhajan, 302

Index

Souza, F.N., 15, 310–11
Soviet cultural festival, *223*
sports and games, xv, 32, 70, 79, 103, 183, 190, 203, *see also under separate sports*
Sports Authority of India, 203
Squash Rackets Federation of India, *402*
squash, 401–*03*
Sreedharan, Chindu, 384
Sreenivasan, *314*
Sri Lanka, 96, 102, 178, 217, 242; Ceylon as, *12*
Sridevi, 219, 221, 290, 377–78
Srinivas Prasanna, E.A., 129
Srinivasa Iyer, Semmangudi, 240
Srinivasa Varadhan, S.R., *361*
Sriramulu, Potti, 37
Srivastava, Sandeep, 338
Star TV, *248*
state animals, 159, 181
States Reorganization Act, 56
States Reorganization Commission, 37
states, integration of, 2
Stein, Joseph Allen, *341*
Subba Rao, P.V., 93
Subbulakshmi, M.S., 158
Subburathinam, Kanaka, 103
Subramaniam, L., 303–4
Subramanyan, K.G., 260
Subway, 272
Sufi Gospel Project, 364
Suitable Boy, A, 256
Sultanpuri, Majrooh, 285
Summer Olympics, 9, 32, 60, 183, 203, 228, 271, 322, 345, 369, 396
Sundar, 63
Sundaram, Vivan, 163–64
Sundari, Sarola, 64, 163
Sunkara, Rishika, 389
Supreme Court of India, Federal Court as, *23*

Suraiya, *34*
Suraj ka Satvan Ghoda, 251
'Swaagatam', 190–91, *see also* Asian Games
Swaminathan, J., 43, ***188***
Swaminathan, M.S., 121–22
Swamy, Arvind, 268
Swarnajayanti Gram Swarozgar Yojana, *293*
Swatantra Party, 9, 74, 135

tabla and other drums, *132–33*
Tabu, 290
Tagore, Abanindranath, 28, 43, 51, 113
Tagore, Dwarkanath, 28
Tagore, Gaganendranath, 43
Tagore, Rabindranath, 20, 28, 43, 112, 365–66
Tagore, Sharmila, 139–*40*, 177
Tamils of Sri Lanka, 217
Tandon, Raveena, 290
Tanvir, Habib, ***173***
Tapp, Ian, 347
Tarakam, Basava, 273
Tarapore, Ardeshir Burzorji, *109*
Tarapur Atomic Power Station, *129*
Tarashankar, 137
Tashkent Agreement, 110
Teachers' Day, 93
technical education, 106
Telangana Rashtra Samithi, 300
Telangana, 300, 380, 389
telegrams, 378
television serials, 227; *Buniyaad*, 203; *Hum Log*, 202; *Khandan*, 203; Ramanand Sagar's *Ramayan*, 227; Ravi Chopra's *Mahabharat*, 227
Telugu Desam Party, 191, 264
Tendulkar, Sachin, *234*, 279
Tendulkar, Vijay, 173, 349
tennis, xv, 17, 271, *see also under players' names*

Index

Teresa (Mother), 178
Territorial Army, *18*
terrorist attack, 312, 344
textiles, bandhani, *26*; bleeding Madras, *27*; ikat, *27*; kalamkari, *27*
Thackeray, Bal/Balasaheb, 111, *373*
Thakar, Vasant, 278
Thakkar, Amritlal Vithaldas, 29
Thakur, Omkarnath (Pranav Rang), 50
Thant, U, *109*
theatre, *173*, *see also* under separate names
Thipsay, Pravin, *226*
Third Theatre, 119
Thoibi, *317–18*
Thombare, Prarthana, 389
Thyagaraja Bhagavathar, M.K., *78*
Tibet, 24, 42, 74–75
Tibetan Buddhism, 74–75
Tomar, Alka, *345*
Transcendental Meditation, 108–9, *see also* Yogi, Maharishi Mahesh
Travancore–Cochin, 13
tribal or adivasi art, *188*
Trinamool Congress, 363, 392
Tripathi, Amish, 359
Tripathi, Suryakant, 123
Tripathi, Vinita, 194
Tripura Merger Agreement, *18*
Tripura National Volunteers, 224
Tripura, 13, *18*, 56, 142, 224
tsunami, *324*
Tulankar, Milind, 108
Twenty Point Programme, 330, 351
Twitter, *384*

Uberoi, Shikha, 389
Uday Shankar Centre for Dance, 138
Uday Shankar India Cultural Centre, 138
Ullman, James Ramsey, 38
Umrigar, P.R., *61*

Union of Saurashtra, 13
United Naga Council (UNC), 398
United Nations, 105
United Progressive Alliance (UPA), 320, 351, 380
Urmila, 102
Usha, P.T., 203–04
Uttar Pradesh, 56, 58, 61, 64, 68, 89, 95, 102, 116, 132, 151–52; United Provinces as, 13

Vaidhya, Rajhesh, 348
Vaidya, A.S., *215*
Vaidyanatha Bhagavathar, Chembai, 153
Vaidyanathan, Nirupama, 389
Vajpayee, A.B., 281, 284, 287–88, *298*, 305–06, 313, 320; visits Japan, 305
Vallathol, Narayana Menon, 72, *266*, 333
Valli, Alarmel, *246*
Valmiki, Om Prakash, 390
Varerkar, Bhargavaram Vitthal, 102–03
Varghese, Poly, 348
Varma, Ravi (Raja), 43
Vasanthakumari, M.L., 158
Vasudevan Nair, M.T., *269*, *314*
Vaswani, Dada J.P., 114
Vaswani, Sadhu T.L., 113
Vaz, George, 85
veena, 76, 122, 158, 171
Venkataraman, Ramaswamy, 223
Venkatesh, 199
Venkatrama Iyer, T.L., 158
Verma, Amitabh, 338
Verma, Aswathi Thirunal Rama, 348
Verma, Binod Bihari, *318*
Verma, Mahadevi, 124
Verma, Nirmal, *293*, 342, 357
Vidhi, Janet, *403*
Vijayakumar, Barbara, 264
Vijayakumar, Kalamandalam, 264

Index

Vijayalakshmi, Subbaraman, *227*
Vindhya Pradesh, 13
Vishva Hindu Parishad, *104*, 249
Visva-Bharati University, *29*
Visvesvaraya, M., *55*
Viswanatha Iyer, Maharajapuram, 240
Visweswaran, R., 303
voting age, 234, *see also* minimum marriageable age
Vyam, Durga Bai, *188*
Vyarawalla, Homai, 369
Vyas, Narayanrao, 50
Vyjayanthimala, 76, 103

Wadekar, Ajit L., 129
Wake Up Sid, 355
Wallis, Maureen, 194
weightlifting, *322*
West Bengal, 13, 29, 51, 53, 56, 88, 116, 152, 163, 169, 225
West Pakistan, xi, 6, 136
Western Himalayan Mountaineering Institute, 87
Whitaker, Romulus, 145

White Revolution, 130
Wildlife Protection Act, 144, 183
wildlife, 34
wind instruments, 4, 79, *see also* shehnai
World Kabaddi League, 382
Wrestling, *345–46*, 360, 380, 396; lifestyle in, *346*

Yadav, Lalu Prasad, 157, 276
Yadav, Mulayam Singh, 250
Yakshagana theatre group, 252
Yanam, 90
Yanaon, 14
Yash Raj Films, 368
Yashpal, 162
Yesudas, K.J., 107
Yogananda, Paramahansa, *34*
Yogoda Satsang Society of India in Ranchi, *34*

Zaheer, Sajjad, 32
Zia-ul-Haq, 224
Zinta, Preity, 290